DATE DUE

DEC 2 0 2010			

Demco, Inc. 38-293

IMPULSIVITY: CAUSES, CONTROL AND DISORDERS

PSYCHOLOGY OF EMOTIONS, MOTIVATIONS AND ACTIONS SERIES

Psychology of Aggression
James P. Morgan (Editor)
2004. ISBN 1-59454-136-1

New Research on the Psychology of Fear
Paul L. Gower (Editor)
2005. ISBN: 1-59454-334-8

Impulsivity: Causes, Control and Disorders
George H. Lassiter (Editor)
2009. ISBN: 978-60741-951-8

PSYCHOLOGY OF EMOTIONS, MOTIVATIONS AND ACTIONS SERIES

IMPULSIVITY: CAUSES, CONTROL AND DISORDERS

GEORGE H. LASSITER
EDITOR

Nova Biomedical Books
New York

Library of Congress Cataloging-in-Publication Data

Impulsivity causes, control, and disorders / [edited by] George H. Lassiter.
  p. ; cm.
Includes bibliographical references and index.
ISBN 978-1-60741-951-8 (hardcover)
1. Impulse control disorders. 2. Compulsive behavior. 3. Impulse. I. Lassiter, George H.
[DNLM: 1. Impulse Control Disorders. WM 190 I344 2009]
RC569.5.I46.I485 2009
616.85'84--dc22

                                                                    2009024603

Published by Nova Science Publishers, Inc. ✦ New York

Contents

Preface   **vii**

Chapter I   Alcohol Abuse and Dependence: Disorders of Control?   **1**
Abigail K. Rose

Chapter II   Obsessive-Compulsive Disorder and the Impulsivity-Compulsivity
Disorder Spectrum: A Review of Research   **31**
*Michael L. Sulkowski, Amy Mariaskin, Cary Jordan
and Eric A. Storch*

Chapter III   Impulsiveness and Suicide Risk: A Literature Review   **59**
*Maurizio Pompili, Antonio Del Casale, Alberto Forte,
Ilaria Falcone, Gaspare Palmieri, Marco Innamorati,
Michela Fotaras, Roberto Tatarelli and David Lester*

Chapter IV   When Working Memory Isn't Effective: The Role of Working
Memory Constraints on Rates of Delayed Discounting
and Substance-Use Problems   **83**
Ana M. Franco-Watkins and Richard E. Mattson

Chapter V   Emotion-based Impulsivity and its Importance for Impulsive
Behavior Outcomes   **105**
*Melissa A. Cyders, Jessica Combs, Regan E. Fried,
Tamika C. B. Zapolski and Gregory T. Smith*

Chapter VI   Genetics Basis of Impulsivity: The Role Serotoninergic
and Dopaminergic Genes   **127**
Laura Mandelli

Chapter VII   The Biological and Sociocognitive Basis of Trait Impulsivity   **149**
Peter J O' Connor

Chapter VIII   Mood Disorders of Female Delinquents in a Juvenile Detention
                   Center: Its Relationship with Impulsivity and Depression
                   Assessments   **167**
                   Michio Ariga, Toru Uehara, Kazuo Takeuchi, Yoko Ishige,
                   Reiko Nakano and Masahiko Mikuni

Chapter IX   The Impact of Impulsivity on Adolescent Performance
                   in an Emotional Go/No-Go Task   **181**
                   Miguel Ángel Muñoz, Marlen Figueroa, Eduardo García,
                   Martina Carmelo, Mercedes Martínez, Ana M. Rodríguez,
                   Rocío Sanjuan and Sonia Rodríguez-Ruiz

Chapter X   A Comparison of the Eysenck Impulsiveness Questionnaire
                   and the Dickman Impulsivity Inventory in a Flemish Sample   **195**
                   L. Claes, H. Vertommen and N. Braspenning

Chapter XI   Psychological and Biological Basis of Impulsive Behavior   **207**
                   Michio Nomura

Chapter XII   The Relationship between Impulsiveness and Rejection Behavior
                   in the Ultimatum Game   **217**
                   Haruto Takagishi, Taiki Takahashi and Toshio Yamagishi

Chapter XIII   The Construct of Impulsivity within the Context of Gender-Specific
                   Adversity and Resilience during Adolescence: Guidelines
                   for Future Work   **227**
                   Roberto Mejia, Christian Heidbreder, Yolanda Torres de Galvis
                   and Lenn Murrelle

Index   **235**

Preface

The term impulsivity is commonly used to describe a person who is prone to act on whim without considering the long-term consequences of his or her actions. Several different definitions and measures have been established to examine impulsive behavior in a variety of populations such as substance abuse addicts, adolescents, brain-damaged patients and those who suffer from eating disorders. Impulsivity is a construct both complex and multi-dimensional. It has been characterized as an inability to inhibit appropriate behaviors or to delay gratification, acting without forethought or sufficient information and the failure to correct inappropriate responses. Its multiple descriptive features have led some to suggest that impulsivity is not a unitary construct, but rather comprises "several related phenomena which are classified together as impulsivity." It has been linked to various negative outcomes including criminality, delinquency, extra marital affairs and gambling. This new book gathers the latest research from around the globe in this field.

Chapter – I Alcohol abuse and dependence are widespread and directly contribute to approximately 1.8 million deaths each year. Alcohol consumption is the number one risk factor for disease burden in developing countries and the third largest risk factor in developed countries. Despite government attempts, alcohol consumption levels are not decreasing, indeed, drinking to levels of intoxication is becoming popular in many countries. This 'binge drinking' pattern of behaviour is associated with both alcohol dependent and non-dependent individuals and poses significant problems in terms of long-term risk of developing alcohol dependence and chronic alcohol-related disorders, such as cirrhosis of the liver, but also more immediate problems including increased risk of accidents, anti-social behaviour, financial and relationship problems. Both alcohol dependent and social drinkers often claim that they drink more than they originally intended. This fact has led some to postulate that alcohol use disorders (AUDs) may involve impaired control processes. However, the nature of this impairment is somewhat harder to determine. Are individuals who have a pre-existing control disorder more at risk of developing an alcohol use disorder or does alcohol consumption lead to short- and long-term biopharmacological changes which support impulsive behiour and development of alcohol use disorders? The following chapter will discuss the theoretical background which links impulsivity with alcohol use and will use empirical evidence to understand what impairment of control can and cannot explain in terms of alcohol use disorders. The chapter will place theories of control and alcohol use in context with other emerging fields of research and will end by outlining what some of the next steps are in understanding this complex and important area of alcohol-related behaviour.

Chapter II - This paper reviews research on the association between obsessive-compulsive disorder (OCD) and obsessive-compulsive spectrum disorders (OCSDs). Since a unidimensional impulsivity-compulsivity dimension has been proposed to classify OCSDs (Bartz and Hollander, 2006), consisting of "compulsive" or anxiety-driven disorders such as OCD on one end of the spectrum and impulse-control disorders (ICDs) on the other end, research on relationships between OCD and various OCSDs has been reviewed to determine if data exist to support a continuous impulsive-compulsive disorder spectrum. Disorders are compared with respect to the following criteria: 1) degrees of co-occurring behaviors and symptomology, 2) phenotypic associations (including comorbidity and familial linkages), 3) neurological and brain-based similarities, and 4), identified response patterns to psychological and medical treatments. In general, there is limited support for a unified impulsivity-compulsivity dimension that includes OCD as a central disorder. However, considerably stronger evidence exists for a narrower cluster of anxiety-driven OCSDs that are characterized by obsessive-compulsive features and body image/sensitization obsessions (e.g., OCD, body dysmorphic disorder, hypochondriasis).

Chapter III - Impulsivity is a complex behavioral construct. Action without planning or reflection is central to most definitions of impulsivity. Thus, impulsivity appears to be associated with a failure of behavioral filtering processes outside of consciousness, with compromised ability to reflect on impending acts or to use knowledge and intelligence to guide behavior. Impulsive behavior, including aggression and suicide attempts, differs from corresponding premeditated behavior by having an inappropriately short threshold for response, lack of reflection, lack of modulation, and lack of potential gain, leading potentially to dissociation between an action and its intent. Impulsivity is a prominent and measurable characteristic of bipolar disorder that can contribute to risk for suicidal behavior. The purpose of this study was to investigate the relationship between impulsivity and severity of past suicidal behavior, a potential predictor of eventual suicide, in patients with bipolar disorder. Although the screening of BD patients for the risk factors is not fool-proof, the consideration of those risk factors is an important component of the clinical assessment of suicidal risk. The clinical unpredictability can be especially challenging with BD patients, given the sometimes rapid shifts in mood (lability), strong reactivity to losses, frustrations or other stressors, impulsivity, disinhibiting effects of commonly abused central depressants including alcohol, comorbid anxiety disorders, and potential adverse effects of excessive use of antidepressants. Impulsivity/aggression has been reported to be related to suicidal behavior in several studies . For example, Mann and colleagues proposed a stress-diathesis model of suicidal behavior. Impulsivity, related to a genetic predisposition and dysfunction of the prefrontal cortex, is part of the diathesis predisposing individuals with suicidal ideation to act upon their impulse. Higher aggression may also contribute to the increased lethality of suicide attempts.

Among all psychiatric disorders, BD carries the highest suicide risk. There is no good explanation as to why BD patients kill themselves more than patients with MDD or schizophrenia. Possibly BD patients are are more prone to dysphoric-irritable mixed states associated with higher degree of discontent and impulsivity. Impulsivity is also a relevant clinical factor in suicidal behavior and is a common trait among persons with BD. However, impulsivity has been tentatively associated primarily with suicide attempts of limited lethality rather than with completed suicide. It is not clear whether relatively high rates of illness recurrence or the presence of rapid cycling (more than four recurrences within a year) increases risk of suicide in mood disorders. There may also be a genetic predisposition to suicide, but it has not been proven that this risk is independent of the risk for BD or depressive illness.

Chapter IV - Research has demonstrated that individuals who pathologically engage in addictive behaviors are in general more impulsive, as suggested by their tendency to discount larger rewards that are delayed in time in favor of immediate, albeit smaller rewards. Additionally, some evidence exists that placing constraints on working memory during the decision making process increased an individual's preference for immediate reward. These findings, taken together, have led some to hypothesize that addictive behavioral disorders might result from working memory deficits because the inability to effectively process real-world discounting tasks (e.g., deciding between the immediate gratification associated with substance use despite the potentially larger rewards associated with abstinence that are displaced further in time). However, recent research indicates that individuals do not necessarily become more impulsive with increasing constraints on working memory; rather, individuals became more variable in their responding. Stately differently, increasing working memory constraints rendered the individual less likely to behave (i.e., decide) in a consistent manner. However, the mechanism by which working memory constraints create variance in responding, as well as the way in which working memory deficits influence the onset and maintenance of addictive behaviors, if not through increasing impulsivity, is currently unclear. The purpose of the current chapter is to specify the process by which working memory constraints create inconsistency in responses during discounting tasks, and use this theoretical account to explain the relationship between working memory deficits and the etiology and maintenance of addictive behavioral disorders. Theoretical and methodological implications regarding basic and applied research on working memory, impulsivity, and their relationship to addictive behaviors are discussed.

Chapter V - Impulsivity has long been considered an important risk factor for a variety of maladaptive behaviors, such as alcohol use, drug use, and eating disorders. However, different authors have used the term to mean different things. In recent years, the construct has been disaggregated into five, separate personality traits. In this chapter, after reviewing the varied definitions of impulsivity that have existed in the literature, the five traits are reviewed and described. Two of them can be best described as deficits in conscientiousness (including lack of persistence in tasks and lack of deliberation before performing tasks), two can be described as emotion-based dispositions (including tendencies to engage in rash actions when experiencing very positive or very negative emotions), and the fifth is sensation seeking. Then a discussion of the differential correlates of each of these dispositions, the clinical implications of their roles in risky behaviors, and the particular importance of emotion-based rash action. By proposing new directions of research for the continued study of impulsive behavior-related disorders, the chapter is concluded.

Chapter VI - The aim of the present chapter is to summarize the current knowledge of genetic basis of impulsive behaviours, which occur across several neuropsychiatric disorders. Impulsivity most frequently characterizes attention-deficit/hyperactivity disorder, substance abuse, binge eating, personality disorders, suicidal behavior, with important ramifications for everyday functioning and quality of life.

The existence of a genetic component and inheritance of impulsivity has been largely demonstrated in families and twins studies. Moreover, in the last years, molecular genetic studies have considerably increased, reporting several positive associations between genetic variants and impulsivity, particularly in regard to genes involved in serotonin and dopaminergic pathways. Indeed, the role of serotonin in impulsivity is well recognized and dopamine system is the neuronal substrate mediating behavioural inhibition.

However, the concept of impulsivity covers a wide range of "actions that are poorly conceived, prematurely expressed, unduly risky, or inappropriate to the situation and that often result in undesirable outcomes" and may be thus made up of several independent factors.

Though varieties of impulsivity, inconsistency in definition and measure, in different psychiatric and non-psychiatric conditions, the present chapter will review genes most consistently associated with impulsivity in both healthy individuals and patients affected by major psychiatric or personality disorders.

Chapter VII - Trait Impulsivity has traditionally been defined in terms of 'impulse control', with those high in Impulsivity thought to lack sufficient levels of restraint. Not surprisingly therefore, Impulsivity has been linked to various negative outcomes including criminality, delinquency, extramarital affairs and gambling. In this review, current and traditional conceptualizations of Impulsivity are critically evaluated and it is argued that Impulsivity is not a one-dimensional, developmentally homogenous trait, but more likely represents a multifaceted biologically and socio-cognitively based characteristic. A model of trait Impulsivity is proposed, which suggests that Impulsivity is comprised of biologically based 'approach' motivation, and *lack* of socio-cognitive 'character' related to restraint. Specifically, it is suggested that approach motivation represents a distal precursor to Impulsivity, and that impulsive individuals are those who fail to learn functional socio-cognitive patterns of behaviour, such as Self Directedness, Goal Orientation and Conscientiousness. From this perspective, approach motivation can lead to positive or negative outcomes. Implications for the prevention and treatment of Impulsivity are discussed.

Chapter VIII - *Backgrounds*: This study aims to compare depression between female participants of adolescent offenders and students, and to clarify relationships of mood variables with comorbidity and impulsivity in a Japanese delinquent sample. *Methods*: 64 females are randomly interviewed at a detention center, and diagnosis was determined using a structured method. The five self-ratings including depression (the DSD), impulsivity (the BIS11), and eating attitudes (the EAT26), were collected. 167 high school and college female students were recruited to compare the DSD. *Results*: By the DSD, the major depressive episodes (MDE) were higher in the offenders than in the controls. In the offenders using a structured interview, 18 (28.1%) were diagnosed with MDE, 21.9% were having dysthymia, and 6.3% had current manic or hypomanic episode. The offenders with MDE showed higher on the DSD significantly than those without mood disorders. Offenders with mood disorders had higher comorbidity including anxiety disorders. The DSD scores were significantly predicted by the EAT26 and the inappropriate attention scores of the BIS11. *Conclusions*:

Depression and mania may be associated with antisocial behaviors in female delinquents. Eating problems and impulsivity were risk factors of depression in female adolescent offenders.

Chapter IX - *Background*. Impulsivity and emotional drive constitute distinctive markers of adolescence, characterized in many instances by sensation seeking and risk taking behaviors. On the other hand, the Go/No-Go task is possibly the experimental paradigm most often used when studying impulsivity and behavioral inhibition in the laboratory. Thus, the aim of this study is to explore the effect of impulsivity on adolescent performance in an emotional Go/No-Go task. *Method*. At this point a set of questionnaires on trait impulsivity (Plutchik Impulsivity Scale; Plutchik and Van Praag, 1989) to a non-clinical sample of 1190 adolescents (from 14 to 18 years old) and selected 49 participants at the two end of the impulsivity continuum: high (n=21) and low impulsive adolescents (n=28). These extreme groups were further tested on neuropsychological measure of motor impulsivity (emotional Go/No-go task). The emotional Go/No-go task provides a measure of motor impulsivity since the participant has to inhibit a behavioural response (press a key) to specific and emotionally relevant stimuli. *Results*. The Go/No-go task indicates that high impulsive adolescents display faster reaction times (both for hits and false alarms) while viewing affective (pleasant and unpleasant) and non-affective pictures, whereas low impulsive participants exhibit faster reaction times only to affective pictures. *Discussion*. High impulsive adolescents revealed impaired emotional responses to the pictures compared to participants with low impulsivity. In sum, the preset study suggests a negative relationship between impulsivity and emotional processing in adolescent population.

Chapter X - Self-report questionnaires are widely used techniques for measuring impulsiveness. Some have developed as a part of more general personality scales, and others specifically for measuring impulsiveness (Luengo et al., 1991). This paper investigated the psychometric properties of one of the latter, the Eysenck Impulsiveness Questionnaire (I.7; Eysenck, Pearson, Easting, and Allsopp, 1985) when applied in a Flemish sample. The factor structure of the Dutch I.7 and the psychometric properties of the instrument are examined. Further, the characteristics of the I.7 subscales were compared with those reported in the original papers. In addition, the items of another impulsivity questionnaire, namely the Dickman Impulsivity Inventory (DII; Dickman, 1990) and the I.7 items were pooled to investigate the extent to which the two scales measure the same variable(s) and to get a better understanding of the impulsiveness construct.

Chapter XI - It has been suggested that impulsive behavior is caused by dysfunctional serotonergic 5-HT neurotransmissions in the central nervous system (CNS). A substantial body of evidence has supported this hypothesis by demonstrating that acute tryptophan depletion, a procedure that transiently decreases 5-HT neurotransmission, has been reported to increase impulsive behaviors. Recently, the conclusions of several studies have been in apparent conflict with the function of the 5-HT2A receptor (one of three major types of the 5-HT receptor family) in impulsivity. Examining whether the polymorphism in the 5-HT2A receptor gene promoter is involved in impulsivity using a Go/No-go task in 71 normal volunteers is next Impulsivity was defined as the number of commission errors (responding when one should not) recorded during a Go/No-go task; a larger number of commission errors indicate greater difficulty in inhibiting impulsive behavior. The participants of the A-

1438A allele group for the 5-HT2A receptor gene made more commission errors under the PR condition (withholding responses to active stimuli were punished and withholding responses to passive stimuli were rewarded) than those in the G-1438G group. From these results, it has been suggested that the possible involvement of the A-1438A polymorphism of the 5-HT2A receptor gene promoter in impulsive behavior.

Chapter XII - The purpose of this study is to examine the relationship between impulsiveness and behavioral responses in an economic game known as the ultimatum game. Thirty-one participants played the role of the responder in repeated one-shot ultimatum game. Following the ultimatum game, participants filled out the Barratt Impulsive Scale (BIS-11; Patton et al., 1995). Results showed that the higher the participant scored on impulsiveness, the more likely they were to accept highly unfair offers. This result implied that rejection behavior in the ultimatum game is less impulsive than accepting behavior.

Chapter XIII - This commentary proposes areas for future development of impulsivity, a construct denoting the inability to inhibit impulsive responses to achieve a goal or to wait for a desired goal. Impulsivity is a multifactorial construct encompassing several processes that include an inability to delay gratification, an inability to withhold a response, acting before all of the relevant information is provided, and decision making that is risky and inappropriate. Delay of gratification and inability to withhold a response are also often referred to as cognitive and motor impulsivity, respectively. Cognitive impulsivity may result from deficits in attention, an inability to discriminate reward magnitude, disruptions in time perception, a misunderstanding of response contingencies, an inability to consider future events, or a distortion in the value of long-term consequences. Similarly, apparent deficits in motor impulsivity may result from disruptions in sensory, motor, or timing abilities, even if the ability to withhold an automatic (pre-potent) response is intact.

In: Impulsivity: Causes, Control and Disorders
Editor: George H. Lassiter

ISBN 978-1-60741-951-8
© 2009 Nova Science Publishers, Inc.

Chapter I

Alcohol Abuse and Dependence: Disorders of Control?

Abigail K. Rose
Division of Psychological Medicine and Psychiatry,
Institute of Psychiatry, Kings College London, London, UK

Abstract

Alcohol abuse and dependence are widespread and directly contribute to approximately 1.8 million deaths each year. Alcohol consumption is the number one risk factor for disease burden in developing countries and the third largest risk factor in developed countries. Despite government attempts, alcohol consumption levels are not decreasing, indeed, drinking to levels of intoxication is becoming popular in many countries. This 'binge drinking' pattern of behaviour is associated with both alcohol dependent and non-dependent individuals and poses significant problems in terms of long-term risk of developing alcohol dependence and chronic alcohol-related disorders, such as cirrhosis of the liver, but also more immediate problems including increased risk of accidents, anti-social behaviour, financial and relationship problems. Both alcohol dependent and social drinkers often claim that they drink more than they originally intended. This fact has led some to postulate that alcohol use disorders (AUDs) may involve impaired control processes. However, the nature of this impairment is somewhat harder to determine. Are individuals who have a pre-existing control disorder more at risk of developing an alcohol use disorder or does alcohol consumption lead to short- and long-term biopharmacological changes which support impulsive behaviour and development of alcohol use disorders? The following chapter will discuss the theoretical background which links impulsivity with alcohol use and will use empirical evidence to understand what impairment of control can and cannot explain in terms of alcohol use disorders. The chapter will place theories of control and alcohol use in context with other emerging fields of research and will end by outlining what some of the next steps are in understanding this complex and important area of alcohol-related behaviour.

Introduction

The practise of consuming alcoholic beverages is an old one. Archaeological finds of beer jugs reveal that the fermenting of sugars from yeast was an intentional act dating back to c10,000 B.C. (Hanson, 1995; Patrick, 1952). Alcohol has long been associated with religious and spiritual practises, the Egyptians and ancient Greeks and Chinese all used alcohol as offerings to their Gods, and the Roman Catholic faith retains the custom of offering wine during the Eucharist. However, the problems associated with alcohol use have also been documented throughout history. The famous illustrations and paintings of William Hogarth capture the excesses and dangers associated with excessive drinking. Interestingly, in Hogarth's famous Beer Street and Gin Lane prints, there seems to be the suggestion that alcohol can be both a good and a bad thing. On the left, the beer drinkers are perceived as happy, able to work and prosperous while, on the right, the gin drinkers are viewed in a depraved and miserable state. Indeed, following the encouragement of the British government in the late 1600's, consumption levels of English gin were very high which, in turn, led to the development of several Acts of parliament aimed at reducing production and consumption of the beverage during the first half of the 18th century.

William Hogarth (1735).

Figure 1. A Rake's Progress, Plate 3: The Tavern Scene (Engraving).

William Hogarth (1751).

Figure 2. Beer Street (left) and Gin Lane (right).

History tells us that there is a cyclical nature to levels of alcohol consumption across countries. However, this fact should not hamper research in to understanding why people drink the way they do or diminish, in any way, the work carried out in the development of new interventions and treatments to help those who are, or are at risk of, developing alcohol use disorders (AUDs).

From a global standpoint, alcohol causes 1.8 million deaths (3.2% of total) and 58.3 million (4% of total) of Disability-Adjusted Life Years (DALYs) world wide per year (World Health Organsiation, 2002). The greatest risk factor for disease burden in developing countries is alcohol, and it remains the third greatest risk factor in developed countries, after tobacco and blood pressure (World Health Organisation, 2004; World Health Organisation, 2002). Although, it is important to realise that the actual levels of disease burden from alcohol is greatest in developed countries. The United States of America, Australia, and many European countries, including the United Kingdom, consistently fall within the top half of countries with the highest levels of alcohol consumption per capita (World Health Organisation, 2004).

Although moderate alcohol consumption is, by many, viewed as a pleasurable past time and social lubricant, there are a host of problems associated with excessive drinking. However, it is first important to define what excessive drinking actually is. Definitions vary from time to time and across countries. Previously, governments often set-out recommended weekly guidelines for alcohol consumption however there has been a shift more recently towards daily benchmarks. This shift occurred to avoid the misconception that it was only quantity, and not pattern, of consumption which was important. For example, it may be suggested that 10 units (1 UK unit = 8g of alcohol; 1 USA unit = 14g of alcohol) of alcohol a week is moderate and very unlikely to lead to significant health or personal problems. However, if 10 units is consumed in one night, rather than equally distributed over the week, this has much greater potential for adverse effects e.g. physical sickness and accidents. Guidelines now focus on daily drinking. In the UK, benchmarks indicate that consumption should not regularly exceed 2-3 units for women and 3-4 units for men. In addition to daily benchmarks, definitions also exist for particular drinking practices. Binge drinking is a significant problem in many countries and there is much media interest in highlighting the problems of binge drinking, and in the same vein, society. Originally, binge drinking was used to describe the very heavy drinking bouts of alcohol dependents individuals which could last for several days. However, the terms 'bingeing' and 'binge drinking' now often stir up scenes of drunken antics of young adults on a Friday and Saturday night in city centres. Linked with such images is the UK binge drinking definition: six or more units of alcohol for women and eight or more units of alcohol for men during any one drinking occasion. In America, heavy episodic drinking is defined as ≥ 4 standard drinks for women and ≥ 5 for men (standard drink: half an ounce [14 g] of alcohol) consumed within a two hour period (Koob and Le Moal, 2008). Harmful drinking is defined as consuming ≥ 50 units per week for men and ≥ 35 units per week for women (UK Department of Health). Although drinking guidelines, terminology, and measurements of alcohol differ across countries, the important issues facing countries experiencing problems with alcohol use in their society are often similar. The strength of alcoholic beverages is rising and the volumes sold in drinking venues, e.g. pubs and bars, are increasing while promotions in shops often include attractive deals on purchasing alcohol in bulk. All these factors can act to increase the amount of alcohol bought and consumed, and it actually becomes fairly easy to consume quantities of alcohol within binge drinking and harmful levels. As such behaviour become easier, instances of heavy drinking are likely to increase and the perception of heavy drinking as a normal behavioural act can be adopted by more people. Such situations may create a vicious cycle and a society where binge drinking increases across age groups, gender, culture and socio-economic status.

Health Problems Associated with Alcohol

Excessive and prolonged alcohol use is associated with a host of health problems. In the UK, levels of cirrhosis of the liver have been rising steadily in both men and women and mortality rates are greater than those associated with certain cancers and dementia (Vas, 2001). Alcohol is mostly metabolised by the liver, and so excessive alcohol use can cause significant damage to this organ. At first fatty deposits form in the liver, from this alcoholic hepatitis may develop if harmful drinking continues. If hepatitis is left untreated, with continued heavy alcohol consumption, it can prove fatal or result in cirrhosis of the liver. If a cirrhosis sufferer fails to stop drinking they will eventually die. However, it often takes considerable time for liver cirrhosis to develop and the increase in rates of cirrhosis probably reflects the growing levels of alcohol consumption over the past few decades (Vas, 2001). In addition, there is a worrying trend for individuals in their thirties and early forties to present with serious alcohol related health problems which suggests increasing levels of alcohol consumption in adolescence and early adulthood. The European School Survey Project on Alcohol and other Drugs (ESPAD) has been collecting data from adolescent populations since 1995 and results show that countries including the UK, Ireland, Denmark, Austria, Czech Republic, and the Netherlands, among others, rate highly on a number of indices such as alcohol consumption, binge drinking and drunkenness (Hibell, et al., 2003). Keeping this in mind, if rates of alcohol consumption do not significantly decrease in the near future, the high and prolonged levels of alcohol use being reported in several countries means that rates of liver cirrhosis, as well as other serious health problems, are likely to increase dramatically over the next few decades. Such increases will, in turn, increase the burden on health services as well as having a significant impact on the personal relationships of the individuals involved.

Excessive alcohol use has a number of other effects; due to its high calorific content individuals who drink excessively often have very poor diets and thus the body does not receive the vitamins, proteins and minerals needed for healthy functioning and maintenance (Grilly, 1998). A well-documented example is Wernicke's encephalopathy resulting from a reduced intake of, and deficient absorption and conversion of, thiamine (vitamin B_1). Thiamine is crucial in maintaining healthy neuronal functioning and prolonged deficiency can lead to neurodegeneration. Degeneration in a number of brain systems leads to Wernicke's encephalopathy which is characterised by memory impairments, confusion, reduced movement or paralysis of the eyes, and ataxia. If left untreated, Wernicke's encephalopathy can progress to Korsakoff's syndrome which is particularly related to neuronal degeneration of the thalamus and mammillary bodies of the hypothalamus. Both regions receive and transmit information from many other brain regions and are crucial in higher cognitive functions, such as learning and memory. Individuals with Korsakoff's Syndrome are often apathetic and lack the insight to recognise they have a serious problem. Due to both anterograde and retrograde amnesia, confabulation – inventing memories to fill in gaps – is quite common. By abstaining from drinking and having an improved diet, sufferers of Korsakoff's Syndrome are likely to make some recovery but may continue to need care, still others fail to show any improvement.

From this brief overview it is clear the excessive alcohol use presents a significant problem, indeed, the negative effects of alcohol from a health (e.g. cirrhosis, dementia, accidents and injury), social (e.g. interpersonal relationships, criminal activity, social functioning), and financial (e.g. lost work productivity, personal finances) perspective is far greater than those associated with illicit drug use. It is, therefore, important to understand how and why people drink the way they do. Only with a fuller understanding of these issues can we hope to develop health policy to educate people about excessive alcohol use and interventions and treatments to help prevent and treat the development of alcohol use disorders.

Excessive alcohol consumption and alcohol dependence are complex phenomena and in addition to the environmental factors which affect drinking behaviour, previous experiences and genetic inheritance also influence the way in which people drink. The following chapter is specifically interested in how alcohol use disorders, as some have suggested (Noel, et al., 2007), may be understood as a disorder of disinhibition. To explore this possibility the chapter will provide an overview of the empirical evidence that suggests alcohol use disorders may be related to inhibitory impairment and some insight in to the pharmacological effects of alcohol on the brain which may lend themselves to disinhibition. The discussion shall highlight the complexities of alcohol phenotypes and argue that a model of alcohol use disorders which focuses on only one mechanism, such as disinhibition in its simplest sense, cannot satisfactorily explain the wide range of alcohol-based research findings. Finally, some possibilities of what research is needed in this area will be introduced.

Inhibition and Impulsivity

As a person matures a number of processes develop, an important one of which is inhibition. Inhibitory mechanisms allow us to refrain from behaving in particular ways and block desires and impulses. The inhibition of certain actions, thoughts, desires and impulses is crucial for healthy and positive integration to society. However, alcohol is synonymous with increased disinhibition and impulsivity, which is often viewed as actions based on impulse and which occur with little cognitive effort or evaluation of potential negative consequences.

Disinhibition is integral to a number of syndromes including hyperactivity, hysteria and sociopathy and is a multifaceted concept. Various definitions for the terms 'disinhibition' and 'impulsivity' have developed and been used throughout the relevant literature. These definitions are linked with a number of constructs including sensation seeking, novelty seeking, risk taking, non-planning and dependence on reward (Acton, 2003).

The nature of behaviours seen following alcohol consumption can be those usually inhibited in normal settings. People may appear to act out of character, for example the normally restrained individual who dances on the table after several cocktails, or show more extreme versions of their personality, for example the argumentative individual who become very aggressive and violent after drinking alcohol. Excessive drinking is positively correlated with suicidal behaviour (O'Connell and Lawlor, 2005), aggression (Swahn, Simon, Hammig, and Guerrero, 2004), drink driving (Lui, et al., 1997), forced sexual activities (O'Brien, et al., 2006), sexual promiscuity (Bushman and Cooper, 1990; Fromme, D'Amico, and Katz, 1999), sexually transmitted infections (Staton, et al., 1999) and absolute and relative levels of nicotine smoking and illicit drug use (Sutherland and Willner, 1998). It has been argued that such actions illustrate alcohol's ability to weaken normal control processes, leading to uncharacteristic and/or extreme forms of behaviour.

Another important phenomenon, and one particularly relevant to the current discussion, is the *alcohol priming* phenotype. This phenotype refers to the finding that initial alcohol consumption can support further drinking. Anecdotal reports show that people often drink more than originally intended, for instance, the student who vows to only go out 'for a few' but ends up spending all their money and wakes up with only hazy recollections of the previous night. It is also common for initial alcohol consumption (a 'slip drink') to be cited as a trigger for relapse by alcoholics (Shaham, Shalev, Lu, de Wit, and Stewart, 2003). Therefore, alcohol priming has been given as a reason for excessive drinking, e.g. binge drinking, and relapse to alcohol following periods of abstinence (Rose and Duka, 2006; Stewart, de Wit, and Eikelboom, 1984; Stockwell, Hodgson, Rankin, and Taylor, 1982).

Within a disinhibitory framework, priming could be linked with a classic theory of drug abuse by Jellinek (1960) which involves control processes. Jellinek differentiated between several different types of alcoholism, some of which he considered to be a disease involving 'loss of control' over drinking behaviour. This model suggested that some individuals could potentially abstain from drinking for relatively long periods of time but had no control over drinking behaviours once initiated; that just one drink would trigger a compulsion to drink excessively leading to a heavy binge drinking session. Such beliefs form the basis of many programmes aimed at helping alcoholics recover, including the 12 step Alcoholics Anonymous program which promotes total abstinence.

However, as already outlined any behaviour is the product of several processes. Although some individuals experience problems with disinhibition others are able to exert control over their actions, for instance, the successful dieter who refrains from eating chocolate even though they crave something sweet. This is the same for drinking behaviour; some people will develop problems with their drinking while other will not. It is therefore important to understand how alcohol exerts its control over inhibitory processes, and how this can lead to continued drinking, at least in some people.

The fact that alcohol does not affect everyone in the same way has led to a substantial amount of research which looks at how personality and specific personality traits and disorders may affect behaviour. Attention Deficit Hyperactivity Disorder (ADHD) was first described during the middle of the 19th century and is characterised by under-controlled and hyperactive behaviour, impulsivity and an inability to pay attention. There are several subtypes of ADHD which reflect differences in levels of these main characteristics. To warrant a diagnosis of ADHD, symptoms should present before the child is 7 years old and continue for at least 6 months. In addition, the behaviour of the child must be seen as pervasive, not normal behaviour for children of a similar age, and must disrupt and lead to problems in at least two spheres of life e.g. family and school (National Institute of Mental Health, 1994 (revised 2001)). Prospective longitudinal research has shown that ADHD is correlated with early drinking onset, for example, Barkley et al (1990) found that 40% of adolescents who had been diagnosed with ADHD as children had consumed alcohol, compared with 22% of adolescents without a history of ADHD. Using a number of behavioural and cognitive measures of disinhibition, Soloff et al (2000) found that 16-21 year olds with high levels of trait impulsivity were significantly more likely to suffer from alcohol use disorders relative to age-matched individuals who reported lower levels of dispositional impulsivity. These are important findings as early onset use of alcohol is highly predictive of alcohol use disorders during adulthood which are often characterised by poorer treatment outcomes. The link between ADHD and alcohol use disorders is found in both men and women. Schubiner et al (2000) reported that women with ADHD had received a greater number of treatment episodes for alcohol problems relative to women without ADHD. However, the evidence that ADHD, a disorder of control, is a specific risk marker for alcohol use disorders is equivocal. Rodriguez and Span (2008) found that ADHD only correlated with frequent and heavy drinking habits in individuals who also held weak expectancies regarding bad hangovers. Further analysis showed that these individuals rated higher on the inattentiveness dimension of ADHD. This finding makes intuitive sense; if someone is inattentive the consequences of actions, for example a bad hangover, are likely to have only minimal impact on behaviour. Although the majority of research shows some link between ADHD and risky drinking behaviours our understanding remains incomplete. More research is needed which investigates the specific aspects of ADHD which might act as a marker for risk of alcohol use disorders.

Those who suffer from drug addiction tend to score higher on a number of personality variables such as, impulsivity, sensation-seeking, lack of constraint and harm avoidance (Conway, Kane, Ball, Poling, and Rounsaville, 2003). Although the concept of an addictive personality per se receives little merit these days, there is some evidence that poly-drug abuse does have links with clusters of personality traits related to social deviance (Conway, et al., 2003). In an attempt to identify personality risk factors for bingeing Baron et al. (1998) discovered six predictors, one of which was impulsivity. Norman et al. (1998) also looked in to risk factors for binge drinking and found that individuals who believed they had less control over their drinking behaviour were more likely to binge drink and to do so frequently (Oei and Morawska, 2004).

Eysenck, one of the most famous psychologists who worked on personality, developed a number of questionnaires including the Eysenck Personality Inventory and the Eysenck Personality Questionnaire. Both of which include dimensions such as extraversion and psychoticism which cover impulsive characteristics. Studies have found that these dimensions positively correlate with self-reported drinking levels and attitude towards alcohol and substance misuse, such that tolerance to substance use is associated with greater disinhibition (Acton, 2003). Conrod (1997) found that individuals who experienced problems with school, work, family, friends and personal functioning due to their drinking habits were those who scored high on the psychoticism scale and presented a disinhibited personality style. The finding that disinhibition is related to alcohol use spans age groups, different cultures and gender. Grau and Ortet (1999) found that both frequency and quantity of alcohol use were highly correlated with impulsivity and sensation-seeking in Spanish women.

Another well-established theory of personality is that of Zuckerman who argued that all individuals have an optimal level of stimulation and introduced the term 'sensation seeking' (Zuckerman, Kolin, Price, and Zoob, 1964). Since then, this particular attribute has gained much attention, illustrated by the number of scales developed to measure it. Zuckerman's Sensation Seeking Scale is one of the best known and identifies individuals high in sensation seeking as those who prefer to experience strong or extreme sensations and novelty, who bore easily of routine, who prefer irregularity and partake in risky activities (Zuckerman, et al., 1964). College samples have shown that high sensation seeking is associated with heavy episodic drink and experience of the negative consequences of drinking alcohol (Yusko, Buckman, White, and Pandina, 2008). High levels of impulsivity and sensation seeking are also found in alcohol dependent patients seeking treatment.

There is evidence that characteristics associated with disinhibition might be more associated with alcohol use in those considered Type II alcoholics (Echeburua, Bravo de Medina, and Aizpiri, 2008). Cloninger separated alcoholism in to Type I or Type II subtypes. He argued that Type I alcoholism tended to develop at a later age often as a result of the expectancies held regarding alcohol's effects which have developed over years of drinking experience, for instance, positive reinforcing effects. Those with Type I alcoholism were more likely to develop psychological rather than physical dependence and experience feelings of guilt and depression concerning their drinking habits. Type II alcoholism is characterised as having an early onset, typically before the age of 25 years, and is associated with disinhibited personalities; individuals who score high on novelty seeking and exhibit other types of disinhibited behaviour such as aggression and other anti-social habits (Cloninger, Sigvardsson, and Bohman, 1988). Longitudinal research has shown that personality traits apparent during childhood are related to risk of alcohol use disorders during adulthood. High novelty seeking and low harm avoidance at age 10 was associated with alcohol abuse before the age of 30 years (Cloninger, et al., 1988). However, there has been some debate as to the usefulness and validity of Cloninger's subtypes. Some have argued that Type II alcoholism actually represents a small part of a primary anti-social personality disorder (Zernig, Saria, Kurz, and O'Malley, 2000). If this is the case it would still hold that disinhibition and impulsivity are risk factors for alcoholism but that when an individual presents with alcohol problems both the primary personality disorder and the co-morbid alcohol problem need to be treated to improve chances of a successful outcome.

Another key model of disinhibition, at least from an historical persepective, is Gray's distinction between two separate control systems based on motivation: a behavioural activation system and a behavioural inhibition system (Gray, 1976). The behavioural activation system is activated by reward cues which stimulate cortical arousal and trigger appetitive and approach behaviours. In contrast, the behavioural inhibition system is activated by punishment and non-reward cues and stimulation leads to aversive and avoidance behaviours (Avila, 2001). These two neuropsychological systems are mutually inhibitory and may be unbalanced in some individuals. Those with a stronger behavioural activation system would perceive a greater number of reward cues in the environment and engage in more approach behaviours, irrespective of the potential negative consequences of the behaviour. In addition, the attenuated behavioural inhibition system would lead to ongoing behaviour even when punishment cues were present. While people with a strong behavioural inhibition system would perceive more punishment or non-reward cues and display a greater degree of inhibition over appetitive behaviours. Therefore disinhibition is associated with an active behavioural activation system and an attenuated behavioural inhibition system.

Research by Avila (2001) looked at how status of the behavioural activation system and behavioural inhibition system related to behaviour on punishment and reward response tasks. The Sensitivity to Punishment and Sensitivity to Reward Questionnaire (SPSRQ) was used to determine the nature of participants' behavioural activation and behavioural inhibition systems. Participants high in sensitivity to punishment (active behavioural inhibition system) showed greater response suppression, whereas those with a low sensitivity to punishment (attenuated behavioural inhibition system) seemed less able to develop expectancies regarding punishment cues and so were less likely to predict when aversive stimuli or consequences would occur. In addition, information regarding punishment seemed less able to exert control over ongoing appetitive behaviour. Participants who had high reward sensitivity (active behavioural activation system) found it difficult to inhibit responding when punishment became more likely, as though the goal-directed behaviour was competing with, and beating, aversive learning.

Due to the nature of the two systems, an overactive behavioural activation system may be linked with the ability of alcohol to act as a reward. For instance, after an initial drink (a prime) the behavioural activation system may become excited and support approach and goal-directed behaviours aimed at acquiring and consuming more alcohol. Empirical evidence for such a distinction between the behavioural activation system and behavioural inhibition system comes from Fillmore and Rush (2001) using a stop signal task. Participants were given 0.55 g/kg of ethanol (approximately 5 UK units of alcohol) or placebo to drink and asked if they wanted to earn alcohol or monetary rewards for good task performance, based on both quick responding and few errors. On the task, participants were instructed to respond to 'go' stimuli as quickly as possible, however, on a small percentage of trials a tone accompanied the stimulus which informed the participant not to respond. In general, error and response latency reflect opposing reward acquisition strategies, the faster one goes the more likely a mistake will be made. Therefore, the best approach is to find the quickest you can respond while still making relatively few errors. The performance of the participants who were given alcohol showed significantly more errors than those given placebo, thus they had chosen the quickest reward strategy, even at the cost of more errors. These results suggest that following alcohol consumption the behavioural activation system was active relative to the behavioural inhibition system (Fillmore, 2003). In terms of alcohol priming, participants given the alcoholic drink were more likely to choose to earn alcohol rewards than the participants given placebo. These findings show that, via effects on behavioural motivation systems, alcohol can support impulsive-like behaviour which may be one way in which initial alcohol consumption can support excessive drinking.

Another task used substantially within disinhibition research is the cued go/no-go task. Both 'go' and 'no-go' stimuli are presented on the computer screen, participants must respond or not respond to these stimuli respectively. Preceding each trial a cue appears on the screen, one precedes the go target approximately 80% of the time, while the other precedes the no-go target 80% of the time. Participants learn an association between these cues and the targets, so that when a 'go' cue occurs the participant can prepare to respond. However, on a minority of trials (approximately 20%) the cues give inaccurate information, thus the participant must suppress their prepotent response, whichever that may be, in order to perform accurately. The cue can occur at various times before the stimulus to assess the time required to successfully alter the prepotent response when 'false' cues occur. Marczinski and Fillmore (2003a, 2003b) found that errors on the cued go/no-go task increased in a linear fashion over placebo and doses of alcohol (0.45 – 0.65 g/kg), as did accurate response latency when stimuli were preceded by invalid cues. A related task is the stop signal model. The participant responds to stimuli which appear on a computer screen, however, on a minority of trials a 'stop' signal can follow the stimuli e.g. 50 or 150ms after the onset of the response stimulus. While comparing the effects of alcohol and amphetamine on behaviour using the stop signal task, de Wit et al., (2000) found that alcohol significantly reduced the ability to inhibit responses in a dose dependent manner even though response execution was unaffected. Mulvihil et al. (1997) also found increased behavioural disinhibition using a stop signal task after a moderate dose of alcohol (men: 0.62 g/kg, women: 0.54 g/kg) was given to male and female participants. Results showed that the impairment related to response inhibition and not response latency (time taken to respond). These findings suggest that alcohol acutely influences behavioural inhibition, rather than behavioural activation, mechanisms as activation of the latter would support decreased latency (Fillmore, 2003a).

Cued tasks, such as the cued go/no-go test, help researchers examine the role of the environment on behavioural output as the participant relies on the cue to prepare for the following event. The fact that individuals perform worse after drinking alcohol, and that this impairment is pronounced on trials that incorporate invalid go cues, rather than on all trials, indicates that after drinking, people rely on environmental cues to a greater extent to determine their behaviour. This suggestion fits within a behaviourist framework; that any drug of abuse, including alcohol, has its effect by altering the degree to which the person relies on, and is controlled by, the environment (Fillmore, 2003b). This finding may also be used to help understand drinking related phenotypes, such as priming. For instance, in many drinking environments, such as a bar or at a party, a person will be surrounded by a host of alcohol related cues including different types of drinks, other people drinking and advertisements for alcohol. If after consuming alcohol the individual relies on cues in the environment to shape their behaviour then, in such contexts, excessive drinking becomes more likely.

The importance of the environment in shaping behaviour during drinking occasions may also suggest that a pure model of disinhibition might not be able to explain all drinking phenomena. For instance, individuals do not always display disinhibited behaviour while drinking alcohol. The alcohol myopia theory proposed by Steele and Josephs (1990) argues that alcohol has two main effects on information processing: to decrease the number of cues a person can attend to and to reduce the amount of information a person can extract from cues and integrate in to their existing knowledge. As alcohol blocks the ability to process information properly, "inhibition conflict" is attenuated. For example, when sober, a person might want to drink when they encounter a facilitatory alcohol cue, such as a pub but, due to work commitments, they decide not to. If the same situation occurred after the individual had consumed alcohol, only the immediate, facilitatory cue of the pub would affect behaviour, rather than the inhibiting cue of work commitments which requires greater information processing. Therefore, if salient cues are conservative, the alcohol myopia theory would predict that alcohol consumption could lead to an increase in less risky and impulsive behaviour relative to when sober. MacDonald et al., (2000) found that after reading a passage of text concerning unprotected sex, intoxicated participants were more likely to report that they would not have unprotected sex following a questionnaire that included inhibitory cues (e.g. regarding contraception) relative to sober participants. As discussed earlier, individuals seems to rely more on contextual cues when drinking alcohol, therefore, if environmental cues are not conducive to certain acts then these behaviours may be less likely to occur. For example, disinhibited sexual behaviour is more likely under the influence of alcohol if the individual is at a party with friends, rather than at a party where family members are also present. Following from this argument, alcohol may not induce a general state of disinhibition but support observed disinhibitory behaviour due its effects on processes of attention allocation and information processing. If this is indeed true, excessive alcohol consumption may be curbed if the drinking environment contained explicit warnings concerning the hazards of alcohol. Unfortunately, each drinking episode does not occur in isolation. Every time a person drinks, sees another person drinking, or listens to a story about drinking, memories and expectations concerning drinking develop. If such expectations are positive then the environmental cues of the drinking environment which match such expectations, e.g. friends having a good time, are likely to have more influence than contextual cues which advertise the potential negative consequences of drinking. When looking at research which investigates both disinhibitory and attentional mechanisms it seems that acute alcohol affects both. A number of studies have used the Stroop task which is a test of interference inhibition. The original task consists of colour words printed in incongruous ink colours, e.g. the word 'red' printed in blue ink. At first participants must simply read out the printed words which provide baseline measures on response latency and error rate. In the second part of the task, participants must ignore the prepotent response, which is the semantic content of the word, and respond with the ink colour that the word is printed in. Participants tend to take longer to complete the second part of the task and make more errors. This impaired response is exacerbated by alcohol, indicating an acute effect of alcohol on impaired inhibition (Rose and Duka, 2007). However, the Stroop task also has modified versions in which the words used potentially have specific meanings to various participant populations. Research has found that social drinkers who have been primed with a dose of alcohol and alcohol dependent individuals show greater levels of disinhibition on the classic Stroop task and alcohol-related Stroop tasks but not on non-alcohol-related modified Stroop tasks (Duka and Townshend, 2004; Fadardi and Cox, 2006; Rose and Duka, 2008). There is also preliminary evidence that children of alcohol dependent parents, who do not differ from age-matched controls in terms of personal drinking habits, show impaired inhibition in alcohol-related Stroop tasks (Zetteler, Stollery, Weinstein, and Lingford-Hughes, 2006). Taken together, these results indicate that an inability to inhibit prepotent responding may be a risk factor for hazardous drinking and alcohol can acutely impair control mechanisms. In addition, an attentional bias for alcohol related stimuli may be an underlying mechanism for the disinhibition observed after acute alcohol consumption in some individuals.

By employing such cognitive and behavioural tasks numerous studies have found that alcohol increases erroneous responding and decreases the ability to suppress inappropriate behaviour (de Wit, et al., 2000; Fillmore and Van Selst, 2002b; Fillmore and Vogel-Sprott, 1995; Fillmore and Vogel-Sprott, 1999). Such findings occur even with relatively small doses of alcohol and when blood alcohol levels are below legal driving limits, highlighting the subjective nature of alcohol effects.

A series of experiments conducted by Bechara et al., (1998, 1999, 2000, 2002) evaluated decision-making functions, and explained disinhibition within an information processing framework. Bechara et al. (2000) developed a gambling task involving four decks of cards. Two decks are associated with smaller rewards but, overall, will result in a greater win while the other two decks are linked with big short-term reward but overall loss. Results showed that participants with disorders of addiction performed worse on the gambling task than non-addicted, matched controls. The drug user's performance was in line with patients suffering frontal lobe damage, showing an apparent inability to take into account long-term consequences when making decisions which, in turn, could lead to disinhibited behaviour and prolonged drug administration.

As already explained, impulsivity is a multifaceted construct and Bechara et al., (2000) argued for a distinction between motor and cognitive impulsivity. Accordingly, motor impulsivity reflects the inability to suppress a prepotent response, whereas cognitive impulsivity is more complex and relates to the inability to delay reward and is, perhaps, more relevant to a type of personality (Crone, Vendel, and van der Molan, 2003). There are, however, other ways by which motoric and cognitive disinhibition may be distinguished. Motor disinhibition may indeed represent a relatively basic activity whereby the execution of a prepotent response becomes habit, and thus difficult to inhibit due to automaticity. Cognitive disinhibition on the other hand may reflect a situation in which more effortful information processing is required to inhibit a particular action and which may not be fully completed by the time a behavioural response is made. If disinhibition is involved in alcohol related phenotypes, such as priming, then it is laudable to assess at what level disinhibition occurs. Such research could shed light on other processes affected by alcohol. For instance, if the more complex, executive functions are disinhibited this may indicate that alcohol has impeded information processing systems, thus initial consumption could prevent the individual deciding between stopping and continuing drinking, which may then lead to the disinhibited behaviour of bingeing.

An experimental assessment of impulsivity based on decision-making, thus a cognitive interpretation of disinhibition, is the delay discounting paradigm. In this task, participants are presented with two rewards, one large and one small, the delivery of the former is delayed but the latter is immediate (e.g. £20 now or £150 in 6 months). These choices are presented to the participant and, by varying either the magnitude of the reward or the delay, the experimenter can gauge the 'indifference point'. From this, participants can be compared and a relative measure of impulsivity given, for instance, someone who claimed that £5 now was equal to £20 in a week would be more impulsive than someone who rated £10 now as equal to £20 in one week. Responses in the delayed discounting task have been found to correlate with trait levels of impulsivity in abstaining alcoholics (Mitchell, Fields, D'Esposito, and Boettiger, 2005). Petry (2001) tested current and detoxified alcoholics and controls and found that discounting larger, delayed rewards was greatest in current alcoholics, followed by abstainers and then controls, indicating acute and chronic effects of alcohol on impulsivity. Several studies have shown that drug users including alcohol, cigarettes and opiates, show greater delay discounting impulsivity scores for monetary rewards than non-addicted, matched controls (Bickel, Odum, and Madden, 1999; Fillmore, 2003b; Kirby, Petry, and Bickel, 1999). Within non-dependent populations, Kollins (2003) and Field et al (2007) found that a number of drug variables including age of first use (alcohol, nicotine, cannabis), number of times passed out from alcohol, frequency of administration of illicit drugs and alcohol, levels of alcohol consumption and binge drinking patterns all positively correlated with impulsivity on a delay discounting task using hypothetical monetary rewards. Using an Experiential Discounting Task, Reynolds et al. (2006) found that alcohol's acute effects also included an increase in impulsive behaviour.

Remaining with the cognitive models of behavioural control, Finn proposed a cognitive modulation model and argued that the behavioural inhibition system is controlled by working memory and conditional associative learning. Furthermore, he argued that individuals differ in terms of their natural level of working memory capacity and conditional associative learning ability. Finn measured participants' working memory capacity and conditional associative learning ability before assessing performance on contingency reversal go/no-go task. In such a task the relationship between the stimuli and the go and no-go responses is reversed half way through the test, therefore, the participant must respond to previous no-go stimuli and inhibit their learnt response to the original go stimuli. Alcohol reduced behavioural inhibition in participants with a naturally low level of working memory capacity only. People with a naturally restricted level of working memory capacity might only be able to process information regarding salient, proximal events such as the positive effects of drinking but not information about more distal events such as family arguments concerning drinking behaviour. In addition, alcohol consumption may acutely reduce working memory capacity resulting in further disinhibited drinking behaviour.

We can integrate the findings from cued tasks and decision-based tasks to understand how acute alcohol effects may trigger impulsive behaviour and support excessive drinking. The discussion has shown that the environment can exert more control over behaviour following alcohol consumption, and we now understand that alcohol may reduce delay discounting. Therefore, when in a drinking environment the alcohol-related cues will encourage continued drinking and the short term rewarding effects of drinking, e.g. staying out with friends and having a good time, will be more salient to the individual than the potential longer term reward of drinking cessation, e.g. saving money and not suffering a hangover in the morning. However, it is important to note that a substantial amount of research using the original delay discounting paradigm fails to show clear acute effects of alcohol (Dougherty, Marsh-Richard, Hatzis, Nouvion, and Mathias, 2008). The finding that different impulsivity tasks generate different types of data, especially with respect to the acute effects of alcohol, highlights the multi-dimensional nature of impulsivity and the need to look at the specific elements of impulsivity and disinhibition which may be related to alcohol behaviours (Dougherty, et al., 2008). One important area of research, which may allow us to understand the links between impulsivity and alcohol, is the biopharmacological basis of impulsivity and the psychopharmacological effects of alcohol and see how these interact and correspond with one another.

Biopharmacological Basis of Alcohol-related Behaviour and Disinhibition

This chapter is not intended to provide an exhaustive description of the biopharmacological basis of alcohol or disinhibition. However, it is useful to include an outline of some of the major systems implicated in these areas, to highlight their complexity and begin to understand some of the neuropharmacological mechanisms underlying alcohol's effect on disinhibition and how impulsivity may impact on alcohol-related behaviour.

Alcohol: Alcohol is both a central nervous system (CNS) depressant and stimulant, dependent on the dose of alcohol administered and the site of action under observation (Little, 1999).

Perhaps the most important effect of alcohol, at least in understanding its addictive potential, is reinforcement. Any effect of a drug which strengthens the relationship between a stimulus and a response is a reinforcer. For example, the positive effects of drinking may strengthen the relationship between the visual cue of the pint of beer (stimulus) and the subsequent consumption of the beer (response). One important point to note is that although reinforcement is often associated with the pleasurable and hedonic effects of alcohol, reinforcement can be both positive and negative. Positive reinforcement confers strengthening of relationships due to the pleasurable effects (e.g. the sociable effects of drinking alcohol) while negative reinforcement strengthens relationships due to removal of an aversive state (e.g. drinking in order to experience the anxiolytic effects of alcohol). At first the positive reinforcing effects of alcohol are usually of primary importance and the incentive properties of drinking motivate the individual to seek out and consume alcohol. After continued and excessive use, dependence on alcohol may develop which may lead to personal and professional problems. In addition, upon cessation of drinking a withdrawal syndrome can be experienced. In an attempt to alleviate this negative state, and perhaps as a way to forget about problems, the individual will commence drinking. Therefore, negative reinforcement often becomes a predominant feature in an individual's motives for drinking and a compulsion to drink can develop, which can see alcohol usurp control over behaviour.

The strong rewarding effects of alcohol are linked with its effects on the brain's reward circuitry which involves the mesocorticolimbic dopamine system. This system involves two of the major dopamine (DA) neural pathways, the first links the ventral tegmental area in the midbrain to the nucleus accumbens situated in the striatum, which is part of the limbic system. The second links the ventral tegmental area with various cortical regions located in the frontal lobes which are involved in control. Animal models of reward and addiction, such as electrical and drug self-administration, often show increases in levels of extracellular dopamine at the terminal regions or firing rates of the ventral tegmentum neurons (Koob and Le Moal, 2008; Moal, 1995). Acute alcohol administration leads to increased neuronal firing of dopamine neurons within the ventral striatum and administration of dopamine antagonists can block or attenuate operant responding for alcohol and drinking behaviour (Di Chiara, 1995; Feldman, Meyer, and Quenzer, 1997). Although dopamine systems seem important in the reinforcing effects of alcohol, it is not sufficient to focus only on the dopaminergic pathways, for example, drugs will still be self-administered following lesions of dopamine neurons (Mucha, Pauli, and Angrilli, 1998). More recently, it has been argued that dopamine mechanisms alert the organism to novel cues which will trigger learning about new and important stimuli (incentive learning). Dopamine mechanimsms may also be involved in recognition of motivationally salient events (e.g. the sight of a favourite pub), based on previous experience and learning, which can allow the individual to adapt and engage in goal-directed behaviour (e.g. to enter the pub and drink alcohol) (Kalivas and Volkow, 2005).

Alcohol's eurphorigenic actions may be due to effects on dopamine and endogenous opioid systems. Much of the research focusing on opioid systems involves administering opioid receptor antagonists and observing what happens to alcohol-related behaviour. An interesting animal study was that of Gonzales and Weiss (1998) who, after training rats to administer alcohol, treated half with naltrexone (a competitive opioid receptor antagonist) and half with an inert substance. Extracellular dopamine levels in the nucleus accumbens were measured before treatment, during a waiting period after treatment, and during alcohol self-administration. During self-administration, vehicle-treated rats consumed more alcohol which correlated with higher dopamine levels. During the 'waiting period', there was an increase in dopamine in both groups, perhaps due to environmental cues signalling alcohol availability. Therefore, naltrexone may specifically inhibit alcohol-stimulated dopamine release by blocking alcohol's effect on the opioid system.

Human research which has incorporated opioid receptor antagonists has also found that alcohol's actions on the opioid systems are important. Following a 12 week treatment regime of either 50 mg of naltrexone or placebo a day, detoxified alcohol dependent individuals in the naltrexone condition reported milder reports of craving, less drinking, lower relapse rates, and longer time to first relapse (O'Brien, Volpicelli, and Volpicelli, 1996). McCaul et al., (2000) treated non-dependent moderate/heavy drinkers with naltrexone (a small or moderate dose: 50mg, 100mg) or placebo before participants consumed alcoholic (either 0.5 or 1.0 g/kg) or non-alcoholic drinks. The results showed that the self-reported pleasurable effects of alcohol and desire to drink decreased in a linear fashion across the naltrexone doses relative to placebo. Drobes et al. (2003) found that non-treatment-seeking alcohol dependent individuals treated with opioid antagonsists (naltrexone or nalmefene) were less likely to choose alcohol following a priming dose (men: 0.4 g/kg, women: 0.34 g/kg). Of those who did choose alcohol, the total amount consumed was less than those treated with placebo. O'Malley et al. (2002) administered naltrexone or placebo before priming non-treatment-seeking alcohol dependent individuals with alcohol (1-1.5 standard drinks). Self-reported alcohol urge was lower in the naltrexone condition and ad lib alcohol consumption was greatest after placebo. Within human research, a number of studies have shown that opioid receptor antagonists reduce self-reported positive effects of alcohol and drinking levels, including frequency of binge drinking in both dependent and social drinkers (Drobes, et al., 2003; McCaul, et al., 2000; Srisurapanont and Jarusuraisin, 2005). Such findings suggest that alcohol's action on the opioid systems may be involved in risk of binge drinking in both dependent and non-dependent drinking populations. Anton et al. (2004) carried out a similar study to O'Malley et al's but provided ad libitum alcohol drinking sessions either immediately or 40 minutes after the alcohol priming session. Naltrexone reduced the amount of alcohol consumed in the delayed, but not immediate, session. In addition, a positive relationship between self-reported feelings of stimulation (a positive subjective effect of alcohol) and ad libitum alcohol consumption was found. However, treatment with naltrexone reversed this relationship. The subjective effects of alcohol are related to the concentration of alcohol within the body. Research shows that the positive and stimulating effects of alcohol correlate with ascending and peak breath alcohol concentrations while the sedative and more negative effects of alcohol are related to the descending portion of the breath alcohol curve (Demmel, Klusener, and Rist, 2004). Rose and Duka (2006) found that priming, following 0.6 g/kg of alcohol, peaked 30-40 minutes following the preload, which related to peak breath alcohol concentration. If naltrexone attenuates the positive reinforcing effects of alcohol, it is likely that this attenuation will be greatest when reinforcing effects are peaking which may explain Anton et al's finding that naltrexone proved most efficacious at reducing drinking levels 40 minutes after the initial alcohol prime.

Disinhibition: Regions of the frontal lobes are believed to exert influence over the execution of both conditioned and reflexive responses (Fowles, 1987). The frontal lobes are subdivided in to several regions and it is likely that different regions are related to different cognitive processes. Dias et al. (1996a) trained marmosets to respond to certain aspects of a stimulus, via discrimination trials, to gain rewards. Lesions were then made to the lateral prefrontal or orbitofrontal cortex and the marmoset's ability to select the appropriate response on the basis of either stimulus-reward relationships (visual discrimination reversal: the animal's ability to correctly reverse their responding in order to maintain reward delivery) or selective attention to particular stimulus attributes (attentional set-shifting: to accurately shift attention to a new salient stimulus attribute and ignore a previously salient attribute which had become redundant) was observed. Lesions to the prefrontal cortex reduced the ability for attentional set-shifting, while orbitofrontal lesions diminished the marmoset's competence at reversing reward-stimulus associations. The key finding was that lesions failed to attenuate the animal's ability to discriminate between, or to maintain attention to, certain stimulus elements and this was taken as evidence that the lesions specifically affected inhibitory control.

Animal studies show lesions within the prefrontal and orbitofrontal cortex leads to perseverative behaviours. Using a primate analogue of the Wisconsin Card Sorting Task, Dias et al. (1996b) tested the effects of lesions to the prefrontal lobe on behaviour. The Wisconsin Card Sorting Task is a neuropsychological test which assesses perseveration and abstract reasoning and it used as a sensitive measure of frontal lobe function. The findings showed that monkeys with prefrontal lesions displayed decreased ability to shift attention. The perseveration of behaviour is important, if an individual is unable to shift their attention once drinking has commenced, then they are likely to continue drinking as their attention is fixed upon alcohol-related cues. This finding again highlights the importance of attention in behavioural control which was discussed earlier.

The importance of dopamine has already been outlined in terms of reward, reinforcement and addiction; that dopamine projections from the ventral tegmental area to limbic areas are involved with attributing incentive value and reward and facilitate motivated behaviour. It has also been proposed that some individuals at risk of developing alcohol use disorders are those governed by reward. It is, therefore, likely that dopamine activity is also involved in control and research supports this possibility. Drugs of abuse, including alcohol, increase dopamine levels in the prefrontal cortex. The importance of dopamine in inhibition is indicated by the observation that hypersensitivity of DA_1 receptors seems to reduce control over approach behaviours (Jentsch and Taylor, 1999). In animal research, disruption of dopamine activity within the frontal cortex can impair animal performance on tasks that require response inhibition (Bubser and Schmidt, 1990). As the frontal lobes are important in higher cognitive function it is likely that the effects of alcohol on these cortical regions will lead to observed behavioural effects as a result of disrupted cognitive processes (Fillmore, 2003b).

Lesions studies also show that disruption within the orbito- and medial-prefrontal cortex can induce hyperactive, compulsive and disinhibited behaviour (Jentsch and Taylor, 1999). Grant et al. (1996) and Childress et al. (1999) have both found that disruption of the frontal regions causes problems with working memory function and control. In a series of studies using a gambling paradigm, Bechara et al., (1998, 1999, 2000a, 2000b, 2001, 2002a, 2002b, 2004) have shown similarities in the risk-taking behaviours of individuals with frontal lesions and those suffering from chronic alcohol abuse, which has suggested some form of control impairment based on decision-making processes. Damasio (1996) found that individuals with orbitofrontal and prelimbic damage showed disinhibition, with respect to strong preferences for immediate, smaller rewards over larger, delayed rewards. As discussed earlier, the inability to delay gratification may be an inherent risk marker for alcohol use disorders. More research is needed which looks at brain function in those with known risks for alcohol use disorders, e.g. offspring of alcoholics. Initial studies suggest that such people may have hyposensitive amygdala function which would reduce input to brain regions associated with control and may support risk-taking behaviours including excessive alcohol use (Glahn, Lovallo, and Fox, 2007).

From this brief introduction of some of the pharmacological mechanisms underlying alcohol related behaviour and control it should be clear that, just as there are many alcohol phenotypes and aspects to disinhibition and impulsivity, there are numerous different biopharmacological systems involved in these areas. Due to such complexity it should not be surprising that alcohol use disorders cannot just be viewed as a 'simple' disorder of disinhibition. The final section of this discussion introduces some of the other factors which are believed to be important in understanding alcohol related issues and some themes for future research which will help our understanding develop further.

Beyond Disinhibition and Future Research

The more sophisticated models of addiction which have been emerging over recent years incorporate a number of processes including motivation, learning, positive and negative reinforcement, personality and attention as well as disinhibition.

Volkow et al., (2003a) proposed a model of addiction which focused on how the choices individuals make are determined by numerous processes which incorporate several brain circuits, including reward, motivation and drive, memory and learning, and control (figure 3). The model proposes that when a person comes in to contact with a previously experienced cue, the memory of past events increases the cue's salience (either positively or negatively, dependent on the nature of past experience). If, at the same time, the individual's internal state is appropriate (e.g. a cue related to drinking and an internal thirst state) then the cue's saliency increases and the motivational/drive state is strengthened. Volkow et al. argued that, unlike natural reinforcers (e.g. food and sex), drug rewards do not lose any of their perceived value which, in turn, increases the individual's reward threshold so that natural reinforcers are not as attractive as drug reinforcers. With regard to alcohol, when a person drinks the brain's reward circuits are strongly activated which leads to high levels of motivation to drink, this action is coupled with the activation of memories of past drinking experiences, and attenuation of the control processes situated in the frontal cortex. The overall effect of the active reward, memory and motivation circuits with the inhibited control system, allows a positive feedback loop to occur which supports prolonged and compulsive drinking, which can be described as disinhibited (Volkow, et al., 2003).

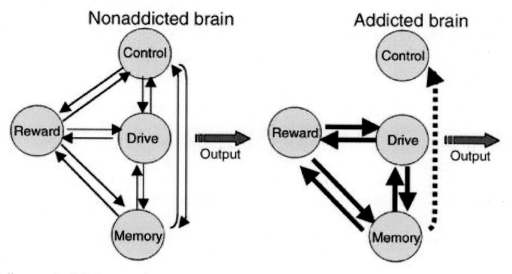

Volkow et al's (2003).

Figure 3. Model consists of four circuits which work together and adapt with experience. Each circuit is associated with a particular concept: saliency (reward), internal state (motivation/drive), learned associations (memory), and conflict resolution (control).

Such models are likely to be more useful when trying to develop a theory of addiction which encompasses the myriad of research findings compared with a model which attempts to explain all findings with one primary mechanism. For instance, disinhibitory aspects of personality may be more related to some of the negative consequences associated with alcohol, e.g. aggression, accidents and injury. Actual drinking levels, and occurrences of binge drinking, may have more to do with positive alcohol reinforcement (Conrod, et al., 1997). When investigating whether binge drinking was related to trait levels of disinhibition or alcohol-induced impulsivity, Rose and Grunsell (2008) used the time estimation and two choice tasks (Dougherty, 2003) within an alcohol priming paradigm (0.6 g/kg alcohol or placebo). It has been suggested that impulsive people may over-estimate the amount of time that has elapsed which, in terms of excessive drinking, may translate in to individuals believing that they are drinking quite slowly and moderately when in actual fact they are drinking heavily. The time estimation task consists of several trials in which participants must estimate a given period of time. The two choice task measures the participant's choice between an immediate small reward and a delayed larger reward. No differences were found in either dispositional impulsivity or alcohol-induced impulsivity between binge and non-binge drinkers. However, binge drinkers showed greater tolerance to the sedative and lightheadedness effects of alcohol. In addition, male binge drinkers reported feeling more stimulated after the alcohol prime relative to placebo. These findings were specifically related to binge status and not typical number of alcohol units consumed per week, suggesting that risk of binge drinking is related more to the subjective, rather than the disinhibiting, effects of alcohol. However, post hoc analysis revealed that dispositional impulsivity, rather than binge status, was related to greater desire for alcohol following a priming drink.

Cloninger found that in addition to novelty seeking, which is associated with impulsivity, harm avoidance and reward dependence are also risk factors for alcohol abuse (Cloninger, et al., 1988). Research is justified which looks at the nature of alcohol abuse and how specific details of the alcohol use disorder and problems experienced by an individual correlate with predominant personality traits.

More research is also needed which allows a clearer understanding of how particular mechanisms affect disinhibition. For example, does alcohol selectively stimulate an attentional bias for alcohol-related stimuli or does it have a more general effect of reducing attentional capacity which may lead to an observable disinhibition over drinking behaviour due to the fact that drinking environments often include salient alcohol-related stimuli. Such research can also help categorise the relationships between particular alcohol effects and specific aspects of disinhibition. For instance, reduced attention capacity and attentional biases may differ in the types of behavioural disinhibition triggered compared with disinhibition induced by prepotent responding. This research will help compare cognitive and behavioural accounts of disinhibition, although it is likely that both play a role in the reciprocal relationship between alcohol and disinhibition.

The preceding discussion has shown how impulsivity and disinhibition are multifaceted constructs and individual elements of these concepts may be related to different aspects of alcohol use disorders and alcohol problems. For example, the inability to ignore small immediate rewards for larger delayed rewards may be a marker for those at risk of developing dependence, while problems with inhibiting prepotent responses might be more the domain of the acute effects of alcohol. Both aspects of impulsivity are important in understanding alcohol related phenotypes and the complex mechanisms underlying alcohol related behaviours. Once a more detailed understanding of disinhibition has been developed, research can look at how the different aspects of disinhibition interact with both acute and chronic alcohol consumption. At present, most research concentrates on discrete aspects of disinhibition and alcohol, for example, impulsive personality traits and risk of alcohol use disorders, levels of disinhibition in clinical alcohol dependent populations or experimental laboratory-based assessments of the acute effects of alcohol on behavioural control. Longitudinal cohort studies could collect data on all these aspects over a number of years and provide important information concerning how these different factors interact. While such research is progressing, we need to use these new findings to develop health policy and educational materials, interventions and treatments which may help reduce excessive drinking and the negative consequences of such behaviour. For example, those who drink excessively primarily due to an impulsive personality may find it very difficult to change their need to partake in risky behaviour, as sensation seeking and novelty are aspects of this personality type. However, it might be possible to take this knowledge and try and direct sensation-seeking behaviour towards another activity such as extreme sports.

The rapidly expanding field of genetic's research will be able to tell us important things about the genetic and heritable basis of alcohol use disorders and disinhibition. Both male and female offspring of alcoholics are more likely to experience alcohol problems and develop alcohol use disorders than individuals without a family history of alcoholism. Midanik (1983) found that women with alcohol problems were more likely to report having at least one first degree relative with an alcohol use disorder. However, such findings are likely to include environmental influences, e.g. the child of an alcoholic may be more exposed to drinking behaviour and so can learn through imitation. However, twin and adoption research have both shown that risk for alcohol use disorders has a significant heritable component. Several cohort studies have shown that children adopted from families with parental alcoholism are more likely to develop alcohol use disorders than children from families without alcoholism even when the adopted environments are similar and free of alcohol-related problems (Agrawal and Lynskey, 2008). In addition, children who have been adopted appear to retain the same level of risk for developing alcohol use disorders than siblings who remain in the original alcohol-related environment (Ball, 2008; Goodwin, et al., 1974). Research focusing on the genetic basis of alcohol use disorders has led to a range of results from approximately 50 – 75% heritability. Some findings suggest heritability to be greater in men than women while other research suggests similar rates across gender (Agrawal and Lynskey, 2008; Ball, 2008). As mentioned earlier, there is growing interest in the role the endogenous opioid system has to play in alcohol related phenotypes. Some research has implicated a genetic variant of the μ-opioid receptor subtype which may interact with, and enhance, alcohol's effects. A single nucleotide polymorphism (A118G SNP) encoded on exon 1 of the OPRM1 gene, leads to an amino acid substitution: Asn40 to Asp40 (Zhang, et al., 2006). The Asp40 variant leads to a μ-receptor subtype with up to three times greater binding of β-endorphin than the more common Asn40 variant (Bond, et al., 1998; Ray and Hutchison, 2004). The A118G SNP is expected to occur in up to 36% of people of European descent (Oslin, et al., 2003) thus it is potentially an important genetic risk factor for alcohol use disorders and may have implications for predicting treatment outcome. Initial findings from the Collaborative Study of the Genetics of Alcoholism (COGA) have identified some potential antecedent risks for alcohol use disorders which may involve disinhibition. Electroencephalography (EEG) studies have shown that alcoholics and those at risk of alcohol use disorders (e.g. offspring of alcoholics) have increased resting beta power (Porjesz and Rangaswamy, 2007). Furthermore, EEG beta frequency has been linked with the GABRA2 gene; GABA$_A$ receptors affect neurons which influence beta frequency (Porjesz, et al., 2002). The GABRA2 gene has been linked with a host of disinhibitory disorders, such as conduct disorder (Dick, et al., 2006; Porjesz and Rangaswamy, 2007). Ongoing genetic research will be able to identify other functional genetic variants as risk, or protective, markers for alcohol and disinhibitory disorders. Such research may well lead to the identification of overlaps in the functional variants identified for alcohol and disinhibitory disorders or variant clusters, which pose increased risk for alcohol-related phenotypes particularly connected with disinhibition.

Conclusion

The preceding discussion has introduced the reader to the idea that alcohol use disorders may be understood within a spectrum of disinhibition disorders. Some of the theories which support this idea have been outlined and empirical evidence has been presented which supports this stance. This is not to say, however, that all cases of alcohol abuse and dependence can be understood as one type of disinhibitory disorder. There is much research which highlights the complexity of both alcohol phenotypes and disinhibition so it should be clear that our understanding of these issues is far from complete. There is no one theory or framework which can provide a global understanding of alcohol use disorders if it only focuses on a single mechanism. With the advancement of experimental, clinical, neuropharmacological, imaging and genetic research, our understanding of addiction is growing rapidly. We are beginning to identify the antecedents of alcohol misuse, some of which are shared with disinhibitory disorders such as attention deficit hyperactivity disorder and conduct disorder. We are also establishing the effects of chronic alcohol use on neuronal mechanisms which may lead to long term damage of cognitive function which can result in behaviour devoid of sufficient planning and awareness of potential consequences. More sophisticated models are being developed which help us understand the complex and reciprocal nature of the circuitary underlying disinhibited drinking behaviour, including learning and memory, motivation and reward, and control. This knowledge can be fed back in to the development of more efficacious interventions and treatments which will improve the quality of life of the many individuals directly and indirectly affected by alcohol.

References

Acton, G. S. (2003). Measurement of impulsivity in a hierarchical model of personality traits: implications for substance use. *Substance Use Misuse, 38*(1), 67-83.

Agrawal, A., and Lynskey, M. T. (2008). Are there genetic influences on addiction: evidence from family, adoption and twin studies. *Addiction, 103*(7), 1069-1081.

Avila, C. (2001). Distinguishing BIS-mediated and BAS-mediated disinhibition mechanisms: a comparison of disinhibition models of Gray (1981, 1987) and of Patterson and Newman (1993). *Journal of Personality and Social Psychology, 80*(2), 311-324.

Ball, D. (2008). Addiction science and its genetics. *Addiction, 103*(3), 360-367.

Barkley, R. A., Fischer, M., Edelbrock, C. S., and Smallish, L. (1990). The adolescent outcome of hyperactive children diagnosed by research criteria: I. An 8-year prospective follow-up study. *Journal of the American Academy of Child and Adolescent Psychiatry, 29*(4), 546-557.

Baron, D., Silberman, A. J., and D'Alonzo, G. E. (1998). The sobering effects of binge drinking. *J. Am. Osteopath. Assoc, 98*(10), 530-531.

Bechara, A., and Damasio, H. (2002). Decision-making and addiction (part I): impaired activation of somatic states in substance dependent individuals when pondering decisions with negative future consequences. *Neuropsychologia, 40*(10), 1675-1689.

Bechara, A., Damasio, H., and Damasio, A. R. (2000). Emotion, decision making and the orbitofrontal cortex. *Cereb. Cortex, 10*(3), 295-307.

Bechara, A., Damasio, H., Damasio, A. R., and Lee, G. P. (1999). Different contributions of the human amygdala and ventromedial prefrontal cortex to decision-making. *J. Neurosci, 19*(13), 5473-5481.

Bechara, A., Damasio, H., Tranel, D., and Anderson, S. W. (1998). Dissociation Of working memory from decision making within the human prefrontal cortex. *J. Neurosci, 18*(1), 428-437.

Bechara, A., Dolan, S., Denburg, N., Hindes, A., Anderson, S. W., and Nathan, P. E. (2001). Decision-making deficits, linked to a dysfunctional ventromedial prefrontal cortex, revealed in alcohol and stimulant abusers. *Neuropsychologia, 39*(4), 376-389.

Bechara, A., Dolan, S., and Hindes, A. (2002). Decision-making and addiction (part II): myopia for the future or hypersensitivity to reward? *Neuropsychologia, 40*(10), 1690-1705.

Bechara, A., and Martin, E. M. (2004). Impaired decision making related to working memory deficits in individuals with substance addictions. *Neuropsychology, 18*(1), 152-162.

Bechara, A., Tranel, D., and Damasio, H. (2000). Characterization of the decision-making deficit of patients with ventromedial prefrontal cortex lesions. *Brain, 123 (Pt 11)*, 2189-2202.

Bickel, W. K., Odum, A. L., and Madden, G. J. (1999). Impulsivity and cigarette smoking: delay discounting in current, never, and ex-smokers. *Psychopharmacology (Berl), 146*(4), 447-454.

Bond, C., LaForge, K. S., Tian, M., Melia, D., Zhang, S., Borg, L., et al. (1998). Single-nucleotide polymorphism in the human mu opioid receptor gene alters beta-endorphin binding and activity: possible implications for opiate addiction. *Proceedings of the National Academy of Science of the USA , 95*(16), 9608-9613.

Bubser, M., and Schmidt, W. J. (1990). 6-Hydroxydopamine lesion of the rat prefrontal cortex increases locomotor activity, impairs acquisition of delayed alternation tasks, but does not affect uninterrupted tasks in the radial maze. *Behavioural Brain Research, 37*(2), 157-168.

Bushman, B. J., and Cooper, H. M. (1990). Effects of alcohol on human aggression: an integrative research review. *Psychological Bulletin, 107*(3), 341-354.

Childress, A. R., Mozley, P. D., McElgin, W., Fitzgerald, J., Reivich, M., and O'Brien, C. P. (1999). Limbic activation during cue-induced cocaine craving. *American Journal of Psychiatry, 156*(1), 11-18.

Cloninger, C. R., Sigvardsson, S., and Bohman, M. (1988). Childhood personality predicts alcohol abuse in young adults. *Alcoholism: Clinical and Experimental Research, 12*(4), 494-505.

Conrod, P. J., Petersen, J. B., and Pihl, R. O. (1997). Disinhibited personality and sensitivity to alcohol reinforcement: independent correlates of drinking behavior in sons of alcoholics. *Alcoholism: Clinical and Experimental Research, 21*(7), 1320-1332.

Conway, K. P., Kane, R. J., Ball, S. A., Poling, J. C., and Rounsaville, B. J. (2003). Personality, substance of choice, and polysubstance involvement among substance dependent patients. *Drug Alcohol Dependence, 71*(1), 65-75.

Crone, E. A., Vendel, I., and van der Molan, M. W. (2003). Decision-making in disinhibited adolescents and adults: insensitivity to future consequences or driven by immediate reward? *Personality and Individual Differences, 35*, 1625 - 1641.

Damasio, A. R. (1996). The somatic marker hypothesis and the possible functions of the prefrontal cortex. *Philos. Trans R. Soc. Lond B Biol. Sci, 351*(1346), 1413-1420.

de Wit, H., Crean, J., and Richards, J. B. (2000). Effects of d-amphetamine and ethanol on a measure of behavioral inhibition in humans. *Behavioural Neuroscience, 114*(4), 830-837.

Demmel, R., Klusener, J., and Rist, F. (2004). Anticipated levels of alcohol-induced sedation and stimulation in relation to estimated blood alcohol concentration. *Journal of Studies on Alcohol, 65*(1), 22-26.

Di Chiara, G. (1995). The role of dopamine in drug abuse viewed from the perspective of its role in motivation. *Drug Alcohol Dependence, 38*(2), 95-137.

Dias, R., Robbins, T. W., and Roberts, A. C. (1996a). Dissociation in prefrontal cortex of affective and attentional shifts. *Nature, 380*(6569), 69-72.

Dias, R., Robbins, T. W., and Roberts, A. C. (1996b). Primate analogue of the Wisconsin Card Sorting Test: effects of excitotoxic lesions of the prefrontal cortex in the marmoset. *Behavioural Neuroscience, 110*(5), 872-886.

Dick, D. M., Bierut, L., Hinrichs, A., Fox, L., Bucholz, K. K., Kramer, J., et al. (2006). The role of GABRA2 in risk for conduct disorder and alcohol and drug dependence across developmental stages. *Behavioural Genetics, 36*(4), 577-590.

Dougherty, D. M. (2003). Laboratory Behavioural Measures of Impulsivity: General Information (Manual). Houston, Texas.

Dougherty, D. M., Marsh-Richard, D. M., Hatzis, E. S., Nouvion, S. O., and Mathias, C. W. (2008). A test of alcohol dose effects on multiple behavioral measures of impulsivity. *Drug Alcohol Dependence, 96*(1-2), 111-120.

Drobes, D. J., Anton, R. F., Thomas, S. E., and Voronin, K. (2003). A clinical laboratory paradigm for evaluating medication effects on alcohol consumption: naltrexone and nalmefene. *Neuropsychopharmacology, 28*(4), 755-764.

Duka, T., and Townshend, J. M. (2004). The priming effect of alcohol pre-load on attentional bias to alcohol-related stimuli. *Psychopharmacology (Berl), 176*(3-4), 353-361.

Echeburua, E., Bravo de Medina, R., and Aizpiri, J. (2008). [Personality variables, psychopathological alterations and personality disorders in alcohol-dependent patients according to Cloninger's typology of alcohol abuse.]. *Psicothema, 20*(4), 525-530.

Fadardi, J. S., and Cox, W. M. (2006). Alcohol attentional bias: drinking salience or cognitive impairment? *Psychopharmacology (Berl), 185*(2), 169-178.

Feldman, R. S., Meyer, J. S., and Quenzer, L. F. (1997). *Principles of Neuropsychopharmacology* (Sinauer Associates Inc ed.).

Field, M., Christiansen, P., Cole, J., and Goudie, A. (2007). Delay discounting and the alcohol Stroop in heavy drinking adolescents. *Addiction, 102*(4), 579-586.

Fillmore, M. I., and Rush, C. R. (2001). Alcohol effects on inhibitory and activational response strategies in the acquisition of alcohol and other reinforcers: priming the motivation to drink. *Journal of Studies on Alcohol, 62*(5), 646-656.

Fillmore, M. T. (2003a). Drug abuse as a problem of impaired control: current approaches and findings. *Behavioral Cognitive Neuroscience Reviews, 2*(3), 179-197.

Fillmore, M. T. (2003b). Drug abuse as a problem of impaired control: current approaches and findings. *Behavioral Cognitive Neuroscience Reviews, 2*(3), 179-197.

Fillmore, M. T. (2003c). Drug Abuse as a Problem of Impaired Control: Current Approaches and Findings. *Behavioral and Cognitive Neuroscience Reviews., 2*(3), 179-197.

Fillmore, M. T., and Van Selst, M. (2002b). Constraints on information processing under alcohol in the context of response execution and response suppression. *Exp. Clin. Psychopharmacology, 10*(4), 417-424.

Fillmore, M. T., and Vogel-Sprott, M. (1995). Expectancies about alcohol-induced motor impairment predict individual differences in responses to alcohol and placebo. *Journal of Studies on Alcohol, 56*(1), 90-98.

Fillmore, M. T., and Vogel-Sprott, M. (1999). An alcohol model of impaired inhibitory control and its treatment in humans. *Experimental and Clinical Psychopharmacology, 7*(1), 49-55.

Fowles, D. C. (1987). Application of behavioural theory of motivation to the concepts of anxiety and impulsivity. *Journal of research of personality, 21,* 417-465.

Fromme, K., D'Amico, E. J., and Katz, E. C. (1999). Intoxicated sexual risk taking: an expectancy or cognitive impairment explanation? *Journal of Studies on Alcohol, 60*(1), 54-63.

Glahn, D. C., Lovallo, W. R., and Fox, P. T. (2007). Reduced amygdala activation in young adults at high risk of alcoholism: studies from the Oklahoma family health patterns project. *Biological Psychiatry, 61*(11), 1306-1309.

Gonzales, R. A., and Weiss, F. (1998). Suppression of ethanol-reinforced behavior by naltrexone is associated with attenuation of the ethanol-induced increase in dialysate dopamine levels in the nucleus accumbens. *Journal of Neuroscience, 18*(24), 10663-10671.

Goodwin, D. W., Schulsinger, F., Moller, N., Hermansen, L., Winokur, G., and Guze, S. B. (1974). Drinking problems in adopted and nonadopted sons of alcoholics. *Archives of General Psychiatry, 31*(2), 164-169.

Grant, S., London, E. D., Newlin, D. B., Villemagne, V. L., Liu, X., Contoreggi, C., et al. (1996). Activation of memory circuits during cue-elicited cocaine craving. *Proceedings of the National Academy of Sciences USA, 93*(21), 12040-12045.

Grau, E., and Ortet, G. (1999). Personality traits and alcohol consumption in a sample of non-alcoholic women. *Personality and Individual Differences 27*(6), 1057 - 1066.

Gray, J. A. (1976). The behavioural inhibition system: A possible substrate for anxiety. In M. P. Feldman and A. Broadhurst (Eds.), *Theoretical and experimental bases of the behaviour therapies.* (pp. 3-41). London.: Wiley.

Grilly, D. M. (1998). *Drugs and Human Behavior.* (3rd ed.). Boston: Allyn and Bacon. USA.

Hanson, D. (1995). *Preventing Alcohol Abuse: Alcohol, Culture and Control.* Wesport CT: Praeger Publishers.

Hibell, B., Andersson, B., Thoroddur Bjarnason, T., Ahlström, S., Balakireva, O., Kokkevi, A., et al. (2003). *The ESPAD Report 2006 Alcohol and Other Drug Use Among Students in 35 European Countries.* Stockholm, Sweden: The Swedish Council for Information on Alcohol and Other Drugs (CAN) and the Pompidou Group at the Council of Europe.

Jellinek, E. M. (1960). *The Disease Concept of Alcoholism.* Highland Park, NJ: Hill House Press.

Jentsch, J. D., and Taylor, J. R. (1999). Impulsivity resulting from frontostriatal dysfunction in drug abuse: implications for the control of behavior by reward-related stimuli. *Psychopharmacology (Berl), 146*(4), 373-390.

Kalivas, P. W., and Volkow, N. D. (2005). The neural basis of addiction: a pathology of motivation and choice. *American Journal of Psychiatry, 162*(8), 1403-1413.

Kirby, K. N., and Petry, N. M. (2004). Heroin and cocaine abusers have higher discount rates for delayed rewards than alcoholics or non-drug-using controls. *Addiction, 99*(4), 461-471.

Kirby, K. N., Petry, N. M., and Bickel, W. K. (1999). Heroin addicts have higher discount rates for delayed rewards than non-drug-using controls. *Journal of Experimental Psychology: General, 128*(1), 78-87.

Kollins, S. H. (2003). Delay discounting is associated with substance use in college students. *Addictive Behavior, 28*(6), 1167-1173.

Koob, G. F., and Le Moal, M. (2008). Addiction and the brain antireward system. *Annual Review of Psychology, 59*, 29-53.

Little, H. J. (1999). The contribution of electrophysiology to knowledge of the acute and chronic effects of ethanol. *Pharmacology and Therapeutics, 84*(3), 333-353.

Lui, S., Seigel, P., Brewer, R., Mokdad, A., Sleet, D., and Serdula, M. (1997). Prevalence of alcohol-impaired driving: results from a national self-reported survey of health behaviors. *Journal of the American Medical Association, 227*, 122-125

MacDonald, T. K., Fong, G. T., Zanna, M. P., and Martineau, A. M. (2000). Alcohol myopia and condom use: can alcohol intoxication be associated with more prudent behavior? *Journal of Personality and Social Psychology, 78*(4), 605-619.

Marczinski, C. A., and Fillmore, M. T. (2003a). Dissociative antagonistic effects of caffeine on alcohol-induced impairment of behavioral control. *Experimental and Clinical Psychopharmacology, 11*(3), 228-236.

Marczinski, C. A., and Fillmore, M. T. (2003b). Preresponse cues reduce the impairing effects of alcohol on the execution and suppression of responses. *Experimental and Clinical Psychopharmacology, 11*(1), 110-117.

McCaul, M. E., Wand, G. S., Eissenberg, T., Rohde, C. A., and Cheskin, L. J. (2000). Naltrexone alters subjective and psychomotor responses to alcohol in heavy drinking subjects. *Neuropsychopharmacology, 22*(5), 480-492.

Midanik, L. (1983). Familial alcoholism and problem drinking in a national drinking practices survey. *Addictive Behavior, 8*(2), 133-141.

Mitchell, J. M., Fields, H. L., D'Esposito, M., and Boettiger, C. A. (2005). Impulsive responding in alcoholics. *Alcoholism: Clinical and Experimental Research, 29*(12), 2158-2169.

Moal, M. (1995). Mesocorticolimbic Dopaminergic Neurons: Functional and Regulatory Roles. In D. Kupfer and F. Bloom (Eds.), *Psychopharmacology - 4th Generation of Progress.* Nashville, USA: American College of Neuropsychopharmacology.

Mucha, R. F., Pauli, P., and Angrilli, A. (1998). Conditioned responses elicited by experimentally produced cues for smoking. *Canadian Journal of Physiology and Pharmacology, 76*(3), 259-268.

Mulvihill, L. E., Skilling, T. A., and Vogel-Sprott, M. (1997). Alcohol and the ability to inhibit behavior in men and women. *Journal of Studies on Alcohol, 58*(6), 600-605.

National Institute of Mental Health (1994, revised 2001). *Attention Deficit Hyperactivity Disorder.* National Institute of Mental Health, National Institutes of Health, US Department of Health and Human Services. Bethesda (MD), USA.

Noel, X., Van der Linden, M., d'Acremont, M., Bechara, A., Dan, B., Hanak, C., et al. (2007). Alcohol cues increase cognitive impulsivity in individuals with alcoholism. *Psychopharmacology (Berl), 192*(2), 291-298.

Norman, P., Bennett, P., and Lewis, H. (1998). Understanding binge drinking among young people: an application of the Theory of Planned Behaviour. *Health Education Research, 13*(2), 163-169.

O'Brien, C., Volpicelli, L., and Volpicelli, J. (1996). Naltrexone in the treatment of alcoholism: a clinical review. *Alcohol, 13*(1), 35-39.

O'Brien, M. C., McCoy, T. P., Champion, H., Mitra, A., Robbins, A., Teuschlser, H., et al. (2006). Single question about drunkenness to detect college students at risk for injury. *Academic Emergency Medicine, 13*(6), 629-636.

O'Connell, H., and Lawlor, B. A. (2005). Recent alcohol intake and suicidality--a neuropsychological perspective. *Irish Journal of Medical Science, 174*(4), 51-54.

O'Malley, S. S., Krishnan-Sarin, S., Farren, C., Sinha, R., and Kreek, M. J. (2002). Naltrexone decreases craving and alcohol self-administration in alcohol-dependent subjects and activates the hypothalamo-pituitary-adrenocortical axis. *Psychopharmacology (Berl), 160*(1), 19-29

Oei, T. P., and Morawska, A. (2004). A cognitive model of binge drinking: the influence of alcohol expectancies and drinking refusal self-efficacy. *Addictive Behavior, 29*(1), 159-179.

Oslin, D. W., Berrettini, W., Kranzler, H. R., Pettinati, H., Gelernter, J., Volpicelli, J. R., et al. (2003). A functional polymorphism of the mu-opioid receptor gene is associated with naltrexone response in alcohol-dependent patients. *Neuropsychopharmacology, 28*(8), 1546-1552.

Patrick, C. (1952). *Alcohol, Culture, and Society* (Vol. Reprint edition by AMS Press, New York, 1970.). Durham, NC: Duke University Press.

Petry, N. M. (2001). Delay discounting of money and alcohol in actively using alcoholics, currently abstinent alcoholics, and controls. *Psychopharmacology (Berl), 154*(3), 243-250.

Porjesz, B., Almasy, L., Edenberg, H. J., Wang, K., Chorlian, D. B., Foroud, T., et al. (2002). Linkage disequilibrium between the beta frequency of the human EEG and a GABAA receptor gene locus. *Proceedings of the National Academy of Sciences USA, 99*(6), 3729-3733.

Porjesz, B., and Rangaswamy, M. (2007). Neurophysiological endophenotypes, CNS disinhibition, and risk for alcohol dependence and related disorders. *Scientific World Journal, 7*, 131-141.

Ray, L. A., and Hutchison, K. E. (2004). A polymorphism of the mu-opioid receptor gene (OPRM1) and sensitivity to the effects of alcohol in humans. *Alcoholism: Clinical and Experimental Research, 28*(12), 1789-1795.

Reynolds, B., Richards, J. B., and de Wit, H. (2006). Acute-alcohol effects on the Experiential Discounting Task (EDT) and a question-based measure of delay discounting. *Pharmacology Biochemistry and Behavior, 83*(2), 194-202.

Rodriguez, C. A., and Span, S. A. (2008). ADHD symptoms, anticipated hangover symptoms, and drinking habits in female college students. *Addictive Behavior, 33*(8), 1031-1038.

Rose, A. K., and Duka, T. (2006). Effects of dose and time on the ability of alcohol to prime social drinkers. *Behavioral Pharmacology, 17*(1), 61-70.

Rose, A. K., and Duka, T. (2007). The influence of alcohol on basic motoric and cognitive disinhibition. *Alcohol Alcohol, 42*(6), 544-551.

Rose, A. K., and Duka, T. (2008). The Effects of Alcohol on Inhibitory Processes. *Behavioural Pharmacology, 19*(4), 284-291.

Rose, A. K., and Grunsell, L. (2008). The subjective, rather than the disinhibiting, effects of alcohol are related to binge drinking. *Alcoholism: Clinical and Experimental Research, 32*(6), 1096-2104.

Schubiner, H., Tzelepis, A., Milberger, S., Lockhart, N., Kruger, M., Kelley, B. J., et al. (2000). Prevalence of attention-deficit/hyperactivity disorder and conduct disorder among substance abusers. *Journal of Clinical Psychiatry, 61*(4), 244-251.

Shaham, Y., Shalev, U., Lu, L., de Wit, H., and Stewart, J. (2003). The reinstatement model of drug relapse: history, methodology and major findings. *Psychopharmacology (Berl), 168*(1-2), 3-20.

Soloff, P. H., Lynch, K. G., and Moss, H. B. (2000). Serotonin, impulsivity, and alcohol use disorders in the older adolescent: a psychobiological study. *Alcoholism: Clinical and Experimental Research, 24*(11), 1609-1619.

Srisurapanont, M., and Jarusuraisin, N. (2005). Opioid antagonists for alcohol dependence. *Cochrane Database Systematic Review*(1), CD001867.

Staton, M., Leukefeld, C., Logan, T. K., Zimmerman, R., Lynam, D., Milich, R., et al. (1999). Risky sex behavior and substance use among young adults. *Health and Social Work, 24*(2), 147-154.

Steele, C. M., and Josephs, R. A. (1990). Alcohol myopia. Its prized and dangerous effects. *American Psychology, 45*(8), 921-933.

Stewart, J., de Wit, H., and Eikelboom, R. (1984). Role of unconditioned and conditioned drug effects in the self-administration of opiates and stimulants. *Psychological Review, 91*, 251 - 268.

Stockwell, T. R., Hodgson, R. J., Rankin, H. J., and Taylor, C. (1982). Alcohol Dependence, Beliefs and the Priming Effect. *Behaviour Research and Therapy, 20*, 513 - 522.

Sutherland, I., and Willner, P. (1998). Patterns of alcohol, cigarette and illicit drug use in English adolescents. *Addiction, 93*(8), 1199-1208.

Swahn, M. H., Simon, T. R., Hammig, B. J., and Guerrero, J. L. (2004). Alcohol-consumption behaviors and risk for physical fighting and injuries among adolescent drinkers. *Addictive Behavior, 29*(5), 959-963.

Vas, A. (2001). Rates of liver cirrhosis rise in England, fall in Europe. *British Medical Journal, 323*(7326), 1388.

Volkow, N. D., Fowler, J. S., and Wang, G. J. (2003). The addicted human brain: insights from imaging studies. *Journal of Clinical Investigation, 111*(10), 1444-1451.

World Health Organisation (2004). *Global Status Report on Alcohol.* Department of Mental Health and Substance Abuse. Geneva.

World Health Organisation (2002). *The World Health Report: Reducing Risks, Promoting Healthy Life*. Geneva.

Yusko, D. A., Buckman, J. F., White, H. R., and Pandina, R. J. (2008). Risk for excessive alcohol use and drinking-related problems in college student athletes. *Addictive Behavior, 33*(12), 1546-1556.

Zernig, G., Saria, A., Kurz, M., and O'Malley, S. S. (2000). *Handbook of Alcoholism*. London, UK: CRC Press.

Zetteler, J. I., Stollery, B. T., Weinstein, A. M., and Lingford-Hughes, A. R. (2006). Attentional bias for alcohol-related information in adolescents with alcohol-dependent parents. *Alcohol Alcohol, 41*(4), 426-430.

Zhang, H., Luo, X., Kranzler, H. R., Lappalainen, J., Yang, B. Z., Krupitsky, E., et al. (2006). Association between two {micro}-opioid receptor gene (OPRM1) haplotype blocks and drug or alcohol dependence. *Human Molecular Genetics, 15*(6), 807-819.

Zuckerman, M., Kolin, E. A., Price, L., and Zoob, I. (1964). Development of a sensation-seeking scale. *Journal of Consulting Psychology, 28*, 477 – 482.

In: Impulsivity: Causes, Control and Disorders
Editor: George H. Lassiter

ISBN 978-1-60741-951-8
© 2009 Nova Science Publishers, Inc.

Chapter II

Obsessive-Compulsive Disorder and the Impulsivity-Compulsivity Disorder Spectrum: A Review of Research

Michael L. Sulkowski,[1]* Amy Mariaskin,[2] Cary Jordan[1] and Eric A. Storch[3]

1. School Psychology Program,
University of Florida, USA
2. Department of Psychology and Neuroscience,
Duke University, USA
3. Departments of Pediatrics and Psychiatry,
University of South Florida, USA

Abstract

This paper reviews research on the association between obsessive-compulsive disorder (OCD) and obsessive-compulsive spectrum disorders (OCSDs). Since a unidimensional impulsivity-compulsivity dimension has been proposed to classify OCSDs (Bartz and Hollander, 2006), consisting of "compulsive" or anxiety-driven disorders such as OCD on one end of the spectrum and impulse-control disorders (ICDs) on the other end, research on relationships between OCD and various OCSDs has been reviewed to determine if data exist to support a continuous impulsive-compulsive disorder spectrum. Disorders are compared with respect to the following criteria: 1) degrees of co-occurring behaviors and symptomology, 2) phenotypic associations (including comorbidity and familial linkages), 3) neurological and brain-based similarities, and 4), identified response patterns to psychological and medical treatments. In general, there is limited support for a unified impulsivity-compulsivity dimension that includes OCD as a central disorder. However, considerably stronger evidence exists for a

* Requests and correspondence to Michael L. Sulkowski, School Psychology Program, Box 117047 University of Florida, Gainesville, FL 32610; e-mail: sulkowsm@ufl.edu.

narrower cluster of anxiety-driven OCSDs that are characterized by obsessive-compulsive features and body image/sensitization obsessions (e.g., OCD, body dysmorphic disorder, hypochondriasis).

Considerable controversy surrounds the proposal of an impulsivity-compulsivity disorder spectrum that contains obsessive-compulsive disorder (OCD) in addition to a variety of other disorders characterized by repetitive behaviors (Abramowitz and Deacon, 2005; Bartz and Hollander, 2006; Hollander, 1993; Lochner and Stein, 2006; Storch, Abramowitz, and Goodman, 2008). Along with this proposal have come suggestions that OCD should be declassified as an anxiety disorder in the forthcoming fifth edition of the Diagnostic and Statistical Manual (DSM-V; American Psychiatric Association, 2000) and repositioned on the "compulsivity" end of this spectrum. The theoretical existence of this spectrum hinges on the strength of the associations between various disorders placed along an impulsivity-compulsivity dimension bounded by anxiety-related compulsive disorders on one end (e.g., OCD, body dysmorphic disorder [BDD]) and impulse-control disorders (ICDs) on the other end (e.g., pathological gambling, trichotillomania). It is the purpose of this chapter to evaluate the validity of such a continuum in light of current research that explores relationships between the disorders.

Although unidimensional in theory, the impulsivity-compulsivity dimension can be subdivided into three clusters, each of which highlights different features of OCSDs: 1) anxiety-driven disorders centered on preoccupations with body image/body sensitization/body weight, 2) ICDs characterized by difficulties with being able to inhibit repetitive thoughts and/or behaviors, and 3) neurologically based disorders marked by repetitive behaviors such as Tourette syndrome, autism, or Sydenham's chorea (Bartz and Hollander, 2006; Hollander et al., 1996). Currently, much of research on the existence of an impulsivity-compulsivity spectrum has compared and contrasted characteristics of OCD with proposed OCSDs by considering the following: 1) Degrees of co-occurring behaviors and common symptomology, 2) phenotypic associations including comorbidity and familial linkages, 3) neurological and brain-based similarities, and 4) identified response patterns to pharmacological treatment. In line with these considerations, a mixed body of research provides varying degrees of support for the existence of a unidimensional impulsivity-compulsivity disorder spectrum. Generally, the extent to which empirical findings support this spectrum depends on the specific OCSD being compared to OCD, as well as selected phenomenological considerations (e.g., comorbidity, neurological similarities). In this manuscript, research will be reviewed on the relationship between OCD and the three suggested OCSD clusters along four phenomenological considerations: comorbidity, phenotypic associations, neurological similarities, and treatment response. In particular, an emphasis will be placed on the relationship between OCD and ICDs as these disorders mark the putative endpoints of the impulsivity-compulsivity spectrum.

OCD and disorders characterized by preoccupations with body image and somatic concerns. A substantial body of research supports the relationship between OCD and OCSDs that involve preoccupation with body image and somatic concerns (Denys et al., 2004; Fontenelle, Mendlowicz, and Versiani, 2005; Grant et al., 2006; LaSalle et al., 2004; du Toit et al., 2001; Zimmerman and Mattia, 1998). In a sample of 239 patients with BDD, Gunstad and Phillips (2003) found that OCD and BDD frequently co-occurred (30%). Additionally, Barsky, Wyshak, and Klerman (1992) reported a significant co-occurrence between OCD and hypochondriasis (7%) in a clinical sample of 76 outpatients with OCD. However, a more recent study by Jaisoorya, Reddy, and Srinath (2003) found higher comorbidity rates of OCD and hypochondriasis in 231 patients (13%) compared to 200 non-clinical control participants (0%). The relatively common co-occurrence of OCD with disorders marked by body image and somatic concerns is not surprising given the functional similarities between the disorders. Specifically, the compulsive behaviors associated with both disorders are preceded by distressing cognitions (e.g., fear of having one's physical appearance scrutinized by others, anxiety about one's health); these behaviors in turn function to reduce anxiety resultant from these distressing cognitions. Thus, although some differences exist in the clinical presentation of OCD, BDD, and hypochondriasis, all of these disorders are anxiety-driven and involve ritualistic anxiety-reducing behaviors.

Family studies indicate that BDD and hypochondriasis occur more frequently in first-degree relatives of patients with OCD (Bienvenu et al., 2000; Black, Goldstein, Noyes, Blum, 1994) than in the family members of control cases. Bienvenu et al. (2000) found BDD to occur in 10 of 343 OCD case probands (4%) as opposed to 2 of 300 control probands (1%). In the same study, hypochondriasis occurred in a comparable number (i.e., not statistically significant) of OCD probands (3%) and controls (1%). Brain imaging studies provide additional support for an association between OCD and the aforementioned body image and somatic concern disorders. Specifically, abnormal activity has been identified in the orbitofrontal subcortical-thalamic pathways and basal ganglion across disorders (Carey, Seedat, Warwick, van Heerden, and Stein, 2004; Saxena et al., 1998; van den Heuvel et al., 2005).

Further support for the relationship between OCD and body image and somatic concern disorders comes from treatment studies. Generally, selective serotonin reuptake inhibitors (SSRIs) are the first line *psychopharmacological* treatment for OCD (Geller et al., 2004), BDD (Phillips, 2002) and hypochondriasis (Fallon et al., 1996), suggesting that serotonin may play an important role in the pathogenesis of these disorders. Further, all of these disorders have been found to respond favorably to variations of cognitive behavioral therapy (CBT). In particular, CBT with exposure and response prevention (ERP) is the best established psychological treatment for OCD (Abramowitz et al., 2005; Chambless et al., 1998) and BDD (Cororve and Gleaves, 2001; Neziroglu et al., 1996; McKay, 1999), and may be equally effective for treating hypochondriasis (Barsky and Ahern, 2004; Visser and Bouman, 2001). Considering the identified comorbidities, phenotypic associations, neurological similarities, and similar responses to pharmacological and psychological interventions between OCD and body image/body sensitization disorders, it seems that an emerging body of research supports a relationship between these disorders.

OCD and neurologically based repetitive disorders. The association between OCD and neurologically based repetitive disorders (i.e., Tourette syndrome, autism) is not as well established in the research literature as is the relationship between OCD and body image/body sensitization disorders. There is evidence suggesting a link between Tourette syndrome and OCD, but less data suggesting a relationship between OCD and autism. A longitudinal study of 101 children with Tourette syndrome revealed that approximately 50% of participants eventually met diagnostic criteria for OCD at some time during the 1.6 year study (Park, Como, Cui, and Kurlan, 1993). Pediatric OCD may also share a similar genetic vulnerability with Tourette syndrome as Grados et al. (2001) found that 7.4% of case relatives of children with OCD ($n = 80$) presented with a tic-related behavior disorder compared to 1% of control participants ($n = 73$). However, a more recent study by Jaisoorya et al. (2003) found that only 3% of OCD patients ($n = 231$) had comorbid Tourette syndrome. Additionally, Pauls et al. (1995) found a 4.6% prevalence rate for tic disorders in the case relatives of OCD patients ($n = 466$), compared to 1% in comparison participants ($n = 100$). As noted by Miguel et al. (1995), repetitive behaviors associated with Tourette syndrome may ostensibly resemble compulsions, yet these behaviors may be consequent to internal sensations or sensory phenomena as opposed to the distressing obsessions associated with OCD.

Several studies suggest that Tourette syndrome may be related to dysfunction in the cortico–striatal–thalamo–cortical circuit (Biswal et al., 1998; Peterson et al., 2001). Specifically, abnormal activity in the basal ganglia, frontal cortex, and limbic structures is implicated in the generation of tics in patients with Tourette syndrome (Stern et al., 2000). Even though similar neural structures have been associated with obsessive and compulsive behaviors in OCD (e.g., basal ganglia, frontal cortex [Saxena et al., 1998]), future research needs to clarify whether neural correlates between OCD and Tourette syndrome are suggestive of an underlying substrate or instead highlight an epiphenomenological relationship between disorders.

Significant differences exist between OCD and Tourette syndrome with regard to first line pharmacological treatments. Whereas SSRIs are most commonly prescribed to treat OCD, they are not effective in treating Tourette syndrome (García-Ruiz, 2001; Jiménez-Jiménez and; Preston, O'Neal, and Talaga, 2006). Generally, dopamine agonists (neuroleptics, atypical antipsychotics) are the first line medications prescribed to decrease tics in patients with Tourette syndrome (Sallee et al., 2000; Scahill et al., 2003). Differences also exist between first line psychological treatments for OCD and Tourette syndrome, as a growing body of research supports the use of habit reversal training for treating Toutrette syndrome (Azrin and Nunn, 1973; Deckersbach, Raucha, Buhlmann, and Wilhelm, 2006; Peterson and Azrin, 1993; Wilhelm, 2003). However, habit reversal therapy differs from CBT in that tics are not motivated by fear/anxiety as in OCD.

The relationship between OCD and autism is not clearly established. Perceived similarities between disorders may stem from focusing on superficially related (yet weakly associated) co-occurring traits across these disorders. In other words, even though both of these disorders are characterized by repetitive behaviors, the behaviors themselves may serve different functions in each disorder. Nevertheless, Leyfer et al. (2006) found that 37% of autistic children also met criteria for OCD in a sample of 109 children. Although the rates were lower, Muris et al. (1998) likewise found elevated rates of OCD in a sample of 44 autistic children. However, a dual association cannot be established between OCD and autism as limited research exists on the prevalence of autism in OCD samples. Even though they are subject to the same methodological considerations that affect comorbidity studies, family studies have attempted to shed some light on the relationship between OCD and autism. One published study by Hollander et al. (2003) found that autistic children (n = 176) were significantly more likely to have parents presenting with obsessive-compulsive traits if they engaged in repetitive behaviors. Additionally, Bolton, Pickles, Murphy, and Rutter (1998) found OCD to be more common in first degree relatives of 126 autistic probands (3%) than in the relatives of 99 intellectually-matched probands with Down syndrome (0%). The practical significance of these findings is questionable however, as a study by Smalley, McCracken, and Tangury (1995) found that 64% of autistic children had a first-degree relative diagnosed with major depressive disorder, and 39% of these same children also had a first degree relative diagnosed with social phobia. Thus, the aforementioned study suggests that the relationship between autism and OCD may not be of any more significance than is the relationship between autism and other mood and anxiety disorders.

Considering the heterogeneity of symptoms in both OCD and autism, it is not surprising that neural correlates vary considerably between these disorders. Additionally, although there is evidence that various brain abnormalities are associated with autism, most neurological studies on autism report mixed findings, have small sample sizes, and have not been sufficiently replicated (Buitelaar and Willemsen-Swinkels, 2000). For example, some studies have identified abnormalities in the limbic system (e.g., hippocampus, amygdala, entorhinal cortex, mammillary body, medial septal nucleus and anterior cingulate gyrus) of patients with autism (Baumen, 1996; Kemper and Bauman, 1993); however, other studies have found widespread abnormalities in the cerebral cortex and brainstem of children with autism and normal functioning in these children's limbic regions (Bailey et al., 1998). Therefore, more research is needed on the structural brain abnormalities identified in both OCD and autistic patients to understand their significance.

Despite the common use of SSRIs to decrease symptoms of anxiety, agitation, and repetitive behavior in OCD and autism (Preston et al., 2006), pharmacological treatment for autism often involves a more complicated combination of medications. In addition to SSRIs, a mixture of atypical antipsychotics (McCracken et al., 2002), antihypertensives (Ratey et al., 1987), anticonvulsants (Luiselli et al., 2000), opioid antagonists (Kolmen, Feldman, Handen, and Janosky, 1995), and stimulants (Handen, Johnson, and Lubetsky, 2000) are used to treat various symptoms of aggression, impulsivity, self-injurious behavior, poor social interaction/communication, distractibility, and repetitive behaviors associated with autism. In contrast to OCD, and due to the complex presentation of symptoms associated with autism, there are no well established psychological treatments for the disorder, although behavioral and social skills interventions appear effective for targeting various behaviors (Eikeseth, Smith, Jahr, and Eldevik, 2002; Lovass, 1987; Schreibman, 2000). One recent case report by Lehmkuhl, Storch, Bodfish, and Geffken (2008) suggests that ERP may be an effective treatment for reducing compulsive behavior in children who have comorbid autism and OCD, but it is unlikely that such an approach would treat repetitive, stereotypic behaviors.

OCD and impulse-control disorders. Impulse control disorders such as trichotillomania, kleptomania, pathological gambling, pyromania, and paraphilias are marked by an individual's failure to resist an impulse, drive, or temptation to perform an act that is harmful to the affected individual or to others (American Psychiatric Association, 2000). Some apparent similarities between OCD and ICDs include repetitive behavior patterns, difficulty controlling life-disruptive impulses, cognitions, or behaviors, and associated distress from feeling unable to control one's will. However, differences between these disorders include the functional relationship between repetitive behaviors and the emotional reactions that people often experience as a result of them. For example, as described in the Diagnostic and Statistical Manual for Psychiatric Disorders, Fourth Edition—Text Revision (American Psychiatric Association, 2000), compulsive behaviors associated with OCD are performed to neutralize anxiety related to distressing cognitions, whereas impulsive behaviors associated with ICDs are often performed to temporarily increase one's pleasure or bring about a certain sensation. Thus, even if individuals with ICDs experience anxiety related to being unable to control their impulsive behaviors, the primary function of these behaviors is not related to anxiety reduction. Obsessive-compulsive disorder is then best characterized as an anxiety-reactive, harm-avoidant disorder in which afflicted individuals are motivated to escape or prevent personal distress arising from specific stimuli/situations. In contrast, many ICDs are better understood as pleasure-enhancing disorders in which affected individuals fail to moderate their involvement in intrinsically rewarding behaviors.[1]

The degree of behavioral inhibition versus disinhibition varies considerably between OCD and ICDs. Compulsions associated with OCD are often attempts to "over control" one's behavior and to prevent the occurrence of, or escape from, a distressing experience (pp. 535; Steketee, Frost, and Cohen, 1998). On the other hand, impulsive behaviors are better characterized by a pervasive pattern of failing to control repetitive pleasure/sensation-seeking behaviors (Grant and Potenza, 2006). Similar to individuals with specific phobias or social anxiety (Muris, Merckelbach, Wessel and van de Ven, 1999), individuals with OCD often take active steps to prevent themselves from coming into contact with an undesired or feared consequence. For example, an individual afflicted with intrusive thoughts of molesting a child may feel extreme anxiety when in proximity to children and may begin to compulsively avoid children or objects that remind him or her of children. In contrast, individuals with ICDs often struggle with being unable to experience desired sensations or experiences. Thus, on the surface, avoidant behaviors associated with ICDs may appear similar to OCD compulsions, but these behaviors are not necessarily anxiety reductive as it is unlikely that they would happen in the absence of negative personal or social consequences. For example, if an individual had unlimited economic resources and there were no negative social consequences associated with pathological gambling, it is not likely that this individual would consider his or her gambling behavior to be problematic.

Comorbidity studies of OCD and ICDs have yielded inconsistent results. In one study that used a small sample ($n = 16$), Fontentelle, Mendlowicz, and Versiani (2005) found 35.5% of OCD patients to have a comorbid ICD, and a study by Matsunaga et al. (2005) also identified a high clinical co-occurrence for these disorders (29%, $n = 153$). However, more recent studies have not replicated these results. Grant et al. (2006) found that 11.6% of 293 OCD patients had a comorbid ICD, and in a sample of 231 patients, Jaisoorya et al. (2003) found an even lower percentage of OCD patients to have a comorbid ICD (8%). Comorbidity differences between these studies are likely due to methodological differences in the measurement of these disorders (e.g., how disorder criteria were operationalized),

---

[1] As a general exception, the hair pulling of patients with trichotillomania may be motivated by a variety of functions that may change across situations (during periods of low vs. high arousal) and features of affect regulation, anxiety-reduction, and self-stimulation.

characteristics of sampled populations, and other unaccounted-for factors. In light of these differences and considering the wide variability within clusters of ICDs, it is difficult to justify combining these disorders to make reliable comparisons to OCD. Therefore, the phenomenological characteristics of OCD will be compared to characteristics of trichotillomania, pathological skin picking, pathological gambling, kleptomania, and paraphilia separately to better elucidate relationships between OCD and ICDs on the putative obsessive-compulsive disorder spectrum. It should be noted that these disorders do not encompass an exhaustive list of ICDs; however, due to the paucity of research associated with certain putative ICDs (e.g., compulsive internet use), some ICDs are not reviewed.

OCD and Trichotillomania. Trichotillomania is a condition in which individuals suffer physical, emotional, economic, and social impairment (Wetterneck, Woods, Norberg, and Begotka, 2006) due to compulsive hair pulling behaviors that are often triggered by feelings of general discomfort (American Psychiatric Association, 2000). Feelings of discomfort in trichotillomania patients may be related to states of irritability, excitement, anxiety, frustration, or dissatisfaction with one's appearance, and can occur in low or high stimulation contexts (Stemberger, Stein, and Mansueto, 2003). Furthermore, the frequency and severity of hair pulling behaviors are largely mediated by environmental variables such as being alone or in the presence of others, and the internal consequence from hair pulling is often described to be self-stimulatory or internally-rewarding to an individual (Stanley et al., 1992). Thus, various antecedents may contribute to a person's motivation for hair pulling and the immediate consequences of pulling (e.g., self-stimulation, grooming, calming feelings) are considerably more diverse in nature than are the presumable anxiety-reducing consequences of OCD rituals. Additionally, although various antecedents and consequences appear to contribute to hair pulling in trichotillomania patients, hair pulling behaviors are rarely preceded by obsessional thoughts (Stein, Simeon, Cohen, and Hollander, 1995; Tükel et al., 2001).

Identified comorbidity rates of OCD and trichotillomania appear to vary depending on the studied sample (i.e., those with primary trichotillomania or OCD). King et al. (1995) found that 13% of trichotillomania patients ($n = 15$) also met criteria for OCD. In a sample of 45 OCD patients, Fontenelle et al. (2005) found that 6.6% of patients also engaged in compulsive hair pulling behaviors. In a sample of 293 patients, Grant et al. (2006) found approximately 1% of OCD patients to have comorbid trichotillomania.

Results on the association between OCD and trichotillomania also appear to vary widely in family studies. In a sample of 16 trichotillomania probands, Lenane et al. (1992) found that 19% of first-degree relatives met lifetime criteria for OCD. Conversely, in a study that assessed the presence of trichotillomania in OCD patients, trichotillomania was present in approximately 4% of 343 OCD case probands as compared to 1% in 200 matched controls (Bienvenu et al., 2000), suggesting a weaker familial link between these disorders. Inconsistent results from comorbidity and family studies indicate a need for additional research to clarify the relationship between OCD and trichotillomania.

Even though both OCD and trichotillomania appear to be related to dysfunction in the striatum, there may be differences in the specific neural regions associated with these disorders. Using brain imaging technology, Stein et al. (1997) did not identify caudate abnormalities in trichotillomania patients that are often identified in OCD patients. In subsequent studies, O'Sullivan et al. (1997) and Stein et al., (2002) found reduced volume and neural activity in trichotillomania patients' left putamen, a region associated with reinforcement learning and motor behavior control (Wellington et al., 2006). Additionally, as suggested by Swedo et al. (1991) and Keuthen et al. (2007) trichotillomania may be related to abnormal activity in the cerebellum that is not generally seen in OCD patients. Collectively, these preliminary findings suggest the possibility of salient neural differences between OCD and trichotillomania (Chamberlain et al., 2007); however, considering the preliminary nature of this research, further investigation is warranted to explore these differences.

Both OCD and trichotillomania patients may respond to tricyclic antidepressant medications such as clomipramine (DeVeaugh-Geiss, Landau, and Katz, 1989; Swedo et al., 1989). However, unlike in OCD, SSRI medications do not appear efficacious in treating trichotillomania. In fact, several studies have found that SSRI medications fail to significantly outperform placebo or wait list controls in reducing hair pulling behaviors in trichotillomania patients (Christenson, Mackenzie, Mitchell, and Callies, 1991; Van Minnen et al., 2003; Streichenwein and Thornby, 1995). Besides clomipramine, no well established pharmacological treatments exist for trichotillomania, even though a variety of medications are often prescribed to treat the disorder (Stemberger et al., 2003). However, considerably more support exists for the use of psychological treatments, namely habit reversal therapy, in the treatment of trichotillomania (Chamberlain et al., 2007; Woods, Wetterneck, and Flessner, 2006). Despite some similarities, the therapeutic methods employed in treating trichotillomania differ considerably from those usually employed in treating OCD (Elliott and Fuqua, 2000). As previously noted, OCD responds best to ERP and cognitive restructuring; on the other hand, treatment for trichotillomania often involves habit reversal strategies, such as teaching patients to attend to unnerving feelings or sensations that precipitate pulling, conducting a functional analysis of antecedents and consequences related to pulling behaviors, and modifying contingencies that exacerbate hair pulling urges (Friman et al., 1984). Whereas CBT for OCD involves confronting anxiety-provoking situations without engaging in anxiety-reducing compulsions, psychotherapy for trichotillomania may involve addressing feelings, sensations, or situations related to hair pulling urges, and developing competing responses to hair pulling urges.

OCD and pathological skin picking. Pathological skin picking has received comparably little empirical attention as compared to other ICDs. Skin picking is considered pathological when the behavior causes visible skin lesions and begins to interfere with an individual's daily functioning. Even though near fatal cases have been reported (O'Sullivan, Phillips, Keuthen, and Wilhelm, 1999), pathological skin picking is still considered a "ego-syntonic" activity and may provide relaxation or calming sensations when an individual is anxious or frustrated (Stein, Hutt, Spitz, and Hollander, 1993; Wilhelm et al.,1999). Specific antecedents for compulsive skin picking include low-stimulation situations/activities (Arnold et al., 1998), attending to cutaneous imperfections such as pimples, scabs, or freckles (Bohne et al., 2002), and the desire to "improve" one's appearance through picking (Stein et al., 1993). Thus, in light of these antecedents, the functional aspects associated with compulsive skin picking appear to overlap with those in both anxiety-driven compulsive disorders (OCD, BDD) and ICDs. For example, some compulsive grooming and skin picking behaviors have been linked to body image and appearance concerns, which is similar in content to the obsessional thoughts experienced by BDD patients (O'Sullivan et al., 1999; Phillips and Taub, 1995). Also, in rare cases, skin picking can occur in OCD patients with contamination obsessions as a ritualistic way to remove skin contaminants (Arnold, Auchenbach, and McElroy, 2001). Other skin picking behaviors, however, seem analogous to compulsive behaviors found in ICDs (e.g., trichotillomania, kleptomania), particularly when picking stimulates a particular sensation and occurs during times of low stimulation (Wilhelm et al., 1999).

Obsessive-compulsive disorder has been found to commonly co-occur in groups of pathological skin pickers. In a sample of 31 patients, Wilhelm et al. (1999) found that 52% percent of pathological skin pickers met criteria for comorbid OCD. In the same study, pathological skin picking was highly comorbid with Axis I disorders in general, as 65% of the sample met diagnostic criteria for an anxiety disorder and 44% met criteria for a mood disorder. Therefore, despite high comorbidity findings, it is unclear whether a unique relationship exists between OCD and pathological skin picking, particularly since skin picking seems to co-occur with a variety of psychiatric disorders (Gupta, Gupta, and Haberman, 1986; O'Sullivan et al., 1999; Phillips and Taub, 1995; Wilhelm et al., 1999). A study by Cullen et al. (2001) provides support for such a relationship between OCD and pathological skin picking, as 13.5% of the 80 sampled OCD patients were found to have comorbid skin picking symptoms. Further, this study also found evidence for a genetic link between OCD and pathological skin picking, as skin picking rates were significantly greater in OCD probands (13.5%) than in community-selected probands (4.7%). In a sample of 343 OCD patients, Bienvenu et al. (2000) provide support for an even stronger link between OCD and pathological skin picking, with 24% of OCD probands and 7% of first-degree relatives of OCD probands evincing skin picking behavior.

Little research has explored the neurological underpinnings of pathological skin picking, but research exploring the condition in patients with Prader-Willi Syndrome – a developmental disorder in which up to 69% of individuals demonstrate compulsive skin picking (Symons et al., 1999) – suggests that dysfunction in the orbitofrontal cortex and regions of the limbic system might be related to compulsive picking (Dimitropoulos et al., 2000; Walley and Donaldson, 2005). If this research generalizes to pathological skin pickers as a whole, it appears that there may be some neural dysfunction similarities between OCD and pathological skin picking. However, considering that no published studies have directly compared the neural characteristics of these disorders, potential similarities are preliminary in nature.

Current pharmacological treatments for pathological skin picking are similar to treatments for both OCD and ICDs (e.g., pathological gambling, trichotillomania). Generally, SSRIs are the first-line treatment for skin picking and have been effective in reducing skin picking behaviors as demonstrated by their performance in double-blind, placebo-controlled studies (Bloch, Elliott, Thompson, and Koran, 2001; Simeon et al., 1997). In addition, case reports suggest that opioid antagonists (Lienemann and Walker, 1989) and atypical antipsychotics (Garnis-Jones, Collins, and Rosenthal, 2000) may be effective in reducing skin picking behaviors. Regarding psychological treatment for pathological skin picking, preliminary data suggest that habit reversal training is a promising treatment for reducing skin excoriation and other compulsive picking behaviors in patients (Rosenbaum and Ayllon,

1981; Twohig and Woods, 2001). Habit reversal training for pathological skin picking generally involves identifying antecedents to picking, teaching competing responses (e.g., clenching fists tightly in response to picking urges), generalizing these responses to various settings and situations, and symbolic rehearsal (i.e., practicing competing responses in the presence of a therapist [Arnold et al., 2001]). When pathological skin picking co-occurs within the context of an anxiety-driven disorder such as BDD, cognitive therapy techniques commonly used with OCD patients may also be employed in its treatment. One published study by Deckersbach et al. (2002) successfully combined cognitive restructuring with habit reversal training for a subtype of pathological skin pickers who presented with body image preoccupations or picked compulsively during high-anxiety periods.

OCD and pathological gambling. Pathological gambling is characterized by a persistent failure to resist the impulse to gamble. Unlike OCD, pathological gambling correlates strongly with other forms of sensation-seeking behavior (Hollander and Wong, 1995). Prior to engaging in gambling, pathological gamblers often report feeling a sense of tension that compels these individuals to gamble. These feelings of tension then often give way to a subjectively reported "rush" feeling when gambling occurs (Lesieur, 1992). The rush associated with gambling is often described as being euphoric, motivating, and addictive; however, after gambling, pathological gamblers often suffer from regret and other negative emotions associated with losing control of their behavior. In contrast to OCD, in which patients are motivated to escape from or prevent personal distress arising from specific stimuli/situations, pathological gamblers are motivated by the internal reward they experience in the process of gambling (Black and Moyer, 1998). At the cognitive level, it is unclear whether these disorders are marked by similar dysfunctional cognitions. One study found that pathological gamblers endorsed experiencing OCD-related obsessional thoughts (Blaszczynski, 1999), but a later study did not replicate these findings (Anholt et al., 2004). Obsessional thoughts associated with pathological gambling might be related to guilt or regret associated with the negative consequences of gambling. In contrast, OCD-related obsessions are more likely to be driven by anxiety or disgust (e.g., engaging in unwanted aggressive behaviors, being contaminated). Furthermore, to the extent that OCD-related obsessions include self-conscious qualities such as guilt, the guilt is likely to be for perceived rather than indicative of having done actual harm such as would be the case if someone gambled away a family member's money.

Research indicates that pathological gambling is rarely comorbid with OCD. In a sample of 85 OCD patients, du Toit et al. (2001) found less that 1% of patients with OCD engaged in pathological gambling. These results were later replicated by Jaisoorya et al. (2003) in a larger sample of 231 OCD patients. Similarly, evidence for a familial link between the two disorders is also lacking, as two family studies did not find comorbidity rates beyond what would be expected in a non-clinical population (Bienvenu et al., 2000; Black, Goldstein, Noyes, and Blum, 1994).

Similarly to OCD and various other psychiatric disorders, dysfunction in regions of the prefrontal cortex has been implicated in both OCD and pathological gambling (Cavedini et al., 2002). However, research suggests that dysfunction in the ventromedial prefrontal cortex, a region associated with processing risk and fear (Bechara, Darnasio, Damasio, and Lee, 1999), may have a unique influence on the etiology of pathological gambling behavior

(Potenza et al., 2003). Neuropsychological research conducted with pathological gamblers indicates that these individuals display relative weaknesses in executive functioning, selective attention, and response inhibition (Goudriaan, Oosterlaan, de Beurs, and van den Brink, 2006; Kertzman et al., 2006; Rugle and Melamed, 1993). Even though OCD patients and pathological gamblers appear to be affected by deficits related to executive functioning and response inhibition, pathological gamblers do not present with consistent dysfunction in regions commonly implicated in the pathogenesis of OCD, such as the caudate nucleus (Saxena et al., 1998).

Clomipramine and SSRIs are often used to treat pathological gambling since both disorders may be characterized by abnormal serotonin activity (Hollander et al., 2000; Hollander et al., 1992; Kim et al., 2002). However, since pathological gamblers often have dysfunction in the dopamine and norepinephrine systems (Bergh, Eklund, Sodersten, Nordin, 1997), other medications such as opioid antagonists (Kim, Grant, Adson, and Shin, 2001) and mood stabilizers (Pallanti, Quercioli, Sood, and Hollander, 2002) may be more effective in reducing impulsive behavior. Research suggests that effective psychological treatment for pathological gambling is often multisystemic and may involve group treatment, social support, cognitive restructuring, and emotion regulation skill instruction (Ladouceur, Sylvain, Letarte, Giroux, and Jacques, 1998). Generally when cognitive-behavioral methods are used to treat pathological gambling, they are similar to techniques used with substance abuse disorders (Loeber et al., 2006), such as cue-exposure and response prevention (Symes and Nicki, 1997). Although cue-exposure and response prevention has parallels with ERP for OCD, cue-exposure and response prevention may pair aversive stimuli with gambling in an attempt to neutralize the positive feelings associate with risk-taking (Greenberg and Rankin, 1982). Therefore, in contrast to ERP, the mechanisms at work behind cue exposure and response prevention are not driven by anxiety and contain a strong counter-conditioning component.

OCD and kleptomania. Kleptomania is characterized by a failure to resist an impulse to steal unneeded objects; an increasing sense of tension or arousal before committing the theft; and an experience of pleasure, gratification, or release at the time of theft (American Psychiatric Association, 2000). In contrast to how OCD compulsions often focus on preventing something undesirable from happening (e.g., compulsively praying to prevent a violent action from happening), compulsive behaviors associated with kleptomania are related to an inability or lack of desire to inhibit the urge to steal (Presta et al., 2002). As in pathological gambling, even though intrusive thoughts play a role in both OCD and kleptomania, these thoughts are markedly different across disorders. Namely, OCD-related obsessions are often ego-dystonic in nature, but since stealing may be motivated by an impulse or the desire to experience a rush sensation, thoughts that immediately precede stealing may be ego-syntonic to the individual (Wiedemann, 1998). Instead of being motivated to neutralize anxiety and prevent negative occurrences in the future as is often the case with OCD-related rituals, stealing behavior is often pleasurable and any anxiety that ensues from compulsive stealing may be accounted for by negative social contingencies (e.g., fear of getting caught, social disapproval).

Comorbidity research on OCD and kleptomania indicates that individuals with kleptomania often present with obsessive-compulsive symptoms, but that patients with OCD rarely present with features of kleptomania. In a sample of 20 patients with kleptomania, Presta et al. (2002) found that 60% of the sampled group evinced comorbid OCD. However, another study found only one subject to have comorbid OCD in a sample of 22 kleptomaniacs (Grant and Kim, 2002). Further, in a study of 19 patients with kleptomania, Dannon et al. (2004) identified only two individuals with OCD, and Baylé et al. (2003) did not find any patients (0%) to present with comorbid OCD in 11 kleptomaniac patients. Additionally, all of these studies found compulsive stealing to be highly comorbid with other axis I mood and anxiety disorders, which makes it difficult to assess whether the disorder shares a specific relationship with OCD or an association with high levels of psychopathology in general (McElroy, Hudson, Pope, and Keck, 1991). Studies that have investigated the presence of compulsive stealing behaviors in patients with OCD also failed to identify a significant relationship between the two disorders. In a sample of 231 OCD patients, Jaisoorya et al. (2003) did not identify a single case of kleptomania and du Toit et al. (2001) identified only 2.4% of 85 OCD patients as manifesting comorbid compulsive stealing symptoms.

Only one published study by Bienvenu et al. (2000) has explored the familial association between OCD and kleptomania. In this study, the authors only found kleptomania symptoms in about 3% of 343 OCD probands, compared to 0% in 200 matched controls. To date, few brain imaging studies have been conducted with individuals who engage in compulsive stealing; however, a study by Grant, Correia, and Brennan-Krohn (2006) suggests that the disorder may be associated with decreased white matter in inferior frontal brain regions, such as the orbitofrontal cortex, that are related to inhibiting impulsive behaviors. Research by Grant, Odlauga, and Wozniaka (2007) corroborates this finding and further suggests that dysfunction in the orbitofrontal cortex might partially explain kleptomaniac patient's decreased executive functioning abilities. Even if the orbitofrontal cortex is implicated in both OCD and kleptomania, a close look at neuropsychological research suggests that significant cognitive differences exist between disorders. For example, individuals with OCD have been found to demonstrate significant weaknesses in cognitive inhibition (Bohne, Keuthen, Tuschen-Caffier, and Wilhelm, 2005), set shifting (Okasha et al., 2000), and attentional processing (Hartston and Swerdlow, 1999), but research on kleptomaniacs examining similar factors has not identified such deficits in that population (Grant, Odlaug, and Wozniak, 2007).

Although most of the research on pharmacological treatment for kleptomania comes from single-case studies and studies with small sample sizes, it appears that pharmacological treatment for the disorder is similar to treatments prescribed for pathological gambling, including the use of SSRIs (Lepkifker et al., 1999; McElroy et al, 1991) opioid antagonists (Grant and Kim, 2002), and mood stabilizers (Kmetz, McElroy, Collins, 1997). As with OCD, it appears that SSRI medication may be a promising treatment for kleptomania. However, unlike pharmacological treatment for OCD, opioid anatagonists may be more efficacious than SSRIs in decreasing compulsive stealing behaviors (Grant, 2005). Psychological treatments for kleptomania, like those for pathological gambling, employ specific cognitive and behavioral strategies aimed at offsetting a person's impulse or urge to steal. In particular, possible treatment strategies include aversion conditioning and covert sensitization such as using imaginal exposure to pair the urge to steal with nausea and vomiting (Glover, 1985; McConaghy and Blaszczynski, 1988), covert sensitization paired with exposure and response prevention (Gauthier and Pellerin, 1982), cognitive restructuring and problem-solving techniques (Kohn and Antonuccio, 2002). Despite the paucity of research that exists to validate these techniques with kleptomaniacs, it is clear that significant differences exist in the currently employed psychological treatments for OCD and kleptomania. More specifically, psychological treatment for kleptomania aims to neutralize a pleasurable experience (i.e., the rush associated with stealing) to stop socially undesirable behavior, while treatment for OCD aims to reduce symptoms via exposure to anxiety-provoking stimuli.

OCD and paraphilia. To be considered a paraphilia, an activity must constitute the sole means of sexual gratification for the afflicted individual over a period of six months, and either cause clinically significant distress or impairment in social, occupational, or other important areas of functioning (American Psychiatric Association, 2000). In contrast to the estimated third of OCD patients who experience distressing sexual obsessions (Rasmussen and Tsuang, 1986), individuals with paraphilias experience extreme erotic pleasure from their recurrent thoughts (Kafka, 2006). Therefore, when differentiating between paraphilia and OCD, two important considerations must be taken into account: the nature of the obsessive thought (i.e., ego-syntonic vs. dystonic), and the function of the expressed behaviors. In other words, it is important to consider whether sexual thoughts are pleasurable or distressing to an individual and whether compulsive behaviors are related to fulfilling or avoiding these thoughts. An individual's willingness to engage in sexual activity also serves as a distinguishing characteristic between OCD and paraphilia. Whereas paraphilia is characterized by impulsive and compulsive sexual activity, individuals with OCD rarely act on their sexual obsessions (Freund and Steketee, 1989) and often report experiencing low levels of sexual desire, arousal, as well as high levels of sexual disgust (Fontenelle et al., 2007; Vulink, Denys, Bus, and Westenberg, 2006).

In a sample of 88 patients with paraphilias, Kafka and Hennen (2002) found that 6.6% of the sample had comorbid OCD, a proportion of individuals lower than those related to dysthymic disorder (69.1%), depression (39.1%), ADHD (35.8%), social phobia (26.1%), conduct disorder (16.6%), generalized anxiety disorder (9.1%), or panic disorder (7.5%). In a sample of 36 patients with paraphilias, Black, Kehrberg, Flumerfelt and Schlosser (1997) found a significant co-occurrence of paraphilia and OCD (14%); however, higher co-occurrence rates were identified between paraphilia and substance abuse disorders (64%), phobic disorders (42%), personality disorders (44%), and major depression and dysthymia (39%) than were identified between paraphilia and OCD.

Low percentages of comorbid paraphilia and repetitive sexual behaviors are found in OCD samples. In a sample of 85 OCD patients, du Toit et al. (2001) found that 4.7% of patients exhibited co-occurring life-disruptive sexual urges, and in a sample of 231 patients, Jaisoorya et al. (2003) found that an even smaller percentage (0.4%) of OCD patients demonstrated comorbid sexual urges that interfered with daily functioning. There are no extant family studies that have directly investigated the occurrence of compulsive sexual behavior in OCD probands, but one case study does attempt to explore the relationship between these disorders.

Due to the heterogeneity of behaviors manifested in paraphilia and its high comorbidity with a wide variety of other psychiatric disorders, a clear understanding of the unique neural mechanisms associated with compulsive sexual behavior has not been obtained. Research on hypersexual actions suggests that compulsive sexual behavior is established and maintained by excessive excitation in the central nervous and endocrine systems, coupled with decreased functioning in neural regions associated with behavioral inhibition (Ragan and Martin, 2000). Therefore, in addition to impairment in specific neural regions implicated in inhibition (e.g., the orbitofrontal cortex), other brain regions such as the hypothalamus and pituitary complex have been linked to sexual behavior (Styne and Grumback, 2007). Even though different biological processes may instigate compulsive behaviors in OCD (e.g., obsessional thoughts) and paraphilic patients (e.g., compulsive sexual behaviors), both disorders may be related to dysfunction in brain regions associated with behavioral inhibition such as in the orbitofrontal cortex. However, as is the case with all of the reviewed disorders, neural correlations are but a piece of a larger network of pathogenetic factors and are currently far from being conclusive.

A study by Stein et al. (1992) compared SSRI treatment responses for three treatment groups: patients with paraphilias, those with non-paraphilic sexual addictions (i.e., excessive non deviant sexual behavior, Goldsmith et al., 1998), and those with sexual obsessions. Patients with OCD-related obsessional thoughts responded the best to treatment, paraphilic patients demonstrated the lowest treatment response, and individuals with nonparaphilic sexual addictions were between the two. Subsequent studies have found that patients with paraphilias respond favorably to relatively large doses of SSRIs (Kafka and Hennen, 2000) but medications such as antiadrongens (Bradford and Pawlak, 1993) and opioid antagonists (Raymond, Grant, Kim, and Coleman, 2002) with known anti-arousal tendencies may be more effective in paraphilia symptom reduction. Due to the marked behavioral differences between OCD patients and individuals with paraphilias, it is not surprising that different psychological interventions are used to treat each disorder. Instead of exposing patients with paraphilias to situations that could increase the likelihood of acting out their obsessions and possibly causing harm to the self or others, interventions such as sexual satiation (Laws and Marshall, 1990), covert sensitization (Johnston, Hudson, and Marshall, 1992), aversive stimulation (Laws, 2001), and aversive behavioral rehearsal (Wickramasekera, 1976) have all been used with varying degrees of success with patients who demonstrate compulsive sexual behaviors. Currently no well established pharmacological or psychological treatment exists for paraphilias.

Summary

This paper reviewed the relationship between OCD and various OCSDs to provide a balanced and comprehensive inquiry into evidence for a putative impulsive-compulsive spectrum of disorders. Based on a review of current research, it appears that there may be a unique relationship between OCD and anxiety-driven body image disorders and disorders marked by somatic concerns, such as BDD and hypochondriasis. These disorders commonly co-occur and familial association studies indicate that BDD and hypochondriasis present more frequently in first-degree relatives of patients with OCD than in controls, suggesting a possible genetic link between these disorders. Brain imaging studies involving patients with

OCD, BDD and hypochondriasis, although preliminary in nature, have suggested that abnormalities in similar neural regions are present in these groups, thus providing additional support for a potential shared etiology of the aforementioned disorders. Lastly, additional support for the relationship between OCD and body image/somatic concern disorders is provided by the overlap in the most effective treatments for these disorders, namely SSRI medication and CBT. Moreover, despite the different clinical presentations of BDD, OCD and hypochondriasis, the compulsive behaviors associated with each are largely driven by anxiety-provoking thoughts. In other words, even though OCD patients' washing behavior may be driven by fears of contamination, BDD patients' excessive grooming habits may stem from body image concerns, and a hypochondriac's frequent trips to the doctor's office may be related to concerns about his or her health, all of these disorders have anxiety as a core element that drives the compulsive behaviors of those who are affected (Storch et al., 2008).

The relationship between OCD and neurologically based repetitive disorders is not clearly established. Research suggests some notable similarities between OCD and Tourette syndrome, but evidence for a link between OCD and autism is tenuous. Comorbidity results suggest that obsessive-compulsive behaviors frequently occur in Tourette syndrome patients but that tic disorders occur less frequently in OCD patients. Nevertheless, some research does suggest that OCD and Tourette syndrome co-occur frequently (Park et al., 1993), particularly in pediatric populations (Grados et al., 2001). Mixed results have been found in family studies exploring the association between OCD and Tourette syndrome (Jaisoorya et al., 2003; Pauls et al., 1995), which renders reaching conclusions about proposed familial links between these disorders difficult. Obsessive-compulsive disorder and Tourette syndrome appear to be related to dysfunction in similar neural regions (Biswal et al., 1998; Peterson et al., 2001; Saxena et al., 1998), but differences in response to pharmacological treatments in each of these disorders suggests differences with respect to neural or structural substrates. Whereas SSRIs have demonstrated effectiveness in the treatment of OCD, they are not effective in treating Tourette syndrome (Jiménez-Jiménez and García-Ruiz, 2001; Preston et al., 2006). Significant differences also exist between first line psychological treatments for OCD and Tourette syndrome. Exposure and ritual prevention is the best established treatment for OCD, whereas habit reversal training has yielded the best results in decreasing tic behaviors in Tourette syndrome patients (Peterson and Azrin, 1993; Wilhelm et al., 2003). Even though repetitive behavior may be a common feature of both OCD and Tourette syndrome, markedly different behavioral functions appear to drive these compulsive behaviors. As previously noted, no clear associations appear to exist between OCD and autism. Although some studies have identified comorbidity and familial associations with respect to these disorders (e.g., Bolton et al., 1998; Hollander et al., 2003), findings must be interpreted in light of significant differences in the clinical presentation of these disorders, neurological discrepancies, and differential responses to pharmacological and psychological treatments. Also salient differences appear to exist in the nature of behaviors exhibited between OCD and autistic patients and in each disorder's shared comorbidities with other psychiatric disorders. That is, different behavioral functions characterize the compulsive behaviors of these disorders, and associations between OCD and autism might be best explained by the fact that both these disorders tend to manifest within the context of a variety of other psychiatric disorders (Abramowitz and Deacon, 2005; Smalley et al., 1995).

Since the relationship between OCD and ICDs is crucial to the existence of an obsessive-compulsive spectrum, this review sought to clarify the associations between OCD and the following ICDs: trichotillomania, pathological skin picking, pathological gambling, kleptomania, and paraphilia.

Comorbidity rates of ICDs and OCD vary, but research generally suggests that obsessive-compulsive symptoms occur more frequently in individuals with particular ICDs (i.e. trichotillomania, skin picking) than do impulse control behaviors in samples of individuals diagnosed with OCD (Cullen et al., 2001; Fontanelle at al., 2005; Grant et al., 2006; King et al., 1995; Wilhelm at al., 1999). Other research shows that ICDs such as pathological gambling, kleptomania, and paraphilia co-occur infrequently with OCD (Baylé et al., 2002; du Toit at al., 2001; Kafka and Hennen, 2002; Jaisoorya et al., 2003). Family studies examining OCD and ICDs have yielded mixed results, with the most promising connections again emerging for skin-picking and trichotillomania with OCD, as opposed to the other ICDs (Bienvenue et al., 2000; Black et al., 1998; Lenane et al., 1992). However, as yet no clear genetic links have emerged for any of the disorders and OCD. Although some similarities have been noted in the neural regions implicated in OCD and those implicated in ICDs (e.g. the striatum, the prefrontal cortex), there are notable differences as well (Cavedini et al., 2002; Grant et al., 2007; Ragan and Martin, 2000; Stein et al., 1997). Specifically, differences have been noted in the role of the caudate nucleus, the left putamen, and the cerebellum (Keuthen et al., 2007; Stein et al., 1997; Swedo et al., 1991; Wellington et al., 2006) between trichotillomania and OCD. Moreover, some impulse control issues are associated with dysfunction in reward centers, a connection which has not been found in OCD (Blum et al., 2000; Bergh et al., 1997). Commonly used treatments for ICDs share some overlap with those effective in treating OCD, though the similarities are largely confined to mediation rather than psychosocial treatment. That is, SSRIs (for skin picking, gambling, kleptomania and paraphilia), tricyclic antidepressants (for trichotillomania) and adjunctive anti-psychotics (for skin picking) have yielded favorable results with both ICDs and OCD. Aside from some shared cognitive-behavioral elements, psychological treatments for ICDs and OCD are highly discrepant.

Implications

The findings of this review are relevant to the continuing debate over the possible reclassification of OCD on an impulsivity-compulsivity disorder spectrum in the forthcoming DSM-V. Although all reviewed disorders are characterized by repetitive behaviors, it is clear that there are major phenomenological differences between OCD and most proposed OCSDs. Considering comorbidity, familial, neurological, and treatment research studies, the closest associations emerged between OCD and anxiety-driven disorders characterized by body image/sensitization obsessions. These disorders are all characterized by obsessive thoughts and anxiety reducing compulsions; thus, at both surface and deeper levels, anxiety appears to be the "glue" that conjoins these disorders. In light of the limited evidence for a broad impulsive-compulsive disorder spectrum containing both anxiety-driven compulsive disorders and ICDs, it may be appropriate to reevaluate the scope of this disorder spectrum.

Perhaps a more limited cluster of disorders containing OCD, BDD, and hypochondriasis better captures the important features of putative OCSDs.

References

Abramowitz, J. S., and Deacon, B. J. (2005). The OC spectrum: A closer look at the arguments and the data. Handbook of OCD: Concepts and Controversies. New York: Springer.

Abramowitz, J. S., Whiteside, S. P., and Deacon, B. J. (2005). The effectiveness of treatment for pediatric obsessive-compulsive disorder: A meta-analysis. *Behavior Therapy*, 36, 55-63.

American Psychiatric Association. (2000). Diagnostic and statistical manual of mental disorders – Fourth edition, Text Revision. Washington, DC: Author.

Anholt, G., Emmelkamp, P., Cath, D., van Oppen, P., Nelissen, H., and Smit, J. (2004). Do patients with OCD and pathological gambling have similar dysfunctional cognitions? *Behaviour Research and Therapy*, 42, 529-537.

Arnold, L. M., Auchenbach, M. B., and McElroy, S. L. (2001). Psychogenic excoriation. clinical features, proposed diagnostic criteria, epidemiology and approaches to treatment. *CNS Drugs*, 15, 351-359.

Arnold, L. M., McElroy, S. L., Mutasim, D. F., Dwight, M. M., Lamerson, C. L., and Morris, E. M. (1998). Characteristics of 34 adults with psychogenic excoriation. *Journal of Clinical Psychiatry*, 59, 509-514.

Azrin, N. H. and Nunn, R. G. (1973). Habit reversal: a method of eliminating nervous habits and tics. *Behaviour Research and Therapy*, 11, 619-628.

Bailey, A., Luthert, P., Dean, A., Harding, B., Janota, I., Montgomery, M., Rutter, M., Lantos, P. (1998). A clinicopathological study of autism. *Brain*, 121, 889-905.

Barsky, A. J., and Ahern, D. K. (2004). Cognitive behavior therapy for hypochondriasis: A randomized controlled trial. *Journal of the American Medical Association*, 291, 1464-1470.

Barsky, A., Wyshak, G., and Klerman, G. (1992). Psychiatric comorbidity in DSM-III-R hypochondriasis. *Archives of General Psychiatry*, 49, 101-108.

Bartz, J. A., and Hollander, E. (2006). Is obsessive-compulsive disorder an anxiety disorder? Progress in Neuro-Psychopharmacology and Biological Psychiatry, 30, 338-352.

Bauman, M.L. (1996). Brief report: neuroanatomic observations of the brain in pervasive developmental disorders. *Journal of Autism and Developmental Disorders* 26, 199-203.

Baylé, F. J., Caci, H., Millet, B., Richa, S., and Olie, J. P. (2003). Psychopathology and comorbidity of psychiatric disorders in patients with kleptomania. *American Journal of Psychiatry*, 160, 1509-1513.

Bechara, A., Damasio, H., Damasio, A. R., and Lee, G. P. (1999). Different contributions of the human amygdala and ventromedial prefrontal cortex to decision-making. *Journal of Neuroscience*, 19, 5473.

Bergh, C., Eklund, T., Sodersten, P., and Nordin, C. (1997). Altered dopamine function in pathological gambling. *Psychological Medicine*, 27, 473-475.

Bienvenu, O. J., Samuels, J. F., Riddle, M. A., Hoehn-Saric, R., Liang, K. Y., Cullen, B. A. M., et al. (2000). The relationship of obsessive–compulsive disorder to possible spectrum disorders: Results from a family study. *Biological Psychiatry*, 48, 287-293.

Biswal, B., Ulmer, J. L., Krippendorf, R. L., Harsch, H. H., Daniels, D. L., Hyde, J. S., et al. (1998). Abnormal cerebral activation associated with a motor task in tourette syndrome. *American Journal of Neuroradiology*, 19, 1509-1512.

Black, D. W., Goldstein, R. B., Noyes, R.,Jr, and Blum, N. (1994). Compulsive behaviors and obsessive-compulsive disorder (OCD): Lack of a relationship between OCD, eating disorders, and gambling. *Comprehensive Psychiatry*, 35, 145-148.

Black, D. W., Kehrberg, L. L., Flumerfelt, D. L., and Schlosser, S. S. (1997). Characteristics of 36 subjects reporting compulsive sexual behavior. *American Journal of Psychiatry*, 154, 243-249.

Black, D. W., and Moyer, T. (1998). Clinical features and psychiatric comorbidity of subjects with pathological gambling behavior. *Psychiatric Services*, 49, 1434-1439.

Blanchard, E. B., Wulfert, E., Freidenberg, B. M., and Malta, L. S. (2000). Psychophysiological assessment of compulsive gamblers' arousal to gambling cues: A pilot study. *Applied Psychophysiology and Biofeedback*, 25, 155-165.

Blaszczynski, A. (1999). Pathological gambling: An impulse control, addictive or obsessive-compulsive disorder?. *Anuario de Psicología*, 30, 93-109.

Bloch, M. R., Elliott, M., Thompson, H., and Koran, L. M. (2001). Fluoxetine in pathologic skin-picking open-label and double-blind results. *Psychosomatics*, 42, 314-319.

Blum, K., Braverman, E. R., Holder, J. M., Lubar, J. F., Monastra, V. J., Miller, D., et al. (2000). Reward deficiency syndrome: A biogenetic model for the diagnosis and treatment of impulsive, addictive, and compulsive behaviors. *Journal of Psychoactive Drugs,* 32, 101-112.

Bohne, A., Keuthen, N., Tuschen-Caffier, B., and Wilhelm, S. (2005). Cognitive inhibition in trichotillomania and obsessive-compulsive disorder. *Behaviour Research and Therapy*, 43, 923-942.

Bohne, A., Wilhelm, S., Keuthen, N. J., Baer, L., and Jenike, M. A. (2002). Skin picking in german students. prevalence, phenomenology, and associated characteristics. *Behavior Modification,* 26, 320-339.

Bolton, P., Pickles, A., Murphy, M. and Rutter, M. (1998). Autism, affective and other psychiatric disorders: Patterns of familial aggregation. *Psychological Medicine*, 28, 385-395.

Bradford, J. M., and Pawlak, A. (1993). Double-blind placebo crossover study of cyproterone acetate in the treatment of the paraphilias. *Archives of Sexual Behavior*, 22, 383-402.

Carey, P., Seedat, S., Warwick, J., van Heerden, B., and Stein, D. J. (2004). SPECT imaging of body dysmorphic disorder. *Journal of Neuropsychiatry and Clinical Neurosciences*, 16, 357-359.

Cavedini, P., Riboldi, G., Keller, R., D'Annucci, A., and Bellodi, L. (2002). Frontal lobe dysfunction in pathological gambling patients. *Biological Psychiatry*, 51, 334-341.

Chamberlain, S. R., Menzies, L., Sahakian, B. J., and Fineberg, N. A. (2007). Lifting the veil on trichotillomania. *American Journal of Psychiatry*, 164, 568-574.

Chambless, D. L., Baker, M. J., Baucom, D. H., Beutler, L. E., Calhoun, K. S., Crits-Christoph, P., et al. (1998). Update on empirically validated therapies, II. *The Clinical Psychologist*, 51, 3-16.

Christenson, G. A., Mackenzie, T. B., Mitchell, J. E., and Callies, A. L. (1991). A placebo-controlled, double-blind crossover study of fluoxetine in trichotillomania. *American Journal of Psychiatry*, 148, 1566-1571.

Cororve, M. B., and Gleaves, D. H. (2001). Body dysmorphic disorder: A review of conceptualizations, assessment, and treatment strategies. *Clinical Psychology Review*, 21, 949-970.

Cullen, B., Samuels, J., Bienvenu, O., Grados, M., Hoehn-Saric, R., Hahn, J., et al. (2001). The relationship of pathologic skin picking to obsessive-compulsive disorder. *Journal of Nervous and Mental Disease*, 189, 193-195.

Cryan, E. M., Butcher, G. J., and Webb, M. G. (1992). Obsessive-compulsive disorder and paraphilia in a monozygotic twin pair. The British Journal of Psychiatry. *Journal of Mental Science*, 161, 694-698.

Dannon, P. N., Lowengrub, K. M., Iancu, I., and Kotler, M. (2004). Kleptomania: Comorbid psychiatric diagnosis in patients and their families. *Psychopathology*, 37, 76-80.

Deckersbach, T., Rauch, S., Buhlmann, U., and Wilhelm, S. (2006). Habit reversal versus supportive psychotherapy in tourette's disorder: A randomized controlled trial and predictors of treatment response. *Behaviour Research and Therapy*, 44, 1079-1090.

Deckersbach, T., Wilhelm, S., Keuthen, N. J., Baer, L., and Jenike, M. A. (2002). Cognitive-behavior therapy for self-injurious skin picking. A case series. *Behavior Modification*, 26, 361-377.

Denys, D., de Geus, F., van Megen, H., and Westenberg, H. (2004). Use of factor analysis to detect potential phenotypes in obsessive-compulsive disorder. *Psychiatry Research*, 128, 273-280.

DeVeaugh-Geiss, J., Landau, P., and Katz, R. (1989). Treatment of obsessive compulsive disorder with clomipramine. *Psychiatric Annals*, 19, 97-101.

Dimitropoulos, A., Feurer, I. D., Roof, E., Stone, W., Butler, M. G., Sutcliffe, J., et al. (2000). Appetitive behavior, compulsivity, and neurochemistry in prader-willi syndrome. *Mental Retardation and Developmental Disabilities Research Reviews*, 6, 125-130.

du Toit, P. L., van Kradenburg, J., Niehaus, D., and Stein, D. J. (2001). Comparison of obsessive-compulsive disorder patients with and without comorbid putative obsessive-compulsive spectrum disorders using a structured clinical interview. *Comprehensive Psychiatry*, 42, 291-300.

Eikeseth, S., Smith, T., Jahr, E., and Eldevik, S. (2002). Intensive behavioral treatment at school for 4-to 7-year-old children with autism: A 1-year comparison controlled study. *Behavior Modification*, 26, 49-61.

Fallon, B., Schneier, F., Marshall, R., and Campeas, R. (1996). The pharmacotherapy of hypochondriasis. *Psychopharmacology Bulletin*, 32, 607-611.

Friman, P., and O'Connor, W. (1984). The integration of hypnotic and habit reversal techniques in the treatment of trichotillomania. *The Behavior Therapist*, 7, 166-167.

Fontenelle, L. F., de Souza, W. F., de Menezes, G. B., Mendlowicz, M. V., Miotto, R. R., Falcao, R., et al. (2007). Sexual function and dysfunction in brazilian patients with obsessive-compulsive disorder and social anxiety disorder. *The Journal of Nervous and Mental Disease,* 195, 254-257.

Fontenelle, L. F., Mendlowicz, M. V., and Versiani, M. (2005). Impulse control disorders in patients with obsessive-compulsive disorder. *Psychiatry and Clinical Neurosciences*, 59, 30-37.

Freidenberg, B. M., Blanchard, E. B., Wulfert, E., and Malta, L. S. (2002). Changes in physiological arousal to gambling cues among participants in motivationally enhanced cognitive-behavior therapy for pathological gambling: A preliminary study. *Applied Psychophysiology and Biofeedback*, 27, 251-260.

Freund, B., and Steketee, G. (1989). Sexual history, attitudes and functioning of obsessive-compulsive patients. *Journal of Sex and Marital Therapy*, 15, 31-41.

Elliott, A., and Fuqua, R. (2000). Trichotillomania: Conceptualization, measurement, and treatment. *Behavior Therapy*, 31, 529-545.

Garnis-Jones, S., Collins, S., and Rosenthal, D. (2000). Treatment of self-mutilation with olanzapine. *Journal of Cutaneous Medicine and Surgery*, 4, 161-163.

Gauthier, J., and Pellerin, D. (1982). Management of compulsive shoplifting through covert sensitization. *Journal of Behavior Therapy and Experimental Psychiatry*, 13, 73-75.

Geller, D. A., Wagner, K. D., Emslie, G., Murphy, T., Carpenter, D. J., Wetherhold, E., et al. (2004). Paroxetine treatment in children and adolescents with obsessive-compulsive disorder: A randomized, multicenter, double-blind, placebo-controlled trial. *Journal of the American Academy of Child and Adolescent Psychiatry*, 43, 1387-1396.

Glover, J. H. (1985). A case of kleptomania treated by covert sensitization. *The British Journal of Clinical Psychology*, 24, 213-214.

Goldsmith, T., Shapira, N., Phillips, K., and McElroy, S. (1998). Conceptual foundations of obsessive-compulsive spectrum disorders. Obsessive-compulsive disorder: Theory, research, and treatment (pp. 397-425).

Goudriaan, A. E., Oosterlaan, J., de Beurs, E., and van den Brink, W. (2006). Neurocognitive functions in pathological gambling: A comparison with alcohol dependence, tourette syndrome and normal controls. *Addiction,* 101, 534-547.

Grados, M. A., Riddle, M. A., Samuels, J. F., Liang, K. Y., Hoehn-Saric, R., Bienvenu, O. J., et al. (2001). The familial phenotype of obsessive-compulsive disorder in relation to tic disorders: The Hopkins OCD family study. *Biological Psychiatry*, 50, 559-565.

Grant, J. E. (2005) Outcome Study of Kleptomania Patients Treated With Naltrexone: A Chart Review. *Clinical Neuropharmacology, 28,* 11-14.

Grant, J. E., Correia, S., and Brennan-Krohn, T. (2006). White matter integrity in kleptomania: A pilot study. *Psychiatry Research*, 147, 233-237.

Grant, J. E., and Kim, S. W. (2002). Clinical characteristics and associated psychopathology of 22 patients with kleptomania. *Comprehensive Psychiatry*, 43, 378-384.

Grant, J. E., and Kim, S. W. (2002). An open-label study of naltrexone in the treatment of kleptomania. *Journal of Clinical Psychiatry*, 63, 349-356.

Grant, J. E., Mancebo, M. C., Pinto, A., Eisen, J. L., and Rasmussen, S. A. (2006). Impulse control disorders in adults with obsessive compulsive disorder. *Journal of Psychiatric Research*, 40, 494-501.

Grant, J. E., Odlaug, B. L., and Wozniak, J. R. (2007). Neuropsychological functioning in kleptomania. *Behaviour Research and Therapy*, 45, 1663-1670.

Grant, J. E., and Potenza, M. N. (2006). Escitalopram treatment of pathological gambling with co-occurring anxiety: An open-label pilot study with double-blind discontinuation. *International Clinical Psychopharmacology*, 21, 203-209.

Greenberg, D., and Rankin, H. (1982). Compulsive gamblers in treatment. *British Journal of Psychiatry*, 140, 364-366.

Gunstad, J., and Phillips, K. A. (2003). Axis I comorbidity in body dysmorphic disorder. *Comprehensive Psychiatry*, 44, 270-276.

Gupta, M. A., Gupta, A. K., and Haberman, H. F. (1986). Neurotic excoriations: A review and some new perspectives. *Comprehensive Psychiatry*, 27, 381-386.

Handen, B. L., Johnson, C. R., and Lubetsky, M. (2000). Efficacy of methylphenidate among children with autism and symptoms of attention-deficit hyperactivity disorder. *Journal of Autism and Developmental Disorders*, 30, 245-255.

Hartston, H. J., and Swerdlow, N. R. (1999). Visuospatial priming and stroop performance in patients with obsessive compulsive disorder. *Neuropsychology*, 13, 447-457.

Hollander, E. (1993). Obsessive-compulsive spectrum disorders: An overview. *Psychiatric Annals*, 23, 355–358.

Hollander, E., Anagnostou, E., Chaplin, W., Esposito, K., Haznedar, M. M., Licalzi, E., et al. (2005). Striatal volume on magnetic resonance imaging and repetitive behaviors in autism. *Biological Psychiatry*, 58, 226-232.

Hollander, E., DeCaria, C. M., Finkell, J. N., Begaz, T., Wong, C. M., and Cartwright, C. (2000). A randomized double-blind fluvoxamine/placebo crossover trial in pathologic gambling. *Biological Psychiatry*, 47, 813-817.

Hollander, E., Frenkel, M., Decaria, C., Trungold, S., and Stein, D. J. (1992). Treatment of pathological gambling with clomipramine. *American Journal of Psychiatry*, 149, 710-711.

Hollander, E., King, A., Delaney, K., Smith, C. J., and Silverman, J. M. (2003). Obsessive-compulsive behaviors in parents of multiplex autism families. *Psychiatry Research*, 117, 11-16.

Hollander, E., Kwon, J., Stein, D., and Broatch, J. (1996). Obsessive-compulsive and spectrum disorders: Overview and quality of life issues. *Journal of Clinical Psychiatry*, 57, 3-6.

Hollander, E., and Wong, C. M. (1995). Body dysmorphic disorder, pathological gambling, and sexual compulsions. *Journal of Clinical Psychiatry*, 56, 7-12.

Jaisoorya, T. S., Reddy, Y. C., and Srinath, S. (2003). The relationship of obsessive-compulsive disorder to putative spectrum disorders: Results from an Indian study. *Comprehensive Psychiatry*, 44, 317-323.

Jimenez-Jimenez, F. J., and Garcia-Ruiz, P. J. (2001). Pharmacological options for the treatment of tourette's disorder. *Drugs*, 61, 2207-2220.

Johnston, P., Hudson, S. M., and Marshall, W. L. (1992). The effects of masturbatory reconditioning with nonfamilial child molesters. *Behaviour Research and Therapy*, 30, 559-561.

Kafka, M. P. (2006). Paraphilia-related disorders. *Principles and Practice of Sex Therapy.* New York: Guilford Press.

Kafka, M. P., and Hennen, J. (2002). A DSM-IV axis I comorbidity study of males (n= 120) with paraphilias and paraphilia-related disorders. Sexual Abuse: *A Journal of Research and Treatment*, 14, 349-366.

Kafka, M. P., and Hennen, J. (2000). Psychostimulant augmentation during treatment with selective serotonin reuptake inhibitors in men with paraphilias and paraphilia-related disorders: A case series. *Journal of Clinical Psychiatry*, 61, 664-670.

Kemper, T.L., and Bauman, M.L. (1993). The contribution of neuropathologic studies to the understanding of autism. *Behavioural Neurology*, 11, 175-187.

Kertzman, S., Lowengrub, K., Aizer, A., Nahum, Z. B., Kotler, M., and Dannon, P. N. (2006). Stroop performance in pathological gamblers. *Psychiatry Research*, 142, 1-10.

Keuthen, N. J., Makris, N., Schlerf, J. E., Martis, B., Savage, C. R., McMullin, K., et al. (2007). Evidence for reduced cerebellar volumes in trichotillomania. *Biological Psychiatry*, 61, 374-381.

Kim, S. W., Grant, J. E., Adson, D. E., and Shin, Y. C. (2001). Double-blind naltrexone and placebo comparison study in the treatment of pathological gambling. *Biological Psychiatry,* 49, 914-921.

Kim, S. W., Grant, J. E., Adson, D. E., Shin, Y. C., and Zaninelli, R. (2002). A double-blind placebo-controlled study of the efficacy and safety of paroxetine in the treatment of pathological gambling. *The Journal of Clinical Psychiatry*, 63, 501-507.

King, R. A., Scahill, L., Vitulano, L. A., Schwab-Stone, M., Tercyak, K. P.,Jr, and Riddle, M. A. (1995). Childhood trichotillomania: Clinical phenomenology, comorbidity, and family genetics. *Journal of the American Academy of Child and Adolescent Psychiatry*, 34, 1451-1459.

Kmetz, G. F., McElroy, S. L., and Collins, D. J. (1997). Response of kleptomania and mixed mania to valproate. *American Journal of Psychiatry*, 154, 580-581.

Kohn, C. S., and Antonuccio, D. O. (2002). Treatment of kleptomania using cognitive and behavioral strategies. Clinical Case Studies, 1, 25.

Kolmen, B. K., Feldman, H. M., Handen, B. L., and Janosky, J. E. (1995). Naltrexone in young autistic children: A double-blind, placebo-controlled crossover study. *Journal of the American Academy of Child and Adolescent Psychiatry,* 34, 223-231.

Ladouceur, R., Sylvain, C., Boutin, C., Lachance, S., Doucet, C., Leblond, J., et al. (2001). Cognitive treatment of pathological gambling. *Journal of Nervous and Mental Disease*, 189, 774-780.

Ladouceur, R., Sylvain, C., Letarte, H., Giroux, I. and Jacques, C. (1998). Cognitive treatment of pathological gamblers. *Behaviour Research and Therapy* 36, 1111–1120.

LaSalle, V. H., Cromer, K. R., Nelson, K. N., Kazuba, D., Justement, L., and Murphy, D. L. (2004). Diagnostic interview assessed neuropsychiatric disorder comorbidity in 334 individuals with obsessive-compulsive disorder. *Depression and Anxiety,* 19, 163-173.

Laws, D. R. (2001). Olfactory aversion: Notes on procedure, with speculations on its mechanism of effect. Sexual Abuse : *A Journal of Research and Treatment*, 13, 275-287

Laws, D., and Marshall, W. (1990). A conditioning theory of the etiology and maintenance of deviant sexual preference and behavior. Handbook of Sexual Assault: Issues, Theories, and Treatment of the Offender. New York: Plenum Publishers..

Lehmkuhl, H. D., Storch, E. A., Bodfish, J. W., and Geffken, G. R. (2008). Brief report: Exposure and response prevention for obsessive compulsive disorder in a 12-year-old with autism. *Journal of Autism and Developmental Disorders*, 38, 977-981.

Lenane, M. C., Swedo, S. E., Rapoport, J. L., Leonard, H., Sceery, W., and Guroff, J. J. (1992). Rates of obsessive compulsive disorder in first degree relatives of patients with trichotillomania: A research note. *Journal of Child Psychology and Psychiatry, and Allied Disciplines*, 33, 925-933.

Lepkifker, E., Dannon, P. N., Ziv, R., Iancu, I., Horesh, N., and Kotler, M. (1999). The treatment of kleptomania with serotonin reuptake inhibitors. *Clinical Neuropharmacology*, 22, 40-43.

Lesieur, H. R. (1992). Compulsive gambling. *Society*, 29, 43-50.

Leyfer, O. T., Folstein, S. E., Bacalman, S., Davis, N. O., Dinh, E., Morgan, J., et al. (2006). Comorbid psychiatric disorders in children with autism: Interview development and rates of disorders. *Journal of Autism and Developmental Disorders*, 36, 849-861.

Lienemann, J., and Walker, F. D. (1989). Reversal of self-abusive behavior with naltrexone. *Journal of Clinical Psychopharmacology*, 9, 448-449.

Lochner, C., Seedat, S., du Toit, P. L., Nel, D. G., Niehaus, D. J., Sandler, R., et al. (2005). Obsessive-compulsive disorder and trichotillomania: A phenomenological comparison. *BMC Psychiatry*, 5, 2-13.

Lochner, C., and Stein, D. J. (2006). Does work on obsessive-compulsive spectrum disorders contribute to understanding the heterogeneity of obsessive-compulsive disorder? *Progress in Neuro-Psychopharmacology and Biological Psychiatry*, 30, 353-361.

Loeber, S., Croissant, B., Heinz, A., Mann, K., and Flor, H. (2006). Cue exposure in the treatment of alcohol dependence: Effects on drinking outcome, craving and self-efficacy. *British Journal of Clinical Psychology*, 45, 515-529.

Lovaas, O. I. (1987). Behavioral treatment and normal educational and intellectual functioning in young autistic children. *Journal of Consulting and Clinical Psychology*, 55, 3-9.

Luiselli, J. K., Blew, P., Keane, J., Thibadeau, S., and Holzman, T. (2000). Pharmacotherapy for severe aggression in a child with autism: "open label" evaluation of multiple medications on response frequency and intensity of behavioral intervention. *Journal of Behavior Therapy and Experimental Psychiatry*, 31, 219-230.

Marzagao, L. R. (1972). Systematic desensitization treatment of kleptomania. *Journal of Behavioral Therapy and Experimental Psychiatry*, 3, 327-328.

Matsunaga, H., Kiriike, N., Matsui, T., Oya, K., Okino, K., and Stein, D. J. (2005). Impulsive disorders in Japanese adult patients with obsessive-compulsive disorder. *Comprehensive Psychiatry*, 46, 43-49.

McConaghy, N., and Blaszczynski, A. (1988). Imaginal desensitization: A cost-effective treatment in two shop-lifters and a binge-eater resistant to previous therapy. *Australian and New Zealand Journal of Psychiatry*, 22, 78-82.

McCracken, J. T., McGough, J., Shah, B., Cronin, P., Hong, D., Aman, M. G., et al. (2002). Risperidone in children with autism and serious behavioral problems. *New England Journal of Medicine*, 347, 314-320.

McDougle, C. J., Kem, D. L., and Posey, D. J. (2002). Case series: Use of ziprasidone for maladaptive symptoms in youths with autism. *Journal of the American Academy of Child and Adolescent Psychiatry*, 41, 921-927.

McElroy, S. L., Hudson, J. I., Pope, H. G., and Keck, P. E. (1991). Kleptomania: Clinical characteristics and associated psychopathology. *Psychological Medicine*, 21, 93-108.

McElroy, S. L., Pope, H. G.,Jr, Hudson, J. I., Keck, P. E.,Jr, and White, K. L. (1991). Kleptomania: A report of 20 cases. *The American Journal of Psychiatry*, 148, 652-657.

McElroy, S. L., Pope, H. G.,Jr, Keck, P. E.,Jr, Hudson, J. I., Phillips, K. A., and Strakowski, S. M. (1996). Are impulse-control disorders related to bipolar disorder? *Comprehensive Psychiatry*, 37, 229-240.

McKay, D. (1999). Two-year follow-up of behavioral treatment and maintenance for body dysmorphic disorder. *Behavior Modification*, 23, 620-632.

Miguel, E. C., Coffey, B. J., Baer, L., Savage, C. R., Rauch, S. L., and Jenike, M. A. (1995). Phenomenology of intentional repetitive behaviors in obsessive-compulsive disorder and tourette's disorder. *Journal of Clinical Psychiatry,* 56, 246-255.

Muris, P., Merckelbach, H., Wessel, I., and van de Ven, M. (1999). Psychopathological correlates of self-reported behavioural inhibition in normal children. *Behaviour Research and Therapy,* 37, 575-584.

Muris, P., Steerneman, P., Merckelbach, H., Holdrinet, I., and Meesters, C. (1998). Comorbid anxiety symptoms in children with pervasive developmental disorders. *Journal of Anxiety Disorders*, 12, 387-393.

Neziroglu, F., McKay, D., Todaro, J., and Yaryura-Tobias, J. A. (1996). Effect of cognitive behavior therapy on persons with body dysmorphic disorder and comorbid axis II diagnoses. *Behavior Therapy*, 27, 67-77.

Okasha, A., Rafaat, M., Mahallawy, N., El Nahas, G., El Dawla, A. S., Sayed, M., et al. (2000). Cognitive dysfunction in obsessive-compulsive disorder. *Acta Psychiatrica Scandinavica*, 101, 281-285.

O'Sullivan, R. L., Phillips, K. A., Keuthen, N. J., and Wilhelm, S. (1999). Near-fatal skin picking from delusional body dysmorphic disorder responsive to fluvoxamine. *Psychosomatics*, 40, 79-81.

O'Sullivan, R. L., Rauch, S. L., Breiter, H. C., Grachev, I. D., Baer, L., Kennedy, D. N., et al. (1997). Reduced basal ganglia volumes in trichotillomania measured via morphometric magnetic resonance imaging. *Biological Psychiatry*, 42, 39-45.

Pallanti, S., Quercioli, L., Sood, E., and Hollander, E. (2002). Lithium and valproate treatment of pathological gambling: A randomized single-blind study. *The Journal of Clinical Psychiatry*, 63, 559-564.

Park, S., Como, P. G., Cui, L., and Kurlan, R. (1993). The early course of the tourette's syndrome clinical spectrum. *Neurology,* 43, 1712-1715.

Pauls, D. L., Alsobrook, J. P., Goodman, W., Rasmussen, S., and Leckman, J. F. (1995). A family study of obsessive-compulsive disorder. *American Journal of Psychiatry*, 152, 76-84.

Peterson, A., and Azrin, N. (1993). Behavioral and pharmacological treatments for tourette syndrome: A review. *Applied and Preventive Psychology*, 2, 1-242.

Peterson, B. S., Staib, L., Scahill, L., Zhang, H., Anderson, C., Leckman, J. F., et al. (2001). Regional brain and ventricular volumes in tourette syndrome. *Archives of General Psychiatry*, 58, 427-440.

Phillips, K. A. (2002). Pharmacologic treatment of body dysmorphic disorder: Review of the evidence and a recommended treatment approach. *CNS Spectrums*, 7, 453-60, 463.

Phillips, K. A., and Taub, S. L. (1995). Skin picking as a symptom of body dysmorphic disorder. *Psychopharmacology Bulletin*, 31, 279-288.

Potenza, M. N., Leung, H. C., Blumberg, H. P., Peterson, B. S., Fulbright, R. K., Lacadie, C. M., et al. (2003). An FMRI stroop task study of ventromedial prefrontal cortical function in pathological gamblers. *American Journal of Psychiatry*, 160, 1990-1994.

Presta, S., Marazziti, D., Dell'Osso, L., Pfanner, C., Pallanti, S., and Cassano, G. B. (2002). Kleptomania: Clinical features and comorbidity in an italian sample. *Comprehensive Psychiatry*, 43, 7-12.

Preston, J., O'Neal, J.H., and Talaga, M.C. (2006). Child and adolescent clinical psychopharmacology made simple. Oakland, CA: Preston.

Rachman, S. (1997). A cognitive theory of obsessions. *Behaviour Research and Therapy*, 35, 793-802.

Ragan, P. W., and Martin, P. R. (2000). The psychobiology of sexual addiction. *Sexual Addiction and Compulsivity*, 7, 161-175.

Rasmussen, S. A, and Tsuang, M. T. (1986). Clinical characteristics and family history in DSM-III obsessive-compulsive disorder. *American Journal of Psychiatry*, 143, 317-322.

Ratey, J. J., Bemporad, J., Sorgi, P., Bick, P., Polakoff, S., O'Driscoll, G., et al. (1987). Open trial effects of beta-blockers on speech and social behaviors in 8 autistic adults. *Journal of Autism and Developmental Disorders*, 17, 439-446.

Raymond, N. C., Grant, J. E., Kim, S. W., and Coleman, E. (2002). Treatment of compulsive sexual behaviour with naltrexone and serotonin reuptake inhibitors: Two case studies. *International Clinical Psychopharmacology*, 17, 201-205.

Rosenbaum, M. S., and Ayllon, T. (1981). The behavioral treatment of neurodermatitis through habit-reversal. *Behaviour Research and Therapy*, 19, 313-318.

Rugle, L., and Melamed, L. (1993). Neuropsychological assessment of attention problems in pathological gamblers. *Journal of Nervous and Mental Disease*, 181, 107-112.

Salkovskis, P. M. (1985). Obsessional-compulsive problems: A cognitive-behavioural analysis. *Behaviour Research and Therapy*, 23, 571-583.

Sallee, F. R., Kurlan, R., Goetz, C. G., Singer, H., Scahill, L., Law, G., et al. (2000). Ziprasidone treatment of children and adolescents with tourette's syndrome: A pilot study. *Journal of the American Academy of Child and Adolescent Psychiatry*, 39, 292-299.

Saxena, S., Brody, A. L., Schwartz, J. M., and Baxter, L. R. (1998). Neuroimaging and frontal-subcortical circuitry in obsessive-compulsive disorder. *British Journal of Psychiatry*. Supplement, 35, 26-37.

Scahill, L., Leckman, J. F., Schultz, R. T., Katsovich, L., and Peterson, B. S. (2003). A placebo-controlled trial of risperidone in tourette syndrome. *Neurology*, 60, 1130-1135.

Schreibman, L. (2000). Intensive Behavioral/Psychoeducational treatments for autism: Research needs and future directions. *Journal of Autism and Developmental Disorders*, 30, 373-378.

Schwartz, S. A., and Abramowitz, J. S. (2003). Are nonparaphilic sexual addictions a variant of obsessive-compulsive disorder? A pilot study. *Cognitive and Behavioral Practice*, 10, 372-377.

Simeon, D., Cohen, L. J., Stein, D. J., Schmeidler, J., Spadaccini, E., and Hollander, E. (1997). Comorbid self-injurious behaviors in 71 female hair-pullers: A survey study. *Journal of Nervous and Mental Disease*, 185, 117-119.

Smalley, S. L., McCracken, J., and Tanguay, P. (1995). Autism, affective disorders, and social phobia. *American Journal of Medical Genetics*, 60, 19-26.

Stanley, M., Swann, A., Bowers, T., and Davis, M. (1992). A comparison of clinical features in trichotillomania and obsessive-compulsive disorder. *Behaviour Research and Therapy*, 30, 39-44.

Stein, D. J., Coetzer, R., Lee, M., Davids, B., and Bouwer, C. (1997). Magnetic resonance brain imaging in women with obsessive-compulsive disorder and trichotillomania. *Psychiatry Research*, 74, 177-182.

Stein, D. J., Hollander, E., Anthony, D. T., Schneier, F. R., Fallon, B. A., Liebowitz, M. R., et al. (1992). Serotonergic medications for sexual obsessions, sexual addictions, and paraphilias. *Journal of Clinical Psychiatry*, 53, 267-271.

Stein, D. J., Hutt, C. S., Spitz, J. L., and Hollander, E. (1993). Compulsive picking and obsessive-compulsive disorder. *Psychosomatics*, 34, 177-181.

Stein, D. J., Simeon, D., Cohen, L. J., and Hollander, E. (1995). Trichotillomania and obsessive-compulsive disorder. *Journal of Clinical Psychiatry*, 56, 28-34.

Stein, D. J., van Heerden, B., Hugo, C., van Kradenburg, J., Warwick, J., Zungu-Dirwayi, N., et al. (2002). Functional brain imaging and pharmacotherapy in trichotillomania. single photon emission computed tomography before and after treatment with the selective serotonin reuptake inhibitor citalopram. Progress in Neuro-Psychopharmacology and Biological Psychiatry, 26, 885-890.

Steketee, G., Frost, R. O., and Cohen, I. (1998). Beliefs in obsessive-compulsive disorder. *Journal of Anxiety Disorders*, 12, 525-537.

Stemberger, R. M. T., Stein, D. J., and Mansueto, C. S. (2003). Behavioral and pharmacological treatment of trichotillomania. *Brief Treatment and Crisis Intervention*, 3, 339-352.

Stern, E., Silbersweig, D. A., Chee, K. Y., Holmes, A., Robertson, M. M., Trimble, M., et al. (2000). A functional neuroanatomy of tics in tourette syndrome. *Archives of General Psychiatry*, 57, 741.

Storch, E. A., Abramowitz, J., and Goodmen, W. K. (2008). Where does obsessive-compulsive disorder belong in the DSM-V? *Depression and Anxiety*, 25, 336-347.

Streichenwein, S. M., and Thornby, J. I. (1995). A long-term, double-blind, placebo-controlled crossover trial of the efficacy of fluoxetine for trichotillomania. *American Journal of Psychiatry*, 152, 1192-1196.

Styne, D. M., and Grumbach, M. M. (2007). Control of puberty in humans. New York: Humana Press.

Swedo, S. E., Rapoport, J. L., Leonard, H., Lenane, M., and Cheslow, D. (1989). Obsessive compulsive disorder in children and adolescents: Clinical phenomenology of 70 consecutive cases. *Archives of General Psychiatry*, 46, 335-341.

Swedo, S. E., Rapoport, J. L., Leonard, H. L., Schapiro, M. B., Rapoport, S. I., and Grady, C. L. (1991). Regional cerebral glucose metabolism of women with trichotillomania. *Archives of General Psychiatry*, 48, 828-833.

Symes, B. A., and Nicki, R. M. (1997). A preliminary consideration of cue-exposure, response-prevention treatment for pathological gambling behaviour: Two case studies. *Journal of Gambling Studies*, 13, 145-157.

Symons, F. J., Butler, M. G., Sanders, M. D., Feurer, I. D., and Thompson, T. (1999). Self-injurious behavior and prader-willi syndrome: Behavioral forms and body locations. *American Journal of Mental Retardation*, 104, 260-269.

Tukel, R., Keser, V., Karali, N. T., Olgun, T. O., and Calikusu, C. (2001). Comparison of clinical characteristics in trichotillomania and obsessive-compulsive disorder. *Journal of Anxiety Disorders*, 15, 433-441.

Twohig, M. P., and Woods, D. W. (2001). Habit reversal as a treatment for chronic skin picking in typically developing adult male siblings. *Journal of Applied Behavior Analysis*, 34, 217-220.

van den Heuvel, O. A., Veltman, D. J., Groenewegen, H. J., Witter, M. P., Merkelbach, J., Cath, D. C., et al. (2005). Disorder-specific neuroanatomical correlates of attentional bias in obsessive-compulsive disorder, panic disorder, and hypochondriasis. *Archives of General Psychiatry*, 62, 922-933.

van Megen, D. D., de geus, H.H., Westenberg, H.G. (2004). Axis I and II comorbidity in a large sample of patients with obsessive-compulsive disorder. *Journal of Affective Disorders*, 80, 155-162.

van Minnen, A., Hoogduin, K. A., Keijsers, G. P., Hellenbrand, I., and Hendriks, G. J. (2003). Treatment of trichotillomania with behavioral therapy or fluoxetine: A randomized, waiting-list controlled study. *Archives of General Psychiatry*, 60, 517-522.

Verdellen, C. W., Keijsers, G. P., Cath, D. C., and Hoogduin, C. A. (2004). Exposure with response prevention versus habit reversal in tourettes's syndrome: A controlled study. *Behaviour Research and Therapy*, 42, 501-511.

Visser, S., and Bouman, T. K. (2001). The treatment of hypochondriasis: Exposure plus response prevention vs cognitive therapy. Behaviour Research and Therapy, 39, 423-442.

Vulink, N. C., Denys, D., Bus, L., and Westenberg, H. G. (2006). Sexual pleasure in women with obsessive-compulsive disorder? *Journal of Affective Disorders*, 91, 19-25.

Walley, R., and Donaldson, M. (2005). An investigation of executive function abilities in adults with prader-willi syndrome. *Journal of Intellectual Disability Research*, 49, 613-625.

Wellington, T. M., Semrud-Clikeman, M., Gregory, A. L., Murphy, J. M., and Lancaster, J. L. (2006). Magnetic resonance imaging volumetric analysis of the putamen in children with ADHD: Combined type versus control. *Journal of Attention Disorders*, 10, 171-180.

Wetterneck, C. T, Woods, D. W., Norberg, M. N., and Begotka, A. M. (2006). The social and economic impact of trichotillomania: results from two nonreferred samples. *Behavioral Interventions*, 21, 97-109.

Wiedemann, G. (1998). Kleptomania: Characteristics of 12 cases. *European Psychiatry*, 13, 67-77.

Wickramasekera, I. (1976). Aversive behavior rehearsal for sexual exhibitionism. *Behavior Therapy*, 7, 167–176.

Wilhelm, S. (2003). Habit reversal versus supportive psychotherapy for tourette's disorder: A randomized controlled trial. *American Journal of Psychiatry*, 160, 1175-1177.

Wilhelm, S., Otto, M. W., Lohr, B., and Deckersbach, T. (1999). Cognitive behavior group therapy for body dysmorphic disorder: A case series. *Behaviour Research and Therapy*, 37, 71-75.

Woods, D. W., Wetterneck, C. T., and Flessner, C. A. (2006). A controlled evaluation of acceptance and commitment therapy plus habit reversal for trichotillomania. *Behaviour Research and Therapy*, 44, 639-656.

Zimmerman, M., and Mattia, J. I. (1998). Body dysmorphic disorder in psychiatric outpatients: Recognition, prevalence, comorbidity, demographic, and clinical correlates. *Comprehensive Psychiatry*, 39, 265-270.

In: Impulsivity: Causes, Control and Disorders
Editor: George H. Lassiter

ISBN 978-1-60741-951-8
© 2009 Nova Science Publishers, Inc.

Chapter III

Impulsiveness and Suicide Risk: A Literature Review

Maurizio Pompili, Antonio Del Casale,
Alberto Forte, Ilaria Falcone, Gaspare Palmieri, Marco Innamorati,
Michela Fotaras, Roberto Tatarelli and David Lester
Department of Psychiatry - Sant'Andrea Hospital,
Sapienza University of Rome, Italy

Abstract

Impulsivity is a complex behavioral construct. Action without planning or reflection is central to most definitions of impulsivity. Thus, impulsivity appears to be associated with a failure of behavioral filtering processes outside of consciousness, with compromised ability to reflect on impending acts or to use knowledge and intelligence to guide behavior. Impulsive behavior, including aggression and suicide attempts, differs from corresponding premeditated behavior by having an inappropriately short threshold for response, lack of reflection, lack of modulation, and lack of potential gain, leading potentially to dissociation between an action and its intent. Impulsivity is a prominent and measurable characteristic of bipolar disorder that can contribute to risk for suicidal behavior. The purpose of this study was to investigate the relationship between impulsivity and severity of past suicidal behavior, a potential predictor of eventual suicide, in patients with bipolar disorder. Although the screening of BD patients for the risk factors is not fool-proof, the consideration of those risk factors is an important component of the clinical assessment of suicidal risk. The clinical unpredictability can be especially challenging with BD patients, given the sometimes rapid shifts in mood (lability), strong reactivity to losses, frustrations or other stressors, impulsivity, disinhibiting effects of commonly abused central depressants including alcohol, comorbid anxiety disorders, and potential adverse effects of excessive use of antidepressants. Impulsivity/aggression has been reported to be related to suicidal behavior in several studies . For example, Mann and colleagues proposed a stress-diathesis model of suicidal behavior. Impulsivity, related to a genetic predisposition and dysfunction of the prefrontal cortex, is part of the diathesis predisposing individuals with suicidal ideation to act upon their impulse. Higher aggression may also contribute to the increased lethality of suicide attempts.

Among all psychiatric disorders, BD carries the highest suicide risk. There is no good explanation as to why BD patients kill themselves more than patients with MDD or schizophrenia. Possibly BD patients are are more prone to dysphoric-irritable mixed states associated with higher degree of discontent and impulsivity. Impulsivity is also a relevant clinical factor in suicidal behavior and is a common trait among persons with BD. However, impulsivity has been tentatively associated primarily with suicide attempts of limited lethality rather than with completed suicide. It is not clear whether relatively high rates of illness recurrence or the presence of rapid cycling (more than four recurrences within a year) increases risk of suicide in mood disorders. There may also be a genetic predisposition to suicide, but it has not been proven that this risk is independent of the risk for BD or depressive illness.

Introduction

Impulsiveness is the trait of acting suddenly on impulse without reflection. For Plato, impulsiveness was an essential function of the soul. It had three strings - the highest made it sound more serious, the lower more acute, the plant intermediate. Plato compares the first to the rational faculty of the soul, the second to the concupiscent faculty, the third to the impulsive faculty, which has the function of mediating between the two opposites (Plato, 360 B.C.). For Aristotle, impulsiveness misunderstands reason, although it seems to give reason something to listen to. However, because of the warmth and vivacity of its nature, impulsiveness feels, but does not listen to, reason's orders. Impulsiveness is related also to courage. It seems, in fact, that individuals acting impulsively are courageous. Courage can be defined as impulsiveness with a choice and awareness of purpose. Aristotle thought of impulsiveness as an important feature of youth. Youths are full of courage and impulsive and hopeful. Impulsivity makes them able to not fear. Nobody is afraid when angry. Moreover, the hope for success makes them bold (Aristotle, 1998). For Kant, impulsiveness was characteristic of the Hippocratic type "Choleric" type, set among other traits such as excitability and aggression (Kant, 1833).

For classical psychopathology, decisions are prompted by a confrontation between (1) a primary impulse (*Drang*), devoid of content and direction; (2) some instinctive drive (*Triebe*), unconsciously tending to an end; and (3) an act of will (*Willensakt*), which manifests itself as a conscious representation of the end, resulting in the discharge of motor or psychological consequences (Lipps, 1907; Lotze, 1852; Wentscher, 1910). In Freud's psychoanalytic theory, impulse is understood in terms of "drive" - as *a dynamic process consisting of a push that stretches the body to a target* (Freud, 1905). Jaspers thought that, for instinctive actions, impulses pass without impediment and without an act of will, but under hidden control of the personality (Jaspers, 1959).

More recently, Barratt and colleagues (1997) proposed a tripartite model of impulsive behavior, assuming the existence of *motor impulsiveness* (the tendency to act without thinking), *cognitive impulsiveness* (the tendency to make quick decisions), and *not-planned impulsiveness* (a mode of behavior characterized by poor assessment of the consequences). Moeller and colleagues (2001) have recently defined impulsivity as a "predisposition toward rapid, unplanned reactions to internal or external stimuli without regard to the negative consequences of these reactions to themselves or others". Schmidt (2003) viewed unplanned impulsivity as the result of an attention disorder and a deficit in *mentalizing* processes. Fonagy and colleagues (2002) stated that impulsivity of borderline patients may be due to a lack of awareness of their own emotional states associated with the absence of symbolic representation of emotions. Patients in such condition find themselves in states of emotional arousal that are beyond self-control, since mentalization is an essential component of affect regulation. Finally, in DSM IV–TR, impulsiveness is considered to be a personality trait, defined as *the incapacity/powerlessness to resist an impulse, thrust or temptation to perform a dangerous act for the subject or other people.*

Abnormal impulsiveness is associated with many psychiatric disorders, such as Axis I substance abuse and bipolar disorder, and cluster B personality disorders. The association between these disorders and impulsivity is at least partly due to the manner in which these disorders have been conceptualized, with a lack of behavioral inhibition being an element of all of these disorders (Moeller et al., 2001). For example, impulsivity is one of the DSM-IV-TR diagnostic criteria for borderline personality disorder, and it is highly predictive of borderline psychopathology (Links, Heslegrave, and van Reekum, 1999). In bipolar disorder, impulsivity is ubiquitous in all the stages of the illness (Corruble, Damy, and Guelfi, 1999; Swann, Anderson, Dougherty, and Moeller, 2001; Swann, Janicak et al., 2001). For Moeller and colleagues (2001), impulsivity could have any of several relationships to bipolar disorder depending on the way in which it is measured. For example, it is related to susceptibility, to episodes of illness or to prodromal episodes, to risk of complications like suicide or substance abuse, to response to treatments, and to pathophysiology of illness. Several studies have reported an association among substance abuse and impulsivity (Allen, Moeller, Rhoades, and Cherek, 1998; Kirby, Petry, and Bickel, 1999; Madden, Petry, Badger, and Bickel, 1997; Mitchell, 1999; Moss, Yao, and Panzak, 1990; Patton, Stanford, and Barratt, 1995; Vuchinich and Simpson, 1998). However, the question of whether the higher level of impulsivity is a factor leading to or resulting from substance abuse has not been answered (Moeller et al., 2001).

Impulsivity is also a risk factor for suicide. In suicidal behavior, two different situations in which impulsiveness is involved can be identified. In the first, impulsiveness is directly involved in the suicide act, influencing the way it happens. In the second, impulsiveness is a personal behavioral trait, influencing the individual's reaction to stressors and personal loss. These two factors can interact with each other to determine the lethality of the suicidal act (Hull-Blanks, Kerr, and Robinson Kurpius, 2004). Suicide attempts in impulsive patients are usually less dangerous and lethal than suicide attempts in non-impulsive patients. Impulsiveness is, therefore, linked to both higher suicide risk and lower lethality.

In recent years, it has been recognized that people who attempt or complete suicide have a unique predisposition, resulting in part from certain personality traits, including impulsivity–aggression (Baca-Garcia et al., 2001; Baca-Garcia et al., 2005; Dumais et al., 2005; Hull-Blanks et al., 2004; M. A. Oquendo, Currier, and Mann, 2006; Pompili et al., 2008; Zouk, Tousignant, Seguin, Lesage, and Turecki, 2006). Maser et al. (2002) conducted a 14-year study of 955 moderately to severely ill affective probands seeking treatment at one of five university-affiliated hospitals (mostly patients with major depression). Among these patients, 36 committed suicide, 120 attempted suicide, and 373 had no recorded suicide attempt. Comparing these three groups on clinical and intake personality variables, only those who complete suicide after 12 months were predicted by personality factors and impulsivity, and not those who completed suicide within 12 months of intake.

Research suggests that impulsive–aggressive traits are part of a developmental cascade that increases suicide risk among a subset of suicides, maybe predisposing them to higher psychopathology and comorbidity, defined as the presence of more than one psychiatric disorder. For example, in a study by Turecki (2005), comorbidity was found especially in subjects with disorders characterized by the presence of impulsive–aggressive traits, whereas subjects without these traits had levels of comorbidity that were not significantly different from those of controls. The patients with higher levels of comorbidity were characterized by a suicidal life trajectory beginning early in childhood. The results of this study also indicated that suicidal behavior had a different "natural history" in younger and older subjects, with impulsivity–aggression playing a more substantial role in young completed suicides. Suicide in older adults was more often the consequence of a planned act, often in a physically ill and depressed subject. Turecki hypothesized that early life stressors, such as a history of parental rejection, negligence, indifference and abuse, may trigger dysfunctional behavior, providing a platform for the abnormal expression of impulsivity combined with aggressive behavior.

The aim of this chapter is to review the literature concerning the association among impulsivity and suicide risk.

Materials and Methods

We performed careful MedLine, Excerpta Medica, PsycLit, and PsycInfo searches for the period 1980 to 2008. The following search terms were used: "Suicid*" (which comprises suicide, suicidal, suicidality, and other suicide-related terms), "Impulsiveness" or "Impulsivity". Only articles published in English peer-reviewed journals were included. A total of 353 articles were located, and the most relevant articles were selected. We excluded studies that mentioned suicide but were not clear about follow-up period, the method of statistical analysis, the diagnosis criteria and the number of patients studied. We also avoided studies that mention impulsiveness but were not clear about its role in the suicide risk or its link with suicidal behavior.

Impulsiveness and Suicide Risk Assessment

Several researchers argued that impulsivity is fundamental in the assessment of suicidal risk. For example, Bryan and Rudd (Bryan and Rudd, 2006) reviewed literature about the assessment of suicidality and identified a number of areas that have been demonstrated empirically to be essential to risk assessment: a predisposition to suicidal behavior; identifiable precipitants or stressors; the patient's symptomatic presentation; the presence of hopelessness; the nature of suicidal thinking; previous suicidal behavior; abnormal impulsivity and self-control; and protective factors. The authors suggested that clinicians should assess the patient's subjective sense of self-control and compare it with objective identifiers of self-control such as engagement in impulsive or self-destructive behaviors and methods for coping with stress. Moreover, impulsivity may be more significant as an indicator of future suicide attempts than a specific suicide plan since many suicide attempts are reactions to an environmental event. Because impulsivity is a stable trait, impulsive multiple attempters should be considered to be individuals with a chronic, stable suicide risk.

Some researchers have tried to determine if there are some specific clinical features in impulsive suicide attempters. Wyder and De Leo (2007) investigated the pattern of suicidal ideation before an impulsive attempt. The researchers contacted by telephone a randomized and stratified population of 5,130 residents in Brisbane, Australia, and those who reported previous suicidal behavior were sent a questionnaire by mail. Sixty-two percent of those who reported having attempted suicide described their attempt as impulsive. Surprisingly, 27% of self-defined "impulsive" attempters also reported making plans, and 22% of this group described the suicidal process as continuous. In addition, 29% of the self-defined "non-impulsive" attempters did not report making any plans, and 68% of this group reported their suicidal process as fluctuating. One quarter of the sample (26%) reported a pattern consistent with an impulsive attempt as previously defined, whereas most participants (41%) described a mixture of patterns. In this study, the impulsive attempters did not significantly differ from the non-impulsive attempters in regards to age, gender and motivations for the attempt in question. They were three times less likely to believe that their attempt would cause death than non-impulsive attempters (25% vs. 75%). Depressed attempters were five times more likely to belong to non-impulsive group (84% compared to 16% in the impulsive group). The researchers concluded that this study identified a relatively small proportion of impulsive attempters and that the questionnaire used to assess trait impulsiveness did not help to differentiate impulsive from non-impulsive attempters, leaving open the best method for searching for objective detectors of impulsiveness.

Not all the literature demonstrates a direct correlation between impulsivity and suicidal ideation. Dear (2000) explored the association between dysfunctional impulsivity and suicidal ideation in a sample of prisoners, half of whom had a history of attempted suicide. Dysfunctional impulsivity was positively correlated with depression and with measures of suicidal ideation. However, when depression was controlled for, using partial correlation coefficients, the positive correlation was not significantly different from zero, but when suicidal ideation was controlled for, the association between depression and dysfunctional impulsivity remained significant, although weak. Dear concluded that any association between dysfunctional impulsivity and suicidal ideation was probably mediated by depression. Lester (1993) found a significant negative correlation between suicidal ideation and functional impulsivity in college students but no significant association between suicidal ideation and dysfunctional impulsivity, while Lester (1990) found an association between impulsivity and a history of threatening suicide in college students, but not between impulsivity and current suicidal ideation.

Impulsiveness and Suicide Risk in Children and Adolescents

Renaud et al. (2008) evaluated psychiatric risk factors for child and adolescent suicide and explored the association between impulsiveness-aggression and other personality traits and completed suicide. Fifty-five consecutive young suicide victims, aged 11–18 years, were matched with 55 living youths for age (within 2 years), sex (43 males and 12 females) and geographic area. Psychiatric diagnoses in the suicides were made by means of the psychological autopsy method. The Brown–Goodwin History of Aggression inventory (BGHA) (Brown and Goodwin, 1986) was used to assess lifetime aggressive behaviors across childhood and adolescence, and the BIS was used to assess impulsive behaviors. The Buss–Durkee Hostility Inventory (BDHI) (Buss and Durkee, 1957) was used to assess the overall tendency of individuals to aggress, and Three-Dimensional Personality Questionnaire (Luby, Svrakic, McCallum, Przybeck, and Cloninger, 1999) was used to assess temperament dimensions, more specifically novelty seeking, harm avoidance, and reward dependence. Measures were completed using proxy-based interview with a key respondent best acquainted with the subject in question. The mean levels of impulsive behaviors, using the total score on the BIS, were significantly higher in completed suicides than in comparison subjects. Mean levels of lifetime aggressive behaviors and overall tendency to aggression (using the total scores on the BGHA and the BDHI, respectively) were also significantly higher in suicides than in comparison subjects. In univariate analyses, higher levels of impulsive and aggressive behaviors were associated with the risk of suicide in children and adolescents. However, a multivariate analyses failed to evidence for a significant association between suicide risk and impulsivity. Only the presence of depressive disorders, substance/alcohol abuse disorders and disruptive disorders resulted independent predictors of suicide risk. The authors hypothesized that these personality traits may underlie the main predictors or that depression in tandem with impulsive and aggressive behaviors could signal mixed states of mood disorders.

Joiner's (2005) interpersonal–psychological theory of attempted and completed suicide proposed an indirect pathway between impulsive behavior and suicide. Joiner argued that, to complete suicide, an individual must have both the desire and the capability to die by suicide. Impulsivity does not necessarily increase the risk of suicide, but it may lead an individual to acquire the capability for suicide after exposure to some stressor.

Witte *et al.* (2008) studied the association between impulsivity (measured via the Youth Risk Behaviour Survey items rather than through previously validated measures) and suicidality in three groups of adolescents: attempted suicides without prior planning, adolescents who only planned suicide without attempting it and adolescents who both planned and attempted suicide. As expected, adolescents who had planned suicide without attempting it were significantly less impulsive than those who had attempted without planning and those who had both planned and attempted suicide. However, adolescents who had made a suicide attempt without prior planning were less impulsive than those who had both planned and attempted. For the authors, the latter result is in conflict with the view that impulsivity is directly related to suicidal behavior. It may be that the relationship between impulsivity and suicide is indirect in that impulsive individuals are more likely to engage in suicidal behavior because impulsivity makes one more likely to be exposed to painful and provocative stimuli (T. E. Joiner, 2005)

Impulsivity and Suicide Risk in Affective Disorders

There is little research on impulsivity and specific affective disorders. Impulsivity is considered to be inherent in mania and is a prominent part of its diagnostic criteria (First, Spitzer, Gibbon, Williams, and Benjamin, 1996). However, the relationship between manic symptoms and specific aspects of impulsiveness has not yet been investigated.

In the case of depression, there is even less information. At first glance, depression may seem to be less strongly related to impulsivity than is mania. However, a combination of depression and impulsivity is important in suicidal behavior (Soloff, Lynch, Kelly, Malone, and Mann, 2000). Corruble *et al.* (1999) focused on clinical impulsivity, as rated by the Impulsivity Rating Scale and the BIS, at admission and after 4 weeks of treatment in depressed patients. In the total sample, impulsivity scores decreased significantly between baseline and after 4 weeks of treatment. The scale and the questionnaire scores correlated slightly with each other, suggesting some differences in impulsivity assessment between patients and clinicians. The two subgroups of patients, attempters and those who had never attempted suicide, differed neither in sociodemographic variables and antidepressant treatments, nor in terms of depression and general psychopathology assessments. However, attempters scored higher on the impulsivity measures than controls, both at the baseline and after four weeks of treatment. These results suggest that impulsivity may be both a trait and a state in depressed attempted suicides.

Several studies have confirmed the association of impulsivity-aggression and suicidality in depressed patients (Corruble et al., 1999; Malone, Szanto, Corbitt, and Mann, 1995; Stein, Apter, Ratzoni, Har-Even, and Avidan, 1998; Weissman, Fox, and Klerman, 1973). For example, Dumais *et al.* (2005) investigated 104 men over the age of 18 who committed suicide during a major depressive episode, matching for age with a group of 74 living men who had a current major depressive episode of sufficient severity as to merit treatment in a specialized psychiatric outpatient clinic, but without a history of medically serious suicide attempts. Psychiatric diagnoses were obtained by proxy-based interview using the Structured Clinical Interview for DSM-IV Axis I Disorders (SCID-I) (Spitzer, Williams, Gibbon, and First, 1992), in addition to the Structured Clinical Interview for DSM-IV Personality Disorders (SCID-II) (First et al., 1996). The SCID-I was used to investigate 71 suicide victims and all comparison subjects. Before the SCID-I, the Schedule for Affective Disorders and Schizophrenia for School-Age Children (Chambers et al., 1985), an interview, modified to include questions adapted from the Interview Schedule for Children (Kovacs, 1985), was used to assess personality disorders. The BGHA was used to assess lifetime aggressive behaviors across three separate stages of life (childhood, adolescence, and adulthood). The BIS was used for the investigation of impulsive behaviors. Finally, the Temperament and Character Inventory (Cloninger, Przybeck, Svrakic, and Wetzel, 1994) was used to collect data by assessing four basic temperament and three character dimensions. The proxy-based measures indicated a higher prevalence of extreme impulsivity and total lifetime aggressivity in subjects who committed suicide, and this association was stronger for the younger men (18 to 40 years old). However, this association may have been mediated by the presence of cluster B personality disorders and alcohol abuse.

Oquendo *et al.* (2005) analyzed impulsivity in Posttraumatic Stress Disorder (PTSD) comorbid with major depression. Subjects with a lifetime history of PTSD and controls without a history of PTSD did not differ significantly in age or income. Subjects with lifetime PTSD were significantly more likely to be female, nonwhite, and unmarried and to have fewer years of education than subjects without PTSD. Furthermore, subjects with lifetime PTSD had significantly higher rates of comorbid cluster B personality disorders than subjects without PTSD, but not of substance abuse or head injury. The group with lifetime PTSD had higher impulsivity (on the BIS) and hostility scores (on the BDHI), but not higher lifetime aggression scores (on the BGHA) than subjects without lifetime PTSD. Patients with lifetime PTSD were significantly more likely to have made a suicide attempt than patients without lifetime PTSD. However, contrary to the authors' hypothesis, the groups did not differ in suicidal ideation after adjustment for depression severity, or in suicidal intent at the time of the most lethal attempt. In this study, lifetime aggression was not higher in patients with a lifetime history of PTSD than in patients without such history, suggesting that major depression and PTSD do not have an additive effect on aggression. It is noteworthy that levels of impulsivity and hostility were higher in the group with lifetime PTSD, while the level of aggression was not.

Some researchers have suggested that patients with bipolar disorder have higher levels of impulsivity than patients with major depressive disorder. Zalsman *et al.* (2006) studied 307 attempted suicides with affective disorders diagnosed with the SCID-I and SCID-II. Lifetime aggression and impulsivity were rated using the BGHA and the BIS. Significantly higher levels of lifetime aggression and impulsivity were found in the bipolar group. Of note, within the bipolar group, but not in those with major depressive disorders, men reported suicidal acts with higher lethality. The conclusion is that there are clinical differences in impulsivity between suicide attempters with affective disorders.

Swann *et al.* (2008) hypothesized that depression and mania are differentially related to impulsivity, and the strongest differences involve symptoms related to *activation* rather than mood. They recruited a sample of 83 subjects with diagnoses of bipolar I disorder according to DSM-IV, 17 of whom met DSM-IV criteria for depression, 16 for mania, and 17 for a mixed state. Impulsivity was assessed using the BIS, and symptoms were rated using the Change Version of the Schedule for Affective Disorders and Schizophrenia (SADS-C) (Spitzer and Endicott, 1978). For all subjects, attentional impulsivity correlated significantly but weakly with depression factor scores and with mania factor scores. Motor impulsivity correlated weakly but significantly with mania factor scores, and non-planning impulsivity correlated weakly but significantly with depression factor scores. Suicidality scores (measured with the SADS-C) correlated with attentional impulsivity. Swann et al. concluded that attentional-cognitive impulsivity correlates with both depression and mania, motor impulsivity with mania, and non-planning impulsivity with depression. They also argued that impulsivity is correlated most strongly with hyperactivity in mania and with hopelessness or anhedonia in depression.

Michaelis *et al.* (2004) assessed trait impulsivity and hostility among 52 bipolar subjects with and without lifetime suicide attempts. Trait levels of impulsivity were assessed using the BIS, and hostility was assessed using the BDHI. Compared to the nonattempters, the attempters had significantly higher levels of overall hostility and subcomponents of hostility, and a trend toward higher overall impulsivity. There was a significant moderate association between hostility and impulsivity for the attempted suicides, but not for nonattempters.

There are, however, discordant research results. For example, Oquendo *et al.* (2000) did not find any significant differences between attempters and nonattempters in lifetime impulsivity. However, these studies suggest that is important for clinicians to maintain a close vigilance for suicidal behaviors in subjects with bipolar disorders, with a need for both pharmacological and psychotherapeutic interventions to diminish the levels of impulsivity.

High levels of impulsivity may be linked with bipolar disorder comorbid with substance abuse (Antelman and Caggiula, 1996; Quintin et al., 2001). Swann *et al.* (2004) recruited subjects with bipolar disorder (45 subjects), and non-bipolar subjects (36 subjects) with and without substance abuse. Diagnoses were made using the SCID-I, and the severity of symptoms was rated using the SADS-C. Impulsivity was assessed using the BIS, and laboratory performance impulsivity was measured using the continuous performance test (Dougherty, Bjork, Marsh, and Moeller, 2000). The results indicated that comorbidity of bipolar disorder and a substance abuse history was correlated with increased BIS impulsivity, even after controlling for age and sex. The BIS score appeared to be a stable measure of impulsivity in bipolar disorder patients, regardless of whether or not mania was present (Swann, Anderson et al., 2001). Performance impulsivity was amplified in manic compared with interepisode subjects, despite their substance abuse history, and was increased in interepisode subjects with substance abuse as well as manic subjects without substance abuse.

Pompili *et al.* (2008) examined clinical, personality and sociodemographic predictors of suicide risk in a sample of inpatients with major affective disorders. Participants were 74 inpatients (37 men, 37 women) consecutively admitted to three psychiatric acute wards located in Rome. The patients showed either psychotic-like symptoms, suicidal behavior, or aggressive behavior. Inclusive criteria were diagnosis of a DSM-IV-TR major affective disorder (unipolar major depressive disorder or bipolar disorder type I, currently experiencing a depressive episode). Patients completed the Mini International Neuropsychiatric Interview (MINI) Italian Version 5.0.0 (Sheehan et al., 1998), the Beck Hopelessness Scale (BHS) (Beck, Weissman, Lester, and Trexler, 1974), the Aggression Questionnaire (Buss and Perry, 1992), the BIS, the Hamilton Rating Scale for Depression (Hamilton, 1960, 1967) and the Hamilton scale for Anxiety (Hamilton, 1959). Patients reported high average scores on hopelessness, and over 52% had scores higher than 9, indicating high suicide intent. When considering the differences between the group with high risk of suicide and the group with low risk as measured by the BHS, several differences were identified. The patients with high risk reported more severe depressive and anxious symptomatology and more impulsivity and hostility. To identify the best predictors of the BHS total score, sociodemographic and clinical variables were entered as predictors in a multiple regression model. In the first step, the best predictor was the BIS, and the model explained 31% of the variability of the BHS scores. The second step added the use of antidepressants as a predictor, with the model explaining another 13% of the variability of the BHS scores. The third step added anxiety/somatization as predictor (with an additional 6% of the variability explained). The last step added the use of mood stabilizers as negative predictor, that is, as a protective factor. The four predictors explained 50% of the variance in BHS scores. Thus, high impulsivity was able to predict suicide even when controlling for diagnosis, anxiety and depression severity, and sociodemographic variables, variables identified as important risk factors for suicide by the US Surgeon General in "*Call to action to prevent suicide*" (US Public Health Service, 1999).

The conclusion is that impulsiveness and aggression may be risk factors for suicidal behavior in affective disorder patientss and may play a role as a diathesis, predisposing individuals with acute disorders (*stressors*) to act upon their suicidal ideation.

Serotonin, Impulsiveness and Suicide Risk

Suicidal behavior appears to be associated with a deficient serotonergic system, and it has also been postulated that serotonin (5-hydroxytryptamine or 5-HT) is involved in impulsive behavior (Soubrié, 1986). Impulsive aggression, or a history of aggressive behavior, may be even more closely related to low serotonergic function than impulsivity alone (Coccaro, 1992; V. M. Linnoila and Virkkunen, 1992).

Acute tryptophan depletion (ATD), which involves depleting the 5-HT precursor L-Tryptophan (Trp), is a powerful technique to inspect lowered serotonin function (Booij, Van der Does, and Riedel, 2003). The rationale is to lower 5-HT levels and then observe any symptoms forced by the procedure, thereby allowing the researcher to establish causal relationships between serotonin levels and behavior (Young, Smith, Pihl, and Ervin, 1985). It has frequently been confirmed that ATD leads to a transient symptom exacerbation in a subsample of remitted depressed patients (Booij et al., 2003; Delgado et al., 1990). Some authors have also demonstrated that ADT has a larger depressive response on impulsivity in remitted depressed patient than in patients who have no history of suicide ideation (Booij et al., 2006; Booij et al., 2002).

The serotonin transporter (5-HTT) gene, which is mapped to chromosome 17q11.1-q12, is one of the major genes known to influence serotonergic transmission. Heinz *et al.* (2000) reported that S (s/s or s/l alleles) individuals have lower levels of serotonergic activity than L (l/l) individuals. Therefore, S individuals, with lower levels of serotonergic activity, should show higher levels of impulsivity and aggressive behavior than L individuals. This study suggested that serotonin transporter genotype in the promoter area is not associated with high levels of impulsivity on the BIS or with aggressive behavior on a modified version of the BGHA.

Giegling *et al.* (2007) studied a group of Tachykinin Receptor 1 markers (TACR): RS 3771810; RS 3771825; RS 726506; RS 1477157, spanning the gene in 167 patients who had attempted suicide, 92 completed suicide, and in 312 healthy subjects, in order to examine the action of substance P – a neurotransmitter involved in the modulation of depression, anxiety and suicidal-related behaviors. Substance P is found in brain areas which are implicated in these behaviors, such as the locus coeruleus, ventral striatum, cerebral cortex, hippocampus and several amygdaloidal nuclei (Caberlotto et al., 2003). Giegling found that the haplotype block, including RS3771825, RS726506 and RS1477157, is not associated with suicidal behavior. However, a weak association between the T-G-G haplotype and impulsive suicidal behavior was observed.

In a study by Lindstrom *et al.* (2004), patients were recruited from the medical emergency room after having been admitted for a suicide attempt. The patients were rated according to the Suicidal Intent Scale (Beck, Schuyler, and Herman, 1974). Five of the patients (all men) made violent suicide attempts. Two patients had previously made a suicide attempt. No patient had so far completed suicide. Six patients had a mood disorder, one a social phobia, and three had an adjustment disorder, while two patients did not have an axis I DSM IV-disorder. One patient with a major depressive disorder had comorbid alcoholism. Half of the patients received a diagnosis of DSM-IV personality disorder. Patients and controls completed the Marke Nyman Temperament scale (Engstrom, Nyman, and Traskman-Bendz, 1996). The results indicated that radiopharmaceutical 123-iodine (123-I-beta-CIT) is a potent ligand for both dopamine and serotonin reuptake sites, and it can be used for single photon emission computed tomography camera measurements of the three-dimensional regional brain distribution. With single photon emission computed tomography camera, the 5-HTT (5-Hydroxytryptamine Transporter) uptake was studied, analyzing the distribution of brain radioactivity. In the suicide attempters, there was a significant positive correlation between whole brain 5-HTT and reflecting impulsivity.

Roggenbacha *et al.* (2002) studied the role of 5-hydroxyindolacetic acid (5-HIAA) in the cerebrospinal fluid and examined whether this factor could be used as a peripheral indicator of deficient serotonergic neurotransmission that is known to be associated with suicidal behavior, depression, impulsivity and aggression. Patients were studied after a suicide attempts or a history of suicidal behavior. The results indicated that a suicidal act is not necessarily associated with peripheral indicators of serotonergic neurotransmission.

Other research indicates reduced levels of 5-HIAA (the breakdown product of 5-HT) in the cerebrospinal-fluid of suicidal patients (Asberg, 1997; Brunner and Bronisch, 1999; Mann, 1999; Mann, Oquendo, Underwood, and Arango, 1999) and in impulsive and/or violent individuals (Golden et al., 1991; Roy and Linnoila, 1988), but not in depressed individuals (Maes and Meltzer, 1995). Linnola *et al.* (1983) reported a lower level of 5-HIAA in 27 violent offenders who were impulsive as compared to nine violent offenders who showed premeditation for the act. Virkunnen *et al.* (1987) found a lower concentration of 5-HIAA in violent offenders than in non-violent arsonists and healthy controls. However, there were many confounding factors in these studies, such as alcoholism and depression (Coccaro, Kavoussi, Cooper, and Hauger, 1997; Coccaro, Kavoussi, Hauger, Cooper, and Ferris, 1998; Cremniter et al., 1999; Lidberg, Belfrage, Bertilsson, Evenden, and Asberg, 2000; M. Linnoila et al., 1983; Virkkunen et al., 1987).

Sequeira *et al.* (2003) investigated the three most common mutations/polymorphisms observed in Wolfram syndrome (WFS) that may result in an increased vulnerability to some psychiatric disorders, in particular, mood disorders and suicidal behaviors, mainly impulsive ones. WFS1 was one of genes that causes Wolfram syndrome (Inoue et al., 1998; Strom et al., 1998). WFS is a rare autosomal recessive neurodegenerative disorder characterized by the early onset of non-immune insulin-dependent diabetes mellitus, diabetes insipidus, progressive optic atrophy, and deafness.

Sequeira *et al.* (2003) analyzed the three most common mutations/polymorphisms in WFS (H611R, R456H, I333) in a sample of 111 people who attempted suicide and 129 normal controls. The results supported the hypothesis that H611R is involved in the predisposition to impulsive behavior and attempting suicide. Authors also found that those patients had higher scores of BIS measures.

Several studies have documented the efficacy of lithium in reducing suicide risk (Bocchetta et al., 1998; Gonzalez-Pinto et al., 2006; Guzzetta, Tondo, Centorrino, and Baldessarini, 2007; Muller-Oerlinghausen, 2001; Muller-Oerlinghausen, Muser-Causemann, and Volk, 1992; Nilsson, 1995; Thies-Flechtner, Muller-Oerlinghausen, Seibert, Walther, and Greil, 1996; Tondo, Jamison, and Baldessarini, 1997), but fewer studies have looked at changes in impulsivity as a main outcome of lithium treatment. In a review of the research, Kovacsics *et al.* (2008) concluded that lithium appears to reduce impulsivity, although only a few double-blind placebo-controlled studies have been conducted to assess lithium's effect on impulsivity (Dorrego, Canevaro, Kuzis, Sabe, and Starkstein, 2002; Hollander, Pallanti, Allen, Sood, and Baldini Rossi, 2005; Swann, Bowden, Calabrese, Dilsaver, and Morris, 2002). Additional well-controlled studies examining the effects of lithium on impulsivity are needed validate this effect.

Impulsiveness and Suicide Risk in Personality Disorders

In a study of 164 completed suicides, Zouk *et al.* (2006) found that impulsive suicides (as defined by scores on the BIS) met a greater number of the criteria for cluster B disorders (OR=19.12; 95% CI: 5.08–72.01) and were more likely to meet full criteria for cluster B diagnoses, particularly borderline (OR 13.60; 95% CI: 2.89–63.95) and antisocial personality disorders (OR 20.50; 95% CI: 2.55–164.90). Surprisingly, mean cluster C, but not cluster A traits, were increased among impulsive suicides. Moreover, impulsive suicides were four to five times more likely to have two or more comorbid Axis I and Axis II diagnoses. Impulsive suicides were more likely to have experienced severe indifference, rejection, and neglect from either parent during their childhood, and were more likely to have experienced and to have been affected by a short duration trigger event occurring within one week of their suicide than were the non-impulsive suicides. Impulsive suicides were characterized by higher measures of aggressive behavior, a higher prevalence of lifetime substance abuse/dependence, as well as high levels of comorbidity of Axis I and II diagnoses. These findings suggest that most of the factors commonly recognized as increasing the risk for suicide are frequently present in suicides with high levels of impulsivity.

Brodsky *et al.* (1997) hypothesized that specific features of borderline personality disorder (impulsivity and childhood trauma - a possible etiological factor in the development of impulsivity) would be associated with suicidal behavior. Information on lifetime history of suicidal behavior was obtained from 214 inpatients diagnosed with borderline personality disorder using a structured clinical interview. In an analysis of covariance that controlled for lifetime major depression and substance abuse diagnoses, patients with borderline personality disorder who met the criterion for impulsivity had more past suicide attempts than those who did not meet the impulsivity criterion. Other features of borderline personality disorder did not correlate with suicidal behavior.

Soloff *et al.* (2000) compared 81 inpatients with borderline personality disorder, (including 49 patients with borderline personality disorder plus a major depressive episode) with 77 inpatients with only a major depressive episode on measures of depressed mood, hopelessness, impulsive aggression, and suicidal behavior. Patients with borderline personality disorder (with and without major depression) had higher scores on all measures of impulsive aggression as compared to the depressed patients. The lifetime number of suicide attempts was independently predicted by both impulsivity (assessed by using the BGHA) and hopelessness (representing depressed mood) in all three groups. This finding suggests that clinicians should be aware of synergies between specific clinical characteristics, such as hopelessness and impulsivity, and suicidal behavior.

Impulsiveness and Suicide Risk in Alcohol-Dependent Patients

Wojnar *et al.* (2008) explored correlates of impulsive and non-impulsive suicide attempts among a treated population of 154 alcohol-dependent patients consecutively admitted for addiction treatment. Three measures of impulsivity were used: the BIS, eight questions related to impulsiveness from the Impulsiveness Facet of the NEO Personality Inventory—Revised (NEOPI-R), and a computerized measure of inhibitory control as an objective neurophysiologic measure of behavioral impulsivity. The Michigan Alcoholism Screening Test (Selzer, 1971) was used as an index of lifetime severity of alcohol dependence. Bivariate comparisons of those with and without a prior attempt indicated that suicide attempters scored higher than other patients on impulsivity as measured by both the NEOPI-R and the BIS, but there was no significant difference between the two groups with respect to behavioral impulsivity as measured by response inhibition times in the stop-signal task. Comparing those who made an impulsive suicide attempt to those who reported a non-impulsive attempt, the impulsive attempters less frequently reported a family history of attempted or completed suicide and were less likely than non-impulsive attempters to be employed at the time of assessment. Moreover, individuals who had made an impulsive suicide attempt in the past had longer stop reaction times in the behavioral laboratory measure of impulsiveness than those who had engaged in non-impulsive attempts, and impulsive attempters were more likely to have used alcohol before or during an attempt than non-impulsive attempters. Individuals making non-impulsive attempt were more likely to have a history of sexual abuse in their childhood (OR=7.17) and a family history of suicide (OR=4.09), and were more impulsive on the NEO-PI-R (OR=2.27) than patients without a suicide attempt. The only significant factor that distinguished patients with impulsive suicide attempts from patients without a suicide attempt and from patients with a non-impulsive suicide attempt was a higher level of behavioral impulsivity (OR=1.84–2.42).

Wojnar *et al.* (2008) examined the influence of suicidality on relapse in 154 alcohol-dependent patients consecutively admitted to four addiction treatment facilities in Warsaw, Poland. Of the eligible patients, 76.6% completed a standardized follow-up assessment at 12 months. The measure of impulsivity was the BIS, and the BHS was used to measure the extent of negative attitudes about the future as perceived by patients. The Alcohol Time-Line Follow-Back Interview was used to evaluate the frequency of alcohol use during the one-year follow-up period. The authors found that, among the attempters, in 62.1% of cases the last suicide attempt was impulsive. Interestingly, the report of a prior impulsive attempt was correlated with an increased odds of relapse of 3.02 (95% CI = 1.25–7.26). Moreover, patients with a history of impulsive suicide attempts relapsed earlier than patients without a prior impulsive attempt. In a logistic regression analysis, even after controlling for many variables (baseline demographics, severity of psychopathology, severity of depression, impulsivity, hopelessness, and severity of pre-treatment alcohol use), making an impulsive suicide attempt was significantly related to a higher likelihood of post-treatment relapse (OR = 2.81; 95% CI = 1.13–6.95). The researchers hypothesized that impulsive suicide attempts could reflect a level of serotonergic hypo-functioning that could be relevant for understanding relapse in alcohol-dependent individuals.

Koller *et al.* (2002) recruited inpatient alcohol-dependent subjects from an addiction treatment ward. All of the patients included into the study were older than 18 years and met ICD-10 and DSM-IV criteria for alcohol dependence. The alcohol-dependence and depression criteria and the patient's history of suicide attempts were assessed using the Semi-structured Interview for Assessment of Genetics in Alcoholism (Bucholz et al., 1994; Hesselbrock, Easton, Bucholz, Schuckit, and Hesselbrock, 1999) and a comprehensive psychiatric examination by one of the authors.

All patients were assessed two weeks after admission and after alcohol withdrawal, free of any psychopharmacological treatment. To assess the history of impulsive and aggressive behavior, the following measures were employed: the BDHI , including the assault and irritability sub-scores, and an adapted version of the BGHA. Seventy-six (41.7 %) patients reported at least one suicide attempt, and 63 (36.6 %) reported a history of at least one episode of major depression. Age and age of onset of alcoholism did not significantly differ across the groups. However, suicidal alcohol-dependent subjects had a significantly higher alcohol intake per day compared to the non-suicidal group. Alcohol-dependent subjects with a history of violent suicide attempts had significantly higher scores on the BDHI assault scale, compared to alcoholics without suicide attempts. BGHA scale scores tended to be higher in alcohol-dependent subjects with a history of violent suicide attempts as compared those without suicide attempts. Patients with a concurrent borderline personality disorder showed significantly higher values in the BDHI assault scores, the BDHI irritability scores and the BGHA aggression scores.

Conclusions

Impulsivity plays an important role in suicidal behavior. Research has demonstrated that impulsive individuals are more likely to engage in painful and provocative experiences that may make them less fearful about death.

According to Joiner's interpersonal-psychological theory of suicide (T. E. Joiner, Jr. et al., 2005; Van Orden, Witte, Gordon, Bender, and Joiner, 2008), three proximal are necessary and sufficient causes for a person to commit suicide: (1) feelings of perceived burdensomeness; (2) a sense of thwarted belongingness; (3) an acquired capability to self-harm lethally. State impulsivity leads people to engage in risky behaviors that over time instil in them the capability to enact serious self-harm (should they develop the desire to do so). If individuals with trait impulsivity experience burdensomeness and thwarted belongingness, they will be at a high risk for death by suicide.

It is common these days for mental health practitioners to assess suicidal risk in patients, prisoners and other high-risk groups using validated suicide assessment instruments (such as standardized inventories to assess suicidal thinking and planning). The research reviewed in this chapter indicates that a thorough and adequate assessment program for suicide should also include measures of impulsivity and aggressiveness. Both trait and state measures of impulsivity may be useful since current behavior depends not only upon the current mood state but also upon the individual's stable long-term traits.

References

Allen, T. J., Moeller, F. G., Rhoades, H. M., and Cherek, D. R. (1998). Impulsivity and history of drug dependence. *Drug and Alcohol Dependence, 50*(2), 137-145.

Antelman, S. M., and Caggiula, A. R. (1996). Oscillation follows drug sensitization: implications. *Critical Reviews in Neurobiology, 10*(1), 101-117.

Aristotle. (1998). *The Nicomachean ethics. Book VII.* Oxford: Oxford University Press.

Asberg, M. (1997). Neurotransmitters and suicidal behavior. The evidence from cerebrospinal fluid studies. *Annals of the New York Academy of Sciences, 836*, 158-181.

Baca-Garcia, E., Diaz-Sastre, C., Basurte, E., Prieto, R., Ceverino, A., Saiz-Ruiz, J., et al. (2001). A prospective study of the paradoxical relationship between impulsivity and lethality of suicide attempts. *Journal of Clinical Psychiatry, 62*(7), 560-564.

Baca-Garcia, E., Diaz-Sastre, C., Garcia Resa, E., Blasco, H., Braquehais Conesa, D., Oquendo, M. A., et al. (2005). Suicide attempts and impulsivity. *European Archives of Psychiatry and Clinical Neuroscience, 255*(2), 152-156.

Barratt, E. S., Stanford, M. S., Kent, T. A., and Felthous, A. (1997). Neuropsychological and cognitive psychophysiological substrates of impulsive aggression. *Biological Psychiatry, 41*(10), 1045-1061.

Beck, A. T., Schuyler, D., and Herman, I. (1974). Development of suicidal intent scales. In A. T. Beck, H. L. P. Resnik and D. Lettieri (Eds.), *The prediction of suicide* (pp. 45–56). Bowie: Charles Press.

Beck, A. T., Weissman, A., Lester, D., and Trexler, L. (1974). The measurement of pessimism: the hopelessness scale. *Journal of Consulting and Clinical Psychology, 42*(6), 861-865.

Bocchetta, A., Ardau, R., Burrai, C., Chillotti, C., Quesada, G., and Del Zompo, M. (1998). Suicidal behavior on and off lithium prophylaxis in a group of patients with prior suicide attempts. *Journal of Clinical Psychopharmacology, 18*(5), 384-389.

Booij, L., Swenne, C. A., Brosschot, J. F., Haffmans, P. M., Thayer, J. F., and Van der Does, A. J. (2006). Tryptophan depletion affects heart rate variability and impulsivity in remitted depressed patients with a history of suicidal ideation. *Biological Psychiatry, 60*(5), 507-514.

Booij, L., Van der Does, A. J., and Riedel, W. J. (2003). Monoamine depletion in psychiatric and healthy populations: review. *Molecular Psychiatry, 8*(12), 951-973.

Booij, L., Van der Does, W., Benkelfat, C., Bremner, J. D., Cowen, P. J., Fava, M., et al. (2002). Predictors of mood response to acute tryptophan depletion. A reanalysis. *Neuropsychopharmacology, 27*(5), 852-861.

Brodsky, B. S., Malone, K. M., Ellis, S. P., Dulit, R. A., and Mann, J. J. (1997). Characteristics of borderline personality disorder associated with suicidal behavior. *American Journal of Psychiatry, 154*(12), 1715-1719.

Brown, G. L., and Goodwin, F. K. (1986). Cerebrospinal fluid correlates of suicide attempts and aggression. *Annals of the New York Academy of Sciences, 487*, 175-188.

Brunner, J., and Bronisch, T. (1999). Neurobiologische Korrelate suizidalen Verhaltens / Neurobiological correlates of suicidal behavior. *Fortschritte der Neurologie, Psychiatrie, 67*(9), 391-412.

Bryan, C. J., and Rudd, M. D. (2006). Advances in the assessment of suicide risk. *Journal of Cinical Psychology, 62*(2), 185-200.

Bucholz, K. K., Cadoret, R., Cloninger, C. R., Dinwiddie, S. H., Hesselbrock, V. M., Nurnberger, J. I., Jr., et al. (1994). A new, semi-structured psychiatric interview for use in genetic linkage studies: a report on the reliability of the SSAGA. *Journal of Studies on Alcohol, 55*(2), 149-158.

Buss, A. H., and Durkee, A. (1957). An inventory for assessing different kinds of hostility. *Journal of Consulting Psychology, 21*(4), 343-349.

Buss, A. H., and Perry, M. (1992). The aggression questionnaire. *Journal of Personality and Social Psychology, 63*(3), 452-459.

Caberlotto, L., Hurd, Y. L., Murdock, P., Wahlin, J. P., Melotto, S., Corsi, M., et al. (2003). Neurokinin 1 receptor and relative abundance of the short and long isoforms in the human brain. *The European Journal of Neuroscience, 17*(9), 1736-1746.

Chambers, W. J., Puig-Antich, J., Hirsch, M., Paez, P., Ambrosini, P. J., Tabrizi, M. A., et al. (1985). The assessment of affective disorders in children and adolescents by semistructured interview. Test-retest reliability of the schedule for affective disorders and schizophrenia for school-age children, present episode version. *Archives of General Psychiatry, 42*(7), 696-702.

Cloninger, C. R., Przybeck, T. R., Svrakic, D. M., and Wetzel, R. D. (1994). *The Temperament and Character Inventory (TCI): a guide to its development and use*. St Louis: Washington University.

Coccaro, E. F. (1992). Impulsive aggression and central serotonergic system function in humans: an example of a dimensional brain-behavior relationship. *International Clinical Psychopharmacology, 7*(1), 3-12.

Coccaro, E. F., Kavoussi, R. J., Cooper, T. B., and Hauger, R. L. (1997). Central serotonin activity and aggression: inverse relationship with prolactin response to d-fenfluramine, but not CSF 5-HIAA concentration, in human subjects. *The American Jjournal of Psychiatry, 154*(10), 1430-1435.

Coccaro, E. F., Kavoussi, R. J., Hauger, R. L., Cooper, T. B., and Ferris, C. F. (1998). Cerebrospinal fluid vasopressin levels: correlates with aggression and serotonin function in personality-disordered subjects. *Archives of General Psychiatry, 55*(8), 708-714.

Corruble, E., Damy, C., and Guelfi, J. D. (1999). Impulsivity: a relevant dimension in depression regarding suicide attempts? *Journal of Affective Disorders, 53*(3), 211-215.

Cremniter, D., Jamain, S., Kollenbach, K., Alvarez, J. C., Lecrubier, Y., Gilton, A., et al. (1999). CSF 5-HIAA levels are lower in impulsive as compared to nonimpulsive violent suicide attempters and control subjects. *Biological Psychiatry, 45*(12), 1572-1579.

Dear, G. E. (2000). Functional and dysfunctional impulsivity, depression, and suicidal ideation in a prison population. *The Journal of Psychology, 134*(1), 77-80.

Delgado, P. L., Charney, D. S., Price, L. H., Aghajanian, G. K., Landis, H., and Heninger, G. R. (1990). Serotonin function and the mechanism of antidepressant action. Reversal of antidepressant-induced remission by rapid depletion of plasma tryptophan. *Archives of General Psychiatry, 47*(5), 411-418.

Dorrego, M. F., Canevaro, L., Kuzis, G., Sabe, L., and Starkstein, S. E. (2002). A randomized, double-blind, crossover study of methylphenidate and lithium in adults with attention-deficit/hyperactivity disorder: preliminary findings. *The Journal of Neuropsychiatry and Clinical Neurosciences, 14*(3), 289-295.

Dougherty, D. M., Bjork, J. M., Marsh, D. M., and Moeller, F. G. (2000). A comparison between adults with conduct disorder and normal controls on a continuous performance test: differences in impulsive response characteristics. *Psychological Record, 50*, 203-219.

Dumais, A., Lesage, A. D., Alda, M., Rouleau, G., Dumont, M., Chawky, N., et al. (2005). Risk factors for suicide completion in major depression: a case-control study of impulsive and aggressive behaviors in men. *American Journal of Psychiatry, 162*(11), 2116-2124.

Engstrom, G., Nyman, G. E., and Traskman-Bendz, L. (1996). The Marke-Nyman Temperament (MNT) Scale in suicide attempters. *Acta Psychiatrica Scandinavica, 94*(5), 320-325.

First, M. B., Spitzer, R. L., Gibbon, M., Williams, J. B. W., and Benjamin, L. (1996). *Structured clinical interview for DSM-IV Axis II personality disorders (SCID-II), version 2.0.* New York: Biometric Research Department, Psychiatric Hospital.

Fonagy, P., Gergely, G., Jurist, E. L., and Target, M. (2002). *Affect Regulation, Mentalization, and the Development of the Self.* New York: Other Press.

Freud, S. (1905). *Tre saggi sulla teoria sessuale* (1989 ed.). Torino: Boringhieri.

Giegling, I., Rujescu, D., Mandelli, L., Schneider, B., Hartmann, A. M., Schnabel, A., et al. (2007). Tachykinin receptor 1 variants associated with aggression in suicidal behavior. *American Journal of Medical Genetics. Part B, Neuropsychiatric Genetics: the Official Publication of the International Society of Psychiatric Genetics, 144B*(6), 757-761.

Golden, R. N., Gilmore, J. H., Corrigan, M. H., Ekstrom, R. D., Knight, B. T., and Garbutt, J. C. (1991). Serotonin, suicide, and aggression: clinical studies. *The Journal of Clinical Psychiatry, 52 Suppl*, 61-69.

Gonzalez-Pinto, A., Mosquera, F., Alonso, M., Lopez, P., Ramirez, F., Vieta, E., et al. (2006). Suicidal risk in bipolar I disorder patients and adherence to long-term lithium treatment. *Bipolar Disorders, 8*(5 Pt 2), 618-624.

Guzzetta, F., Tondo, L., Centorrino, F., and Baldessarini, R. J. (2007). Lithium treatment reduces suicide risk in recurrent major depressive disorder. *Journal of Clinical Psychiatry, 68*(3), 380-383.

Hamilton, M. (1959). The assessment of anxiety states by rating. *British Journal of Medical Psychology, 32*, 50-55.

Hamilton, M. (1960). A Rating Scale for depression. *Journal of Neurology, Neurosurgery, and Psychiatry, 23*, 56-62.

Hamilton, M. (1967). Development of a rating scale for primary depressive illness. *British Journal of Social and Clinical Psychology, 6*(4), 278-296.

Heinz, A., Jones, D. W., Mazzanti, C., Goldman, D., Ragan, P., Hommer, D., et al. (2000). A relationship between serotonin transporter genotype and in vivo protein expression and alcohol neurotoxicity. *Biological Psychiatry, 47*(7), 643-649.

Hesselbrock, M., Easton, C., Bucholz, K. K., Schuckit, M., and Hesselbrock, V. (1999). A validity study of the SSAGA--a comparison with the SCAN. *Addiction (Abingdon, England), 94*(9), 1361-1370.

Hollander, E., Pallanti, S., Allen, A., Sood, E., and Baldini Rossi, N. (2005). Does sustained-release lithium reduce impulsive gambling and affective instability versus placebo in pathological gamblers with bipolar spectrum disorders? *The American Journal of Psychiatry, 162*(1), 137-145.

Hull-Blanks, E. E., Kerr, B. A., and Robinson Kurpius, S. E. (2004). Risk factors of suicidal ideations and attempts in talented, at-risk girls. *Suicide and Life-Threatening Behavior, 34*(3), 267-276.

Inoue, H., Tanizawa, Y., Wasson, J., Behn, P., Kalidas, K., Bernal-Mizrachi, E., et al. (1998). A gene encoding a transmembrane protein is mutated in patients with diabetes mellitus and optic atrophy (Wolfram syndrome). *Nature genetics, 20*(2), 143-148.

Jaspers, K. (1959). *Allgemeine Psychopathologie*. Berlin: Springer-Verlag.

Joiner, T. E. (2005). *Why people die by suicide*. Cambridge: Harvard University Press.

Joiner, T. E., Jr., Conwell, Y., Fitzpatrick, K. K., Witte, T. K., Schmidt, N. B., Berlim, M. T., et al. (2005). Four studies on how past and current suicidality relate even when "everything but the kitchen sink" is covaried. *Journal of Abnormal Psychology, 114*(2), 291-303.

Kant, I. (1833). *Anthropologie in pragmatischer Hinsicht*. Leipzig: Berlag von Immanuel Muller.

Kirby, K. N., Petry, N. M., and Bickel, W. K. (1999). Heroin addicts have higher discount rates for delayed rewards than non-drug-using controls. *Journal of Experimental Psychology, 128*(1), 78-87.

Koller, G., Preuss, U. W., Bottlender, M., Wenzel, K., and Soyka, M. (2002). Impulsivity and aggression as predictors of suicide attempts in alcoholics. *European Archives of Psychiatry and Clinical Neuroscience, 252*(4), 155-160.

Kovacs, M. (1985). The Children's Depression, Inventory (CDI). *Psychopharmacology bulletin, 21*(4), 995-998.

Kovacsics, C. E., Goyal, H. K., Thomas, K. J., and Gould, T. D. (2008). The antisuicidal efficacy of lithium: a review of the clinical literature and underlying pharmacology. *The International Journal on Disability and Human Development, 1*(3).

Lester, D. (1990). Impulsivity and threatened suicide. *Personality and Individual Differences, 11*(10), 1097-1098.

Lester, D. (1993). Functional and dysfunctional impulsivity and depression and suicidal ideation in a subclinical population. *The Journal of General Psychology, 120*(2), 187-188.

Lidberg, L., Belfrage, H., Bertilsson, L., Evenden, M. M., and Asberg, M. (2000). Suicide attempts and impulse control disorder are related to low cerebrospinal fluid 5-HIAA in mentally disordered violent offenders. *Acta Psychiatrica Scandinavica, 101*(5), 395-402.

Lindstrom, M. B., Ryding, E., Bosson, P., Ahnlide, J. A., Rosen, I., and Traskman-Bendz, L. (2004). Impulsivity related to brain serotonin transporter binding capacity in suicide attempters. *European Neuropsychopharmacology, 14*(4), 295-300.

Links, P. S., Heslegrave, R., and van Reekum, R. (1999). Impulsivity: core aspect of borderline personality disorder. *Journal of Personality Disorders, 13*(1), 1-9.

Linnoila, M., Virkkunen, M., Scheinin, M., Nuutila, A., Rimon, R., and Goodwin, F. K. (1983). Low cerebrospinal fluid 5-hydroxyindoleacetic acid concentration differentiates impulsive from nonimpulsive violent behavior. *Life Sciences, 33*(26), 2609-2614.

Linnoila, V. M., and Virkkunen, M. (1992). Aggression, suicidality, and serotonin. *The Journal of Clinical Psychiatry, 53 Suppl*, 46-51.

Lipps, T. (1907). *Vom Fühlen, Wollen und Denken. Eine psychologische Skizze*. Leipzig: Barth.

Lotze, H. R. (1852). *Medizinische Psychologie oder Physiologie der Seele*. Leipzig: Weidmann.

Luby, J. L., Svrakic, D. M., McCallum, K., Przybeck, T. R., and Cloninger, C. R. (1999). The Junior Temperament and Character Inventory: preliminary validation of a child self-report measure. *Psychological Reports, 84*(3 Pt 2), 1127-1138.

Madden, G. J., Petry, N. M., Badger, G. J., and Bickel, W. K. (1997). Impulsive and self-control choices in opioid-dependent patients and non-drug-using control participants: drug and monetary rewards. *Experimental and Clinical Psychopharmacology, 5*(3), 256-262.

Maes, M., and Meltzer, H. Y. (1995). The serotonin hypothesis of major depression. In F. E. Bloom and D. J. Kupfer (Eds.), *Psychopharmacology: the fourth generation of progress* (pp. 933–944). New York: Raven Press.

Malone, K. M., Szanto, K., Corbitt, E. M., and Mann, J. J. (1995). Clinical assessment versus research methods in the assessment of suicidal behavior. *The American Journal of Psychiatry, 152*(11), 1601-1607.

Mann, J. J. (1999). Role of the serotonergic system in the pathogenesis of major depression and suicidal behavior. *Neuropsychopharmacology, 21*(2 Suppl), 99S-105S.

Mann, J. J., Oquendo, M., Underwood, M. D., and Arango, V. (1999). The neurobiology of suicide risk: a review for the clinician. *Journal of Clinical Psychiatry, 60 Suppl 2*, 7-11; discussion 18-20, 113-116.

Maser, J. D., Akiskal, H. S., Schettler, P., Scheftner, W., Mueller, T., Endicott, J., et al. (2002). Can temperament identify affectively ill patients who engage in lethal or near-lethal suicidal behavior? A 14-year prospective study. *Suicide and Life-Threatening Behavior, 32*(1), 10-32.

Michaelis, B. H., Goldberg, J. F., Davis, G. P., Singer, T. M., Garno, J. L., and Wenze, S. J. (2004). Dimensions of impulsivity and aggression associated with suicide attempts among bipolar patients: a preliminary study. *Suicide and Life-Threatening Behavior, 34*(2), 172-176.

Mitchell, S. H. (1999). Measures of impulsivity in cigarette smokers and non-smokers. *Psychopharmacology, 146*(4), 455-464.

Moeller, F. G., Barratt, E. S., Dougherty, D. M., Schmitz, J. M., and Swann, A. C. (2001). Psychiatric aspects of impulsivity. *The American Journal of Psychiatry, 158*(11), 1783-1793.

Moss, H. B., Yao, J. K., and Panzak, G. L. (1990). Serotonergic responsivity and behavioral dimensions in antisocial personality disorder with substance abuse. *Biological Psychiatry, 28*(4), 325-338.

Muller-Oerlinghausen, B. (2001). Arguments for the specificity of the antisuicidal effect of lithium. *European Archives of Psychiatry and Clinical Neuroscience, 251 Suppl 2*, II72-75.

Muller-Oerlinghausen, B., Muser-Causemann, B., and Volk, J. (1992). Suicides and parasuicides in a high-risk patient group on and off lithium long-term medication. *Journal of Affective Disorders, 25*(4), 261-269.

Nilsson, A. (1995). Mortality in recurrent mood disorders during periods on and off lithium. A complete population study in 362 patients. *Pharmacopsychiatry, 28*(1), 8-13.

Oquendo, M., Brent, D. A., Birmaher, B., Greenhill, L., Kolko, D., Stanley, B., et al. (2005). Posttraumatic stress disorder comorbid with major depression: factors mediating the association with suicidal behavior. *American Journal of Psychiatry, 162*(3), 560-566.

Oquendo, M. A., Currier, D., and Mann, J. J. (2006). Prospective studies of suicidal behavior in major depressive and bipolar disorders: what is the evidence for predictive risk factors? *Acta Psychiatrica Scandinavica, 114*(3), 151-158.

Oquendo, M. A., Waternaux, C., Brodsky, B., Parsons, B., Haas, G. L., Malone, K. M., et al. (2000). Suicidal behavior in bipolar mood disorder: clinical characteristics of attempters and nonattempters. *Journal of Affective Disorders, 59*(2), 107-117.

Patton, J. H., Stanford, M. S., and Barratt, E. S. (1995). Factor structure of the Barratt impulsiveness scale. *Journal of Cinical Psychology, 51*(6), 768-774.

Plato. (360 B.C.). *The Republic*. Retrieved December 20 2008, from http://classics.mit.edu/Plato/republic.html

Pompili, M., Innamorati, M., Raja, M., Falcone, I., Ducci, G., Angeletti, G., et al. (2008). Suicide risk in depression and bipolar disorder: do impulsiveness-aggressiveness and pharmacotherapy predict suicidal intent? *Neuropsychiatric Disease and Treatment, 4*, 247-255.

Quintin, P., Benkelfat, C., Launay, J. M., Arnulf, I., Pointereau-Bellenger, A., Barbault, S., et al. (2001). Clinical and neurochemical effect of acute tryptophan depletion in unaffected relatives of patients with bipolar affective disorder. *Biological Psychiatry, 50*(3), 184-190.

Renaud, J., Berlim, M. T., McGirr, A., Tousignant, M., and Turecki, G. (2008). Current psychiatric morbidity, aggression/impulsivity, and personality dimensions in child and adolescent suicide: a case-control study. *Journal of Affective Disorders, 105*(1-3), 221-228.

Roggenbach, J., Muller-Oerlinghausen, B., and Franke, L. (2002). Suicidality, impulsivity and aggression--is there a link to 5HIAA concentration in the cerebrospinal fluid? *Psychiatry Research, 113*(1-2), 193-206.

Roy, A., and Linnoila, M. (1988). Suicidal behavior, impulsiveness and serotonin. *Acta Psychiatrica Scandinavica, 78*(5), 529-535.

Schmidt, C. (2003). Impulsivity. In E. F. Coccaro (Ed.), *Aggression. Psychiatric assessment and treatment*. New York-Basel: Marcel Dekker Inc.

Selzer, M. L. (1971). The Michigan alcoholism screening test: the quest for a new diagnostic instrument. *The American Journal of Psychiatry, 127*(12), 1653-1658.

Sequeira, A., Kim, C., Seguin, M., Lesage, A., Chawky, N., Desautels, A., et al. (2003). Wolfram syndrome and suicide: Evidence for a role of WFS1 in suicidal and impulsive behavior. *American Journal of Medical Genetics. Part B, Neuropsychiatric Genetics: the Official Publication of the International Society of Psychiatric Genetics, 119*(1), 108-113.

Sheehan, D. V., Lecrubier, Y., Sheehan, K. H., Amorim, P., Janavs, J., Weiller, E., et al. (1998). The Mini-International Neuropsychiatric Interview (M.I.N.I.): the development and validation of a structured diagnostic psychiatric interview for DSM-IV and ICD-10. *Journal of Clinical Psychiatry, 59 Suppl 20*, 22-33;quiz 34-57.

Soloff, P. H., Lynch, K. G., Kelly, T. M., Malone, K. M., and Mann, J. J. (2000). Characteristics of suicide attempts of patients with major depressive episode and borderline personality disorder: a comparative study. *American Journal of Psychiatry, 157*(4), 601-608.

Soubrié, P. (1986). Reconciling the role of central serotonin neurons inhuman and animal behavior. *Behavioral and Brain Sciences, 9*, 319 -364.

Spitzer, R. L., and Endicott, J. (1978). *Schedule for Affective Disorders and Schizophrenia: change Version* (3rd ed.). New York: Biometrics Research, New York State Psychiatric Institute.

Spitzer, R. L., Williams, J. B., Gibbon, M., and First, M. B. (1992). The Structured Clinical Interview for DSM-III-R (SCID). I: History, rationale, and description. *Archives of General Psychiatry, 49*(8), 624-629.

Stein, D., Apter, A., Ratzoni, G., Har-Even, D., and Avidan, G. (1998). Association between multiple suicide attempts and negative affects in adolescents. *Journal of the American Academy of Child and Adolescent Psychiatry, 37*(5), 488-494.

Strom, T. M., Hortnagel, K., Hofmann, S., Gekeler, F., Scharfe, C., Rabl, W., et al. (1998). Diabetes insipidus, diabetes mellitus, optic atrophy and deafness (DIDMOAD) caused by mutations in a novel gene (wolframin) coding for a predicted transmembrane protein. *Human Molecular Genetics, 7*(13), 2021-2028.

Swann, A. C., Anderson, J. C., Dougherty, D. M., and Moeller, F. G. (2001). Measurement of inter-episode impulsivity in bipolar disorder. *Psychiatry Research, 101*(2), 195-197.

Swann, A. C., Bowden, C. L., Calabrese, J. R., Dilsaver, S. C., and Morris, D. D. (2002). Pattern of response to divalproex, lithium, or placebo in four naturalistic subtypes of mania. *Neuropsychopharmacology, 26*(4), 530-536.

Swann, A. C., Dougherty, D. M., Pazzaglia, P. J., Pham, M., and Moeller, F. G. (2004). Impulsivity: A link between bipolar disorder and substance abuse. *Bipolar Disorders, 6*(3), 204-212.

Swann, A. C., Janicak, P. L., Calabrese, J. R., Bowden, C. L., Dilsaver, S. C., Morris, D. D., et al. (2001). Structure of mania: depressive, irritable, and psychotic clusters with different retrospectively-assessed course patterns of illness in randomized clinical trial participants. *Journal of Affective Disorders, 67*(1-3), 123-132.

Swann, A. C., Steinberg, J. L., Lijffijt, M., and Moeller, F. G. (2008). Impulsivity: differential relationship to depression and mania in bipolar disorder. *Journal of Affective Disorders, 106*(3), 241-248.

Thies-Flechtner, K., Muller-Oerlinghausen, B., Seibert, W., Walther, A., and Greil, W. (1996). Effect of prophylactic treatment on suicide risk in patients with major affective disorders. Data from a randomized prospective trial. *Pharmacopsychiatry, 29*(3), 103-107.

Tondo, L., Jamison, K. R., and Baldessarini, R. J. (1997). Effect of lithium maintenance on suicidal behavior in major mood disorders. *Annals of the New York Academy of Sciences, 836*, 339-351.

Turecki, G. (2005). Dissecting the suicide phenotype: the role of impulsive-aggressive behaviours. *Journal of Psychiatry and Neuroscience, 30*(6), 398-408.

US Public Health Service. (1999). *The Surgeon General's Call to Action to Prevent Suicide.* Washington, DC: US Public Health Service.

Van Orden, K. A., Witte, T. K., Gordon, K. H., Bender, T. W., and Joiner, T. E., Jr. (2008). Suicidal desire and the capability for suicide: tests of the interpersonal-psychological theory of suicidal behavior among adults. *Journal of Consulting and Clinical Psychology, 76*(1), 72-83.

Virkkunen, M., Nuutila, A., Goodwin, F. K., and Linnoila, M. (1987). Cerebrospinal fluid monoamine metabolite levels in male arsonists. *Archives of General Psychiatry, 44*(3), 241-247.

Vuchinich, R. E., and Simpson, C. A. (1998). Hyperbolic temporal discounting in social drinkers and problem drinkers. *Experimental and Clinical Psychopharmacology, 6*(3), 292-305.

Weissman, M., Fox, K., and Klerman, G. L. (1973). Hostility and depression associated with suicide attempts. *American Journal of Psychiatry, 130*(4), 450-455.

Wentscher, E. (1910). *Der Wille. Versuch einer psychologischen Analyse.* Leipzig/Berlin: Teubner.

Witte, T. K., Merrill, K. A., Stellrecht, N. E., Bernert, R. A., Hollar, D. L., Schatschneider, C., et al. (2008). "Impulsive" youth suicide attempters are not necessarily all that impulsive. *Journal of Affective Disorders, 107*(1-3), 107-116.

Wojnar, M., Ilgen, M. A., Czyz, E., Strobbe, S., Klimkiewicz, A., Jakubczyk, A., et al. (2008). Impulsive and non-impulsive suicide attempts in patients treated for alcohol dependence. *Journal of Affective Disorders.*

Wojnar, M., Ilgen, M. A., Jakubczyk, A., Wnorowska, A., Klimkiewicz, A., and Brower, K. J. (2008). Impulsive suicide attempts predict post-treatment relapse in alcohol-dependent patients. *Drug and Alcohol Dependence, 97*(3), 268-275.

Wyder, M., and De Leo, D. (2007). Behind impulsive suicide attempts: indications from a community study. *Journal of Affective Disorders, 104*(1-3), 167-173.

Young, S. N., Smith, S. E., Pihl, R. O., and Ervin, F. R. (1985). Tryptophan depletion causes a rapid lowering of mood in normal males. *Psychopharmacology, 87*(2), 173-177.

Zalsman, G., Braun, M., Arendt, M., Grunebaum, M. F., Sher, L., Burke, A. K., et al. (2006). A comparison of the medical lethality of suicide attempts in bipolar and major depressive disorders. *Bipolar Disorders, 8*(5 Pt 2), 558-565.

Zouk, H., Tousignant, M., Seguin, M., Lesage, A., and Turecki, G. (2006). Characterization of impulsivity in suicide completers: clinical, behavioral and psychosocial dimensions. *Journal of Affective Disorders, 92*(2-3), 195-204.

In: Impulsivity: Causes, Control and Disorders
Editor: George H. Lassiter

ISBN 978-1-60741-951-8
© 2009 Nova Science Publishers, Inc.

Chapter IV

When Working Memory Isn't Effective: The Role of Working Memory Constraints on Rates of Delayed Discounting and Substance-Use Problems

*Ana M. Franco-Watkins and Richard E. Mattson**

Auburn University,
Department of Psychology, Auburn, USA

Abstract

Research has demonstrated that individuals who pathologically engage in addictive behaviors are in general more impulsive, as suggested by their tendency to discount larger rewards that are delayed in time in favor of immediate, albeit smaller rewards. Additionally, some evidence exists that placing constraints on working memory during the decision making process increased an individual's preference for immediate reward. These findings, taken together, have led some to hypothesize that addictive behavioral disorders might result from working memory deficits because the inability to effectively process real-world discounting tasks (e.g., deciding between the immediate gratification associated with substance use despite the potentially larger rewards associated with abstinence that are displaced further in time). However, recent research indicates that individuals do not necessarily become more impulsive with increasing constraints on working memory; rather, individuals became more variable in their responding. Stately differently, increasing working memory constraints rendered the individual less likely to behave (i.e., decide) in a consistent manner. However, the mechanism by which working memory constraints create variance in responding, as well as the way in which working memory deficits influence the onset and maintenance of addictive behaviors, if not

* Address correspondence to: Ana M. Franco-Watkins or Richard E. Mattson, Auburn University, Department of Psychology, Auburn, AL 36830, USA. Email: afrancowatkins@auburn.edu or rem0003@auburn.edu.

through increasing impulsivity, is currently unclear. The purpose of the current chapter is to specify the process by which working memory constraints create inconsistency in responses during discounting tasks, and use this theoretical account to explain the relationship between working memory deficits and the etiology and maintenance of addictive behavioral disorders. Theoretical and methodological implications regarding basic and applied research on working memory, impulsivity, and their relationship to addictive behaviors are discussed.

Introduction

The term impulsivity is commonly used to describe a person who is prone to act on whim without considering the long-term consequences of his or her actions. Several different definitions and measures have been established to examine impulsive behavior in a variety of populations (i.e., substance abuse addicts, adolescents, brain-damaged patients, etc). Impulsivity is a construct both complex and multidimensional. It has been characterized as an inability to inhibit inappropriate behaviors (e.g., Newman, 1987) or to delay gratification (e.g., Mischel, Shoda, and Rodriguez, 1989), acting without forethought or sufficient information (e.g., Dickman, 1985), and the failure to correct inappropriate responses (e.g., Schachar and Logan, 1990). Its multiple descriptive features have led some to suggest that impulsivity is not a unitary construct, but rather comprises "several related phenomena which are classified together as impulsivity" (Evenden, 1999; p. 348). As such, it is not surprising that a consistent and integrative definition of impulsivity has yet to emerge (Buss and Plomin, 1997; Mitchell, 1999; Parker and Bagby, 1997). Most recently, some researchers (Reynolds, Penfold, and Patak, 2008) advocated for three behavioral dimensions underlying impulsivity: impulsive decision making, impulsive inattention, and impulsive disinhibition. In this chapter, we primarily focus on a behavioral task often used to measure impulsive decision making; namely, the delayed discounting (DD) task.

In what follows, we first provide a conceptual and psychometric background on delay discounting and its use as a measure of impulsivity. We then provide a review of a recent debate addressing whether taxing working memory increases impulsivity followed by a description of two theoretical models that might account for responses on the DD task under working memory constraints. Finally, a novel theoretical perspective connecting working memory constraints, decision making in the laboratory, and substance use disorders is provided.

Delay Discounting of Rewards: Conceptual and Pyschometric Considerations

The discounting of delayed rewards. The propensity to discount larger delayed rewards in favor of smaller immediate rewards is referred to as delay discounting or temporal discounting. This phenomenon occurs in real-world situations (cf. Lowenstein and Thaler, 1997), as well as in laboratory settings (Green and Myerson, 2004; Kirby and Marakovic,

1995; Rachlin, Raineri, and Cross, 1991). Whether or not a delayed reward is discounted is a function of the (a) length of time between the immediate and delayed reward, and (b) relative magnitude between the two rewards. The probability of selecting the immediate reward increases as the relative value of the delayed reward quickly depreciates from its absolute magnitude as time to receipt increases. Although the general tendency is for all individuals to eventually discount delayed rewards, differences exist as to when the immediate reward is preferred over the delayed reward (Green, Fry, and Myerson, 1994).

The DD task. Within laboratory settings, the typical delayed discounting paradigm involves presenting individuals with a series of options between an immediate reward and a larger reward that is delayed in time (e.g., "would you prefer $150 now or $500 in one year?"). In many studies, a staircase method is used to ascertain the degree of discounting by asking participants to choose between an immediate reward of progressively increasing (or decreasing) step values (e.g., ranging from $1 to $499) and a fixed delay reward (e.g., $500 in 1 year). At some point during the progression, the individual's preference reverses, indicating the point at which they roughly equate the value of the immediate and delay rewards. Delay discounting is assessed by examining preferences at a range of time periods (e.g., 1 month, 6 months, 1 year, 3 years, 5 years, and 10 years).

Typically, a hyperbolic function is used to assess delay discounting because value is discounted at a faster rate over short delays but asymptotes as the length of delay increases (Green and Myerson, 2004; Kirby, 1997). This hyperbolic function is modeled using the following equation:

$$V = A / (1 + k\,D) \tag{Eq. 1}$$

where V refers to value, A represents the monetary amount in the option, k reflects the rate of discounting, and D is the delay time. The free parameter k indicates one's propensity to select smaller immediate reward over larger delayed ones. Larger values of k indicate a faster rate at which the delayed reward is disregarded.

Use of k as a measure of impulsivity. Although it is common in the delay discounting literature to define impulsivity as higher rates of discounting (k), this interpretation can potentially lead to conceptual and interpretational problems. In particular, there is a risk of confusing the behavioral topography with the underlying construct. Impulsivity is often considered a biologically-based temperamental characteristic (e.g., Cloninger, 1987) shaped over time by environmental determinants (e.g., Soubrie, 1986) that manifests in observable behavior (e.g., greater rate of delayed discounting). If k is of theoretical interest, then the appropriate terminology is the *rate of delay discounting;* the term *impulsivity* carries additional and unnecessary explanatory value (e.g., a temperamental characteristic thought to account for overt behavior). If the extent to which k is determined by impulsivity is of interest, then defining impulsivity in terms of k is potentially tautological.

Nonetheless, using k as an *indicator* of impulsivity is not necessarily problematic on either conceptual or empirical grounds. Specifically, individuals who demonstrate higher rates of discounting for delayed rewards are assumed to be higher on the underlying dispositional continuum of impulsivity. However, treating the continuous distribution of k values and impulsivity as one and the same is problematic. The rate at which an individual discounts delayed rewards is an observable response pattern that has multiple proximal determinants (e.g., working memory capacity), whereas as impulsivity is one such (likely primary) determinant of k. In other words, k and impulsivity caanot be treated as synonymous because k values are not solely determined by one's level of impulsivity. We heretofore use k to refer to the rate of delay discounting and *impulsivity* to indicate one putative and internal hypothetical determinant.

The reason for making this distinction extends beyond the academic and is germane to the purpose of the present chapter. Failure to differentiate k values from the construct of impulsivity can render difficult the interpretation of intervening variables. In the present case, we examine whether or not working memory constraints can increase the rate at which rewards are discounted across periods of delay. It is assumed that changes in the observed behavior occur because working memory potentially mediates or moderates the relationship between one's discounting rate and biologically- and environmentally- determined position on the underlying continuum of impulsivity.

Working Memory and the Rate Discounting Delayed Rewards

Since the inception of Baddeley and Hitch's (1974) seminal tripartite model of working memory, the construct of working memory and its associated properties has been constantly evaluated and redefined (Baddeley, 2002; Postle, 2006). Working memory can be summarized as a *"brain system for holding and manipulating a small amount of information temporarily"* (Cowan and Morey, 2006, p. 139). The limited-capacity for controlled attention is assumed to be a fundamental component of the working memory (Baddeley, 2002; Baddeley and Hitch, 1974; Engle, 1996) that relies on frontal lobe functioning (Andres, 2003; Baddeley, Della Sala, Popgagno, and Spinnler, 1997; Smith and Jonides, 1999; Stuss and Alexander, 2000). The ability to engage in controlled attention is assumed to be a domain-free, general capability that enables participants to maintain memory representations in an active state in face of distracting or interfering stimuli (Jarrold and Towse, 2006; Kane, Bleckley, Conway, and Engle, 2001). These memory representations are assumed to reflect task-relevant stimuli in the environment, action plans, or goal states (Kane and Engle, 2003).

Accordingly, working memory plays an integral role in decision-making, particularly in situations where task-relevant and –irrelevant information must be discriminated between or when multiple dimensions of task-relevant information require simultaneous consideration in order to maximize rewards and minimize costs. In the DD task, an individual's ability to respond optimally is contingent on their ability to simultaneously retain and manipulate four pieces of information based on two separate dimensions: the magnitude disparity and temporal delay between the two rewards. The amount of information that can be maintained in working memory is limited to approximately 3-4 items (Cowan, 2001, 2005; Vogel and Machizawa, 2004; Vogel, McCollough and Machizawa, 2005). Thus, taxing working memory by placing additional attentional demands on the system might lead to suboptimal responding in the DD task if the ability to retain and manipulate these two dimensions of task-relevant information is required to generate optimal responses.

Suboptimal responding on the DD task. Before discussing exactly how taxing working memory might underlie suboptimal responding in delay discounting, it is important to define exactly what is meant by "suboptimal responses". Defining suboptimal responding for decisions in which one of the two dimensions is held constant (relative magnitude or temporal delay) is straightforward. Holding temporal delay constant, the suboptimal solution is to select the smaller reward (e.g., $10 today versus $100 today), whereas the suboptimal response when reward magnitude is invariant is to select the delayed option (e.g., $10 today versus $10 in 2 years).[2] On the other hand, defining suboptimal responding when both dimensions are varied is complicated because there is no objective optimal solution; rather, the option representing the maximal reward value when magnitude is prorated by delay is *inherently subjective*. In other words, the strategy for maximizing the overall subjective reward on the DD task is based on ideographically determined criteria for the optimal distribution of rewards over time for a given individual, which we denote as θ. To the extent that all other determinants of an individual's responses to the DD task are controlled (e.g., working memory constraints), θ should solely be determined by one's biologically-based and environmentally-shaped position on the temperamental continuum of impulsivity. Therefore, it follows that k becomes an increasingly valid indicator of θ under these hypothetically controlled conditions. Alternatively stated, if k for a given participant was known, then his or her specific responses to any given set of options in the DD task could be completely predicted using Eq. 1, which would equal the individual's subjective criteria for reward maximization (θ) determined by their underlying level of impulsivity. Suboptimal performance on the DD task can therefore be conceptualized as responses that do not conform to what would be predicted by a best-fitting value for k, when $k = \theta$.[3]

Although it is currently unknown how and in what sequence the temporal reweighing of reward magnitudes are computed and compared in working memory, the extent to which these processes are impaired should lead to responses in the DD task that deviate from θ (i.e., resulting in suboptimal responding). Even if one correctly assumes that extraneous determinants cannot be practically removed from DD task response variability in research settings, and that estimates of k will therefore be imperfect indicators of θ (i.e., will deviate from subjective optimal responding), it can still be assumed that responses occurring under no additional attentional demands on working memory would be a closer indicator of θ than

---

2 Although the increased utility of higher over lower magnitude rewards is considered here as self-evident, that immediate rewards are more optimal than delayed rewards requires clarification. For any given reward or commodity (e.g., food) and the level of its associated need state (e.g., hunger), its practical utility (e.g., sustaining biological function) operates only in the present moment. Although delayed rewards become more or less optimal when the current and projected level of need and reward scarcity is low and high, respectively, they are ultimately only preferred because at some point they will be accessed by the organism in the present moment. If the only variable parameter modeled by the DD task is the length of delay (i.e., reward magnitude, need, and projected scarcity are held constant), then the optimal choice will always be the one that is more immediate.

3 Note that this does not suggest different values of k across individuals can be more or less adaptive, and therefore more or less optimal based upon some external and objective anchor point. However, the extent to which a particular value of k is adaptive or maladaptive will fluctuate in response to environmental contingencies. For example, a greater tendency to select small immediate rewards would be more adaptive in situations where the probability that larger will rewards will still be accessible rapidly decreases as a function of time (i.e., a bird in

when working memory was taxed. However, the exact pattern of suboptimal responses caused by taxing working memory processes is currently under debate. Next, we outline two different interpretations of the effect of taxing working memory in a DD task.

Impulsivity or inconsistency? According to Hinson, Jameson, and Whitney (2003), individuals whose working memory is taxed will resort to a more "simple" strategy by which the relative immediacy of the reward will predominate decision making, as it may "become too difficult or time consuming to properly weight the value of a larger reward over an extended period of time" (p. 299). In other words, limiting the capacity of working memory impairs the ability to adjust the larger reward value by the amount of delay; responses will deviate from θ towards immediate response because the value of the smaller reward does not require any temporal adjustment. The result of a shift towards immediate rewards is to increase k, making participants appear more impulsive when working memory is taxed. In support of this hypothesis, Hinson et al. (2003) demonstrated that *normal* individuals (i.e., those without addiction or prefrontal brain damage) obtained higher k values when they engaged in a cognitive load task (used to constrain working memory resources) while making decisions in a DD task. Their results indicated that the discounting rate increased (as indexed by k) in the load condition ($k = .646$) compared to the control condition ($k = .301$). Therefore, under working memory constraints, an individual's responses appear to become less optimal in favor of reward immediacy versus reward magnitude. Alternatively stated, they demonstrate "performance that is consistent with greater impulsiveness" (Hinson et al., 2003, p. 301).

In a reanalysis of the data from Hinson et al.'s (2003) experiment, Franco-Watkins, Pashler, and Rickard (2006) provided initial support for an alternative account: the *random response model*. Although an increase in the number of immediate rewards selected under cognitive load would increase the average k value, it was reasoned that an increase in random responding under load would also be sufficient to produce this effect if there was a propensity to select the delay reward more often under control conditions (when no additional constraints are placed on working memory). Specifically, because the Hinson et al.'s experiment had a response bias where the delay option appeared to be more advantageous and was selected more often (i.e., on average 75% of the time) when working memory load was not taxed, then an increase in random responding would tend to shift responses towards the immediate reward, thereby increasing the average value of k without requiring a consistent shift in decision criterion reflective of greater impulsivity.

As noted above, if k perfectly summarized an individual's response pattern on the DD task, one could accurately predict an individual's response for a given set of options by inserting his or her k value into Eq. 1 and solving for (V). However, a k value could still be calculated if participants were responding completely at random, but this value would be unable to predict the individual's response pattern because random responses are by nature unpredictable. To test whether or not the average k value increased across trials as a function of random responding, Franco-Watkins et al. plotted the difference in the average k values across load and control conditions for each participant against the difference in erroneous predictions (based on their best fitting k). If Hinson et al.'s model was correct, increasingly

---

the hand is better than two in the bush). Although particular values of k might be more or less adaptive in

positive difference score values (i.e., increasingly "impulsive" behavior) would be uncorrelated with increasingly erroneous predictions (i.e., random responding). If the consistency of each participant's response were comparable across conditions, then k should not yield a difference in the number of erroneous predictions even though the average value of k increased as a function of cognitive load. However, a significant correlation was found, $r = .88$, $p < .01$, indicating that k values increased across conditions solely as a function of the number of erroneous responses. Furthermore, the apparent increase in impulsivity (increase in k) was limited to only a few outlier subjects and the load task appeared to have little effect on performance for most subjects (c.f., Hinson and Whitney, 2006). Franco-Watkins et al. provided a simulation to support that the increase in k in the cognitive load condition for the outlier subjects could be fully accounted for by an increase in random responding (which is discussed later in more detail).

Recently, Franco-Watkins, Rickard and Pashler (in press) extended their findings by first correcting for the prior response bias. The correction for the bias was sufficient to reduce the dominance of preferring the delayed reward to 55 % in the control condition (compared to 75% in Hinson et. al's experiment). Furthermore, the mean k associated with load ($k = .309$) and control ($k = .329$) conditions were not statistically different ($p > .05$).[4] In a second experiment, they introduced a more cognitively demanding load task coupled with a modified version of a standard DD task (i.e., all steps presented to participants, but in a random presentation order). Although the k values differed slightly from previous experiments, the mean discounting rate did not differ between the load ($k = .437$, SD $= 1.32$) and control ($k = .360$, SD $= .55$) conditions for the \$500 reward, $d = .08$ nor between the load ($k = .281$, SD $= .53$) and control ($k = .250$, SD $= .98$) conditions for the \$10,000 reward, $d = .04$.[5] In addition, the number of intransitive responses across load and control conditions was examined. An intransitive response occurred when a participant preferred the immediate reward option on a given trial (e.g., \$50 now versus \$500 in one month) despite having opted for the delayed reward when presented with a larger immediate reward (\$150 now versus \$500) on a different trial. It was shown that a significantly greater number of intransitive errors occurred under cognitive load, further supporting the hypothesis that working memory constraints create inconsistent or random responding in the DD task.

Deterministic Models for Random Responding

The evidence thus far does not seem to indicate that taxing working memory results in a significant increase in the rate at which delayed rewards are discounted over time, even when the DD task eliminated the response bias or a more demanding cognitive load task was

---

specific environments, there is no inherently maladaptive value of k.

4 It is notable that values of k obtained in the modified task are similar to the value of k observed in Hinson et al.'s Experiment 1 control condition ($k = .301$).

5 To support the notion that taxing executive processes of working memory do not increase "impulsive" decisions, Fellows and Farah (2004) did not find differences in discounting rates between patients with non-frontal and frontal lobe (ventromedial and dorsolateal frontal cortex) damage using a delay discounting task with shorter delay reward time frame (i.e., extending to six months).

introduced (Franco-Watkins et al., in press). Rather, cognitive load appears to increase response inconsistency or suboptimal responding with respect to *k*, and had no effect on the rate of discounting (as measured by *k*). In particular, the probability that an individual would select a given response was randomly distributed at chance levels around *k*. That their responding became more random, however, does not indicate that it lacked a cause. Assuming a deterministic model, responses that appear random are analogous to unexplained variance in a statistical model. In particular, the parameters that bring patterns to static are simply unknown, with the latter being referred to as random error. In the words of Leucippus, "[n]othing occurs by chance...there is a reason and necessity for everything" (as quoted in Jammer, 1973; p. 587). What are the conditions that account for the ostensibly random responding across DD task trials when working memory is taxed? We propose two related models that potentially address this question: the *alternating strategies for response optimization* model and the *local proactive interference* hypothesis.

   Alternate strategies for response optimization. As was previously discussed, the most optimal strategy for subjective reward maximization (i.e., optimal responding) is to exactly prorate the reward magnitudes by their temporal delay. Optimal responding requires working memory processes because comparison of the options entails combining and evaluating the values associated with each option according to some algorithm (Eq. 1). When this process is disrupted by working memory constraints, Hinson et al. (2003) hypothesized that individuals would increasingly rely on a simpler optimization strategy. Under such conditions, however, consistently selecting the smaller immediate reward option represents only one possible simplified strategy. As noted by Franco-Watkins et al. (in press), an alternative optimization strategy under working memory constraints is to consistently select the larger magnitude reward irrespective of time delay. In either strategy, information from one of the two task-relevant dimensions (magnitude of rewards or temporal delay) is at some point completely discarded, with individuals becoming increasingly "impulsive" or "conservative." Neither solution, however, appears to accurately capture and model the observed data.

   Although responses based on either dimension (magnitude of reward or temporal delay) is more optimal than responses based on neither (i.e., completely random responding), other more optimal maximization strategies that are more computationally simple than comparing temporally prorated reward magnitudes are conceivable. One possible strategy is to respond based on *either* the difference between the reward magnitudes *or* the differences between temporal delays based on some idiographic cut-off point. For example, one could always select the higher reward when the length of time delay is short (e.g., 1 year) and the smaller reward when the delays are long (e.g., 3 years). This strategy is more optimal than consistently selecting delayed or immediate rewards because high rewards over short delays will be selected more frequently and relatively small increases in magnitude over long delays will not be selected. Although this process is less optimal than when temporal proration is used (e.g., large magnitude rewards beyond the cut-off point would never be selected), the algorithm upon which responses are based is computationally simpler and therefore an advantage under taxing cognitive load conditions. It is also possible the task dimension with the predominant disparity between options (e.g., absolute differences in reward magnitude versus temporal delays) drives response selection. For instance, information regarding time delays will be completely discarded on trials where the magnitude disparity (e.g., $500) is more prominent than the temporal disparity (e.g., 5 months). Rewards are not temporally prorated and compared, but selecting the most prominent dimension will lead to more optimal responding than consistently selecting either dimension (e.g., only time or only magnitude) on ambiguous trials.

An additional strategy is that responses are solely based on parameter values for the delayed reward option only. Using this strategy, the individual decides only whether a particular reward magnitude (e.g., $150) is worth a particular time delay (e.g., 5 years). This strategy is particularly optimal given that the delay for the immediate reward (i.e., "now") is invariant across DD task trials, coupled with the fact that the immediate reward is always smaller. In this case, the information that is most variable (i.e., magnitude and time for the delayed reward) receives a higher levels of activation in working memory whereas more stable information (e.g., "now") or parameter relationships (e.g., immediate < delay) descend to lower levels of activation in working memory. Again, the solution is less optimal than temporal proration with respect to achieving θ, but the computation is easier and therefore more optimal under cognitive load. As such, it is likely more effective in achieving θ than consistently shifting responses to either reward magnitude or time delay because it is more sensitive to the parameters values of the reward options.

Presenting an exhaustive list of alternative optimization strategies to the DD task is beyond the scope of this chapter. However, the above exemplars provide the basis for the following theorem: the most optimal response strategy for a given magnitude-delay pairing is the one that generates a response closest to what would be predicted by k under θ at a given capacity for computation in working memory. Under no cognitive load, temporal proration is the optimal strategy because it is a simpler computationally solution that generates responses closer to θ. Temporal proration becomes less optimal as cognitive load increases because it exceeds computationally capacity. Although several algorithms under a given degree of cognitive load might exist, the most optimal of these is the one that most closely replicates what the responses would be under no cognitive load (i.e., θ).

Importantly, any hypothetical optimization strategy that exists in between response consistency (choosing either immediate or delayed) and temporal proration will generate a set of nonrandom responses that appear random under Eq. 1. Using this equation to estimate k when the temporal proration strategy was not used will produce an erroneous value; the temporal discounting function mischaracterizes the data because a different decision-making algorithm was employed. For example, responses based solely on the difference between time delays irrespective of reward magnitude would lead to a step function; the point at which the immediate reward is selected occurs at a particular delay interval (e.g., a delay of 3 years). This response pattern would appear random when compared to predictions based on Eq. 1 (as was demonstrated by Franco-Watkins et al., 2006, in press) because the individual utilized a different algorithm to generate responses. However, the overall value of k for participants did not significantly change, suggesting perhaps that the responses matched θ to a lesser degree, but using k to predict the exact nature of those responses yielded inconsistencies. In sum, participants might be consistent with respect to some decision-making algorithm, but only appeared to be random because their responses were not consistent with what would be predicted by Eq. 1 using a best fitting value of k.

Two additional issues relevant to this model require discussion. First, none of the alternative strategies noted above (if employed consistently) would produce the intransitivities found by Franco-Watkins et al. (in press). This is theoretically problematic, but it is possible that the increased task difficulty forced participants to select response options at random, as the degree of working memory constraints reduced the ability for any computational strategy. Alternatively, an interaction effect might exist between the specific parameters of a given trial and the type of optimization strategy employed. Even under cognitive load, basing decisions on the temporal discounting function might occur under conditions when the disparity between item parameters is obvious (e.g., $1 now or $999 in 1 day), for example, but revert to increasingly simpler strategies as differences between rewards converge around the point of indifference. If the decision-making strategy differed across trials, then no singular mathematic function would accurately characterize the response data, and the number of inconsistencies based on Eq. 1 would be randomly distributed across magnitude-delay pairs. In other words, different algorithms would be necessary to accurately predict responses for rewards that differed in proximity from the point of indifference.

Local proactive interference. Hinson and Whitney (2006) suggested that the inconsistent responding found by Franco-Watkins et al. (2006) occurred as a result of a global proactive interference (PI) increasingly placing demands on working memory as the DD task progressed. In support of this contention, they demonstrated that k increased across successive blocks of 20 trials; an effect observed only in the load condition and not in the control condition. This would support the contention that individuals tended to select more immediate rewards as a function of working memory constraints, but that this effect only emerged when PI buildup sufficiently taxed working memory on later trials. Although this model perhaps accounts for the findings of Franco-Watkins et al.'s initial reanalysis of Hinson et al.'s data (2003), it does not explain the later findings using a more demanding cognitive load task. Specifically, if PI was necessary to increase immediate responding because the initial cognitive load task was by itself insufficient, then a more taxing cognitive task should be by itself sufficient to generate this effect. However, Franco-Watkins et al. (in press) found no evidence for a global proactive interference across trials in the DD task.

Although PI buildup across DD task trials is perhaps not the operative process underlying random responding, it is conceivable that PI affects responding more locally and to a lesser extent. In particular, it is possible that on some trials, rewards from a previous trial are still active in working memory and potentially affect decision making on the subsequent trial. Because under ordinary circumstances one of the functions of working memory is to inhibit task-irrelevant information, during taxing situations these abilities are diminished and may allow task-irrelevant information from previous trials to impact current responding. In proactive interference memory tasks, individuals with higher working memory capacity tend to be better at suppressing task-irrelevant information than individuals with lower working memory capacity (Kane and Engle, 2000). That is, the ability to inhibit (suppress) interfering task-irrelevant information differentiates individuals on working memory capacity. However, under a cognitive load, all individuals, regardless of their working memory capacity, performed similarly in that all were susceptible to PI intrusions.

In the DD task, the extent to which PI interference carries-over from one trial to the next might also depend on the relative nature of the proximal items. For example, items that are more similar in parameter values might increase the PI effect whereas the effect of PI may be less when the difference in task-relevant versus task-irrelevant information across trials are more clearly differentiated. The individual's weighting function for temporal proration will therefore change as a function of the relative (dis)similarity of specific reward options and their associated level of local PI.

Another possible account for the effects of PI can be derived from the work of Mischel and colleagues (e.g., Mischel and Baker, 1975), who have shown that selecting the immediate versus delayed rewards may influence subsequent behaviors in predictable ways. Their work suggests that conflict is inherent in a forced-choice situation between rewards over varying delays, and that selection of a larger but delayed reward increases the value of an immediate reward as a function of time. The conflict situation is thought to generate feelings of frustration that increases the probability that the individual will select an available immediate reward to terminate the negative affective state associated with the conflict (c.f., Atkinson and Birch, 1974; Birch and Atkinson, 1970). Also, if the levels of inherent conflict increase as parameter values converge on the point of indifference, the commensurate increase in negative affect would proportionally increase the probability of selecting the immediate reward. Although the nature of their delay task differs from the DD task currently under consideration, it is possible that a given response to DD task trials is similarly affected by selecting a delayed reward on a previous item. In particular, selecting a delayed reward generates an emotional response that increases the probability of selecting an immediate reward on the subsequent trial. Theoretically, the level of frustration carried-over to the subsequent trial will be larger if the preceding trial was near the point of indifference (and the delayed reward was selected). Current trials that approach the point of indifference may need a relatively smaller degree of frustration to shift responding. Therefore, the extent to which this effect will shift responding to an immediate reward that otherwise would not have been selected depends on the relative nature of the two trials.

In general, the local PI model suggests that the valuation of a particular reward-delay pair might be influenced by responding on previous trials, potentially resulting from cognitive (i.e., item similarity) or motivation determinants (i.e., termination of frustration following the selection of a delayed reward). Irrespective of the exact mechanism, one appealing feature about this model is that the effect that PI has on any particular response would be distributed randomly across trials because DD task items are administered at random. As such, the randomness in responding observed by Franco-Watkins and colleagues might capture the randomly distributed effects of PI.

Working Memory, Response Variability and Substance-Use Disorders

A large body of empirical findings shows that greater discounting rates are associated with real-world impulsive behavior, such as the use of psychoactive and addictive substances.[6] With respect to this relationship, Kirby and Perty (2004) posit that the reason why negative consequences of drug use are dismissed by abusers is that the negative effects are delayed in time compared to the immediate positive effects associated with use, which in turn, results in greater discounting of the negative effects in lieu of immediate rewards. Furthermore, the DD task appears to be well suited for studying these relationships. According to Vuchinich and Tucker (1998), the DD task represents the choice faced by individuals with a substance-use disorder: select the immediate rewards of substance intoxication or the delayed, but more highly valued outcomes associated with abstinence. This contention has similarly been supported by empirical research. A disposition to decrease reward values at higher rates over time, as indexed by relatively higher k values on the DD task, is shown to correlate with various substances of abuse, such as alcohol (Dom, D'haene, Hulstijn, and Sabbe, 2006; MacKillop, Mattson, Anderson MacKillop, Castelda, and Donovick, 2007; Petry, 2001), tobacco (Bickel, Odum, and Madden, 1999; Mitchell, 2004; Reynolds, Richards, Horn, and Karraker, 2004), cocaine (Kirby and Petry, 2004), and heroin (Kirby, Petry, and Bickel, 2004). Furthermore, individuals with co-occurrences of addictive behaviors (i.e., pathological gamblers with substance abuse disorders) have higher discounting rates than individuals with only one addictive behavior (i.e., pathological gamblers without substance abuse; Petry, 2001).

Similar relationships have been found between working memory impairments and substance abuse disorders. For example, Bechara and Martin (2004) have shown impaired decision-making and working memory capacity in individuals with substance use disorders. Additionally, Bechara (2005) demonstrated that patients with damage to the ventromedial frontal lobe as well as some substance-abuse addicts had comprised decision making (as evidenced by signs of disinhibition and poor impulse control) in a gambling task. Although cross-sectional in nature, these data render plausible Hinson et al.'s (2003) hypothesis that increases in impulsivity account for the association between working memory impairments and substance use disorders.

These data notwithstanding, concluding that increases in the rate of delay discounting mediate the association between working memory deficits and substance-use disordersis premature. As demonstrated by Franco-Watkins and colleagues (2006, in press), working memory deficits do not predict increased rates of delay discounting, thus, hampering the theoretical feasibility of a mediating relationship. However, definitively concluding that relative rates of delay discounting do not play a mediating role in the causal link between working memory deficits and substance use behaviors is perhaps equally as premature. Inconsistent responses relative to k might naturally increase the base rates of substance use behaviors beyond what they would have been otherwise, and the processes associated with these high-risk behaviors are potentially sufficient to increase the probability of future occurrences. It also should be noted that current findings regarding this relationship between individuals with addiction and more impulsive responses in delay discounting tasks are solely correlational in nature. Although there is some evidence that performance on a delay discounting task predicts vulnerability to cocaine self-administration using non-human

---

6 Given space constraints and the greater breadth of empirical findings, the following sections will focus solely on the relationship between working memory impairments, impulsivity, and substance use, as opposed to other

subjects (Perry, Larson, German, Madden, and Carroll, 2005), the causal link between impulsivity and addiction in humans remains a matter of debate amongst researchers. Specifically, it is as equally possible that substance use behavior increases rates of discounting.

The lack of findings regarding causal associations between working memory, delayed discounting, and substance use is problematic for theory development. Specifically, the number of possible combinations between these variables is large and the ability to rule out opposing hypotheses is constrained by the dearth of this empirical evidence. As such, only three likely alternative accounts for the relationship between these aforementioned variables are presented. First, given that the rate of delayed discounting is only one aspect of the larger and multidimensional construct of impulsivity, it is alternatively possible that the association between working memory deficits and increase substance use is mediated by a different mechanism related to impulsivity. Second, working memory deficits do not bear a proximal relationship with decisions to use substances, but rather lead to other functional and emotional impairments that increase the likelihood of substance use as a coping mechanism. Third, substance use predicts working memory deficits, as opposed to the inverse, or an unaccounted for (third) variable better accounts for the co-occurrence of the two. Each of these theoretical models will be addressed below in turn.

Suboptimal response variability hypothesis. The hypothesis that working memory deficits increase the incidence of addictive disorders is theoretically contingent upon the assumption that individuals who are subjected to the former would not have otherwise developed the latter. Specifically, this causal relationship is only plausible to the extent that no third variable better accounts for the correlation between the two (a possibility that is discussed in more detail below). Another possibility is that individuals with low premorbid (i.e., prior to or controlling for working memory deficits) values of k are more likely to develop substance use disorders following impairments in working memory. Based on this assumption, we speculate that an increase in risk occurs because working memory impairments cause variability in suboptimal responding relative to k (under no working memory constraints) in real-world DD situations. As suboptimal variability in DD responding only has been shown in laboratory studies, this hypothesis is predicated on the assumption that working memory deficits will similarly increase the frequency and variability of suboptimal responding in real-world DD situations (e.g., whether or not to use a psychoactive substance). This hypothesis also rests on two additional bases.

First, suboptimal responding will necessarily increase the base rate frequency of high-risk behaviors even when premorbid values of k are low and $k = 0$. This is because low k values represent a low base rate of responses in which the smaller reward is chosen over the larger delayed reward, and an increase in suboptimal response variability therefore can only shift the distribution of immediate versus delayed responses in a single direction (i.e., an increase and decrease in immediate versus delayed rewards, respectively). This premise is supported by the findings of Franco-Watkins et al. (2006); they demonstrated that the base rate of immediate reward responses exponentially increased beyond initial values of k

---

high-risk behaviors and impulse-control problems.

(obtained from participants during the control condition) when random responding was modeled at an incremental rate of 5%.

Second, an increase in the base rate of suboptimal responding creates the necessary conditions for a substance use disorder to develop, given that substances of abuse carry an addictive potential. Alternatively stated, a tendency for selecting immediate over delayed rewards consistently across trials is not a necessary precondition for habitual engagement in substance use; habitual responding can emerge from variability in initial responding because psychoactive substances are addictive. For example, the probability that an individual will administer a psychoactive substance increases after the initial use because the commensurate reduction in unpleasant withdrawal effects becomes negatively reinforcing. Additional usages, however, are associated with subsequent withdrawal, the effects of which increase in magnitude as greater amounts of that substance are required to produce similar magnitudes of negative reinforcement (Solomon, 1980). The individual may increasingly select the immediate reward in real-world DD decisions because its subjective magnitude increases as a function of use. However, this shift would occur because of the operant processes following substance use, not because working memory impairments shift their preference for immediate rewards. Considered together, for individuals who would not otherwise engage in substance use, variability in responding – resulting from working memory impairment - during real-world DD situations involving substance use would necessarily increase the frequency with which these substances were used and potentially result in a cycle of addictive behaviors that otherwise, given an intact working memory capacity, would not have occurred.

It is also notable that a marginal increase in suboptimal response variability may be influential in substance use maintenance and relapse. Evidence regarding the abstinence violation effect (Marlatt, 1979) suggests that the probability of continued use markedly increases after even a single administration of a substance. Hence, even the most minor deviation from a consistent decision-making criterion of delayed responding can vastly increase the frequency of subsequent use. Even if increases in suboptimal response variability do not cause substance-use disorders to develop in individuals with working memory impairments, the high prevalence of such problems in this population relative to a normal population might result because those with working memory deficits are more likely to remain addicted.

Other forms of impulsivity as a mediator of high-risk behaviors. Hinson et al. (2003) suggest that the overall frequency of high-risk behavior potentially occurs because the individual's suboptimal responses consistently favor the immediate and smaller reward, irrespective of the specific nature of the reward (e.g., money, psychoactive substances, sexual intercourse, etc.). In contrast, the suboptimal response variability hypothesis, by modeling the addictive potential of particular rewards, suggests that substance use disorders can result from variability in suboptimal responding in real-world DD situations. The former model assumes that increased impulsivity precedes habitual high-risk behaviors, whereas the latter one posits that a general tendency to select small and immediate rewards prior to disorder onset is theoretically unnecessary.[7] It is possible that neither model is completely accurate. An

---

7 The correlational association between higher *k* values and substance use behaviors prevents a causal interpretation; as such, this relationship needs to be assumed for Hinson et al.'s (2003) interpretation to be

increase in impulsive behavior, resulting from working memory deficits, may indeed increase substance use, but the increase in impulsive behavior does not result from a shift in the rate of delay discounting. As was previously noted, a greater tendency for selecting small but immediate rewards over larger ones delayed in time is but one of many descriptive characteristics of impulsive behavior. It is possible that some other dimension of impulsivity increases as a function of impairments in working memory, and that this relationship may better account for the association between deficits in working memory and high-risk behaviors.

As an example, Schachar and Logan (1990) define impulsivity as an inability to alter behavior as a function of experience; environmental feedback for inappropriate responses does not influence learning by association. Even when working memory is intact, these associations might become even more difficult as the direct or associated consequences of a behavior occur at points further in time (e.g., the role of temporal contiguity in learned responding), or if the relationship between response and outcome cannot be deduced, reasoned, or understood by the individual. The ability to learn from the consequences of high-risk behaviors may become increasingly difficult, however, provided the severity of the working memory impairment. The effects of working memory constraints on reasoning ability (e.g., Gilhooly, Logie, and Wynn, 2002; Logie and Salway, 1990; Messier, Klauer, and Naumer, 2001) are known and well documented. In addition, Bechara and colleagues (e.g., Bechara, Damasio, Tranel, and Anderson, 1998) have demonstrated that working memory impairments resulting from brain damage impair implicit associative learning in the Iowa Gambling Task (IGT; Bechara, Damasio, Damasio, and Anderson, 1994).[8] To the extent that individual's with working memory deficits can neither associate nor understand the consequences associated with their high-risk behavior, their decision-making strategy will be disproportionally influenced by immediate response options. It should be noted, that increases in the frequency of high-risk behavior does depend on an increased preference for immediate rewards because delayed options are more difficult to incorporate in real-time decision-making calculation. Rather, the information cannot be incorporated into the decision-making process because task-relevant information regarding alternative response options (e.g., delayed consequences of present behavior) is simply unknown despite previous experience with relevant environmental contingencies. Although several other hypotheses regarding the causal influence of working memory impairment on high-risk behaviors, only one model was presented because the sole purpose of the aforementioned discussion was to demonstrate that an alternative account for the observed association is possible (for a similar model, see Finn, Justus, Mazas, and Steinmetz 1999; also see Kimberg and Farah, 1993).

Distal mediation models. The models discussed so far posit that working memory has an indirect effect of high-risk behaviors as a result of some proximal mediating process, such as increases in suboptimal response variability or deficits in associative learning (i.e., impulsive

---

plausible. However, the response variability hypothesis does not need to make this assumption because greater consistency in and frequency of immediate responding results from, rather than predicts, the use of psychoactive substances.

8 Briefly, the IGT requires an individual to develop implicit, as opposed to declarative knowledge about a prefixed but unknown optimal strategy for maximizing rewards and minimizing costs across 100 trials (see Bechara et al., 1998 for an overview of the IGT).

responding). An alternative possibility is that the indirect effects of working memory impairment on high-risk behaviors occur as a function of a more protracted process in which such impairments are a distal predictor of variables that operate locally on future decision making. More specifically, impairments in decision making might create functional difficulties across several life domains, the confluence of which may generate a set of establishing operations (i.e., environmental conditions that make a particular behavior more or less likely) for future substance use. For example, populations with working memory deficits (e.g., attention deficit disorder) have a higher prevalence of employment or educational difficulties (e.g., Ponsford, Oliver, Curran, and Ng, 2000) and marital problems (e.g., Wilens, Faraone, and Biederman, 2004; Wood and Yurdakul, 1997), both of which are associated with increases in substance use disorders (e.g., Fals-Stewart, Birchler, and O'Farrell, 1999). In other words, the association between working memory impairments and increased substance use is mediated by life stressors caused by the former and subsequently impacts the latter. Individuals with working memory deficits may be no more likely to engage in high-risk behavior initially following problem onset (e.g., traumatic brain injuries; TBI), but more immediate impairments in judgment and decision making that do emerge create the types of situations and emotional difficulties that potentially underlie impulse-control disorders (even for individuals that do not have such deficits). However, whether or not negative long-term outcomes result from working memory deficits in particular, as opposed to other comorbid problems in individuals with such impairments is currently unclear. Specifically, it is possible that conditions associated with working memory deficits (e.g.,TBI) might predispose individuals to psychiatric conditions that increase the likelihood of substance-use disorders (e.g., posttraumatic stress disorder; Bryant and Harvey, 1998).

High-risk behavior as an etiological determinant of working memory deficits. A final hypothesis we considered was that working memory impairments do not predict substance use disorders, but rather that that substance-use disorders predict TBI that result in working memory impairments. For example, histories of substance-use disorders are found to exist prior to or as a precipitating factor of TBI. Corrigan (1995) found that one third to one half of TBI cases had alcohol-related problems, and that such problems were associated with repeat hospitalization and injuries, acute complication, and poorer neuropsychological outcomes. Furthermore, that TBI results in working memory impairments has been shown empirically (e.g., Christodoulou et al., 2001). Taken together, the apparent association between working memory deficits and substance abuse may occur because TBI often results from substance-use related disorders, and working memory deficits result from TBI.

It is also possible that the correlation between working memory deficits and substance use behavior emerges as a function of a third variable, potentially in the form of a shared set of etiological determinants, which raise the likelihood of occurrence of both problems. Koponen et al. (2002) found that 11.7% of patients developed an alcohol-use problem *following* TBI. For these patients, TBI was perhaps an etiological determinant of both working memory deficits and substance-use problems, therefore representing a third variable that accounts for the ostensible relationship between the two outcomes. In sum, working memory deficits might not underlie substance-use problems, but substance-use problems might predict later working memory impairments or share a particular etiology that account for their apparent association.

Conclusions

In this chapter, we discussed the connections and relationships between the DD task, impulsivity and working memory constraints. Although the DD task is typically construed as behavioral measure of impulsivity, we argue that treating higher rates of discounting (k) as analogous to one's level of impulsivity is problematic. Rather, we contend that is more appropriate to focus on the behavior resultant from DD task responses as indicative of one's rate of delay discounting (k). We focused primarily on the issue of whether taxing working memory changes the rate at which rewards are discounted across periods of delay in the DD task by presenting two opposing viewpoints: an impulsive decision strategy and a random decision strategy. To this juncture, there seems to be little support that taxing working memory in normal participants increases the rate of which the immediate reward is preferred. We outlined how taxing working memory can lead to inconsistent responses and not necessarily more "impulsive" responses.

Several models might account for underlying processes associated with inconsistent choices or suboptimal responses found in the DD task under cognitive load. Two applicable models: the *alternating strategies for response optimization* model and *local proactive interference* hypothesis were presented as plausible accounts for the observed behavior. Although it is likely that both models might account for variability in responding to the DD task, these two models have yet to be evaluated.

On the surface, response variability under working memory constraints might appear to have little explanatory power to account for real-world impulsive behaviors exhibited by those who engage in addictive substances. However, we present several plausible hypotheses linking working memory, response variability and substance-use problems. We note that the relationship is still primarily based on correlations rather than an established causal chain across these variables. Although the interest in and research attempting to connect these constructs into a cohesive theory to account for both laboratory and real-world situations is laudable, the development of such a theory is in its infancy. As such, the prospect of research focuses on integrating clinical, cognitive, and behavioral processes to investigate underlying mechanisms of impulsivity and addiction remains an exciting arena for continued research.

References

Andres, P. (2003). Frontal cortex and the central executive of working memory: Time to revise our view. *Cortex, 39,* 871-895.

Atkinson, J. W., and Birch, D. (1974). The Dynamics of Action. New York: Wiley.

Baddeley, A. D. (2002). Is working memory still working? *European Psychologist, 7,* 85-97.

Baddeley, A., Della Sala, S., Popagno, C., and Spinnler, H. (1997). Dual-task performance in dysexecutive and nondysexecutive patients with a frontal lesion. *Neuropsychology, 11,* 187-194.

Baddeley, A. D., and Hitch, G. J. (1974). Working memory. In G. A. Bower (Ed.), *Recent advances in learning and motivation* (Vol. 8, pp. 47-90). New York: Academic Press.

Bechara, A. (2005). Decision making, impulse control and loss of willpower to resist drugs: A neurocognitive perspective. *Nature Neuroscience, 8,* 1458-1463.

Bechara, A. Damasio, A. R., Damasio, H., Anderson, S. W. (1994). Insensitivity to future consequences following damage to the prefrontal cortex. *Cognition, 50,* 7-15.

Bechara, A., Damasio, H., Tranel, T., and Anderson, S. W. (1998). Dissociation of working memory from decision making within the human prefrontal cortex. *The Journal of Neuroscience, 18,* 428-437.

Bechara, A., and Martin, E. M. (2004). Impaired decision making related to working memory deficits in individuals with substance addictions. *Neuropsychology, 18,* 152-162.

Bickel, W. K., Odum, A. L., Madden, G. J. (1999). Impulsivity and cigarette smoke: delay discounting in current, never, and ex-smokers. *Psychopharmacology, 146,* 447-454.

Birch, D., and Atkinson, J. W. (1974). Comments on the discussion. In B. Weiner (Ed.). Cognitive Views of Human Motivation (p. 71-84). New York: Academic Press.

Bryant, R. A., and Harvey, A. G. (1998). Relationship between acute stress disorder and posttraumatic stress disorder following mild brain injury. *American Journal of Psychiatry, 155,* 625-629.

Buss, A. H., and Plomin, R. (1997). *A Temperament Theory of Personality Development.* New York: Wiley.

Cloninger, C. R. (1987). A systematic method for clinical description and classification of personality variants. *Archives of General Psychiatry, 44,* 573-990.

Christodoulou, C., DeLuca, J., Ricker, J. H., Madigan, N. K., Bly, B. M., Lange, G., Kalnin, A. J., Liu, W-C., Steffener, J., Diamond, B. J., Ni, A. C. (2001). Functional magnetic resonance imaging of working memory impairment after traumatic brain injury. *Journal of Neurology, Neurosurgery, and Psychiatry, 71,* 161-168.

Corrigan, J. D. (1995). Substance abuse as a mediating factor in outcome from traumatic brain injury. *Archives of Physical Medicine and Rehabilitation, 76,* 302-309.

Cowan, N. (2001). The magical number 4 in short-term memory: A reconsideration of mental storage capacity. *Behavioral and Brain Sciences, 24,* 87-185.

Cowan, N. (2005). *Working memory capacity.* New York: Psychology Press.

Cowan, N., and Morey, C. C. (2006). Visual working memory depends on attentional filtering. *Trends in Cognitive Science, 10,* 139-141.

Dickman, S. J. (1985). Impulsivity and perception: individual differences in the processing of the local and global dimension of stimuli. *Journal of Personality and Social Psychology, 48,* 133-149.

Dixon, M.R., Marley, J., and Jacobs, E. A. (2003). Delay discounting by pathological gamblers. *Journal of Applied Behavior Analysis, 36,* 449-458.

Dom, G., D'haene, P., Hilstijn, W., and Sabbe, B. (2006). Impulsivity in abstinent early- and late-onset alcoholics: differences in self-report measures and a discounting task. *Addiction, 101,* 50-59.

Engle, R. W. (1996). Working memory and retrieval: An inhibition-resource model (pp. 89-119). In J. T. Richardson, R. W. Engle, L. Hasher, R. H. Logie, E. R. Stoltzfus, R. T. Zacks , *Working memory and human cognition.* New York: Oxford University Press.

Evenden, J. L. (1999). Varieties of impulsivity. *Psychopharmacology, 146,* 348-361.

Fals-Stewart, W., Birchler, G. R., and O'Farrell, T. J. (1999). Drug-abusing patients and their intimate partners: Dyadic adjustment, relationship stability, and substance use. *Journal of Abnormal Psychology, 108,* 11-23.

Fellows, L. K., and Farah, M. J. (2004). Dissociable elements if human foresight: a role for the ventromedial frontal loves in framing future, but not in discounting future rewards. *Neuropsychologia, 43,* 1214-1221.

Finn, P. R., Justus, A., Mazas, C., Steinmetz, J. E. (1999). Working memory, executive process and the effects of alcohol on Go/No-Go learning: testing a model of behavioral regulation and impulsivity. *Psychopharmacology, 146,* 465-472.

Franco-Watkins, A.M., Pashler, H., and Rickard, T. (2006). Does working memory load lead to greater impulsivity? Commentary on Hinson, Jameson, and Whitney's (2003). *Journal of Experimental Psychology: Learning, Memory, and Cognition.*

Franco-Watkins, A.M., Rickard, T., and Pashler, H. (in press). Taxing executive processes does not necessarily increase impulsive decision making. *Experimental Psychology.*

Gilhooly, K. J., Logie, R. H., and Wynn, V. E. (2002). Syllogistic reasoning task and working memory: Evidence from sequential presentation of premises. *Current Psychology: Developmental, Learning, Personality, and Social, 21,* 111-120.

Green, L., Fry, A. S., and Myerson, J. (1994). Discounting delayed rewards: A life-span comparison. *Psychological Science, 5,* 33-36.

Green, L., and Myerson, J. (2004). A discounting framework for choice with delay and probabilistic rewards. *Psychological Bulletin, 130,* 769-792.

Hinson, J. M., Jameson, T. L., and Whitney, P. (2003). Impulsive decision making and working memory. *Journal of Experimental Psychology: Learning, Memory, and Cognition, 29,* 298-306.

Hinson, J. M., and Whitney, P. (2006). Working memory load and decision making: A reply to Franco-Watkins, Pashler, and Rickard (2006). *Journal of Experimental Psychology: Learning, Memory, and Cognition, 32,* 448-450.

Jammer, M. (1973). Indeterminacy in physics. In P. P. Wiener (Ed.) *Dictionary of the History of Ideas.* New York: Charles Scribner's Sons.

Jarrold, C. and Towse, J. N. (2006). Individual differences in working memory. *Neuroscience, 139,* 39-50.

Kane, M. J., Bleckley, M. K., Conway, A. R. A, and Engle, R. W. (2001). A controlled-attention view of working-memory capacity. *Journal of Experimental Psychology: General, 130,* 169-183.

Kane, M. J., and Engle, R. W. (2000) Working-memory capacity, proactive interference, and divided attention: Limits on long-term memory retrieval. *Journal of Experimental Psychology: Learning, Memory, and Cognition, 26,* 336-358.

Kane, M. J., and Engle (2003). Working-memory capacity and the control of attention: The contributions of goal neglect, response competition, and task set to Stroop interference. *Journal of Experimental Psychology: General, 132,* 47-70.

Kimberg, D.Y., and Farah, M.J. (1993). A unified account of cognitive impairments following frontal lobe damage: The role of working memory in complex, organized behavior. *Journal of Experimental Psychology: General, 4,* 411-428.http://www.ncbi.nlm.nih.gov/entrez/query.fcgi?cmd=Retrieveanddb=PubMedandlist_uids=9427330anddopt=Abstract

Kirby, K. N. (1997). Bidding on the future: Evidence against normative discounting of delayed rewards. *Journal of Experimental Psychology: General, 126,* 54-70.

Kirby, K. N., and Marakovic, N. N. (1995). Modeling myopic decisions: Evidence for hyperbolic delay-discounting within participants and amounts.

Kirby, K. N., and Petry, N. M. (2004). Heroin and cocaine abusers have higher discount rates for delay rewards than alcoholics and non-drug-using controls. *Addiction, 99, 461-471.*

Kirby, K. N., and Petry, N. M., and Bickel, W. K. (2004). Heroin addicts have higher discount rates for delayed rewards than non-drug-using controls. *Journal of Experimental Psychology: General, 128,* 78-87.Kimberg, D. Y., D'Esposito, M., and Farah, M. J. (1997). Effects of bromocriptine on human subjects depend on working memory capacity. *NeuroReport, 8,* 3581-3585.

Koponen, S., Taiminen, T., Portin, R., Himanen, L., Isoniemi, H., Heinonen, H., Hinkka, S., and Tenovou, O. (2002). Axis I and II psychiatric disorders after traumatic brain injury: A 30-year follow-up study. *American Journal of Psychiatry,* 159, 1315 -1321.

Loewenstein, G. and Thaler, R.H. (1997). Intertemporal choice. In W. M. Goldstein and R. M. Hogarth (Eds.), *Reseacrh on judgment and decision making: Currents, connections, and controversies* (pp. 365-378.). Cambridge, England: Cambridge University Press.

Logie, R. H., and Salway, A. F. S. (1990). Working memory and modes of thinking: A secondary task approach. In. K. J. Gihooly, M. T. G. Keane, R. H. Logie and G. Erdos (Eds.), *Lines of thinking: Reflections on the psychology of thought, Vol.2: Skills, emotion, creative processes, individual differences and teaching thinking* (pp. 99-113). Oxford, England: John Wiley and Sons.

MacKillop, J., Mattson, R. E., Anderson MacKillop, E., J., Castelda, B. A., and Donovick, P. J. (2007). Multidimensional assessment of impulsivity in undergraduate hazardous drinkers and controls. *Journal of Studies on Alcohol and Drugs,* 68, 785-788.

Marlatt, G. A. (1979). A cognitive-behavioral model of the relapse process. In N. A. Krasnegor (Ed.), *Behavior Analysis and Treatment of Substance Abuse.* Rockville, Maryland: National Institute for Drug Abuse.

Meiser, T., Klauer, K. C., and Naumer, B. (2001). Propositional reasoning and working memory: the role of prior training and pragmatic content. *Acta Psychologica, 106,* 303-327.Mischel, W., and Baker, N. (1975). Cognitive appraisals and transformations in delay behavior. *Journal of Personality and Social Psychology, 31,* 254-261.

Mischel, W., and Baker, N. (1975). Cognitive appraisals and transformations in delay behavior. *Journal of Personality and Social Psychology, 31,* 254-261.

Mischel, W., Shoda, Y., and Rodriguez, M. L. (1989). Delay of gratification in children. *Science, 244,* 933-938.

Mitchell, S. H. (1999). Measures of impulsivity in cigarette smokers and nonsmokers. *Psychopharmacology, 146,* 455-464.

Mitchell, S. H., (2004). Measuring impulsivity and modeling its association with cigarette smoking. *Behavioral and Cognitive Neuroscience Reviews, 3,* 261-275.

Newman, J. P. (1987). Reaction to punishment in extraverts and psychopaths: Implications for the impulsive behavior of disinhibited individuals. *Journal of Research on Personality, 21,* 464-480.

Parker, J. D. A., Bagby, R. M. (1997). Impulsivity in adults: A critical review of measurement approaches. In C. D. Webster and M. A. Jackson (Eds.) Impulsivity: Theory, Assessment, and Treatment (pp. 142-157). New York: Guilford.

Perry, J. L., Larson, E. B., German, J. P., Madden, M. E., and Carroll, M. E. (2005). Impulsivity (delay discounting) as a predictor of acquisition of IV cocain self-administration in female rats. *Psychopharmacology, 178*, 193-201.

Petry, N. M. (2001). Pathological gamblers, with and without substance abuse disorders, discount delayed rewards at high rates. *Journal of Abnormal Psychology, 110*, 482-487.

Ponsford, J. L., Oliver, J. H., Curran, C., and Ng, K. (2000). Factors predicting return to work following mild traumatic brain injury: A discriminant analysis. *The Journal of Head Trauma Rehabilitation, 15*, 1103-1112

Postle, B.R. (2006). Working memory as an emergent property of the mind and brain. *Neuroscience*, 139, 23-38.

Rachlin, H., Raineri, A., and Cross, D. (1991). Participantive probability and delay. *Journal of the Experimental Analysis of Behavior, 55*, 233-244.

Reynolds, B., Richards, J. B., Horn, K., and Karraker, K. (2004). Delay discounting and probability discounting as related to cigarette smoking status in adults. *Behavioural Processes, 65*, 35-42.

Reynolds, B., Penfold, R.B., and Patak, M. (2008). Dimensions of impulsive behavior in adolescents: Laboratory behavioral assessments. *Experimental and Clinical Psychopharmacology, 16*, 124-131.

Schachar, R., and Logan, G. D. (1990). Impulsivity and inhibitory control in normal development and childhood psychopathology. *Developmental Psychology, 26*, 710-720.

Smith, E. E., and Jonides, J. (1999). Storage and executive processes in the frontal lobes. *Science, 283*, 1657-1661.

Solomon, R. L. (1980). The opponent-process theory of acquired motivation: the costs of pleasure and the benefits of pain. *The American Psychologist, 35*, 691-712.

Soubrie, P. (1986). Reconciling the role of central serotonin neurons in human and animal behavior. *Behavioral and Brain Sciences, 9*, 319-364.

Stuss, D. T., and Alexander, M. P. (2000). Executive functions and the frontal lobes: a conceptual view. *Psychological Research, 63*, 289-298.

Vogel, E. K., and Machizawa, M. G. (2004, April 15). Neural activity predicts individual differences in visual working memory capacity. *Nature, 428*, 748-751.

Vogel, E. K., McCollough, A. W., and Machizawa, M. G. (2005, November 24). Neural measures reveal individual dofferences in controlling access to working memory. *Nature, 438 (24)*, 500-503.

Vuchinich , R. E., and Tucker, J. A. (1998). Choice, behavioral economics, and addictive behavior patterns. In W. R. Miller and N. Heather (eds.) Treating Addictive Behaviors (2nd ed.). New York: Plenum Press.

Wilens, T. E., Faraone, S. V., and Biederman, J. (2004). Attention-Deficit/Hyperactivity Disorder in Adults. *Journal of the American Medical Association, 292*, 619-623.

Wood, R. L., and Yurdakul, L. K. (1997). Chane in relationship status following traumatic brain injury. *Brain Injury, 11*, 491-502.

In: Impulsivity: Causes, Control and Disorders
Editor: George H. Lassiter

ISBN 978-1-60741-951-8
© 2009 Nova Science Publishers, Inc.

Chapter V

Emotion-based Impulsivity and its Importance for Impulsive Behavior Outcomes

Melissa A. Cyders
Indiana University Purdue University Indianapolis, USA

*Jessica Combs, Regan E. Fried,
Tamika C. B. Zapolski and Gregory T. Smith*
University of Kentucky, USA

Abstract

Impulsivity has long been considered an important risk factor for a variety of maladaptive behaviors, such as alcohol use, drug use, and eating disorders. However, different authors have used the term to mean different things. In recent years, the construct has been disaggregated into five, separate personality traits. In this chapter, after reviewing the varied definitions of impulsivity that have existed in the literature, we review and describe the five traits. Two of them can be best described as deficits in conscientiousness (including lack of persistence in tasks and lack of deliberation before performing tasks), two can be described as emotion-based dispositions (including tendencies to engage in rash actions when experiencing very positive or very negative emotions), and the fifth is sensation seeking. We then discuss the differential correlates of each of these dispositions, the clinical implications of their roles in risky behaviors, and the particular importance of emotion-based rash action. We conclude by proposing new directions of research for the continued study of impulsive behavior-related disorders.

Definition of Impulsivity

Impulsivity is a notoriously difficult concept to succinctly define, yet incredibly important to the field of personality as evidenced by its presence in every major model of personality (Miller, Flory, Lynam and Leukefeld, 2003). Over the past few decades, efforts have been made in research to define the construct in a satisfactory way (Costa and McCrae, 1992; Evenden, 1999). This is a difficult task, as one of the only aspects that researchers can agree on with respect to impulsivity is that it is a broad and multifaceted construct with several related dimensions, including acting without thinking, sensation seeking, and failures of persistence (Bagby, Joffe, Parker, and Schuller, 1993; Depue and Collins, 1999; Evenden, 1999; Eysenck and Eysenck, 1977; Petry, 2001; Whiteside and Lynam, 2001). These various definitions are similar in that they all describe impulsivity as one factor or a group of factors relating to a tendency to fail to analyze and reflect before engaging in a behavior and lack of consideration of the results of the behavior (Evenden, 1999).

Of the varied definitions, each appears to be related to maladaptive behaviors and each makes intuitive sense (Anestis, Selby and Joiner, 2007a). Researchers have used the label "impulsivity" to refer to many things, including acting without forethought, the inability to concentrate, adventuresomeness, novelty seeking, failures of inhibitory control, inability to delay reward, failures of persistence, sensation seeking, and the tendency to become easily distracted (Buss and Plomin, 1975; Depue and Collins, 1999; Eysenck and Eysenck, 1977; Reed and Derryberry, 2005; Whiteside and Lynam, 2001). Some of the definitions neglect negative affect as an integral part of the construct (Eysenck and Eysenck, 1977; Gray, 1970; Patton, Stanford, and Barratt, 1995). Others are based primarily upon behavior (Barratt, 1993), while others define it operationally as a laboratory response to certain events (Bickel and Marsch, 2001). Still others view impulsivity as a collection of traits characteristic of an individual's personality (Eysenck and Eysenck, 1977). A brief review of the histories of different definitions of impulsivity is important for understanding the significance of the concept in research now.

One of the earliest conceptualizations of impulsivity comes from Buss and Plomin (1975) who first suggested that impulsivity was part of their four factor model of temperament, along with emotionality, activity, and sociability. Their definition of impulsivity was that of a multidimensional temperament which had inhibitory control as its core aspect. Other aspects of impulsivity included the tendency to consider alternatives and consequences before decision making (decision time), the ability to remain with a task despite competing temptations (persistence) and the tendency to become bored and need to seek new stimuli (boredom or sensation seeking). Eysenck and Eysenck's work started in a similar time frame, and their definition of impulsivity has been adapted and molded as research has progressed. Their initial attempt (1968) at clarifying the construct led to impulsivity's inclusion as a subscale of extraversion on their three factor theory of personality (also including neuroticism and psychoticism). In 1977, the authors then subdivided impulsivity into narrow impulsiveness, risk-taking, non-planning and liveliness, eventually moving to a two-part subdivision of impulsivity (Eysenck and Eysenck, 1985) under extraversion (as venturesomeness and sensation seeking) and psychoticism (as impulsiveness).

Tellegen (1982, 1985) described impulsivity as one of the three factors that determines the manner and intensity in which individuals respond to emotional stimuli. In his model, one's rating when comparing one's level of impulsivity to one's level of control provides for an overall constraint score. Cloninger and colleagues posited that impulsivity was in fact an aspect of novelty-seeking, which is one of their four dimensions of personality (Cloninger, Przybeck, and Svrakic, 1991; Cloninger, Svrakic, and Przybeck, 1993). Their conceptualization of impulsivity was influenced heavily by their focus on hypothesized physiological predispositions and described it as an automatic response to novel stimuli that occurs at a preconscious level, due to the biological tendencies of the individual. Zuckerman, Kuhlman and colleagues included impulsivity (called impulsive-sensation seeking) as a factor of their alternative five factor model, describing it as both lack of planning, i.e., the tendency to act without thinking; and seeking experiences and risks for the sake of excitement (Zuckerman, Kuhlman, Thornquist, and Kiers, 1991; Zuckerman, Kuhlman, Joireman, Teta and Kraft, 1993).

Another more behaviorally based definition emerged in 1993, suggesting that impulsivity encompassed actions that appeared poorly conceived and prematurely expressed (Daruna and Barnes, 1993). This definition also included actions that were unduly risky or inappropriate to the situation and often resulted in consequences that were undesirable. Other researchers focused on impulsivity as a cluster of lower-order personality characteristics, including sensation-seeking, risk-taking, novelty seeking, boldness, adventuresomeness, boredom susceptibility, unreliability and orderliness (Depue and Collins, 1999), while those seeking an operational definition defined impulsivity as the selection of a small and immediately available reward over a larger, delayed reward (Bickel and Marsch, 2001).

The Disaggregation of Impulsivity

Psychometric and validity theorists came to recognize the necessity of disaggregating multidimensional constructs and focusing validation and theory testing on lower-level, unidimensional entities (Edwards, 2001; Hough and Schneider, 1995, McGrath, 2005; Schneider, Hough, and Dunnette, 1996, Smith, Fischer, and Fister, 2003; Smith and McCarthy, 1995). When one uses a single score from a multidimensional measure (i.e., more than one construct contributes to the score), one risks averaging the predictive variance of one construct with the nonpredictive variance of another (Smith et al., 2003). The result is that the broad measure's correlation with a criterion will be lower than that of the most predictive construct and higher than that of the nonpredictive constructs.

Even more problematic, two individuals could have the same score, even though they differ on the component constructs that led to the score. For example, consider the NEO-PI-R Neuroticism scale, which has six facets, two of which are anxiety and angry hostility. Two individuals could obtain the same score on the overall Neuroticism scale, even though one may have reported high levels of angry hostility and low levels of anxiety, while the other reported low levels of angry hostility and high levels of anxiety. To the degree that this is true, correlations between Neuroticism and measure of other constructs produce ambiguous empirical results and unclear implications for theory.

As Whiteside and Lynam (2001) noted, many measures of "impulsivity" include items representing more than one of the many constructs tied to that term. This reality, together with the psychometric theory recognition of the need to study unidimensional constructs, points clearly to the need to disaggregate the construct of "impulsivity."

To this end, Whiteside and Lynam (2001) sought to identify the facets of impulsivity that are common across measures and place them within the framework of a well-validated personality model: the Five Factor Model (FFM: McCrae and Costa, 1990). The FFM was chosen because it is well-validated, comprehensive, and because it includes several separate traits that have been formerly described as impulsivity.

They conducted a series of factor analyses on an extensive list of "impulsivity" measures, and they identified four separate dimensions on three different broad personality domains that capture some aspect of what had formerly been described as impulsivity. Their four factor solution explained 66% of the variance in an extensive set of impulsivity measures. The first factor, lack of premeditation, reflects the inability to delay action in favor of careful thinking and planning. The second factor, which they labeled urgency, reflects the tendency to act rashly in response to intense negative affect. The third factor, sensation seeking, reflects the tendency to seek out novel and thrilling experience. The fourth factor, lack of perseverance, reflects the inability to remain focused on a task.

Each of these four factors appeared to have an analogue among the lower order facets of the NEO-PI-R (lack of premeditation was related to low deliberation, urgency to impulsiveness, sensation seeking to excitement seeking, and perseverance to low self-discipline); this finding supports both the convergent and discriminant validity of the four constructs. Smith et al. (2007) developed an interview assessment of the four traits and conducted a Multitrait-Multimethod matrix analysis (MTMM: Campbell and Fiske, 1959). There was convergent validity in the assessment of each construct across methods and discriminant validity between the different constructs, even when measured with the same method.

Cyders et al. (2007) proposed a fifth disposition towards rash action, called positive urgency, which reflects the tendency to act rashly in response to extreme positive emotion. Although such a disposition was not present in previous theories of impulsivity, there was much evidence to support their hypothesis. For instance, positive mood has been identified as a trigger to resume gambling among recently recovering pathological gamblers (Holub, Hodgins, and Peden, 2005) and the motive to drink to enhance an already existing positive mood is related to increases in drinking, drinking-related problems, and involvement in risky behaviors for college students (Cooper, Agocha, and Sheldon, 2000). Additionally, experimentally induced positive mood states have been shown to increase risk for impulsive action (Yuen and Lee, 2003).

Because there was no representation of positive emotion based rash action in previous impulsivity measures, Cyders et al. (2007) developed a 14 item measure of positive urgency that they demonstrated to be content valid and unidimensional. Through factor analyses, they demonstrated that positive urgency was separate from the four factors identified by Whiteside and Lynam (2001) and from other models, too, such as Gray's (1987) behavioral activation system framework.

Delineation of the Structure of Impulsivity

Two separate factor analytic studies have examined the structural relations of the different dispositions. The first set of analyses, conducted prior to the identification of positive urgency, compared five models of the relations among the four constructs identified by Whiteside and Lynam (Smith et al., 2007). The first model tested the fit of a single, unitary impulsivity construct. The second model tested was a four-factor model with four constructs that were not presumed to share a common, broad trait core. The third was a hierarchical model that recognized the four constructs as facets of one common, overall impulsivity trait. The fourth and fifth were three factor models composed of urgency, sensation seeking, and a lack of planning/lack of persistence composite. The fourth model combined lack of planning and lack of persistence to be one trait, while the fifth model specified them as distinct facets of a broad trait reflecting low conscientiousness. This fifth model fit the data best and is the most consistent with the NEO-PI-R operationalization of the four facets. It was also replicated using an interview assessment of the traits.

This analysis demonstrated several important implications about the structure of impulsivity. First, model one fit the data poorly thus providing further evidence that impulsivity is not well represented as a single, unidimensional construct. Impulsivity is instead best represented by three distinct but related dispositions: Urgency, sensation seeking, and lack of conscientiousness: lack of planning and lack of perseverance are separate facets of this broader trait of lack of conscientiousness. The value of separating the two low conscientiousness traits was indicated both by these factor analysis results and by findings indicating different external correlates for the two traits (Smith et al., 2007).

The second factor-analytic study incorporated positive urgency and provided further clarification of the relations among the dispositions. In this study, three separate models were tested: Model one consisted of the low conscientiousness trait composed of two facets, sensation seeking, positive urgency, and negative urgency. Model two combined positive urgency and negative urgency into one trait for a three factor model. Finally model three was a three factor model with negative and positive urgency specified as distinct facets of an overall urgency construct. The third model fit the data best, demonstrating that the urgency traits are distinct facets of a broader disposition. This structure was identified using both interview and questionnaire assessments (Cyders and Smith, 2007).

These five dispositions toward rash action have recently been identified in children as young as nine years old (Zapolski, Annus, Fried, Combs, and Smith, 2008). Zapolski et al. (2008) found the same factor structure with this young sample, and they also found that the traits had different external correlates in children, just as they do in adults. We return to the traits' external correlates below.

To summarize, the five dispositions appear to be best understood in the following way: lack of planning and lack of perseverance are distinct facets of a broad disposition reflecting deficits in conscientiousness; negative urgency and positive urgency are distinct facets of a broader, emotion based disposition toward rash action; and sensation seeking represents a third disposition (Cyders and Smith, 2007, 2008a). Although the five dispositions are correlated with one another, they do not appear to be related to an overall impulsivity construct. The five dispositions can be observed in adults, college students, adolescents, and children and are important for a variety of behavioral and clinical outcomes. Next, we discuss the unique external correlates of the five dispositions.

External Correlates of the Five Dispositions

Consistent with theory and the previously described factor analytic and MTMM studies, the five dispositions have differential external correlates; these findings further support the trait measures' construct validity and predictive validity.

Sensation seeking. Sensation seeking appears to relate to involvement in and pursuit of risky behaviors that provide sensation, but not to problems experienced because of that involvement. For example, sensation seeking is related to involvement in risky behaviors such as bungee-jumping, skate-boarding, and parachuting (Cyders and Smith, 2008b). Sensation seeking is also related to the frequency of engagement in risk-taking behaviors such as alcohol use, intoxication, and gambling, but not to problem levels of engagement in these behaviors (Cyders and Smith, 2007; Cyders et al., 2007a; Fischer, Smith, Annus, and Hendricks, 2007; Fischer and Smith, 2007; Smith et al., 2007). Likewise, Sensation Seeking longitudinally predicts increases in the quantity of alcohol consumed among first year college students, but not increases in alcohol-related problems (Cyders, Flory, Rainer, and Smith, 2009). It thus appears that although individuals high in sensation seeking are likely to seek out and engage in risky behaviors, their involvement in those behaviors is not primarily characterized by negative outcomes.

Lack of premeditation and lack of perseverance. Consistent with the idea of a broad trait with two distinct facets, Lack of Perseverance and Lack of Premeditation have similar relations with some external criteria as well as unique relations with others. Lack of Premeditation and Lack of Perseverance are both related to poor school performance but only lack of perseverance is related to attentional difficulties. (Miller et al, 2003; Smith et al., 2007; Zapolski et al., 2008). It appears then that deficits in conscientiousness overall contribute to poor school performance and that lack of perseverance may uniquely contribute to poor performance through its relationship to attention difficulties. Both traits are also related to symptoms of Obsessive Compulsive Disorder but in distinct ways: Lack of perseverance is positively related to obsessing and negatively related to ordering, Lack of premeditation is positively related to ordering and checking symptoms, while Lack of Perseverance is negatively related to ordering and positively related to obsessing symptoms (Zermatten and Van der Linden, 2008).

Lack of premeditation seems to play a unique role in several problem behaviors. It is related to binge eating and problem gambling (Fischer and Smith, 2004; Smith et al., 2007) suggesting that the inability to delay action and carefully consider the consequences of one's actions puts individuals at risk and is related to problematic risky behavior. Lack of premeditation also predicts maladaptive risk taking beyond the role of sensation seeking, but plays no role in adaptive risk taking (Fischer and Smith, 2004). Thus while some individuals high in sensation seeking can engage in risky behaviors without experiencing negative outcomes, those who are also high in Lack of Premeditation may experience more problems due to their tendency to act quickly without careful thought.

Lack of perseverance predicts increases in risky sex among college students (Zapolski, Cyders, and Smith, 2009). Its role in risky sexual behavior is hypothesized to be primarily through condom use: Condom use requires consistent performance of both the tasks of purchasing condoms and using them, even when one, or one's partner, might not feel inclined to do so. Thus, executing condom use may tend to be difficult for those who can not stay on task. Interestingly, Lack of perseverance is also negatively associated with antisociality, suggesting that the ability to persist on tasks may facilitate antisociality (Smith et. al, 2007).

Negative and positive urgency. When the five traits are studied together, only the two urgency traits correlate with problem levels of involvement in risky behavior (Cyders and Smith, 2007; Cyders and Smith, 2008a, 2008b; Cyders et al., 2007; Cyders et al., 2008; Fischer, Smith, Annus, and Hendricks, 2007; Fischer and Smith, 2007; Smith et al., 2007). The urgency traits are both cross-sectionally and prospectively related to a number of problem behaviors including alcohol consumption and alcohol related problems (Cyders, et al., 2009; Miller et al., 2003; Whiteside, Lynam, Miller, and Reynolds, 2005), risky sexual behavior and illegal drug use (Zapolski et al., 2009), binge eating and purging (Anestis, Selby, Fink, and Joiner, 2007b; Anestis, Selby, and Joiner, 2007a; Fischer, Smith, Anderson, and Flory, 2003; Fischer, Anderson and Smith, 2004; Smith et al., 2007), gambling (Cyders et al., 2007; Cyders and Smith, 2008b; Smith et al., 2007), and excessive shopping (Billieux, Rochat, Rebetez, and Van der Linden, 2008). This may explain why, for instance, alcoholics have higher levels of negative urgency than controls (Castellani and Rugle, 1995; Fischer et al., 2004; Whiteside and Lynam, 2003).

Although the two urgency traits both represent emotion-based dispositions to rash action, they do have distinct roles in impulsive behavior. Positive urgency explains substantial variance in positive mood-based risky behavior and negative urgency does not (Cyders and Smith, 2007). Likewise, negative urgency explains substantial variance in negative mood based risky behavior and positive urgency does not (Cyders and Smith, 2007). Consistent with evidence that negative mood is a precipitant for binge eating (Smyth et al., 2007) and with evidence that some individuals drink problematically to enhance a positive mood (Cooper, 1994), (a) negative urgency relates to binge eating behavior, but positive urgency does not and (b) positive urgency differentiates alcoholic women from eating disordered women (Cyders et al., 2007). The two traits also interact with Cooper's (1994) drinking motives in distinct ways. Positive urgency interacts with drinking to enhance motives and negative urgency does not, and negative urgency interacts with drinking to cope motives while positive urgency does not (Cyders et. al, 2007a).

Positive urgency's relation to risky behavior has also been supported in longitudinal and experimental work. Positive urgency uniquely predicts increases in the amount of alcohol consumed on any given drinking occasion and problems associated with alcohol use during the first year of college, while sensation seeking predicts increases in the frequency with which alcohol is consumed (Cyders et al., 2009). Positive urgency also uniquely predicted increases in risky sexual behaviors, drug use, and gambling behaviors during the first year of college (Cyders and Smith, 2008b; Zapolski et al., 2009). Additionally, during experimentally-induced positive mood states, only positive urgency predicted increases in alcohol consumption and increases in negative outcomes from gambling (Cyders et al., 2008).

The Unique and Important Role
of Emotion-Based Impulsivity

Given that among the five dispositions toward rash action negative and positive urgency have unique predictive roles for a variety of maladaptive and problematic behaviors, it is important to provide a theoretical framework for understanding these traits as specific risk factors for maladaptive behaviors. First, we will review the adaptive and maladaptive roles of emotions. Next, we discuss how the urgency traits may be related to brain system and neurotransmitter functioning. Finally, we will suggest ways in which the urgency traits may play a particularly important role for treatment of risky behavior syndromes.

The basic role of emotions. Basically, emotions signal needs and thus serve to facilitate action. Many studies have shown that emotional processing areas of the brain, such as the amygdala, are fundamentally connected to motor cortex regions, especially the anterior cingulated cortex (Devinsky, Morrel, and Vogt, 1995). These motor cortex regions have been shown to become excited, showing increased activity levels, during period of emotional arousal (Bremner et al., 1999; Rauch et al., 1996; Hajcak et al., 2007). Interestingly, this activation of motor cortex regions is fundamentally adaptive, in that it brings one's attention to the activating event that precipitated the emotion and activates the individual to address the need at hand.

To specify further, this emotional activation helps humans to plan actions consistent with the needs of the current situation. Often this process produces adaptive results. The experience of anger or fear and can lead one to take steps to improve their situation, perhaps by asserting themselves or seeking safety. The experience of attraction to another can lead one to take steps to initiate an interaction. However, it is important to note that not all emotional experiences lead to an adaptive use of problem solving skills to address the need that precipitated the emotion. Often, one cannot act immediately to meet one's emotional need, and so one instead seeks to modulate the intensity of the emotion (Cyders and Smith, 2008a). In some cases, though, individuals use maladaptive means of emotion modulation. For example, some individuals will use drugs, alcohol, gambling, shopping, or self-harm behaviors in order to distract oneself from the emotion and/or the precipitating need of the situation. To the extent that distraction is used, the emotional experience can result in more maladaptive choices and behaviors (Cyders and Smith, 2008a).

Researchers have recently begun to appreciate the role of emotions in risk-taking behaviors. Emotional experiences, both positive and negative, have been shown to undermine rational decision making (Bechara 2004, 2005; Dolan, 2007; Dreisbach, 2006; Shiv, Lowenstein, and Bechara, 2005), impair one's ability to continue self-control behaviors (Muraven and Baumeister, 2000; Tice and Bratslavsky, 2000; Tice, Bratslavsky, and Baumeister, 2001), lead to less discriminative use of information (Forgas, 1992; Forgas and Bower, 1987; Gleicher and Weary, 1991), and lead to poor decision-making outcomes (Slovic, Finucane, Peters, and MacGregor, 2004). Even positive emotions, which have long been ignored as an important factor in risk-taking behaviors, can interfere with one's orientation toward long-term goals, increase one's distractability (Dreisbach and Goschke, 2004), and make one more optimistic about positive outcomes of a situation (Nygren, Isen, Taylor, and Dulin, 1996; Wright and Bower, 1992).

The urgency traits and brain systems. Emotion and action are fundamentally linked, and we view negative and positive urgency as representations of individual differences in the degree to which one's emotion-based actions are rash. It follows that there might well be brain systems expressing the emotion–action connection. As mentioned above, there are many connections, both anatomically and functionally, between motor cortex regions and emotional processing areas of the brain. More generally, however, there are many connections among the amygdala and areas of the brain that are thought to control planful behaviors, such as the orbitofrontal cortex (OFC), the ventromedial prefrontal cortex (vmPFC), and other areas of the prefrontal cortex (PFC: Barbas, 2007; Bechara, 2005). These connections are reciprocal. It appears that there is "bottom-up" processing, in which activation of the amygdala signals which events are salient to the PFC, and also "top-down" processing, in which the OFC and related areas modulate responsiveness in the amygdala and elsewhere, in part as a function of information processing and orientation to one's long-term goals (Cardinal, Parkinson, Hall, and Everitt, 2002; Cyders and Smith, 2008a; Lewis and Todd, 2007).

At times, one's strong emotions may increase the likelihood that one will act in ways inconsistent with one's long-term goals (e.g., yelling at one's boss or pursuing an otherwise ill-advised sexual liaison). At these times, modulation of one's affect by the OFC appears to play a crucial role in avoiding rash, ill-considered behavior. Davidson (2003) describes affect-guided planning as the process in which one maintains an affective connection to one's long-term goals and anticipates outcomes of behaviors in terms of those goals: This process is a hallmark of rational, adaptive decision making and allows one to maintain long-term goals despite strong emotional pulls in different directions (Cyders and Smith, 2008a). And individuals with damage to the OFC, perhaps vmPFC, tend to show diminished affect-guided planning. They tend to act in less adaptive and more rash ways following emotional arousal (Bechara, 2004; Bechara, Damasio, Damasio, and Anderson, 1994; Bechara, Tranel, Damasio and Damasio, 1996; Cardinal et al., 2002; Damasio, Grabowski, Frank, Galaburda, and Damasio, 1994; Spinella, 2007; see review by Cyders and Smith, 2008a).

It may be the case that variation in neurotransmitter functioning in this system contributes to individual differences in affect-guided planning or its reverse, negative and positive urgency. Generally speaking, low levels of serotonin (5HT) and high levels of dopamine (DA) have been shown to be related to increased emotional experiences and impulsive action (Cardinal and Everitt, 2004; Cools et al., 2005; Depue, 1995; Depue and Collins, 1999; Frankle et al., 2005; Krakowski, 2003; Morgan, Impallomeni, Pirona, and Rogers, 2006; Spear, 2000; Spoont, 1992; Stuettgen, Hennig, Reuter, and Netter, 2005; Winstanley, Dalley, Tehobald, and Robbins, 2004; Winstanley, Eagle, and Robbins, 2006; Winstanley, Theobald, Dalley, Glennon, and Robbins, 2004; Zald and Depue, 2001). Additionally, 5HT and DA interact: serotonergic systems, which appear to be important for information processing, modulate certain dopaminergic pathways that seem to underlie approach behaviors (Patterson and Newman, 1993; Spoont, 1992). It is thus possible that 5HT activity contributes to the process by which the OFC modulates affect-driven action as a function of its role in facilitating information processing. Thus, low levels of 5HT, and resulting higher levels of DA, may constitute facilitative conditions for reduced affect-guided planning or increased levels of positive and negative urgency.

Overall, it appears that positive and negative urgency have important biological underpinnings that may involve the dual activation of (1) related brain processes, (2) reciprocal modulation of brain regions, and (3) neurotransmitter systems that underlie both approach behaviors and emotional experiences (Cyders and Smith, 2008a). This evidence, in combination with the evidence that positive and negative urgency are uniquely related to problematic levels of maladaptive behaviors, leads one to consider the importance of these traits for treatment settings.

The Urgency Traits and Treatment

We next will discuss the existing and potentially future role of the urgency traits in clinical treatment for risky behaviors. We first will discuss general theories of prevention of risky behaviors, will acknowledge where, in existing treatments, affect-based treatments are present, and propose a more complete role of the urgency traits in therapeutic treatments.

Prevention of risky behaviors. The literal definition of prevention is to "stop something from happening." However, stopping behaviors related to psychological dysfunction from ever occurring is a difficult task, in part because (a) researchers lack the capacity to predict subsequent behavior perfectly and (b) personality and environmental events interact to contribute to the emergence of dysfunction, and these interactions are often outside the control of the clinician. Romano and Hage (2000) attempted to clarify the understanding of prevention by providing five dimensions of prevention. According to Romano and Hage (2000), at least one or more of these dimensions need to be present in order to classify an effort as "preventative." The five dimensions are as follows: 1) stops (prevents) a problem behavior from ever occurring, 2) delays the onset of a problem behavior, 3) reduces the impact of an existing problem behavior, 4) strengthens knowledge, attitudes, and behaviors that promote emotional and physical well-being, and 5) supports institutional, community, and government policies that promote physical and emotional well-being.

All these definitions, except perhaps for the first, appear to be especially applicable for the assessment of impulsivity-like personality traits and subsequent engagement in risky behaviors. For example, it has been shown that children who demonstrate externalizing behaviors experience a higher number of controllable negative life events over the course of development (Masten, Neemann, and Andenas, 1994). We believe it may be the case that emotion-based impulsivity traits are a factor that influences the likelihood of expressing these behaviors. Therefore, teaching skills to manage emotion may (a) delay the onset of problem behaviors, (b) reduce the frequency or severity of problem behaviors, and (c) help individuals successfully manage their mental well-being. And recognition of this risk process may lead to support for other policies that promote emotional and physical well-being.

Existing treatments utilizing rash action traits. Many treatments for engagement in risky behaviors have included some focus on emotions. One such treatment is Dialectical Behavioral Therapy (DBT), which was created as an affect management treatment for individuals diagnosed with Borderline Personality Disorder (BPD: Linehan, 1993). BPD is a personality disorder characterizing pervasive instability in mood, interpersonal relationships, and self-image. Additionally, many individuals diagnosed with BPD also report engaging in parasuicidal behaviors, such as cutting, as a maladaptive attempt to help manage their mood. The main goals of DBT are to teach clients how, given their affective intensity, to learn more adaptive ways to manage their mood.

Within DBT training are three core modules: emotion regulation, distress tolerance, and interpersonal effectiveness. Through the teaching and application of the skills taught in DBT, individuals are able to better adjust their emotional reaction to a stimulus depending on the context, cope with intense emotions without use of maladaptive behaviors, and effectively relay their feelings about precipitating events that led to the intense mood with others. Individuals are also taught how to inhibit ill-advised mood-dependent action such as avoiding "blowing up" and also how to behave consistently with one's goals, leading to attainment of goals rather than failing to do so as a result of overreacting to a stimulus.

Another area in which affect-based treatment has been utilized is alcohol treatment. The main goal of most alcohol treatment programs is for clients to be completely abstinent from the drug. This is a difficult feat, given the estimate that approximately 50% of alcoholic patients relapse within three months after completion of treatment (Leamon, Wright, and Myrick, 2008). Understanding why individuals do lapse or completely relapse into pretreatment alcohol use is important for clinicians working with this population. However, more important may be the need to identify what factors place individuals at risk for relapse and focusing treatment on management and/or removal of these factors from the client's environment. Thus, a common component of many treatment programs is relapse prevention (Etheridge, Hubbard, Anderson, Craddock, and Flynn, 1997).

Relapse prevention is a treatment intervention designed to teach clients a wide range of cognitive and behavioral coping skills to avoid a brief return to substance use (lapse), or a protracted return to previous levels of use (relapse), following a period of moderation or abstinence. Marlatt and Gordon (1985) developed a model for relapse prevention based on social-cognitive psychology. Use of the model has led to strong evidence for an empirically-based typology of five situations that present high risk for relapse: negative emotional states, interpersonal conflict, social pressure, positive emotional states, and coping levels. Additionally, the first three situations were reported to account for 75 percent of all relapses, leaving positive emotional states and coping to account for the remaining 25 percent (Marlatt and Gordon, 1985). More recently, researchers have used Marlatt's model to identity eight more specific categories of risk: unpleasant emotions, physical discomfort, pleasant emotions, testing personal control, urges and temptations to use, conflict with others, social pressure to use, and pleasant times with others (Annis, 1982). The inclusion of both positive and negative mood emphasizes the importance of both in understanding alcohol use, but also sheds light on the need to understand the underlying personality characteristics lending someone to engage in these and similar risky behaviors.

The treatment approach, based on Marlatt's model, is for clinicians to help their clients identify the environmental and emotional characteristics of situations that were associated as potentially high risk situations for relapsing. The clinician needs to help the client examine situations that precipitate the client's exposure to the high risk situations (i.e., lifestyle factors and urges/cravings), as well as identify the client's typical response to exposure to the high risk factors. Then, focus is placed on teaching the client strategies to be able to recognize and cope with high-risk situations (Larimer, Palmer, and Marlatt, 1999). Such strategies would include teaching the client to recognize warning signs (e.g., peer pressure, positive expectancies about drinking, and being in a bar) and to learn to take some overt action to reduce vulnerability, such as leaving the environment or avoiding the situation entirely. However, under circumstances when the client is unable to physically escape the situation, the model recommends teaching the client effective coping skills (e.g., assertive communication skills, anger management, and positive self talk).

Recently, distress tolerance skills training from DBT have also been applied effectively to drug/alcohol use. The focus is on learning to participate in other, more adaptive activities when distressed instead of engaging in the addictive behavior (Robins and Chapman, 2004). Combining these specific skills with established substance abuse treatment programs or models may be an important contribution in increasing the efficacy of substance abuse treatment.

Further Areas of Application of the Urgency Traits

Although much work has been conducted on addressing affect guided rash action within the personality and substance abuse literatures, many other psychological disorders involving affect dysregulation and impulsive behavior have not yet benefited from treatments targeting these processes. One possibility is bulimia nervosa, which is a type of eating disorder characterized by engagement in binge eating episodes that are accompanied by compensatory behaviors, such as vomiting, abuse of laxatives, or diuretics, fasting, or excessive exercise (Peterson and Mitchell, 1999). The most common treatment for bulimia nervosa is cognitive behavioral therapy, although other models of therapy, such as interpersonal and family-based therapy are also used. Within the CBT model of treatment, the underlying conceptualization of bulimia nervosa is that the disorder is maintained due to the interaction of five core domains: low self-esteem, extreme concerns with shape and weight, restrictive dieting, binge eating, and self-induced vomiting (Anderson and Maloney, 2001). CBT models focus most of the treatment on behavioral change through cognitive restructuring and altering current patterns of eating.

However, negative urgency is by far the single best impulsivity-like predictor of binge eating (Fischer, Smith, and Cyders, 2008) and, as predicted by urgency theory, women with bulimia nervosa binge eat when they are experiencing high levels of negative affect (Smyth et al., 2007). It thus appears that specifically addressing the association between negative urgency and bulimic symptoms might fruitfully be included in intervention programs, as well as specific techniques not only to teach skills on decreasing the level of distress the client is experiencing, but also to teach skills on how to mitigate the client's tendency to engage in rash actions when distressed.

More recently, studies have shown that the distress tolerance components of DBT can also be used to address these concerns with affect-based rash action. Clyne and Blampied (2004) provided training in emotion recognition and management, problem solving, assertiveness training, relaxation, and stress management to 11 women with binge eating disorder. The treatment reduced binge eating frequency, stress, and depression over the course of 11 sessions; no participant met criteria for binge eating disorder at follow-up.

Although use of DBT skills is not a common practice in many treatment programs for eating disorders, the success of the Clyne and Blampied study suggests the value of implementing more techniques to address affect based rash action in existing treatment programs.

Final Implications of the Urgency Traits on Treatment

We have argued that information about the role of affect-based rash action in risky behavior involvement suggests the need to address that process in treatment. Yet, the application of many of these affect-based treatments may be difficult to implement if identification of the client' precipitating risk factors are unclear, especially when the client has little insight to these factors or has poor memory. A more effective starting point might be identifying the client's risk for impulsive behavior based on the five traits we have discussed. As mentioned earlier, each is distinct from the others and each predicts different aspects of risky behavior involvement. Thus, by assessment of these traits, the clinician will have more insight as to what types of environments and behaviors a client participants in that may be particularly high-risk for that individual, perhaps even regardless if the client is aware of the possible harm. Moreover, preventive coping skills can be implemented based on the particular nature of the personality risk for impulsive behavior.

For example, if the client is high on sensation seeking, therapy time could be spent identifying high sensation behaviors that the client participants that are problematic and also identifying other behaviors that provide a comparable level of sensation, but are less harmful. For individuals high on positive urgency, the typical coping skills use to manage and alleviate negative mood, such as avoiding situations that elicit negative mood states or learning relaxation skills, do not appear to be particularly appropriate for positive mood states. It is reasonable to teach clients to mange negative moods, due to the adverse outcomes associated with prolonged negative affect, such as depression, suicidal ideation, and harm to other. However, it appears unreasonable to teach someone to be less happy.

Thus a more appropriate course of action for individuals high on positive urgency might be for clinicians to work with their clients in identifying situations that create extremely high positive emotions for the client. The client could be taught alternative behaviors other than the impulsive acts that cause problems when in a positive mood or during celebrations (e.g., rather than drink large quantities of alcohol at a party, do something active such as playing a sport or dancing). Additionally, clinicians can teach their clients how to identify warning signs, during which they become more impulsive, and create reminder cues to help the client remain cognizant of their long-term goals (e.g., career advancement, faithfulness to a significant other). The use of reminder cues has been found to be effective across multiple outcome variables, such as condom use and dieting (Cin, MacDonald, Fong, Zanna, and Elton-Marshall, 2006; Horan and Johnson, 1971). As for negative urgency, the treatment options described above for positive urgency could also be used, in addition to typical affect management treatment procedures, such as anger management and distress tolerance skills from DBT.

Thus, in order to select the most relevant and presumed effective treatment for an individual, clinicians must first identify the specific levels of the rash action traits exhibited by an individual. Assessment tools have been created to assess these impulsivity-like traits and have found to be both reliable and valid across several adult and child populations. Information regarding access to these measures can be provided by contacting the first author of this chapter.

Conclusion

To summarize, impulsivity is a broadly defined concept that has lead many researchers to attempt to further define the different aspects that have been referred to under the rubric of "impulsivity." Five traits have been identified: sensation seeking, negative urgency, positive urgency, lack of perseverance, and lack of deliberation. These traits have unique predictive relationship with outcome behaviors, with negative and positive urgency's role being one of relation to negative problematic outcomes from risk-taking behaviors. Therefore, it is important to understand the potentially maladaptive role that emotions can play in the choices to participate in potentially harmful maladaptive behavior. This relationship between rash action and emotions is likely influenced by neurotransmitter functioning within key brain systems and may explain a large portion of failures to inhibit behaviors. Clinicians can take advantage of these findings by assessing the specific personality underpinnings for a given client's rash action, and thus develop a more targeted, and presumably more effective, intervention.

References

Anderson, D. A., and Maloney, K. C. (2001). The efficacy of cognitive-behavioral therapy on the core symptoms of bulimia nervosa. *Clinical Psychology Review, 21*, 971-988.

Anestis, M. D., Selby, E. A., Fink, E. L., and Joiner, T.E. (2007b). The multifaceted role of distress tolerance in dysregulated eating behaviors. *International Journal of Eating Disorders, 40*, 718-726.

Anestis, M.D., Selby, E.A., and Joiner, T.E. (2007a). The role of urgency in maladaptive Behaviors. *Behaviour Research and Therapy, 45*, 3018-3029.

Annis, H. M. (1982). *Inventory of Drinking Situations (IDS-100).* Toronto, Ontario, Canada: Addition Research Foundation of Ontario.

Bagby, R.M., Joffe, R.T., Parker, J.D.A., and Schuller, D.R. (1993). Re-examination of the evidence for the DSM-III personality disorder clusters. *Journal of Personality Disorders, 7*, 320-328.

Barbas, H. (2007). Specialized elements of orbitofrontal cortex in primates. *Linking Affect to Action: Critical Contributions of the Orbitofrontal Cortex: 1121*, 10-32.

Barratt, E.S. (1993). Impulsivity: integrating cognitive, behavioral, biological, and environmental data. In W. McCowan, J. Johnson, and M. Shure, *The impulsive client: theory, research, and treatment.* Washington, DC: American Psychological Association.

Bechara, A. (2004) The role of emotion in decision-making: Evidence from neurological patients with orbitofrontal damage. *Brain and Cognition, 55*, 30-40.

Bechara, A. (2005). Decision making, impulse control and loss of willpower to resist drugs: a neurocognitive perspective. *Nature Neuroscience, 8* 1458-1463.

Bechara, A., Damasio, A., Damasio, H., and Anderson, S. W. (1994). Insensitivity to future consequences following damage to human prefrontal cortex. *Cognition, 50*, 7–15.

Bechara, A., Tranel, D., Damasio, H., and Damasio, A. R. (1996). Failure to respond autonomically to anticipated future outcomes following damage to prefrontal cortex. *Cerebral Cortex, 6*, 215–225.

Bickel, W. K. and Marsch, L. A. (2001). Toward a behavioral economic understanding of drug dependence: Delay discounting processes. *Addiction, 96*, 73–86.

Billieux, J., Rochat, L., Rebetez, M.M.L., and Van der Linden, M. (2008). Are all facets of impulsivity related to self-reported compulsive buying behavior? *Personality and Individual Differences, 44*, 1432-1442.

Block, J. (1995). A contrarian view of the five-factor approach to personality description. *Psychological Bulletin, 117*, 187-215.

Bremner, J. D., Staib, L. H., Kaloupek, D., Southwick, S. M., Soufer, R., and Charney, D. S. (1999). Neural correlates of exposure to traumatic pictures and sound in Vietnam combat veterans with and without posttraumatic stress disorder: A positron emission tomography study. *Biological Psychiatry, 45*, 806–816.

Buss, A. H., and Plomin, R. (1975). A temperament theory of personality development. New York: John Wiley and Sons.

Campbell, D.T. and Fiske, D.W. (1959). Convergent and discriminant validation by the multitrait-Multimethod matrix. *Psychological Bulletin, 56*, 81-105.

Cardinal, R. N., and Everitt, B. J. (2004). Neural and psychological mechanisms underlying appetitive learning: Links to drug addiction. *Current Opinion in Neurobiology, 14*, 156–162.

Cardinal, R. N., Parkinson, J. A., Hall, J., and Everitt, B. J. (2002). Emotion and motivation: The role of the amygdala, ventral striatum, and prefrontal cortex. *Neuroscience and Biobehavioral Reviews, 26*, 321-352.

Castellani, B., and Rugle, L. (1995). A comparison of pathological gamblers to alcoholics and cocaine misusers on impulsivity, sensation seeking, and craving, *The International Journal of the Addictions*, 30, 275–289.

Cin, S. D., MacDonald, T. K., Fong, G. T., Zanna, M. P., and Elton-Marshal, T. E. (2006). Remembering the message: The use of a reminder cue to increase condom use following a safer sex intervention. *Health Psychology, 25*, 438-443.

Cloninger, C. R., Przybeck, T. R., and Svrakic, D. M. (1991). The Tridimensional Personality Questionnaire: US normative data. *Psychological Reports, 69*, 1047-1057.

Cloninger, C. R., Svrakic, D. M., and Przybeck, T. R. (1993). A psychobiological model of temperament and character. *Archives of General Psychiatry, 50*, 975-990.

Clyne, C., and Blampied, N. M. (2004). Training in emotion regulation as a treatment for binge eating: A preliminary study. *Behaviour Change, 21*, 269-281.

Cools, R., Blackwell, A., Clark, L., Menzies, L., Cox, S., and Robbins, T. W. (2005). Tryptophan depletion disrupts the motivational guidance of goals-directed behavior as a function of trait impulsivity. *Neuropsychopharmacology, 30*, 1362–1373.

Cooper, M.L. (1994). Motivations for alcohol use among adolescents: Development and validation of a Four factor model. *Psychological Assessment, 6*, 117-128.

Cooper, M. L., Agocha, V.B., and Sheldon, M.S. (2000). A motivational perspective on risky behaviors: the role of personality and affect regulatory processes. *Journal of Personality, 68*, 1059-1088.

Costa, P. T., and McCrae, R. R. (1992). Revised NEO personality inventory manual. Odessa, FL: Psychological Assessment Resources.

Cyders, M. A., Flory, K., Rainer, S., and Smith, G. T. (2009). The role of personality dispositions to risky behavior in predicting first year college drinking. *Addiction, 104*, 193-202.

Cyders, M.A. and Smith, G.T. (2007). Mood-based rash action and its components: positive and negative urgency. *Personality and Individual Differences, 43*, 839-850.

Cyders, M.A. and Smith, G.T. (2008b). Clarifying the role of personality dispositions in risk for increased gambling behavior. *Personality and Individual Differences, 45*, 503-508.

Cyders, M. A., and Smith, G. T. (2008a). An emotion-based disposition to rash action: The trait of urgency. *Psychological Bulletin, 134*, 807-828.

Cyders, M.A., Smith, G.T., Spillane, N.S., Fischer, S., Annus, A.M., and Peterson, C. (2007). Integration of impulsivity and positive mood to predict risky behavior: development and validation of a measure of positive urgency. *Psychological Assessment, 19,* 107-118.

Cyders, M. A., Zapolski, T. B., Combs, J., Fried, R., Fillmore, M., and Smith, G. T. (2008). Positive emotion and urgency and their relations to alcohol consumption and gambling behaviors for college students. Manuscript submitted for publication.

Damasio, H., Grabowski, T. J., Frank, R., Galaburda, A. M., and Damasio, A. R. (1994). The return of Phineas Gage: Clues about the brain from the skull of a famous patient. *Science, 264*, 1102–1105.

Daruna, J.H. and Barnes, P.A. (1993). A neurodevelopmental view of impulsivity. In McCown, W.G., Johnson, J.L. and M.B. Shure (eds.), The impulsive client: theory, research and treatment. American Psychological Association, Washington, D.C.

Davidson, R. J. (2003). Darwin and the neural basis of emotion and affective style. *Annals of the New York Academy of Science*, 1000, 316–336.

Depue, R.A., (1995). Neurobiolological factors in personality and depression. *European Journal of Personality, 9*, 413–439.

Depue, R. A., and Collins, P. F. (1999). Neurobiology of the structure of personality: DA, facilitation of incentive motivation, and extraversion. *Behavioral and Brain Sciences, 22*, 491–569.

Devinsky, O., Morrel, M. J., and Vogt, B. A. (1995). Contributions of anterior cingulate cortex to behaviour. *Brain: A Journal of Neurology, 118*, 279–306.

Dolan, R. J. (2007). The human amygdale and orbital prefrontal cortex in behavioural regulation. *Philosophical Transactions of the Royal Society B-Biological Sciences, 362*, 787-799.

Dreisbach, G. (2006). How positive affect modulates cognitive control: The costs and benefits of reduced maintenance capability. *Brian and Cognition, 60*, 11-19.

Dreisbach, G., and Goschke, T. (2004). How positive affect modulated cognitive control: reduced perseveration at the cost of increased distractibility. *Journal of Experimental Psychology – Learning Memory and Cognition, 30*, 343-353.

Edwards, J. R. (2001). Multidimensional constructs in organizational behavior research: An integrative analytical framework. *Organizational Research Methods, 4*, 144–192.

Etheridge, R. M., Hubbard, R. L., Anderson, J., Craddock, S. G., and Flynn, P. M. (1997). Treatment structure and program services in the drug abuse treatment outcome study (DATOS). *Psychology of Addictive Behaviors, 11*, 244-260.

Evenden, J. (1999). Impulsivity: A discussion of clinical and experimental findings. *Journal of Psychopharmacology, 13*, 180-192.

Eysenck, H. J., and Eysenck, S. B. G. (1968). Manual of the Eysenck Personality Inventory. San Diego: Educational and Industrial Testing Service.

Eysenck, S.G.B., and Eysenck, H.J. (1977). The place of impulsiveness in a dimensional system of personality disposition. *British Journal of Social and Clinical Psychology, 16*, 57-68.

Eysenck, H. J., and Eysenck, M. W. (1985). Personality and individual differences: a natural science approach. New York: Plenum Press.

Fischer, S. and Smith, G.T. (2004). Deliberation affects risk taking beyond sensation seeking. *Personality and Individual Differences, 36*, 527-537.

Fischer, S., and Smith, G. T. (2009). Binge eating, problem drinking, and pathological gambling: Linking behavior to shared traits and social learning. *Personality and Individual Differences, 44*, 789-800.

Fischer, S., Anderson, K. G., and Smith, G. T. (2004). Coping with distress by eating or drinking: The role of trait urgency and expectancies. *Psychology of Addictive Behaviors, 18*, 269–274

Fischer, S., Smith, G. T., and Anderson, K. G. (2003a). Clarifying the role of impulsivity in bulimia nervosa. *International Journal of Eating Disorders, 33*, 406–411.

Fischer, S., Smith, G. T., Anderson, K. G., and Flory, K. (2003). Expectancy influences the operation of personality on behavior. *Psychology of Addictive Behaviors, 2*, 108-114.

Fischer, S., Smith, G.T., Annus, A., and Hendricks, M. (2007). The relationship of neuroticism and urgency to negative consequences of alcohol uses in women with bulimic symptoms.

Fischer, S., Smith, G. T., and Cyders, M. A. (2008). Another look at impulsivity: A meta-analytic
review of types of impulsivity and bulimic symptoms. *Clinical Psychology Review, 28*, 1413-1425.

Forgas, J. P. (1992). Affect in social judgments and decisions: A multiprocess model. In M. Zanna (Ed.), *Advances in experimental social psychology.* (pg. 227-275). San Diego, CA: Academic Press.

Forgas, J. P., and Bower, G. H. (1987). Mood effects on person-perception judgments. *Journal of Personality and Social Psychology, 53*, 53-60.

Frankle, W. G., Lombardo, I., New, A. S., Goodman, M., Talbot, P .S., Huang, Y., et al. (2005). Brain 5HT transporter distribution in subjects with impulsive aggressivity: A positron emission study with [1C]McN 5652. *American Journal of Psychiatry, 162,* 915–923

Gleicher, F., and Weary, G. (1991). Effect of depression on quantity and quality of social inferences. *Journal of Personality and Social Psychology, 61,* 105-114.

Grant, J. E., Kushner, M. G., and Kim, S. (2002). Pathological gambling and alcohol use disorder. *Alcohol Research and Health, 26,* 143–150.

Gray, J.A. (1970). The psychophysiological basis of introversion-extroversion. *Behaviour Research and Therapy, 8,* 249-266.

Gray, J.A. (1987). Perspectives on anxiety and impulsivity: A commentary. *Journal of Research in Personality, 21,* 493-509.

Hajcak, G., Molnar, C., George, M. S., Bolger, K., Koola, J., and Nahas Z. (2007). Emotion facilitates action: A transcranial magnetic stimulation study of motor cortex excitability during picture viewing. *Psychophysiology, 44,* 91–97.

Hough, L. M., and Schneider, R. J. (1995). Personality traits, taxonomies, and applications in organizations. In K. R. Murphy (Ed.), *Individuals and Behavior in Organizations* (pp. 31–88). San Francisco, CA: Josey-Bass.

Hohlstein, L. A., Smith, G. T., and Atlas, J. G. (1998). An application of expectancy theory to eating disorders: Development and validation of measures of eating and dieting expectancies. *Psychological Assessment, 10,* 49–58.

Holderness, C. C., Brooks-Gunn, J., and Warren, M. P. (1994). Co-morbidity of eating disorders and substances abuse: Review of the literature. *International Journal of Eating Disorders, 16,* 1–34.

Holub, A., Hodgins, D. C., and Peden, N. E. (2005). Development of the temptations for gambling questionnaire: A measure of temptation in recently quit gamblers. *Addiction Research and Theory,* 13, 179-191.

Horan, J. J. and Johnson, R. G. (1971). Coverant conditioning through a self-management application of the premack principle: Its effects on weight reduction. *Journal of Behaviour Therapy and Experimental Psychiatry, 2,* 243-249.

Krakowski, M. (2003). Violence and 5HT: Influence of impulse control, affect regulation, and social functioning. *Journal of Neuropsychiatry and Clinical Neurosciences, 15,* 294–305.

Larimer, M. E., Palmer, R. S., and Marlatt, G. A. (1999). Relapse prevention: An overview of Marlatt's cognitive-behavioral model. *Alcohol Research and Health, 23,* 151-160.

Leamon, M. H., Wright, T. M., and Myrick, H. (2008). Substance related disorders. In R. E. Hales, S. C. Yudofsky, and G. O. Gabbard (Eds.) *The American Psychiatric Publishing Textbook of Psychiatry.* (pp. 365-706). New York: American Psychiatric Pub.

Lewis, M. D., and Todd, R. M. (2007). The self-regulating brain: Cortical-subcortical feedback and the development of intelligent action. *Cognitive Development, 22,* 406-430.

Linehan, M. M. (1993). *Cognitive-behavioral treatment of borderline personality disorder.* New York: Guilford Press.

Marlatt, G. A. and Gordon, J. R., (1985). *Relapse prevention: Maintenance strategies in the treatment of addictive behaviors.* New York: Guilford Press.

Masten, A.S., Neemann, J., and Andenas, S. (1994). Life events and adjustment in adolescents: The significance of event independence, desirability, and chronicity. *Journal of Research on Adolescence, 4*, 71-97.

McCrae, R.R., and Costa, P.T. Jr (1990). *Personality in Adulthood.* New York: Guilford.

McGrath, R. E. (2005). Conceptual complexity and construct validity. *Journal of PersonalityAssessment, 85,* 112-124.

McGrath, R. E. (2007). Toward validity. Manuscript submitted for publication.

Miller, J., Flory, K., Lynam, D., and Leukefeld, C. (2003). A test of the four-factor model of impulsivity-related traits. *Personality and Individual Differences, 34,* 1403-1418.

Morgan, M. J., Impallomeni, L. C., Pirona, A., and Rogers, R. D. (2006). Elevated impulsivity and impaired decision-making in abstinent ecstasy (MDMA) users compared to polydrug and drug-naive controls. *Neuropsychopharmacology, 31,* 1562–1573.

Muraven, M., and Baumeister, R. F. (2000). Self-regulation and depletion of limited resources: Does self-control resemble a muscle? *Psychological Bulletin, 126,* 247–259.

Nygren, T. E., Isen, A. M., Taylor, P. J., and Dulin, J. (1996). The influence of positive affect on the decision rule in risk situations: Focus on outcome (and especially avoidance of loss) rather than probability. *Organizational Behavior and Human Decision Processes, 66,* 59-72.

Patterson, M. C., and Newman, J. P. (1993). Reflectivity and learning from aversive events: Toward a psychological mechanism for the syndromes of disinhibition. *Psychological Review, 100,* 716–736.

Patton, J.H., Stanford, M.S., and Barratt, E.S. (1995). Factor structure of the Barratt impulsiveness scale. *Journal of Clinical Psychology, 51,* 768-774.

Peterson, C. B., and Mitchell, J. E. (1999). Psychosocial and pharmacological treatment of eating disorders: A review of research findings. *Journal of Clinical Psychology, 55,* 685-697.

Petry, N. (2001). Substance abuse, pathological gambling, and impulsiveness. *Drug and Alcohol Dependence, 63,* 29-38.

Rauch, S., van der Kolk, B. A., Fisler, R., Alpert, N. M., Orr, S. P., and Savage, C. R. (1996). A symptom provocation study of posttraumatic stress disorder using positron emission tomography and script-driven imagery. *Archives of General Psychiatry, 53,* 380-387.

Reed, M.A., and Derryberry, D. (2005). Temperament and response processing- Facilitatory and inhibitory consequences of positive and negative motivational states. *Journal of Research in Personality, 29,* 59-84.

Robins, C. J., and Chapman, A. L. (2004). Dialectical behavior therapy: Current status, recent developments, and future directions. *Journal of Personality Disorders, 18,* 73-89.

Romano, J. L. and Hage, S. M. (2000). Prevention and counseling psychology: Revitalizing commitments for the 21st century. *The Counseling Psychologist, 28,* 733-763.

Schneider, R. J., Hough, L. M., and Dunnette, M. D. (1996). Broadsided by broad traits: How to sink science in five dimensions or less. *Journal of Organizational Behavior, 17,* 639–655.

Shiv, B., Loewenstein, G., and Bechara, A. (2005). The dark side of emotion in decision-making: When individuals with decreased emotional reactions make more advantageous decisions. *Cognitive Brain Research, 23,* 85-92.

Slovic, P., Finucane, M. L., Peters, E., and MacGregor, D. G. (2004). Risk as analysis and risk as feelings: Some thoughts about affect, reason, risk, and rationality. *Risk Analysis, 24,* 311-322.

Smith, G.T., Fischer, S., Cyders, M.A., Annus, A.M., Spillane, N.S., and McCarthy, D.M. (2007). On the validity and utility of discriminating among impulsivity-like traits. *Assessment, 14,* 155-170.

Smith, G. T., Fischer, S., and Fister, S. M. (2003). Incremental validity principles of test construction. *Psychological Assessment, 15,* 467–477.

Smith, G. T., and McCarthy, D. M. (1995). Methodological considerations in the refinement of clinical assessment instruments. *Psychological Assessment, 7,* 300–308.

Smith, G. T., McCarthy, D. M., and Zapolski, T. B. (2007b). Elemental constructs and descriptive hierarchies: Toward increased validity of measurement and theory. Manuscript submitted for publication.

Smyth, J. M., Wonderlich, S. A., Heron, K. E., Sliwinski, M. J., Crosby, R. D., Mitchell, J. E., et al. (2007). Daily and momentary mood and stress are associated with binge eating and vomiting in bulimia nervosa patients in the natural environment. *Journal of Consulting and Clinical Psychology, 75,* 629-638.

Spear, L. P. (2000). Neurobehavioral changes in adolescence. *Current Directions in Psychological Science, 9,* 111–114.

Spinella, M. (2007).The role of prefrontal systems in sexual behavior. *International Journal of Neuroscience, 117,* 369–385.

Spoont, M. R. (1992). Modulatory role of 5HT in neural information processing: Implications for human psychopathology. *Psychological Bulletin, 112,* 330–350.

Stuettgen, M. C., Hennig, J., Reuter, M., and Netter, P. (2005). Novelty seeking but not BAS is associated with high DA as indicated by a neurotransmitter challenge test using mazindol as a challenge substance. *Personality and Individual Differences, 38,* 1597–1608.

Tellegen, A. (1982). *Multidimensional Personality Questionnaire manual.* Minneapolis, MN: University of Minnesota Press.

Tellegen, A. (1985). Structure of mood and personality and their relevance to assessing anxiety, with an emphasis on self-report. In A. H. Tuma, and J. D. Maser, *Anxiety and the anxiety disorders* (pp. 681-706). Minneapolis, MN: University of Minnesota Press.

Tice, D. M., and Bratslavsky, E. (2000). Giving in to feel good: The place of emotion regulation in the context of general self-control. *Psychological Inquiry, 11,* 149–59.

Tice, D. M., Bratslavsky, E., and Baumeister, R. F. (2001). Emotional distress regulation takes precedence over impulse control: If you feel bad, do it! *Journal of Personality and Social Psychology, 80,* 53–67.

Whiteside, S.P. and Lynam, D.R. (2001). The five factor model and impulsivity: using a structural model of personality to understand impulsivity. *Personality and Individual Differences, 30,* 669-689.

Whiteside, S.P. and Lynam, D.R. (2003). Understanding the role of impulsivity and externalizing Psychopathology in alcohol abuse: Applications of the UPPS impulsive behavior scale. *Experimental and Clinical Psychopharmacology, 11,* 210-217.

Whiteside, S.P., Lynam, D.R., Miller, J.D. and Reynolds, S.K. (2005). Validation of the UPPS Impulsive Behavior scale: A four-factor model of impulsivity. *European Journal of Personality, 19*, 559-574.

Winstanley, C. A., Dalley, J. W., Theobald, D. E. H., and Robbins, T. W. (2004). Fractionating impulsivity: Contrasting effects of central 5-HT depletion on different measures of impulsive behavior. *Neuropsychopharmacology, 29*, 1331–1343

Winstanley, C. A., Eagle, D. M., and Robbins, T. W. (2006). Behavioral models of impulsivity in relation to ADHD: Translation between clinical and preclinical studies. *Clinical Psychology Review, 26*, 379–395.

Winstanley, C. A., Theobald, D. E. H., Dalley, J. W., Glennon, J. C., and Robbins, T. W. (2004). 5-HT$_{2A}$ and 5-HT$_{2C}$ receptor antagonists have opposing effects on a measure of impulsivity: Interactions with global 5-HT depletion. *Psychopharmacology, 176*, 376–385.

Wright, W. F., and Bower, G. H. (1992). Mood effects on subjective-probability assessment. *Organizational Behavior and Human Decision Processes, 52*, 276-291

Yuen, K.S., and Lee, T.M.C. (2003). Could mood state affect risk-taking decisions? *Journal of Affective Disorders, 75*, 11-18.

Zald, D.H., and Depue, R.A. (2001). Serotonergic functioning correlates with positive and negative affect in psychiatrically healthy males. *Personality and Individual Differences, 30*, 71–86.

Zapolski, T.C.B., Annus, A.M., Fried, R.E., Combs, J.L., and Smith, G.T. (2008, July). Disaggregating impulsivity traits in children. Paper presented at the annual meeting of the Research Society on Alcoholism, Washington D.C.

Zapolski, T.C.B., Cyders, M.A., and Smith, G.T. (2009). Positive urgency predicts illegal drug use, risky sexual behavior, and smoking. *Psychology of Addictive Behaviors, 23*, 348-354.

Zermatten, A., and Van der Linden, M. (2008). Impulsivity in non-clinical persons with obsessive-compulsive symptoms. *Personality and Individual Differences, 44*, 1824-1830.

Zuckerman, M., Kuhlman, D. M., Joireman, J., Teta, P., and Kraft, M. (1993). A comparison of three structural models of personality: the big three, the big five, and the alternative five. *Journal of Personality and Social Psychology, 65*, 757-768.

Zuckerman, M., Kuhlman, D. M., Thornquist, M., and Kiers, H. (1991). Five (or three) robust questionnaire scale factors of personality without culture. *Personality and Individual Differences, 12*, 929-941.

In: Impulsivity: Causes, Control and Disorders
Editor: George H. Lassiter

ISBN 978-1-60741-951-8
© 2009 Nova Science Publishers, Inc.

Chapter VI

Genetics Basis of Impulsivity: The Role Serotoninergic and Dopaminergic Genes

Laura Mandelli
Institute of Psychiatry, University of Bologna, Italy

Abstract

The aim of the present chapter is to summarize the current knowledge of genetic basis of impulsive behaviours, which occur across several neuropsychiatric disorders. Impulsivity most frequently characterizes attention-deficit/hyperactivity disorder, substance abuse, binge eating, personality disorders, suicidal behavior, with important ramifications for everyday functioning and quality of life.

The existence of a genetic component and inheritance of impulsivity has been largely demonstrated in families and twins studies. Moreover, in the last years, molecular genetic studies have considerably increased, reporting several positive associations between genetic variants and impulsivity, particularly in regard to genes involved in serotonin and dopaminergic pathways. Indeed, the role of serotonin in impulsivity is well recognized and dopamine system is the neuronal substrate mediating behavioural inhibition.

However, the concept of impulsivity covers a wide range of "actions that are poorly conceived, prematurely expressed, unduly risky, or inappropriate to the situation and that often result in undesirable outcomes" and may be thus made up of several independent factors.

Though varieties of impulsivity, inconsistency in definition and measure, in different psychiatric and non-psychiatric conditions, in the present chapter we will review genes most consistently associated with impulsivity in both healthy individuals and patients affected by major psychiatric or personality disorders.

The Role of Serotonin and Dopamine in Impulsive Behaviour

Impulsivity is a multidimensional concept that involves the tendency to act quickly and without reflection, being unrestrained, having difficulty to handle different emotions and delay gratification. Impulsive behavior has a significant implication on several forms of psychopathology, such as attention deficit hyperactivity disorder (ADHD), suicide, substance abuse, personality disorders and antisociality [1]. By this recognition, research related to biological and genetic bases of impulsivity has noticeably increased in the last years.

Earlier studies implicate deficits in serotoninergic function and impaired frontal lobe function in impulsive behavior [2]. The role of frontal cortex in impulsive behavior is well established [3]. People with frontal lobe lesions are more impulsive compared to both normal controls and people with other brain damage. Recently, medication-naïve adolescents with ADHD have been reported showing abnormally reduced brain activation in the right inferior frontal gyrus during a response inhibition task [4]. Serotoninergic neurons project from the raphe throughout the brain to diverse regions, including prefrontal cortex. Loss of impulse control may be thus due to chemical-induced alterations in frontal cortex, other than anatomical damage.

A first evidence of an involvement of serotonin system in impulsivity come from the original work of Soubriè in 1986 [5], reporting that treatments that reduce serotonin (5-HT) activity, significantly attenuate punishment-induced inhibition of behavior. However, since the effect was not limited to reinforced behavior, Soubriè proposed a role for serotonin in impulse control, not limited to punishment or reward. Many other subsequent animal and human studies found support for this hypothesis.

A second source of evidence comes from clinical works, following the work of Asberg et al. [6] that reported patients who committed suicide by impulsive and violent means having lower levels of the 5-HT metabolite 5-hydroxyindole-acetic acid (5-HIAA) in the cerebrospinal fluid than patients committing suicide by poisoning. The reader can find more information about the role of serotonin and impulsive behavior in Lesch et al. [7].

More recently, several studies demonstrate that also modulation of dopamine (DA) levels as well as dopaminergic areas in the brain affect impulsive choice behavior. For instance, systemic administration of D1/D2 antagonists increases impulsive choice behavior [8]. At the opposite, administration of dopaminergic agonists (psychostimulants) promotes self-controlled response [9], though the promoting effect of either impulsivity or self-control of psychostimulants may be dependent on the dose level of the drug [10].

Dopamine innervates frontostriatal and limbic-striatal brain circuits, which are involved in motivated and goal-directed behaviour. Failures of behavioural control may also result from abnormal motivational processes that implicate the ventral striatum, which is moreover strongly connected with ventral/medial regions of prefrontal cortex. It has been shown that high-impulsive individuals respond faster in anticipation of reward and exhibit greater neural activity in the ventral striatum during reward than do low-impulsive subjects [11]. The role of dopamine in behavioural control has been recently reviewed by Cools [12].

Variations in genes regulating 5-HT and DA circuits may account for a large proportion of individual dissimilarity in behavioural control and risk for impulsive-related disorders. To date, a large number of studies investigated serotoninergic and dopaminergic genes, as well as genes involved in other systems such as GABAergic, cholinergic and noradrenergic, mainly focusing on impulsive-related disorders, particularly ADHD and substance abuse. Only recently, genetic investigation has addressed impulsivity as a trait underlying different diagnostic categories.

We will firstly summarize the evidence of the involvement of genetic factors in impulsive-related traits as demonstrated by studies on families and twins briefly discussing some methodological issues. Subsequently, we will review the genes most consistently associated with impulsiveness focusing on genes regulating 5-HT and DA systems.

Is Impulsiveness Genetically Inherited?

In order to determine the genetic influence of complex traits, which are likely caused by a set of genes probably in reciprocal interaction and subjected to epigenetic and environmental factors, two combined approaches do exist. The former is the so called "Formal Genetics", based on families, twin, and adoption studies, which aims to suggest the degree to which illness is familial in the population. Such studies are a first compulsory step to initiate more complex genetic investigations, based on modern "Molecular Genetics" techniques and aimed to find genes variations potentially involved in the pathophysiology of the illnesses.

If a disease has a genetic basis, it is expected to aggregate in families. *Family studies* assess whether family members of affected individuals have high rates of the illness as compared to non-related individuals. By *Twin studies*, it is possible to calculate "heritability", which is a measure of the influence of genetic factors on disease liability as compared to other environmental factors. This aim is achieved by comparing the risk of being affected in monozygotic (MZ) and dizygotic (DZ) twins, which share the same environment but respectively 100% and 50% of their genome. However, environmental issues may bias twin studies, since cultural influences may account for a proportion of observed concordance. *Adoptions studies* or studies comparing on twins reared apart or together are designed to overcome this bias.

By these methods of investigation, it has been estimated that about 30-40% of impulsiveness is explained by genetic factors. First evidence came from a study of Matekunas et al. [13], which reported a correlation ranging from 0.21 to 0.39 in the performance on a behavioural task measuring impulsiveness between 10-years old children and their mothers. Following, Plomin et al. [14] performed the first twin study in order to evaluate heritability of impulsive behaviour. Fifty-four pairs of twins (32 identical and 22 fraternal) were evaluated by a behavioural task measuring response time and errors by the Kagan's Matching Familiar Figures (MFF), a widely employed measure of "reflection-impulsivity" [15]. Re-test after training to impulse control was performed on a sample of twin control pairs in order to evaluate stability of impulsiveness. Scores on test-retest measures of reflection-impulsivity showed no indication that impulse control training was associated with a reduction in impulsivity. The correlation for the identical twins was greater than the correlation for the fraternal twins for MFF latency (respectively 0.77 and 0.54) and errors (respectively 0.48 and

0.36). Heritability estimates for MFF latency ranged from 0.42 and 0.48, suggesting that over 40% of the variance in impulsivity may be due to genetic factors.

A third study [16] was performed on 137 families with 60 identical twins and 77 dizygotic twins evaluated by the Emotionality, activity, sociability and Impulsivity (EASI) Temperament survey [17]. For all scales including impulsiveness, homozygous twins were more similar than dizygotic ones with an average correlation of 0.55 for identical vs. 0.07 for fraternal. Parent-child correlations were also consistent with the hypothesis that impulsive traits have a genetic component, though with a comparable influence observed among dizygotic twins of about 0.13. In a following study, Pedersen et al. [18] evaluated the heritability for neuroticism, extraversion, impulsivity, and monotony avoidance in a large sample of twins both reared apart and together. It was estimated that from 23% to 45% of the total variation was attributable to genetic sources, while shared environment accounted for less than 10% of the variance.

Another source of evidence came from a study by Mattes and Fink in 1987 [19], focused on the personality trait of "having temper outbursts" and associated diagnoses. Result of the study indicated familial transmission of temper problems: an average of 18.2% of probands' relatives had temper problems, compared to 4.3% of relatives of individuals without temper outbursts. Interestingly, the trait of having temper outbursts was more strongly transmitted than were specific diagnoses associated with temper outbursts (e.g. Intermittent Explosive Disorder, Antisocial Personality Disorder or Attention Deficit Disorder).

Coccaro et al. [20] investigated the heritability of self-reported personality traits related to impulsiveness, irritability and behavioral inhibition in 500 healthy monozygotic and dizygotic twin pairs raised together or apart. Results of the study were consistent with a genetic, but not a shared environmental influence for the factor "impulsive irritability".

Confirmatory evidence of a genetic contribution to impulsive behavior also came from studies on animals. Fairbanks et al. [21] investigated 352 adolescent and adult vervet monkeys for a standardized test that measures impulsivity and aggressiveness toward a stranger. A significant genetic contribution to social impulsivity was found, with no significant influence of maternal environment. In mice, not only a substantial genetic contribution to impulsiveness was confirmed, but also the existence of common genetic factors influencing both impulsivity and locomotor activity, further suggesting a shared background for impulsiveness and hyperactivity [22]. Finally, a study confirmed the role of genetic factors in impulsive behaviours, by comparing different strains of mice [23].

Genes Associated to Impulsivity

Modern molecular techniques allow to test genetic variations potentially involved in the pathophysiology of a disorder. *Association studies* directly investigate specific genes, looking for difference in alleles' distribution among affected individuals (probands) and healthy controls. The choice of genes to be tested in case-control studies is a matter of great importance. The most commonly employed method of choice is the *"functional candidate approach"*, based on the selection of genes that are thought to be involved in the biological processes implicated in the disease. An alternative approach is based on results coming from

Linkage studies (aimed to find chromosomal areas in which are located genes of liability by testing a large number of markers), by selection of genes that are located in regions associated to the disease, the so called *"positional candidate approach"*.

The study of genetic basis of impulsivity is complicated by some methodological problems that deserve a brief discussion. First, impulsivity as a trait occurs on a continuum and there is accumulating evidence that impulsivity is a multidimensional factor. For instance, impulsive behaviour has been described as composed of two (disinhibition and impulsive decision making) [24], three (non-planning, disinhibition and thrill-Seeking) [25] or four factors (urgency, lack of premeditation, lack of perseverance and sensation seeking) [26]. Corresponding to the variety of views on impulsivity, theorists have developed several different instruments to evaluate impulsiveness, arising thus a problem of comparability across studies. A presumed "objective" evaluation of impulsivity is the measure of time response and errors in behavioural tasks [15], however tasks differ among studies implying the same problem of generalization of findings. Though we will not enter in the detail of procedures employed by each study, the reader should be aware of the problem, which may explain conflicting results obtained in different investigation.

A second important problem is that impulsivity is a contributing feature to psychiatric and behavioural problems such as attention-deficit/hyperactivity disorder, conduct disorder, bipolar disorder, and personality disorders that feature antisocial, violent, and self-destructive behaviour [1]. Impulsive personality is associated with greater risk for alcohol and substance abuse, criminality, and suicide. For this reason, impulsivity is rarely studied in isolation of these other symptoms. Because patients are usually categorized according to one or more related diagnoses, each representing an heterogeneous constellation of symptoms, impulsivity-related behaviours in patients is usually confounded by disease-specific symptomatology.

Table 1. Strength of evidence of association between genes' variants and impulsive related traits

Gene	Strength of evidence
SERT	++
TPH	+++
TPH2	+
5HTR1B	≈
5HTR2A	+++
5HTR2C	+
MAOA	++
COMT	++
DAT	+++
DRD2	++
DRD3	≈
DRD4	++++

Behaviours characterized by a deficit in impulse control have been studied for association with candidate genes mainly in the serotonergic and dopaminergic systems. In the following sections of the chapter, we will summarize the genes that received more consistent association with impulsiveness as regards these two major brain systems. The strength of association between such genes and impulsiveness is summarized in table 1.

Serotonin and Serotoninergic Genes

A widely investigated gene as potentially involved in impulsivity is the one coding for *SEROTONIN TRANSPORTER* (SERT), a protein responsible of the reuptake of serotonin within the pre-synaptic axon, controlling thus the levels of serotonin and the overall serotoninergic system function. SERT has been associated with impulsive-related disorders such as alcoholism [27], suicide [28], violent suicide [29], borderline personality disorder [30], ADHD [31] and aggressive conduct disorder [32].

As regards specifically impulsiveness, a first study found a significant association with early onset alcoholism associated to impulsive violent behaviour (type II alcoholism) [33]. A subsequent study, evaluating patients with a rating scale for impulsiveness did not find a significant association in alcohol dependent patients [34]. Similarly, no association with impulsiveness was found in drug abusers [35], in individuals referred for a forensic psychiatric examination [36] and schizophrenic patients [37]. However, SERT was found associated with impulsiveness in obese women [38] and in borderline patients [39]. In suicide attempters, the association between SERT and impulsiveness is controversial with two positive studies [40, 41] and a negative report [42]. In ADHD patients two study found positive associations with measures of impulsivity [43, 44], while a third study in Asian patients failed confirm the result [45]. Finally, no consensus does exist in bulimic patients, though only two studies could be found [46, 47].

In healthy individuals, one study found no association between SERT and measures of behavioural impulsivity [48], while one study in adolescent-young adults [49] and three in healthy adults [50-52] reported positive findings. Finally, in adolescents, SERT has been shown to influence externalising behaviours, alone and interacting with socio-economic status [53].

In summary, there is a consistent evidence of an involvement of variations within the SERT gene in modulating impulsive behaviours and the risk for impulsive-related psychiatric conditions.

Another widely investigated gene is *TRYPTOPHAN HYDROXYLASE* (TPH), coding for the rate-limiting enzyme in the biosynthesis of serotonin, influencing thus serotonin levels in the brain. TPH has been associated with violent suicide [54], deliberate self-harm [55], early smoking behaviour [56], suicidal borderline patients [57] and alcohol dependence [58].

In an extreme impulsive group composed of alcoholics and violent offenders, TPH genotype was associated with cerebrospinal fluid 5-hydroxyindoleacetic acid (5-HIAA) concentration, the main metabolite of serotonin in the human body [59]. Subsequently, TPH was associated with suicidality in impulsive offenders [60] and impulsive suicide attempters [61, 62], though a fourth study failed to find an association with impulsivity in suicide attempters [40]. In patients presenting after deliberate self-harm the association between impulsivity and TPH genotype is not clear [55, 63], but given the close relationship between self-harm and suicide, a positive influence may be postulated. In a well characterized sample for impulsivity, a positive association with TPH variation was confirmed [64].

Recently, a second tryptophan hydroxylase isoform has been discovered (TPH2), which is mainly expressed in neuronal tissues, in contrast with the classical TPH isoform mostly expressed in peripheral tissues [65]. THP2 has been associated with suicidal risk [66], ADHD [67] and cluster B personality disorders [68]. As regards impulsiveness, a significant association was found with measures of cognitive and aggressive impulsive traits in ADHD patients [44]. In healthy controls, TPH2 was found associated to reaction times in a behavioural task measuring impulsiveness [69]. Due to the recent discovery of this gene, only few studies are available. However, its involvement in impulsive related behaviours and measures of impulsivity suggest TPH2 as a good candidate gene in impulsiveness.

A third interesting serotoninergic gene involved in impulsivity is the one coding for *Serotonin Receptor 2A* (5HTR2A), associated with ADHD [70], bulimia nervosa (71) criminal behaviour [72], anger related traits in community individuals [73] and extraversive traits in borderline patients [74].

A study on alcohol dependent patients reported a significant association between a measure of impulsivity and genotype for 5HTR2A [75]. A similar result was obtained in a sample of bulimic women [76], hyperactive-impulsive ADHD patients [77] and measures of cognitive impulsiveness in a large sample of ADHD children [44]. No clear evidence does exist in impulsive suicide attempters [78-80]. However, in healthy subjects, the 5HTR2A genotype was significantly associated with a behavioural measure of impulsivity [81].

Two other genes coding for serotonin receptors raised some interest in impulsive behaviours. The first encodes for *Serotonin Receptor 1B* (5HTR1B), which was associated with substance abuse [82], ADHD [70] and antisocial alcoholism in two different populations [83], though not found associated with self-reported impulsive aggression in patients with personality disorders [84] and healthy subjects [69]. The relationship with impulsive suicide attempt is controversial [85, 86]

The second interesting gene is the one encoding for *Serotonin Receptor 2C* (5HTR2C), which has been however poorly investigated in impulsive related disorders. One study on patients presenting after deliberate self-harm found a significant association between high levels of impulsivity and 5HTR2C genotype [63]. Accordingly, in a previous study on suicide attempters, we found a slight association between 5HTR2C genotype and impulsive suicide attempt [79].

The Monoamine-oxidase-A Gene

Monoamine oxidase type A gene (MAOA) encodes for an important enzyme responsible of the degradation of various monoamines, including 5-HT, norepinephrine and dopamine (DA). MAOA has been associated with impulsive related traits such as drug abuse and antisocial traits [87], violent suicide [88], ADHD [89] and borderline personality disorder [90].

A first evidence of an involvement of MAOA in impulsivity came from a study reporting a positive association between a region on the short harm of chromosome X, with a maximal pick at the locus of the MAOA gene, and a form of mild mental retardation characterized by aggressive and impulsive behaviour [91]. A study on transgenic mice lacking the MAOA gene corroborated the finding of an increased impulsive aggressiveness [92]. Recently, low platelet monoamine oxidase A activity has been associated with measure of impulsiveness in healthy adolescents [52].

The MAOA genotype was found significantly associated with the emotive-impulsive cluster B personality disorder, though not with specific measures of impulsiveness [93]. The role of MAOA genotype in early-onset impulsive alcoholics (type II) [94, 95] as well as in behavioural measures of impulsivity in ADHD [96, 97] remains controversial and further studies are required to establish its involvement in impulsive traits characteristics of these patients. However, in a large sample of psychiatric patients, the MAOA genotype was significantly associated with impulsive traits in males [98]. Finally, in healthy subjects MAOA was not found associated with behavioural measures of impulsiveness [69], though a subsequent study reported an association with impulsiveness-related traits (novelty-seeking) in women [99].

Dopamine and Dopaminergic Genes

An important role for dopamine (DA) in impulsive behaviour has been inferred from the therapeutic efficacy of some psychostimulant drugs in the treatment of ADHD. Treatment with low doses of apomorphine or dopamine D2 receptor agonists that reduce dopamine neurotransmission or treatment with dopamine receptor antagonists reduced impulsive action [100]. Moreover, alterations in striatal dopaminergic system have been also observed in impulsive-related disorders [101].

A gene that has received great interest is the one coding for DOPAMINE RECEPTOR D4 (DRD4), as it was associated with the personality trait of novelty seeking, which includes an impulsivity dimension [102]. DRD4 has been also associated with impulsive-related disorders such as Tourette's syndrome [103], pathological gambling [104], ADHD [105] and substance abuse [106, 107].

A study on high and low novelty seeking scorers in a community sample found no association between DRD4 with the overall dimension of NS, but positive on the sub-scale of impulsiveness and exploratory excitability [108]; a further investigation reported a positive association with extraversion and hypomania [99]. In psychiatric patients, DRD4 was found strongly associated with the novelty-seeking sub-scale of impulsivity as well [109], and a recent meta-analysis confirmed an involvement of DRD4 genotype in novelty seeking and impulsiveness [110].

Instead, no association with measures of impulsiveness and related traits was observed in adolescent suicide attempters [111]. Similarly, two studies on ADHD patients evaluating impulsivity traits failed to find a significant association with DRD4 genotype [112, 113]. However, a third study on ADHD reported DRD4 associated with an impulsive response style on neuropsychological tasks that, according to the Authors, could not be explained by

ADHD symptom severity [114]. Two others studies suggested an involvement of DRD4 in hyperactive-impulsive ADHD form [115, 116] and a last one found an association with impulsive behavioural aggression [44].

Recently, DRD4 has been associated with impulsivity in children and it has been shown to moderate the effect of maternal styles [117]. In adolescents, DRD4 influenced externalising behaviours, alone and interacting with socio-economic status [53].

Finally, two independent studies on healthy individuals reported positive association with behavioural measures of impulsivity [118, 119].

A second interesting dopaminergic gene is the one coding for DOPAMINE TRANSPORTER (DAT), responsible of the reuptake of dopamine in the pre-synaptic axon. DAT has been associated with ADHD [120], alcoholism [121], drug abuse [122], antisocial behaviour [123], externalising behaviour [124] and Tourette's syndrome [125].

DAT has been associated with impulsiveness as a trait predominantly in samples of ADHD patients but also in a community sample. Two studies on ADHD children reported levels of hyperactive-impulsive symptoms but not inattentive related to DAT genotype [126, 127]; a behavioural measure of impulsiveness has been associated with DAT1 genotype in two other ADHD samples [44, 128], as well as in the large community sample [129].

CATECHOL-O-METHYLTRANSFERASE is a major enzyme participating to the degradation of catecholamines, including dopamine, epinephrine and norepinephrine. The gene coding for this enzyme (COMT) has been associated with ADHD [130], aggressive and antisocial behaviour in schizophrenic patients [131], alcoholism [32], drug abuse [133] and borderline personality disorder [134].

This gene has been associated with ADHD impulsive-hyperactive form in at least two independent studies [130, 135]. In a community sample evaluated for measures of impulsivity, hostility and lifetime aggression history, COMT genotype was found associated with impulsivity and CNS serotonergic responsivity [136]. However, a recent study failed to find an association with measures of impulsivity in suicidal patients [137]. Finally, two other genes coding for dopamine receptors received some interest, particularly the one coding for DOPAMINE RECEPTOR D2 (DRD2), which was found associated with substance abuse [138], obesity [139], smoking, pathological gambling [140], attention-deficit-hyperactivity disorder (ADHD), Tourette's syndrome and other related compulsive behaviours [125]. A first meta-analysis in 1995, confirmed an association of DRD2 and impulsive-additive-compulsive behaviour [141]. More recently, one study on alcohol dependent patients focused on impulsivity traits and found a significant association with DRD2 genotype [142]. A second one performed on a sample of ADHD cocaine dependent individuals reported a similar association with impulsiveness [143]. In healthy volunteers, a positive association was reported on a behavioural measure of impulsivity [118].

DOPAMINE RECEPTOR D3 gene (DRD3) has been less widely investigated. DRD3 was associated with alcohol dependence [144] and drug abuse [145]. In a sample of violent offenders, a significant association between DRD3 and measures of impulsivity has been reported [146]. The same association has been reported in a sample of alcohol dependent men [147], but not in a sample of ADHD cocaine dependent individuals [143]. To our knowledge, no any study on healthy individuals was performed as regards impulsiveness.

Conclusions

A consistent proportion of behavioural control and impulsive-traits is explained by genetic factors, as evidenced by studies on families, twins and adoptee. There is indeed evidence that about 30-40% of the variance in impulsiveness is attributable to genetic factors and is thus heritable.

Compelling evidence has involved serotoninergic and dopaminergic systems in behavioural control and a large number of studies found genetic variations regulating these systems in impulsive-related disorders such as ADHD and substance abuse. Only recently, genetic investigation has focused on impulsiveness as a trait isolated from other symptoms and only few studies strictly focusing on measures of impulsiveness have been performed so far. However, a certain evidence of an involvement of genes coding for 5-HT and DA regulating factors does exist. In particular, studies quite robustly support the involvement Tryptophan hidroxilase gene (TPH), serotonin receptor 2A (5HTR2A), dopamine transporter (DAT) and dopamine receptor D4 (DRD4) in impulsiveness. Other interesting genes are serotonin transporter (SERT), serotonin receptor 2C (5HTR2C), genes coding for the enzymes monoamine oxydase A (MAOA) and cathecol-o-methyl transferase (COMT), and dopamine receptor D2 (DRD2).

Impulsivity is not a unitary construct and the definition and measurement of impulsivity varies widely across studies, thereby limiting attempts to bridge fields of research to reach consilience. However, studies focused on impulsivity as a trait, overcoming diagnostic categories, are warrant, as they could shed light on neurobiological mechanisms underlying such clinically defined disorders. A more comprehensive approach covering multiple methodologies, such as behavioural, genetic and neuroimaging techniques, would be helpful. Some have also proposed an "endophenotype approach", based on the identification of intervening variables more sensitive to the effects of genetic variation, to overcome present methodological limitations [148].

In conclusion, genetic investigation confirms an involvement of serotonin and dopamine systems in impulsive behaviour and related disorders. Genes may explain individual variability in behavioural control and risk for some psychiatric disorders.

References

[1]   Moeller FG, Barratt ES, Dougherty DM, Schmitz JM, Swann AC. Psychiatric aspects of impulsivity. *Am. J. Psychiatry* 2001;158(11):1783-93.

[2]   Evenden J. Impulsivity: a discussion of clinical and experimental findings. *J. Psychopharmacol.* 1999;13(2):180-92.

[3]   Torregrossa MM, Quinn JJ, Taylor JR. Impulsivity, compulsivity, and habit: the role of orbitofrontal cortex revisited. *Biol. Psychiatry* 2008;63(3):253-5.

[4]   Rubia K, Smith AB, Brammer MJ, Toone B, Taylor E. Abnormal brain activation during inhibition and error detection in medication-naive adolescents with ADHD. *Am. J. Psychiatry* 2005;162(6):1067-75.

[5]   Soubriè P. Reconciling the role of central serotonin neurones in human and animal behaviour. *Behav. Brain Sci.* 1986;9:319-364.

[6]   Asberg M, Traskman L, Thoren P. 5-HIAA in the cerebrospinal fluid. A biochemical suicide predictor? *Arch Gen. Psychiatry* 1976;33(10):1193-7.

[7]   Lesch KP, Merschdorf U. Impulsivity, aggression, and serotonin: a molecular psychobiological perspective. *Behav. Sci. Law* 2000;18(5):581-604.

[8]   Evenden J. The pharmacology of impulsive behaviour in rats V: the effects of drugs on responding under a discrimination task using unreliable visual stimuli. *Psychopharmacology* (Berl) 1999;143(2):111-22.

[9]   Richards JB, Sabol KE, de Wit H. Effects of methamphetamine on the adjusting amount procedure, a model of impulsive behavior in rats. *Psychopharmacology* (Berl) 1999;146(4):432-9.

[10] Isles AR, Humby T, Wilkinson LS. Measuring impulsivity in mice using a novel operant delayed reinforcement task: effects of behavioural manipulations and d-amphetamine. *Psychopharmacology* (Berl) 2003;170(4):376-82.

[11] Cools R, Blackwell A, Clark L, Menzies L, Cox S, Robbins TW. Tryptophan depletion disrupts the motivational guidance of goal-directed behavior as a function of trait impulsivity. *Neuropsychopharmacology* 2005;30(7):1362-73.

[12] Cools R. Role of dopamine in the motivational and cognitive control of behavior. *Neuroscientist* 2008;14(4):381-95.

[13] Matekunas M. Parent-child similarity in reflection-impulsivity: Pardue University; 1972.

[14] Plomin R, Willerman L. A cotwin control study and a twin study of reflection-impulsivity in children. *J. Educ. Psychol.* 1975;67(4):537-43.

[15] Kagan J, Pearson L, Welch L. Modifiability of an impulsive tempo. *J. Educ. Psychol.* 1966; 57(6):359-65.

[16] Plomin R. A twin and family study of personality in young children. *J. Psychol.* 1976; 94(2d Half):233-5.

[17] Buss A, Plomin R. Temperament theory of personality development. Nw York: Wiley-Interscience; 1975.

[18] Pedersen NL, Plomin R, McClearn GE, Friberg L. Neuroticism, extraversion, and related traits in adult twins reared apart and reared together. *J. Pers. Soc. Psychol.* 1988;55(6):950-7.

[19] Mattes JA, Fink M. A family study of patients with temper outbursts. *J. Psychiatr Res.* 1987;21(3):249-55.

[20] Coccaro EF, Bergeman CS, McClearn GE. Heritability of irritable impulsiveness: a study of twins reared together and apart. *Psychiatry Res.* 1993;48(3):229-42.

[21] Fairbanks LA, Newman TK, Bailey JN, Jorgensen MJ, Breidenthal SE, Ophoff RA, et al. Genetic contributions to social impulsivity and aggressiveness in vervet monkeys. *Biol. Psychiatry* 2004;55(6):642-7.

[22] Isles AR, Humby T, Walters E, Wilkinson LS. Common genetic effects on variation in impulsivity and activity in mice. *J. Neurosci.* 2004;24(30):6733-40.

[23] Otobe T, Makino J. Impulsive choice in inbred strains of mice. *Behav. Processes* 2004; 67(1):19-26.

[24] Avila C, Cuenca I, Felix V, Parcet MA, Miranda A. Measuring impulsivity in school-aged boys and examining its relationship with ADHD and ODD ratings. *J. Abnorm. Child Psychol.* 2004;32(3):295-304.

[25] Flory JD, Harvey PD, Mitropoulou V, New AS, Silverman JM, Siever LJ, et al. Dispositional impulsivity in normal and abnormal samples. *J. Psychiatr Res.* 2006;2:2.

[26] Whiteside S, Lynam D. The Five Factor Model and impulsivity: Using a structural model of personality to understand impulsivity. *Personality and Individual Differences* 2001; 30((4)):669–689.

[27] Schmidt L, Rommelspacher H, Lesch KP, Sander T. Variants of the dopamine and serotonin transporter genes and alcohol withdrawal vulnerability. *Am. J. Med. Genet.* 1997; 6:621–622.

[28] Du L, Faludi G, Palkovits M, Demeter E, Bakish D, Lapierre YD, et al. Frequency of long allele in serotonin transporter gene is increased in depressed suicide victims. *Biol. Psychiatry* 1999;46(2):196-201.

[29] Courtet P, Baud P, Abbar M, Boulenger JP, Castelnau D, Mouthon D, et al. Association between violent suicidal behavior and the low activity allele of the serotonin transporter gene. *Mol. Psychiatry* 2001;6(3):338-41.

[30] Ni X, Chan K, Bulgin N, Sicard T, Bismil R, McMain S, et al. Association between serotonin transporter gene and borderline personality disorder. *J. Psychiatr Res.* 2006; 40(5):448-53.

[31] Li J, Wang Y, Zhou R, Zhang H, Yang L, Wang B, et al. Association between polymorphisms in serotonin transporter gene and attention deficit hyperactivity disorder in Chinese Han subjects. *Am. J. Med. Genet B Neuropsychiatr Genet* 2007; 144B(1):14-9.

[32] Sakai JT, Young SE, Stallings MC, Timberlake D, Smolen A, Stetler GL, et al. Case-control and within-family tests for an association between conduct disorder and 5HTTLPR. *Am. J. Med. Genet B Neuropsychiatr Genet* 2006;141B(8):825-32.

[33] Hallikainen T, Saito T, Lachman HM, Volavka J, Pohjalainen T, Ryynanen OP, et al. Association between low activity serotonin transporter promoter genotype and early onset alcoholism with habitual impulsive violent behavior. *Molecular Psychiatry* 1999; 4(4):385-388.

[34] Preuss UW, Soyka M, Bahlmann M, Wenzel K, Behrens S, de Jonge S, et al. Serotonin transporter gene regulatory region polymorphism (5-HTTLPR), [3H]paroxetine binding in healthy control subjects and alcohol-dependent patients and their relationships to impulsivity. P*sychiatry Res.* 2000;96(1):51-61.

[35] Patkar AA, Berrettini WH, Hoehe M, Thornton CC, Gottheil E, Hill K, et al. Serotonin transporter polymorphisms and measures of impulsivity, aggression, and sensation seeking among African-American cocaine-dependent individuals. *Psychiatry Res.* 2002; 110(2):103-15.

[36] Retz W, Retz-Junginger P, Supprian T, Thome J, Rosler M. Association of serotonin transporter promoter gene polymorphism with violence: relation with personality disorders, impulsivity, and childhood ADHD psychopathology. *Behav. Sci. Law* 2004; 22(3):415-25.

[37] Bayle FJ, Leroy S, Gourion D, Millet B, Olie JP, Poirier MF, et al. 5HTTLPR polymorphism in schizophrenic patients: Further support for association with violent suicide attempts. *Am. J. Med. Genet* 2003;119B(1):13-7.

[38] Camarena B, Ruvinskis E, Santiago H, Montiel F, Cruz C, Gonzalez-Barranco J, et al. Serotonin transporter gene and obese females with impulsivity. *Mol. Psychiatry* 2002; 7(8):829-30.

[39] Pascual JC, Soler J, Baiget M, Cortes A, Menoyo A, Barrachina J, et al. Association between the serotonin transporter gene and personality traits in borderline personality disorder patients evaluated with Zuckerman-Zuhlman Personality Questionnaire (ZKPQ). *Actas Esp. Psiquiatr* 2007;35(6):382-6.

[40] Courtet P, Picot MC, Bellivier F, Torres S, Jollant F, Michelon C, et al. Serotonin transporter gene may be involved in short-term risk of subsequent suicide attempts. *Biol. Psychiatry* 2004;55(1):46-51.

[41] Baca-Garcia E, Salgado BR, Segal HD, Lorenzo CV, Acosta MN, Romero MA, et al. A pilot genetic study of the continuum between compulsivity and impulsivity in females: the serotonin transporter promoter polymorphism. *Prog. Neuropsychopharmacol. Biol. Psychiatry* 2005;29(5):713-7.

[42] Baca-Garcia E, Vaquero C, Diaz-Sastre C, Garcia-Resa E, Saiz-Ruiz J, Fernandez-Piqueras J, et al. Lack of association between the serotonin transporter promoter gene polymorphism and impulsivity or aggressive behavior among suicide attempters and healthy volunteers. *Psychiatry Res.* 2004;126(2):99-106.

[43] Retz W, Thome J, Blocher D, Baader M, Rosler M. Association of attention deficit hyperactivity disorder-related psychopathology and personality traits with the serotonin transporter promoter region polymorphism. *Neurosci Lett.* 2002;319(3):133-6.

[44] Oades RD, Lasky-Su J, Christiansen H, Faraone SV, Sonuga-Barke EJ, Banaschewski T, et al. The influence of serotonin- and other genes on impulsive behavioral aggression and cognitive impulsivity in children with attention-deficit/hyperactivity disorder (ADHD): Findings from a family-based association test (FBAT) analysis. *Behav. Brain Funct.* 2008;4:48.

[45] Kim SJ, Badner J, Cheon KA, Kim BN, Yoo HJ, Cook E, Jr., et al. Family-based association study of the serotonin transporter gene polymorphisms in Korean ADHD trios. *Am. J. Med. Genet B Neuropsychiatr Genet* 2005;139B(1):14-8.

[46] Steiger H, Joober R, Israel M, Young SN, Ng Ying Kin NM, Gauvin L, et al. The 5HTTLPR polymorphism, psychopathologic symptoms, and platelet [3H-] paroxetine binding in bulimic syndromes. *Int. J. Eat Disord.* 2005;37(1):57-60.

[47] Wonderlich SA, Crosby RD, Joiner T, Peterson CB, Bardone-Cone A, Klein M, et al. Personality subtyping and bulimia nervosa: psychopathological and genetic correlates. *Psychol. Med.* 2005;35(5):649-57.

[48] Clark L, Roiser JP, Cools R, Rubinsztein DC, Sahakian BJ, Robbins TW. Stop signal response inhibition is not modulated by tryptophan depletion or the serotonin transporter polymorphism in healthy volunteers: implications for the 5-HT theory of impulsivity. *Psychopharmacology* (Berl) 2005;182(4):570-8.

[49] Lee JH, Kim HT, Hyun DS. Possible association between serotonin transporter promoter region polymorphism and impulsivity in Koreans. *Psychiatry Res.* 2003; 118(1): 19-24.

[50] Sakado K, Sakado M, Muratake T, Mundt C, Someya T. A psychometrically derived impulsive trait related to a polymorphism in the serotonin transporter gene-linked polymorphic region (5-HTTLPR) in a Japanese nonclinical population: assessment by the Barratt impulsiveness scale (BIS). *Am. J. Med. Genet B Neuropsychiatr Genet* 2003; 121B(1):71-5.

[51] Walderhaug E, Magnusson A, Neumeister A, Lappalainen J, Lunde H, Refsum H, et al. Interactive effects of sex and 5-HTTLPR on mood and impulsivity during tryptophan depletion in healthy people. *Biol. Psychiatry* 2007;62(6):593-9.

[52] Paaver M, Nordquist N, Parik J, Harro M, Oreland L, Harro J. Platelet MAO activity and the 5-HTT gene promoter polymorphism are associated with impulsivity and cognitive style in visual information processing. *Psychopharmacology* (Berl) 2007; 194(4):545-54.

[53] Nobile M, Giorda R, Marino C, Carlet O, Pastore V, Vanzin L, et al. Socioeconomic status mediates the genetic contribution of the dopamine receptor D4 and serotonin transporter linked promoter region repeat polymorphisms to externalization in preadolescence. *Dev. Psychopathol.* 2007;19(4):1147-60.

[54] Abbar M, Courtet P, Bellivier F, Leboyer M, Boulenger JP, Castelhau D, et al. Suicide attempts and the tryptophan hydroxylase gene. *Mol. Psychiatry* 2001;6(3):268-73.

[55] Pooley EC, Houston K, Hawton K, Harrison PJ. Deliberate self-harm is associated with allelic variation in the tryptophan hydroxylase gene (TPH A779C), but not with polymorphisms in five other serotonergic genes. *Psychol. Med.* 2003;33(5):775-83.

[56] Lerman C, Caporaso NE, Bush A, Zheng YL, Audrain J, Main D, et al. Tryptophan hydroxylase gene variant and smoking behavior. *Am. J. Med. Genet* 2001;105(6):518-20.

[57] Zaboli G, Gizatullin R, Nilsonne A, Wilczek A, Jonsson EG, Ahnemark E, et al. Tryptophan hydroxylase-1 gene variants associate with a group of suicidal borderline women. *Neuropsychopharmacology* 2006;31(9):1982-90.

[58] Anghelescu I, Klawe C, Fehr C, Singer P, Schleicher A, Himmerich H, et al. The TPH intron 7 A218C polymorphism and TCI dimension scores in alcohol-dependent patients: hints to nonspecific psychopathology. *Addict. Behav.* 2005;30(6):1135-43.

[59] Nielsen DA, Goldman D, Virkkunen M, Tokola R, Rawlings R, Linnoila M. Suicidality and 5-hydroxyindoleacetic acid concentration associated with a tryptophan hydroxylase polymorphism. *Archives of General Psychiatry* 1994;51(1):34-8.

[60] Nielsen DA, Virkkunen M, Lappalainen J, Eggert M, Brown GL, Long JC, et al. A Tryptophan Hydroxylase Gene Marker For Suicidality and Alcoholism. *Archives of General Psychiatry* 1998;55(7):593-602.

[61] Rotondo A, Schuebel KE, Bergen AW, Aragon R, Virkkunen M, Linnoila M, et al. Identification of four variants in the tryptophan hydroxylase promoter and association to behavior. *Molecular Psychiatry* 1999;4(4):360-368.

[62] Galfalvy H, Huang YY, Oquendo MA, Currier D, Mann JJ. Increased risk of suicide attempt in mood disorders and TPH1 genotype. *J. Affect Disord.* 2008.

[63] Evans J, Reeves B, Platt H, Leibenau A, Goldman D, Jefferson K, et al. Impulsiveness, serotonin genes and repetition of deliberate self-harm (DSH). *Psychol. Med.* 2000; 30(6):1327-34.

[64] Staner L, Uyanik G, Correa H, Tremeau F, Monreal J, Crocq MA, et al. A dimensional impulsive-aggressive phenotype is associated with the A218C polymorphism of the tryptophan hydroxylase gene: a pilot study in well-characterized impulsive inpatients. *Am. J. Med. Genet* 2002;114(5):553-7.

[65] Walther DJ, Peter JU, Bashammakh S, Hortnagl H, Voits M, Fink H, et al. Synthesis of serotonin by a second tryptophan hydroxylase isoform. *Science* 2003;299(5603):76.

[66] Zill P, Buttner A, Eisenmenger W, Moller HJ, Bondy B, Ackenheil M. Single nucleotide polymorphism and haplotype analysis of a novel tryptophan hydroxylase isoform (TPH2) gene in suicide victims. *Biol. Psychiatry* 2004;56(8):581-6.

[67] Sheehan K, Lowe N, Kirley A, Mullins C, Fitzgerald M, Gill M, et al. Tryptophan hydroxylase 2 (TPH2) gene variants associated with ADHD. *Mol. Psychiatry* 2005; 10(10):944-9.

[68] Gutknecht L, Jacob C, Strobel A, Kriegebaum C, Muller J, Zeng Y, et al. Tryptophan hydroxylase-2 gene variation influences personality traits and disorders related to emotional dysregulation. *Int. J. Neuropsychopharmacol.* 2007;10:309-320.

[69] Stoltenberg SF, Glass JM, Chermack ST, Flynn HA, Li S, Weston ME, et al. Possible association between response inhibition and a variant in the brain-expressed tryptophan hydroxylase-2 gene. *Psychiatr Genet* 2006;16(1):35-8.

[70] Hawi Z, Dring M, Kirley A, Foley D, Kent L, Craddock N, et al. Serotonergic system and attention deficit hyperactivity disorder (ADHD): a potential susceptibility locus at the 5-HT(1B) receptor gene in 273 nuclear families from a multi-centre sample. *Mol. Psychiatry* 2002;7(7):718-25.

[71] Nishiguchi N, Matsushita S, Suzuki K, Murayama M, Shirakawa O, Higuchi S. Association between 5HT2A receptor gene promoter region polymorphism and eating disorders in Japanese patients. *Biol. Psychiatry* 2001;50(2):123-8.

[72] Berggard C, Damberg M, Longato-Stadler E, Hallman J, Oreland L, Garpenstrand H. The serotonin 2A -1438 G/A receptor polymorphism in a group of Swedish male criminals. *Neurosci. Lett.* 2003;347(3):196-8.

[73] Giegling I, Hartmann AM, Moller HJ, Rujescu D. Anger- and aggression-related traits are associated with polymorphisms in the 5-HT-2A gene. *Journal of Affective Disorders* 2006;96(1-2):75-81.

[74] Ni X, Bismil R, Chan K, Sicard T, Bulgin N, McMain S, et al. Serotonin 2A receptor gene is associated with personality traits, but not to disorder, in patients with borderline personality disorder. *Neurosci Lett.* 2006;408(3):214-9.

[75] Preuss UW, Koller G, Bondy B, Bahlmann M, Soyka M. Impulsive traits and 5-HT2A receptor promoter polymorphism in alcohol dependents: possible association but no influence of personality disorders. *Neuropsychobiology* 2001;43(3):186-91.

[76] Bruce KR, Steiger H, Joober R, Ng Ying Kin NM, Israel M, Young SN. Association of the promoter polymorphism -1438G/A of the 5-HT2A receptor gene with behavioral impulsiveness and serotonin function in women with bulimia nervosa. *Am. J. Med. Genet B Neuropsychiatr Genet* 2005;137B(1):40-4.

[77] Reuter M, Kirsch P, Hennig J. Inferring candidate genes for attention deficit hyperactivity disorder (ADHD) assessed by the World Health Organization Adult ADHD Self-Report Scale (ASRS). *J. Neural Transm.* 2006;113(7):929-38.

[78] Zalsman G, Frisch A, Baruch-Movshovits R, Sher L, Michaelovsky E, King RA, et al. Family-based association study of 5-HT(2A) receptor T102C polymorphism and suicidal behavior in Ashkenazi inpatient adolescents. *Int. J. Adolesc. Med. Health* 2005; 17(3):231-8.

[79] Serretti A, Mandelli L, Giegling I, Schneider B, Hartmann AM, Schnabel A, et al. HTR2C and HTR1A gene variants in German and Italian suicide attempters and completers. *Am. J. Med. Genet B Neuropsychiatr Genet* 2007;144(3):291-299.

[80] Saiz PA, Garcia-Portilla MP, Paredes B, Arango C, Morales B, Alvarez V, et al. Association between the A-1438G polymorphism of the serotonin 2A receptor gene and nonimpulsive suicide attempts. *Psychiatr Genet* 2008;18(5):213-8.

[81] Nomura M, Kusumi I, Kaneko M, Masui T, Daiguji M, Ueno T, et al. Involvement of a polymorphism in the 5-HT2A receptor gene in impulsive behavior. *Psychopharmacology* (Berl) 2006;187(1):30-5.

[82] Huang YY, Oquendo MA, Friedman JM, Greenhill LL, Brodsky B, Malone KM, et al. Substance abuse disorder and major depression are associated with the human 5-HT1B receptor gene (HTR1B) G861C polymorphism. *Neuropsychopharmacology* 2003; 28(1): 163-9.

[83] Lappalainen J, Long JC, Eggert M, Ozaki N, Robin RW, Brown GL, et al. Linkage of antisocial alcoholism to the serotonin 5-HT1B receptor gene in 2 populations. *Arch Gen. Psychiatry* 1998;55(11):989-94.

[84] New AS, Gelernter J, Goodman M, Mitropoulou V, Koenigsberg H, Silverman J, et al. Suicide, impulsive aggression, and HTR1B genotype. *Biol. Psychiatry* 2001;50(1):62-5.

[85] Rujescu D, Giegling I, Sato T, Moller HJ. Lack of association between serotonin 5-HT1B receptor gene polymorphism and suicidal behavior. *Am. J. Med. Genet B Neuropsychiatr Genet* 2003;116B(1):69-71.

[86] Zouk H, McGirr A, Lebel V, Benkelfat C, Rouleau G, Turecki G. The effect of genetic variation of the serotonin 1B receptor gene on impulsive aggressive behavior and suicide. *Am. J. Med. Genet B Neuropsychiatr Genet* 2007;144B(8):996-1002.

[87] Contini V, Marques FZ, Garcia CE, Hutz MH, Bau CH. MAOA-uVNTR polymorphism in a Brazilian sample: further support for the association with impulsive behaviors and alcohol dependence. *Am. J. Med. Genet B Neuropsychiatr Genet* 2006; 141B(3):305-8.

[88] Courtet P, Jollant F, Buresi C, Castelnau D, Mouthon D, Malafosse A. The monoamine oxidase A gene may influence the means used in suicide attempts. *Psychiatr Genet* 2005; 15(3):189-93.

[89] Jiang S, Xin R, Lin S, Qian Y, Tang G, Wang D, et al. Linkage studies between attention-deficit hyperactivity disorder and the monoamine oxidase genes. *Am. J. Med. Genet* 2001;105(8):783-8.

[90] Ni X, Sicard T, Bulgin N, Bismil R, Chan K, McMain S, et al. Monoamine oxidase a gene is associated with borderline personality disorder. *Psychiatr Genet* 2007; 17(3):153-7.

[91] Brunner HG, Nelen MR, van Zandvoort P, Abeling NG, van Gennip AH, Wolters EC, et al. X-linked borderline mental retardation with prominent behavioral disturbance: phenotype, genetic localization, and evidence for disturbed monoamine metabolism. *Am. J. Hum. Genet* 1993;52(6):1032-9.

[92] Seif I, De Maeyer E. Knockout Corner: Knockout mice for monoamine oxidase A. *Int. J. Neuropsychopharmacol.* 1999;2(3):241-243.

[93] Jacob CP, Muller J, Schmidt M, Hohenberger K, Gutknecht L, Reif A, et al. Cluster B personality disorders are associated with allelic variation of monoamine oxidase A activity. *Neuropsychopharmacology* 2005;30(9):1711-8.

[94] Saito T, Lachman HM, Diaz L, Hallikainen T, Kauhanen J, Salonen JT, et al. Analysis of monoamine oxidase A (MAOA) promoter polymorphism in Finnish male alcoholics. *Psychiatry Res.* 2002;109(2):113-9.

[95] Hill EM, Stoltenberg SF, Bullard KH, Li S, Zucker RA, Burmeister M. Antisocial alcoholism and serotonin-related polymorphisms: association tests. *Psychiatr Genet* 2002; 12(3):143-53.

[96] Manor I, Tyano S, Mel E, Eisenberg J, Bachner-Melman R, Kotler M, et al. Family-based and association studies of monoamine oxidase A and attention deficit hyperactivity disorder (ADHD): preferential transmission of the long promoter-region repeat and its association with impaired performance on a continuous performance test (TOVA). *Mol. Psychiatry* 2002;7(6):626-32.

[97] Mills S, Langley K, Van den Bree M, Street E, Turic D, Owen MJ, et al. No evidence of association between Catechol-O-Methyltransferase (COMT) Val158Met genotype and performance on neuropsychological tasks in children with ADHD: a case-control study. *BMC Psychiatry* 2004;4:15.

[98] Huang YY, Cate SP, Battistuzzi C, Oquendo MA, Brent D, Mann JJ. An association between a functional polymorphism in the monoamine oxidase a gene promoter, impulsive traits and early abuse experiences. *Neuropsychopharmacology* 2004; 29(8):1498-505.

[99] Golimbet VE, Alfimova MV, Gritsenko IK, Ebstein RP. Relationship between dopamine system genes and extraversion and novelty seeking. *Neurosci. Behav. Physiol.* 2007;37(6):601-6.

[100] van Gaalen MM, Brueggeman RJ, Bronius PF, Schoffelmeer AN, Vanderschuren LJ. Behavioral disinhibition requires dopamine receptor activation. *Psychopharmacology* (Berl) 2006;187(1):73-85.

[101] Tiihonen J, Kuikka J, Bergstrom K, Hakola P, Karhu J, Ryynanen OP, et al. Altered striatal dopamine re-uptake site densities in habitually violent and non-violent alcoholics. *Nat. Med.* 1995;1(7):654-7.

[102] Ebstein RP, Novick O, Umansky R, Priel B, Osher Y, Blaine D, et al. Dopamine D4 receptor (D4DR) exon III polymorphism associated with the human personality trait of Novelty Seeking. *Nat. Genet.* 1996;12(1):78-80.

[103] Grice DE, Leckman JF, Pauls DL, Kurlan R, Kidd KK, Pakstis AJ, et al. Linkage disequilibrium between an allele at the dopamine D4 receptor locus and Tourette syndrome, by the transmission-disequilibrium test. *Am. J. Hum. Genet.* 1996;59(3):644-52.

[104] Perez de Castro I, Ibanez A, Torres P, Saiz-Ruiz J, Fernandez-Piqueras J. Genetic association study between pathological gambling and a functional DNA polymorphism at the D4 receptor gene. *Pharmacogenetics* 1997;7(5):345-8.

[105] LaHoste G, Swanson J, Wigal S, Glabe C, Wigal T, King N, et al. Dopamine D4 receptor gene polymorphism is associated with attention deficit hyperactivity disorder. *Molecular Psychiatry* 1996;1:121-124.

[106] George SR, Cheng R, Nguyen T, Israel Y, O'Dowd BF. Polymorphisms of the D4 dopamine receptor alleles in chronic alcoholism. *Biochem. Biophys. Res. Commun.* 1993; 196(1):107-14.

[107] Kotler M, Cohen H, Segman R, Gritsenko I, Nemanov L, Lerer B, et al. Excess Dopamine D4 receptor (D4DR) exon III seven repeat allele in opioid dependent subjects. *Molecular Psychiatry* 1997;2:251-254.

[108] Keltikangas-Jarvinen L, Elovainio M, Kivimaki M, Lichtermann D, Ekelund J, Peltonen L. Association between the type 4 dopamine receptor gene polymorphism and novelty seeking. *Psychosom. Med.* 2003;65(3):471-6.

[109] Rogers G, Joyce P, Mulder R, Sellman D, Miller A, Allington M, et al. Association of a duplicated repeat polymorphism in the 5'-untranslated region of the DRD4 gene with novelty seeking. *Am. J. Med. Genet* 2004;126B(1):95-8.

[110] Munafo MR, Yalcin B, Willis-Owen SA, Flint J. Association of the dopamine D4 receptor (DRD4) gene and approach-related personality traits: meta-analysis and new data. *Biol. Psychiatry* 2008;63(2):197-206.

[111] Zalsman G, Frisch A, Lewis R, Michaelovsky E, Hermesh H, Sher L, et al. DRD4 receptor gene exon III polymorphism in inpatient suicidal adolescents. *J. Neural Transm.* 2004;111(12):1593-603.

[112] Mill JS, Caspi A, McClay J, Sugden K, Purcell S, Asherson P, et al. The dopamine D4 receptor and the hyperactivity phenotype: a developmental-epidemiological study. *Mol. Psychiatry* 2002;7(4):383-91.

[113] Frank Y, Pergolizzi RG, Perilla MJ. Dopamine D4 receptor gene and attention deficit hyperactivity disorder. *Pediatr Neurol* 2004;31(5):345-8.

[114] Langley K, Marshall L, van den Bree M, Thomas H, Owen M, O'Donovan M, et al. Association of the dopamine D4 receptor gene 7-repeat allele with neuropsychological test performance of children with ADHD. *Am. J. Psychiatry* 2004;161(1):133-8.

[115] Kim YS, Leventhal BL, Kim SJ, Kim BN, Cheon KA, Yoo HJ, et al. Family-based association study of DAT1 and DRD4 polymorphism in Korean children with ADHD. *Neurosci. Lett.* 2005;390(3):176-81.

[116] Lasky-Su J, Banaschewski T, Buitelaar J, Franke B, Brookes K, Sonuga-Barke E, et al. Partial replication of a DRD4 association in ADHD individuals using a statistically derived quantitative trait for ADHD in a family-based association test. *Biol. Psychiatry* 2007; 62(9):985-90.

[117]Sheese BE, Voelker PM, Rothbart MK, Posner MI. Parenting quality interacts with genetic variation in dopamine receptor D4 to influence temperament in early childhood. *Dev. Psychopathol.* 2007;19(4):1039-46.

[118]Eisenberg DT, Mackillop J, Modi M, Beauchemin J, Dang D, Lisman SA, et al. Examining impulsivity as an endophenotype using a behavioral approach: a DRD2 TaqI A and DRD4 48-bp VNTR association study. *Behav. Brain Funct.* 2007;3:2.

[119]Congdon E, Lesch KP, Canli T. Analysis of DRD4 and DAT polymorphisms and behavioral inhibition in healthy adults: implications for impulsivity. *Am. J. Med. Genet. B Neuropsychiatr. Genet.* 2008;147B(1):27-32.

[120]Kuntsi J, McLoughlin G, Asherson P. Attention deficit hyperactivity disorder. *Neuromolecular Med.* 2006;8(4):461-84.

[121]Heinz A, Goldman D, Gallinat J, Schumann G, Puls I. Pharmacogenetic insights to monoaminergic dysfunction in alcohol dependence. *Psychopharmacology* (Berl) 2004; 174(4):561-70.

[122]Palomo T, Kostrzewa RM, Beninger RJ, Archer T. Gene-environment interplay in alcoholism and other substance abuse disorders: expressions of heritability and factors influencing vulnerability. *Neurotox Res.* 2004;6(5):343-61.

[123]Gerra G, Garofano L, Pellegrini C, Bosari S, Zaimovic A, Moi G, et al. Allelic association of a dopamine transporter gene polymorphism with antisocial behaviour in heroin-dependent patients. *Addict. Biol.* 2005;10(3):275-81.

[124]Young SE, Smolen A, Corley RP, Krauter KS, DeFries JC, Crowley TJ, et al. Dopamine transporter polymorphism associated with externalizing behavior problems in children. *Am. J. Med. Genet.* 2002;114(2):144-9.

[125]Comings D, Wu S, Chiu C, Ring R, Gade R, Ahn C, et al. Polygenic inheritance of Tourette syndrome, Stuttering, Attention Deficit Hyperactivity, Conduct and Oppositional Defiant Disorder: the additive and subtractive effect of the three dopaminergic genes DRD2, DbH and DAT1. *American Journal of Medical Genetics* 1996; 67:264-288.

[126]Waldman ID, Rowe DC, Abramowitz A, Kozel ST, Mohr JH, Sherman SL, et al. Association and linkage of the dopamine transporter gene and attention-deficit hyperactivity disorder in children: heterogeneity owing to diagnostic subtype and severity. *Am. J. Hum. Genet.* 1998;63(6):1767-76.

[127]Lee SS, Lahey BB, Waldman I, Van Hulle CA, Rathouz P, Pelham WE, et al. Association of dopamine transporter genotype with disruptive behavior disorders in an eight-year longitudinal study of children and adolescents. *Am. J. Med. Genet. B Neuropsychiatr Genet* 2007;144B(3):310-7.

[128]Kim JW, Kim BN, Cho SC. The dopamine transporter gene and the impulsivity phenotype in attention deficit hyperactivity disorder: a case-control association study in a Korean sample. *J. Psychiatr Res.* 2006;40(8):730-7.

[129]Cornish KM, Manly T, Savage R, Swanson J, Morisano D, Butler N, et al. Association of the dopamine transporter (DAT1) 10/10-repeat genotype with ADHD symptoms and response inhibition in a general population sample. *Mol. Psychiatry* 2005;10(7):686-98.

[130]Eisenberg J, Mei-Tal G, Steinberg A, Tartakovsky E, Zohar A, Gritsenko I, et al. Haplotype relative risk study of catechol-O-methyltransferase (COMT) and attention

deficit hyperactivity disorder (ADHD): association of the high-enzyme activity Val allele with ADHD impulsive-hyperactive phenotype. *Am. J. Med. Genet.* 1999;88(5): 497-502.

[131]Strous RD, Bark N, Parsia SS, Volavka J, Lachman HM. Analysis of a functional catechol-O-methyltransferase gene polymorphism in schizophrenia: evidence for association with aggressive and antisocial behavior. *Psychiatry Res.* 1997;69(2-3):71-7.

[132]Tiihonen J, Hallikainen T, Lachman H, Saito T, Volavka J, Kauhanen J, et al. Association between the functional variant of the catechol-O-methyltransferase (COMT) gene and type 1 alcoholism. *Mol. Psychiatry* 1999;4(3):286-9.

[133]Vandenbergh DJ, Rodriguez LA, Miller IT, Uhl GR, Lachman HM. High-activity catechol-O-methyltransferase allele is more prevalent in polysubstance abusers. *Am. J. Med. Genet.* 1997;74(4):439-42.

[134]Tadic A, Victor A, Baskaya O, von Cube R, Hoch J, Kouti I, et al. Interaction between gene variants of the serotonin transporter promoter region (5-HTTLPR) and catechol O-methyltransferase (COMT) in borderline personality disorder. *Am. J. Med. Genet B Neuropsychiatr Genet* 2008.

[135]Halleland H, Lundervold AJ, Halmoy A, Haavik J, Johansson S. Association between Catechol O-methyltransferase (COMT) haplotypes and severity of hyperactivity symptoms in Adults. *Am. J. Med. Genet B Neuropsychiatr Genet* 2008.

[136]Manuck SB, Flory JD, Ferrell RE, Mann JJ, Muldoon MF. A regulatory polymorphism of the monoamine oxidase-A gene may be associated with variability in aggression, impulsivity, and central nervous system serotonergic responsivity. *Psychiatry Res.* 2000; 95(1):9-23.

[137]Zalsman G, Huang YY, Oquendo MA, Brent DA, Giner L, Haghighi F, et al. No association of COMT Val158Met polymorphism with suicidal behavior or CSF monoamine metabolites in mood disorders. *Arch Suicide Res.* 2008;12(4):327-35.

[138]Blum K, Noble EP, Sheridan PJ, Montgomery A, Ritchie T, Ozkaragoz T, et al. Genetic predisposition in alcoholism: association of the D2 dopamine receptor TaqI B1 RFLP with severe alcoholics. *Alcohol* 1993;10(1):59-67.

[139]Comings DE, Flanagan SD, Dietz G, Muhleman D, Knell E, Gysin R. The dopamine D2 receptor (DRD2) as a major gene in obesity and height. *Biochem. Med. Metab. Biol.* 1993;50(2):176-85.

[140]Comings DE, Rosenthal RJ, Lesieur HR, Rugle LJ, Muhleman D, Chiu C, et al. A study of the dopamine D2 receptor gene in pathological gambling. *Pharmacogenetics* 1996;6(3):223-34.

[141]Blum K, Sheridan PJ, Wood RC, Braverman ER, Chen TJ, Comings DE. Dopamine D2 receptor gene variants: association and linkage studies in impulsive-addictive-compulsive behaviour. *Pharmacogenetics* 1995;5(3):121-41.

[142]Limosin F, Loze JY, Dubertret C, Gouya L, Ades J, Rouillon F, et al. Impulsiveness as the intermediate link between the dopamine receptor D2 gene and alcohol dependence. *Psychiatr Genet* 2003;13(2):127-9.

[143]Ballon N, Leroy S, Roy C, Bourdel MC, Olie JP, Charles-Nicolas A, et al. Polymorphisms TaqI A of the DRD2, BalI of the DRD3, exon III repeat of the DRD4, and 3' UTR VNTR of the DAT: association with childhood ADHD in male African-

Caribbean cocaine dependents? *Am. J. Med. Genet B Neuropsychiatr Genet* 2007; 144B(8): 1034-41.

[144]Sander T, Harms H, Podschus J, Finckh U, Nickel B, Rolfs A, et al. Dopamine D1, D2 and D3 receptor genes in alcohol dependence. *Psychiatr Genet* 1995;5(4):171-6.

[145]Duaux E, Gorwood P, Griffon N, Bourdel MC, Sautel F, Sokoloff P, et al. Homozygosity at the dopamine D3 receptor gene is associated with opiate dependence. *Mol. Psychiatry* 1998;3(4):333-6.

[146]Retz W, Rosler M, Supprian T, Retz-Junginger P, Thome J. Dopamine D3 receptor gene polymorphism and violent behavior: relation to impulsiveness and ADHD-related psychopathology. *J. Neural Transm*. 2003;110(5):561-72.

[147]Limosin F, Romo L, Batel P, Ades J, Boni C, Gorwood P. Association between dopamine receptor D3 gene BaII polymorphism and cognitive impulsiveness in alcohol-dependent men. *Eur. Psychiatry* 2005;20(3):304-6.

[148]Congdon E, Canli T. The endophenotype of impulsivity: reaching consilience through behavioral, genetic, and neuroimaging approaches. *Behav. Cogn. Neurosci. Rev.* 2005; 4(4): 262-81.

In: Impulsivity: Causes, Control and Disorders
Editor: George H. Lassiter

ISBN 978-1-60741-951-8
© 2009 Nova Science Publishers, Inc.

Chapter VII

The Biological and Sociocognitive Basis of Trait Impulsivity

Peter O'Connor
The University of Notre Dame, Australia

Abstract

Trait Impulsivity has traditionally been defined in terms of 'impulse control', with those high in Impulsivity thought to lack sufficient levels of restraint. Not surprisingly therefore, Impulsivity has been linked to various negative outcomes including criminality, delinquency, extramarital affairs and gambling. In this review, current and traditional conceptualizations of Impulsivity are critically evaluated and it is argued that Impulsivity is not a one-dimensional, developmentally homogenous trait, but more likely represents a multifaceted biologically and socio-cognitively based characteristic. A model of trait Impulsivity is proposed, which suggests that Impulsivity is comprised of biologically based 'approach' motivation, and *lack* of socio-cognitive 'character' related to restraint. Specifically, it is suggested that approach motivation represents a distal precursor to Impulsivity, and that impulsive individuals are those who fail to learn functional socio-cognitive patterns of behaviour, such as Self Directedness, Goal Orientation and Conscientiousness. From this perspective, approach motivation can lead to positive or negative outcomes. Implications for the prevention and treatment of Impulsivity are discussed.

Applied versus Taxonomic Conceptualizations of Impulsivity

The most popular conceptualization of Impulsivity in applied research is one of impulse Control (e.g. Braet, Claus, Verbeken and Vlierberghe, 2007; Corruble, Benyamina, Bayle, Falissard, and Hardy, 2003; King and Chassen 2004). From this perspective, impulsive individuals are said to lack foresight (Winstanley, Eagle and Robins, 2006), engage in behaviour that is poorly conceived (Durana and Barnes, 1993) or even 'rash' (Braet et al., 2007). This conceptualization is consistent with current perspectives on psychopathology, which regard many clusters of dysfunctional behaviour as being disorders of impulse control (e.g. Problem Gambling; DSM IV-TR APA, 2000). Indeed empirical research has linked Impulsivity to behaviours generally regarded as risky or even dysfunctional. For example Impulsivity has been found to be associated with delinquency (Levine and Jackson, 2004), extramarital affairs (Buss and Shackelford, 1997), overeating in children (Braet et al., 2007), ADHD (Winstanley et al, 2006) substance abuse (Dawe and Loxton, 2004) and poor job performance (Reio and Sanders-Reio, 2006).

A second method of conceptualising Impulsivity is in terms of its place in the taxonomy of human personality traits (e.g. the Five Factor Model, Costa and McCrae, 1992). Taxonomic, or 'descriptive' models purport that variance in surface level behaviour can be explained by individual differences in a number of broad personality dimensions. In descriptive models, these dimensions are factor analytically based, and thus consist of dimensions which maximally explain variance in a large number of self-reported behaviours. Many descriptive models of personality view Impulsivity as an important dimension of human behaviour (e.g. 'Impulsiveness', Costa and McCrae, 1985; 'Liveliness', Cattell, 2003). Consistent with these models therefore, it is argued that much surface level variance in human behaviour reflects a cluster of behaviours broadly defined as Impulsivity.

From taxonomic personality perspective, Impulsivity does not *necessarily* represent a short-coming or limitation (i.e. lack of restraint), but merely a dimension upon which people vary. Cattell's Liveliness, for example is characterised by animated, spontaneous and enthusiastic behaviour (Cattell, 2003). Overall however, it seems that most descriptive taxonomies of personality do consider Impulsivity to be an inherently negative or dysfunctional trait. For example, Costa and McCrae (1992) measure Impulsiveness as a subscale of neuroticism, and define it as an inability to resist cravings (e.g. food, drugs) or urges. Similarly Hogan (1986) and Buss and Plomin (1975) view Impulsivity at the low end of 'Prudence' and Conscientiousness respectively. Thus, it would appear that applied and taxonomic conceptualisations of Impulsivity are generally consistent; Impulsivity is viewed as a negative trait reflecting the lack of ability to control ones impulses.

The conceptualisation of Impulsivity as 'impulse control' is appealing as it is consistent with Cloninger's (1987) argument that abnormal (pathological) personality traits represent extreme levels of normal personality traits. Specifically, Cloninger argued that a constructive taxonomy of human personality traits should not only be relevant to human behaviour in normal populations, but also be relevant to human behaviour in clinical populations. For example, Impulsivity (which Cloninger termed 'Novelty Seeking') can be considered a primary personality trait, as it not only explains behavioural variance in normal populations, but also characterises a subset of personality disorders (the impulsive cluster of personality disorders). Similarly, Harm Avoidance can also be considered a primary personality trait, as it also explains behavioural variance in both normal and abnormal populations (specifically, this trait is thought to play a role in the fearful cluster of personality disorders). Research has found support for this aspect of Cloninger's model (Svrakic, Draganic, Hill, Bayon, Przybeck, 2002). Thus, the consistent conceptualisation of Impulsivity as 'impulse control' in applied and taxonomic research provides some support for the idea that Impulsivity reflects a general and useful dimension of personality.

A further trait-based conceptualisation of Impulsivity also warrants mention here. Dickman (1990) distinguished between two *types* of Impulsivity. Dysfunctional Impulsivity was defined as the tendency to act with little forethought in situations where such behaviour is not optimal. Thus Dysfunctional Impulsivity has clear overlap with traditional conceptualisations of Impulsivity (i.e. poor impulse control). Functional Impulsivity on the other hand, was defined as the tendency to act with little forethought in situations where such behaviour is optimal. Over three studies, Dickman established a sound factor structure for Functional and Dysfunctional Impulsivity, demonstrated that these two dimensions were only weakly correlated, and also demonstrated that information processing accuracy was related to Functional Impulsivity but not Dysfunctional Impulsivity. Importantly, Dickman (1990) also found that the two types of Impulsivity were differentially related to 'Cognitive Structure', which was defined as "the desire to make decisions based on definite knowledge or probabilities" (p. 97). Specifically, Functional Impulsivity was positively correlated with Cognitive Structure, whereas Dysfunctional Impulsivity was negatively correlated with this scale.

Theoretical Conceptualisations of Impulsivity

Of primary relevance to this chapter, is the *explanation* of trait Impulsivity in terms of prominent theoretical models of personality. Theoretical models of personality are those which attempt to explain stable individual differences in surface level behaviour on the basis of underlying, causal biological and sociocognitive mechanisms. The advantage of such models is that they allow a non-circular, extra-statistical explanation of surface level traits. Descriptive models on the other hand, do not have a theoretical basis and thus can not be used to speculate on the socio-cognitive precursors to personality dimensions. For example, according to the descriptive Five-Factor model of personality, extraverted behaviour is caused by trait Extraversion, because 'Extraversion' emerges as a primary factor when self report measures of surface-level behaviour are factor analysed (circularity). In reality, Extraversion may not be developmentally homogenous, but linked to a number of developmentally distinct pathways. For example, research has linked extraverted behaviour to dopaminergic and serotonergic pathways, as well as sociocognitive mechanisms (see Gillihan, Farah, Sankoorikal, Breland, Brodkin, 2007; Golimbet,; Alfimova, Gritsenko, Ebstein, 2007. Also see Block, 1995, for a critique of the Five Factor model). From this perspective therefore, it is argued that although Impulsivity constitutes a surface level dimension of personality (i.e. people vary in behaviour which could be described as impulsive) this does not mean it has a simple causal mechanism. Indeed several explanatory models of personality can be used to explain variation in impulsive behaviour.

Gray (1982; 1987) proposed arguably the most influential biologically based theory of human personality, and initially considered Impulsivity to play a key role. Gray's theory had its basis in evolutionary psychology, as it was founded on the assumption that fundamental biological systems underlying rodent behaviour could be extended to lower level, biological aspects of human behaviour. Specifically, Gray argued that personality could be largely explained on the basis of two underlying motivational systems; the Behavioural Inhibition System (BIS) and the Behavioural Activation System (BAS). According to this theory, individual differences in the BIS are related to how people react to non-reward or punishment, whereas individual differences in the BAS are related to how people react to reward or potential reward. People high in the BIS tend to avoid fear and anxiety provoking stimuli, whereas people high in the BAS tend to approach potentially rewarding stimuli. These underlying approach and avoidance systems were said to manifest themselves in terms of Anxiety (BIS) and Impulsivity (BAS). Thus from this viewpoint, trait Impulsivity can be thought of as having its basis in an underlying *approach* motivational system.

A similar biological theory of personality was proposed by Cloninger (1987). Cloninger described a biosocial model of personality, based on a synthesis of information from twin research, neurobehavioral studies, and studies of longitudinal development. He argued that primary dimensions of human personality could be explained by biologically-based (temperament) dimensions of Harm Avoidance, Novelty Seeking and Reward Dependence. According to Cloninger, Novelty Seeking reflects variation in approach behaviour, and is thus related to the BAS whereas Harm Avoidance reflects variation in avoidance behaviour and is thus related to the BIS. In this model, Impulsivity is regarded as a subscale of Novelty Seeking, and similar to Gray therefore, Cloninger conceptualised Impulsive type behaviour as having its basis in underlying behavioural activation. An example item from Cloninger's measure of Impulsivity is "I like to make quick decisions so I can get on with what has to be done" (answered either true or false).

From a theoretical perspective therefore, Impulsivity is not seen as solely the failure to inhibit dysfunctional behaviour, but rather as the outcome of underlying behavioural activation (i.e. approach motivation) which might *lead* to the failure to inhibit dysfunctional behaviour. Thus, it seems that Impulsivity has been conceptualised in two different ways depending on whether it has been used in applied and taxonomic or theoretical research. Impulsivity has been defined in terms of 'impulse control' in applied and taxonomic research, whereas it has been defined as the outcome of behavioural activation in theoretical personality research. Indeed, some recent definitions of Impulsivity have incorporated both these components.

Recent *explanations* of Impulsivity have also focussed on both activation and inhibitory mechanisms (e.g. Dawe and Loxton, 2004; Gullo and Dawe, 2008; Jackson 2005). Dawe and Loxton (2004) refer to these to facets of Impulsivity as Rash Impulsivity (lack of restraint) and Reward Drive (activation related to the BAS). Similarly, Jackson focuses on the development of adaptive sociocognitive mechanisms (related to restraint) and Sensation Seeking (undirected approach motivation related to the BAS), in his explanation of impulsive behaviour (Jackson 2005; O'Connor and Jackson 2008).

In the following sections, biological and sociocognitive explanations of Impulsivity are examined in more detail. In particular, perspectives put forward by Gullo and Dawe (2008) and O'Connor and Jackson (2008) will be reviewed in detail, and implications for the measurement of Impulsivity will also be discussed.

Biological and Sociocognitive Explanations of Impulsivity

Cloninger initially argued that the biological basis of Novelty Seeking was related to dopamine activity in the forebrain (Cloninger, 1987). Indeed this is consistent with Gray (1982, 1987; Gray and McNaughton, 2000) who also suggested that dopamine projections play a part in the BAS. Evidence that Novelty Seeking is associated with dopamine levels has been obtained from self-stimulation of dopaminergic neurons in animals and humans (Stellar et al., 1983; Corbett and Wise, 1980; Kelley and Stinus, 1984) and findings that lesions of dopamine stimulating areas (e.g., the ventral tegmentum) reduce spontaneous exploratory behaviour and lead to neglect of novel environmental stimuli (Stellar et al., 1983). More generally, much research has supported the link between approach-type traits related to Impulsivity and dopaminergic pathways (e.g.Ebstein, Nemanov, Klotz, Gritsenko and Belmaker, 1997; Keltikangas-Jarvinen, Raikkonen, Ekelund, Peltonen, 2004; Strobel, Wehr, Michael and Brock, 1999).

A more recent neurobiological model of approach related traits was proposed by Depue and Collins (1999). In contrast to the theories of Cloninger and Gray, Depue and Collins argued that dopaminergic pathways related to BAS reflect trait Extraversion more so than Impulsivity. Specifically, the authors question the role of Impulsivity in Extraversion and convincingly argue that Impulsivity is better interpreted as the interaction between *Agency* (an undirected, approach-type trait) and *Constraint* (a trait related to low Psychoticism and high Conscientiousness, not related to approach or avoidance systems). Consistent with Depue (1995, 1996) and Spoont (1992), Constraint was suggested to be associated with serotonin functioning.

The Constraint component of Impulsivity described by Depue and Collins (1999) resembles the 'impulse control' conceptualisation of Impulsivity described earlier. There is also a clear conceptual overlap between Constraint and Dickman's (1990) Dysfunctional Impulsivity. Indeed, as alluded to earlier, most conceptualisations of Impulsivity acknowledge an element of Restraint (or Constraint), however as noted by Depue and Collins (1999) this trait does not seem to have its basis in approach or avoidance systems. Thus, although the *activation* component of Impulsivity has an established biological basis, and is present in such models as Cloninger (1987), Depue and Collins (1999) and Gray (1987), the theoretical basis of the restraint component of Impulsivity is more ambiguous.

As mentioned above, Depue and Collins (1999) suggested that Constraint was associated with serotonin pathways. Indeed research on behavioural control processes has also hinted at the possibility of a serotoninergic basis (Cools, Roberts and Robbins, 2008), and serotonin has also been linked to disorders of impulse control, such as impulsive aggression (e.g. Coccaro, 1989; Linnoila and Virkkunen, 1992) and mania (e.g. Thakore et al., 1996). However overall, research supporting a relationship between Constraint, (also referred to as 'Rash Impulsivity' at low levels), and serotonin is not strong. Furthermore, it is debatable as to whether the inhibitory effect of serotonin is due specifically to constraint, or more generally the result of the avoidance motivation system (i.e. the BIS). Indeed, research tends to indicate that the latter is more likely, as the link between serotonin and the BIS (or Harm Avoidance) has been widely established (e.g. Lesch et al., 1996; Oscher, et al., 2000; Peirson et al., 1999). For example, research on benzodiazepines (which reduce serotonin activity), has found that serotonin inhibition reduces general levels of anxiety (Deakin, and Graeff, 1991; Fowles, 1980).

Gullo and Dawe (2008) proposed a model of the relationship between Impulsivity and addictive behaviours (the 2-Component Approach to Reinforcing Substances, 2-CARS model). This model focuses on the interplay between two components of Impulsivity which the authors termed Reward Drive (activation related to the BAS) and Rash Impulsivity (lack of restraint). An important feature of the model is that Rash Impulsivity is not defined as the generalised lack of restraint, but specifically defined as the lack of restraint in the context of 'prepotent' or Reward Dependent behaviours (i.e. behaviours initially motivated by reward). From this perspective, Rash Impulsivity can be distinguished from the more general avoidance motivation system (BIS). Gullo and Dawe (2008) use a simple analogy of two motor cars to demonstrate how these components of Impulsivity interact. They liken Reward Drive to the engine of a car; someone with a high Reward Drive has a powerful engine, and thus has difficulty slowing down when necessary. Rash Impulsivity on the other hand is likened to the braking system of a car; someone who has a powerful engine (prepotent/reward driven behaviours) *and* a poor braking system (Rash Impulsivity) will have much difficulty slowing down when necessary. Thus according to this model, Impulsivity has Reward Drive at its basis, but its effects are exacerbated by poor restraint (Rash Impulsivity). An important feature of the 2-CARS model is the focus on the neurophysiological basis of Rash Impulsivity, in particular the orbitofrontal and anterior cingulate cortices (Gullo and Dawe, 2008).

There are however a number of limitations to this model, particularly when it is used to understand Impulsive behaviours *other* than addiction[9]. The primary limitation of this model is its near exclusive focus on the biological basis of Reward Drive and Rash Impulsivity. Specifically, it is argued that clusters of human behaviour (such as Impulsivity), are too complex to be explained solely on the basis of biologically based reward dependent and inhibitory motivations. For example, cognitive research has indicated that the salience of certain stimuli (i.e. power to exert approach or avoidance motivation) is largely dependent on modifiable cognitive processes associated with those stimuli (Cloninger et al., 1993). In the context of addiction for example, impulsive drug related behaviour is not solely dependent on an individual's biological drive to obtain a biologically reinforcing stimuli, but is also dependent on accompanying cognitive processes which affect the desirability of that stimuli. Indeed research into theoretical models of personality suggests that sociocognitive causal mechanisms are at least as important as biological mechanisms in the explanation of behaviour (see Matthews and Gilliland, 1999).

A second limitation of the model described by Dawe and Gullo (2008) is the relatively weak evidence supporting the biological basis of restraint; although much evidence has been obtained to support the link between dopamine and Reward Drive, the same cannot be said for the biological basis of Rash Impulsivity. A third limitation concerns the simplistic rationale regarding how the two components interact to produce impulsive behaviour. As

---

[9] Note that this is primarily a limitation of scope, as the model was originally designed to focus on the relationship between Impulsivity and addiction.

outlined previously, Gullo and Dawe (2008) argue that Impulsive behaviour is due to Reward Drive (a powerful engine) and exacerbated by Rash Impulsivity (a poor braking system). However this model overlooks self-regulatory processes which have recently been shown to have powerful effects on behaviour (e.g. Vande-Walle, Brown, Cron, and Slocum, 1999). In contrast to the model proposed by Gullo and Dawe (2008), self-regulatory theory would suggest that someone with high Reward Drive (a powerful engine) would develop a more effective braking system (thus lower Rash Impulsivity) as a means of controlling their Drive, and functionally adapting to the environment. From this perspective individuals with high Reward Drive *and* Rash Impulsivity should be reasonably uncommon.

Jackson (2005; 2008) proposed a neuropsychological model of learning which, as previously mentioned, has clear relevance to Impulsivity research. Jackson's model is appealing, as unlike the 2-CARS model it places a strong emphasis on the socio-cognitive basis of personality. Similar to the 2-CARS model, Jackson argues for the presence of a biologically based approach mechanism related to dopamine. Jackson refers to this mechanism as 'Sensation Seeking', which he argues is an undirected appetitive learning style (similar to Reward Drive). Jackson argues that this mechanism is evolutionarily adaptive and instinctive, as it provides the underlying drive required for people meet their fundamental biological needs (e.g. sex, food, water etc). According to the model, all behaviour is *initially* motivated by Sensation Seeking, and other dimensions of personality reflect adaptive strategies to re-express this drive in a way that is consistent with society's laws and norms. These socio-cognitive adaptive strategies (referred to as 'learning styles' by Jackson) include Goal Oriented Achiever, Conscientious Achiever, Emotionally Intelligent Achiever, and Deep Learning Acheiver.

Jackson's definition of Sensation Seeking therefore does not presuppose a level of maladaptiveness (as does Zuckerman, 1994), but on the contrary implies that *some* amount of approach motivation is essential. Sensation Seeking is only seen as a problem when people have not developed socio-cognitive adaptive strategies, and hence cannot express this drive in a functional way. For example, according to the model, Sensation Seeking underlies the desire to obtain wealth (i.e. money is a rewarding stimuli). This desire to obtain wealth can be achieved in multiple ways; for example individuals can make plans and set difficult goals (Goal Oriented Achiever), work hard (Conscientious Achiever), obtain social status and befriend influential individuals (Emotionally Intelligent Achiever), or come up with an ingenious idea (Deep Learning Achiever). However, the desire to obtain wealth can also be achieved in dysfunctional ways, such as theft, robbery or illegal activity (e.g. drug dealing). Individuals who have not developed sociocognitive adaptive strategies are likely to engage in these dysfunctional behaviours.

O'Connor and Jackson (2008) provided a comprehensive test of Jackson's model by focussing on the learning style 'Goal Orientation'. Goal Orientation can be broadly defined as the extent to which individuals set mastery goals and focus on process rather than outcome. The authors argued that, for Jackson's model to be tenable, support should be obtained for four key hypotheses. First, Sensation Seeking should be associated with positive *and* negative behaviours; second Goal Orientation should be positively related to functional behaviour and negatively related to dysfunctional behaviour; third, Sensation Seeking should be mediated by Goal Orientation in the prediction of functional behaviour, and fourth,

Mastery Orientation should suppress the relationship between Sensation Seeking and dysfunctional behaviour. Hypotheses were tested over a number of samples and tasks, and good support was found for all four hypotheses. Importantly, it was found that Goal Orientation significantly mediated Sensation Seeking in the prediction of functional behaviour. Furthermore, consistent with the model, it was found that when the effects of Goal Orientation on Sensation Seeking are partialed, Sensation Seeking was a positive predictor of dysfunctional behaviour.

A key component of Jackson's model is that Sensation Seeking is mediated as opposed to moderated by sociocognitive dimensions such as Goal Orientation. Importantly, Jackson argues that Sensation Seekers need to develop socio-cognitive mechanisms such as Goal Orientation, to enable them to functionally adapt to a complex and inconsistent environment. From a statistical point of view, Sensation Seekers therefore should have higher levels of Goal Orientation, as they have a greater need to engage in goal directed behaviour; consequently there should be a positive relationship between these two dimensions. Results presented by O'Connor and Jackson (2008) support this component of Jackson's model.

Although Jackson's model incorporates biological and socio-cognitive mechanisms, and has been well supported (O'Connor and Jackson, 2008) there are nevertheless a number of limitations to this model. First, despite measuring 'Sensation Seeking' which Jackson argues is an undirected approach motivation, Jackson does not specifically discuss where trait Impulsivity fits into his model. It could be inferred that 'dysfunctional' behaviour is actually Impulsivity, as Jackson defines dysfunctional behaviour as the failure to re-express Sensation Seeking functionally (Jackson, 2008). However this seems unlikely as according to the model very few Sensation Seekers should engage in dysfunctional behaviour (O'Connor and Jackson, 2008) and as previously established, a significant amount of normal human behaviour varies along a continuum defined by Impulsivity.

This limitation stems from Jackson's argument for mediation as opposed to moderation. Mediation requires a causal pathway between an IV and a DV via a mediator, and from a statistical point of view, the IV will predominately lead to *either* high or low levels of the DV. A moderated model on the other hand, whereby Sensation Seeking is theorised to be unrelated to Goal Orientation would overcome this limitation, as in this case Sensation Seeking could lead to *both* high and low levels of the DV, depending on the moderator. Indeed a moderated model is broadly consistent with the interpretation of Impulsivity put forward by Depue and Collins (1999), where it was suggested that Impulsivity represents an interaction between Agency and Constraint.

A second limitation of Jackson's model relates to the assumption of linear relationships between Sensation Seeking, sociocognitive variables and indices of functional and dysfunctional behaviour. Specifically, Jackson argues for simple indirect effects between Sensation Seeking and dysfunctional behaviour via sociocognitive variables such as Goal Orientation. Indeed it is likely that these effects exists at *high* levels of Sensation Seeking (i.e. high Sensation Seeking -> high Goal Orientation -> high functional/ low dysfunctional behaviour) but may not be present, or at least not as strong at *moderate* or *low* levels of Sensation Seeking (i.e. low Sensation Seeking -> low Goal Orientation -> low functional/high dysfunctional behaviour). Jackson argues that Sensation Seeking is required for functional behaviour; however it suggested here that individuals with *low* sensation seeking can also develop adaptive strategies to maximise their likelihood of functional behaviour.

A Model of Impulsivity

It is argued that an accurate model of precursors to Impulsivity should be able to explain surface variance in this trait, but not necessarily in terms of a simple causal mechanism. Indeed two recent models of Impulsivity reviewed in this chapter (Gullo and Dawe, 2008; Jackson 2005; 2008) both suggest a multifaceted causal basis for trait Impulsivity. Importantly, both models are broadly consistent with the idea that trait Impulsivity reflects a heightened approach system, combined with an impaired ability to restrain ones behaviour when the situation requires such restraint.

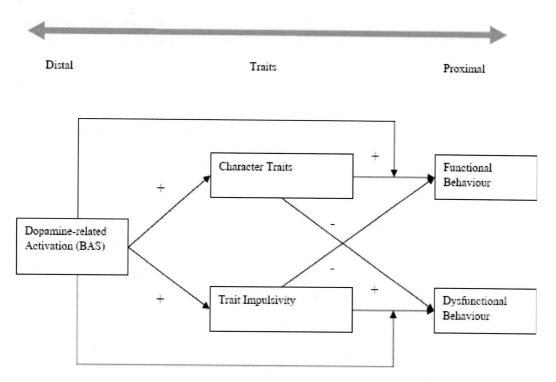

Figure 1. A proposed relationship between Reward Drive, character, trait Impulsivity and functional and dysfunctional behaviour.

The model presented here also incorporates these two components. Specifically, it overlaps with the perspectives put forward by Dawe and Gullo (2008) and Jackson (2005; 2008) however it overcomes important limitations of these perspectives. Specifically, the model proposed in this section incorporates both biological and socio-cognitive elements, clarifies the relationship between Reward Drive and Restraint, and overcomes the problem of non-linear relationships by incorporating a number of moderated-mediated pathways (conditional indirect effects). The model being proposed is illustrated in figure 1; the following section explains this model in detail, and justifies the specific pathways included in the model.

Consistent with Dawe and Gullo (2008), Jackson (2005; 2008), and Depue and Collins (1999) 'Activation' is modelled as the distal, biologically-based mechanism underlying much of Impulsivity. This approach mechanism is undirected and *not* by definition functional or dysfunctional. Activation represents a generalised drive, or desire to approach stimuli when there is a potential for reward. From a measurement point of view, Activation reflects Carver and White's (1994) correlated BAS scales (Reward Responsiveness, Drive and Fun Seeking). This conceptualisation of Activation is different from Jackson's Sensation Seeking, which from a measurement point if view is much more inherently functional (i.e. it has previously been correlated with Goal Orientation at r = 0.63, O'Connor and Jackson, 2008).

As can be seen in Figure 1, Activation is modelled as a biological precursor to Character traits and trait Impulsivity. Character, is made up of a number of surface level traits including Goal Orientation, Self Directedness and Conscientiousness. Theoretically, these traits are likely to develop in people with high levels of Approach, as these traits increase the likelihood that such individuals will be successful in their environment (and are therefore adaptive). Indeed, this reasoning is consistent with supported perspectives put forward by Elliot and Thrash (2002) and O'Connor and Jackson (2008). The proposed model differs from such perspectives however, in suggesting that only a subset of Approach motivated individuals will develop such traits. It is argued that people who do not develop such traits will display high levels of trait Impulsivity. Thus because Activation leads to *either* Character or Trait Impulsivity, only weak bivariate relationships should exist between Activation and the two traits illustrated in Figure 1.

It is argued however, that *within the model*, moderate to strong relationships should exist between Activation and the two traits illustrated in Figure 1. It is emphasised that these relationships should only be present when they are tested in the context of the model (i.e. either using standardised regression or structural equation modelling). Importantly, it is argued that the relationship between Activation and Trait Impulsivity should be visible when variance related to Character has been removed from Activation. The reverse is also true; the relationship between Activation and Character should be visible when the variance related to trait Impulsivity has been removed from Activation (i.e. when trait Impuslivity has been controlled).

From an explanatory point of view, it is important to identify factors influencing the development of Character traits in Approach motivated individuals. For brevity, these potential causes have not been included in the Figure 1; however a number of factors are thought to play a role. First, it is likely that other neurobiological mechanisms play a role here. For example the orbitofrontal and anterior cingulate cortices have been related to inhibitory control (e.g. Goldstein et al., 2006; see also Gullo and Dawe, 2008). Similarly, as mentioned previously, serotonin has been related to Constraint (Depue, 1995, 1996; Spoont, 1992), and more generally, to behavioural inhibition (Lesch et al., 1996; Oscher, et al., 2000; Peirson et al., 1999).

However, consistent with Jackson (2005; 2008) it is argued that trait Impulsivity (termed 'dsyfunctional behaviour' by Jackson) results from insufficient learning of alternative, adaptive strategies in Approach motivated individuals. In particular it is argued that character development is dependent on exposure to key learning situations and stimuli throughout life. Arguably, the developmental stage of greatest importance to adult personality is infancy (see

Bretherton, 1996). During infancy, babies form attachments of varying quality with their primary caregivers. Bowlby (1973) argued that babies who form secure attachments with their primary caregiver are likely to develop positive 'internal working models' of the world. Because securely attached babies tend to have caregivers who are responsive and caring, Bowlby (1973) argued that they form a general perception of others as being trustworthy and helpful. Indeed, recently published longitudinal research has established that infant attachment quality has implications on facets of adult personality, in particular romantic relationships (Simpson et al, 2007). Furthermore, research is consistent with the idea that attachment style is related self-regulatory competence later in life (Gunnar, 1998), and recent research has also linked Impulsive/Aggressive traits with insecure adult attachment styles (Fossati et al., 2005).

In addition to attachment style, a number of other environmental factors likely influence the development of character in approach motivated individuals. Importantly, it is argued that a stimulating learning environment is necessary for the attainment of functional character traits. Aspects of a stimulating learning environment include adequate social interaction, external reinforcement for positive, goal directed behaviours and formal education from competent teaching staff. Indeed research supports the links between such environmental factors and the development of disorders of impulse control. For example, Hurtig et al., (2007) demonstrated environmental factors such as low SES status, dysfunctional families, and lack of parental interest predicted more severe forms of ADHD in adolescents.

A further factor likely to influence character development in an individual, involves the desire to make decisions based on prior information (termed Cognitive Structure; Jackson, 1967). Dickman demonstrated that this variable was correlated at 0.28 with Functional Impulsivity and at -0.51 with Dysfunctional Impulsivity. It therefore follows that Cognitive Structure influences whether an individual high in Approach will develop Functional Impulsivity or Dysfunctional Impulsivity. Similar to what has been argued previously, it is suggested that environmental factors influence whether individuals will learn that that informed decision making is adaptive in society. Of particular importance is the level of exposure to potential learning situations.

To reiterate, it is argued that Approach motivation is expressed at the trait level as either character or trait Impulsivity, depending largely on environmental factors. As illustrated in Figure 1, it is argued that character traits (Goal Orientation, Self Directedness and Conscientiousness) have positive relationships with functional behaviour, and negative relationships with dysfunctional behaviour. Indeed research has linked each of these traits to functional behaviours (e.g. Goal Orientation and workplace factors, Fisher and Ford, 1998; Kozlowski et al., 2001; VandeWalle, et al., 1999; VandeWalle and Cummings, 1997; Self Directedness and university performance, Ham et al., 2006; Conscientiousness and job performance, Barrick and Mount, 1991; Hurtz and Donovan, 2000). Trait Impulsivity on the other hand is modelled as being positively related to dysfunctional behaviour and negatively related to functional behaviour. Research reviewed previously has linked Impulsivity to dysfunctional behaviour (e.g. Braet et al., 2007; Levine and Jackson, 2004).

An important component of the model not yet described is the conditional indirect effect theorised to occur between Approach motivation and proximal behaviours. Throughout this chapter, the focus has been on understanding the development and consequences of *high*

Impulsivity. Indeed this focus is reflective of Impulsivity research in general. Thus, linear relationships of precursors to, and consequences of Impulsivity are generally based on a thorough consideration of high Approach/Impulsivity, rather than additionally considering precursors to, and consequences of *low* Impulsivity. One reason for this narrow focus appears to be the reliance on statistical tests focussing on the magnitude of linear relationships; statistical tests involving non-linear relationships tend to be much more complex. However recently techniques for assessing 'conditional indirect effects' or 'moderated-mediated' pathways have been developed (see Preacher, Rucker and Hayes, 2007).

In the proposed model therefore, it is argued that the relationship between Activation, character and functional behaviour will exist at high levels of Activation, but will only be weak at low levels of Activation. Similarly, it is argued that the relationship between Activation, Impulsivity and dysfunctional behaviour will exist at high levels of Activation, but will only be weak at low levels of Activation. Specifically, failure to develop character is not considered problematic at low levels of Activation and hence should not be negatively associated with functional behaviour or positively associated with dysfunctional behaviour. These proposed moderated-mediated pathways have been illustrated in Figure 1.

It is argued that the model illustrated in Figure 1 has a number of theoretical and practical implications. From a theoretical point of view, it specifies the developmental precursors of Impulsivity, and focuses on the role of both biological and socio-cognitive mechanisms. Importantly, it conceptualises Impulsivity as an inherently dysfunctional *surface level* trait, however views the biological basis of Impulsivity as being undirected and thus having potential for functional or dysfunctional proximal behaviours.

From a practical point of view, the proposed model has implications for the potential treatment and prevention of disorders related to Impulsivity. According to the model, approach motivation leads to trait Impulsivity (which is pathological at extreme levels) when adaptive socio-cognitive traits fail to develop. Thus, to ensure prevention of disorders of impulse control, it is important to ensure that individuals have stimulating learning environments, which would allow important socio-cognitive traits to mature. Similarly, it is argued that Impulsive individuals can learn more functional strategies of adapting to the environment (and thus improve their impulse control), through interventions such as behaviour modification programs. When Impulsive individuals are reinforced for engaging in functional and adaptive strategies, it is likely that new and adaptive behavioural patterns will emerge in their personalities.

Although the model proposed in Figure 1 is heavily based on pre-existing research, it has not been tested. Further research is required to test this model, and also test whether behavioural interventions based on this model are effective. Importantly, the entire model needs to be tested at the same time, as most of the pathways are only hypothesised to exist in the context of the entire model. For this reason, the model should only be tested with a large sample size using structural equation methodology.

Conclusion

The purpose of this chapter was to explain 'trait Impulsivity' particularly in regards to recent, explanatory models of personality. Research has been reviewed from a number of areas, including applied psychology, trait psychology and personality psychology, and two broad conceptualisations of trait impulsivity were identified. First, much applied research and descriptive trait research define Impulsivity in terms of impulse control; specifically impulsive individuals are said to lack impulse control. Second, theoretical personality research tends to focus on biologically-based behavioural activation (or approach motivation), and suggests that Impulsivity is the behavioural outcome of this biologically based construct. Recently, a number of recent researchers combine these two perspectives conceptualisations, particularly when attempting to model the biological and/or socio-cognitive basis of Impulsivity (e.g. Depue and Collins, 1999; Gullo and Dawe, 2008; Jackson, 2005; 2008).

In this chapter a model of Impulsivity was proposed, which incorporates supported elements of recent models, but overcomes several important limitations in these models. Importantly, the proposed model includes both biological and socio-cognitive constructs; provides a mechanism by which Approach motivation can lead to both character and Trait Impulsivity, and is not restricted by the assumption of linearity which characterises previous models. Importantly, it was suggested that the relationship between Approach, character/Trait Impulsivity and proximal behaviours is strongest at high levels of approach.

To conclude, trait impulsivity can be conceptualised in terms of impulse control, and has typically been associated with negative or dysfunctional behaviours. It is argued that trait Impulsivity has its distal basis in dopamine-related approach motivation (BAS), and that trait Impulsivity reflects the inability of approach motivated individuals to express their heightened levels of activity in a functional way. Specifically, it is suggested that a stimulating learning environment enables approach motivated individuals to develop character traits (including Goal Orientation, Self Directedness and Conscientiousness) whereas a lack of exposure to critical learning situations fosters the development of trait Impulsivity. Indeed, it is argued that trait Impulsivity does not represent an underlying dysfunctional mechanism, but manifests itself to be dysfunctional when appropriate learning does not take place.

References

American Psychological Association (2000). Diagnostic and statistical manual of mental disorders, Fourth Edition – Text Revision. D. C.: American Psychiatric Press.

Barrick, M. R., and Mount, M. K. (1991). The Big Five personality dimensions and job performance: A meta-analysis. *Personnel Psychology*, 44, 1-26.

Block, J. (1995). A contrarian view of the five-factor approach to personality description. *Psychological Bulletin*, 117, 187-215.

Bowlby, J. (1973). Attachment and Loss: Vol. 2. Separation. New York: Basic Books.

Bretherton, I. (1996). Internal working models of attachment relationships as related to resilient coping. In G. G. Noam, and K. W. Fischer (Eds.), Development and vulnerability in close relationships. Mahwah, NJ: Erlbaum.

Buss, A. H., and Plomin, R. (1975). A temperament theory of personality development. New York: Wiley.

Carver, C. S., and White, T., L. (1994). Behaviour inhibition, behavioural activation, and affective responses to impending reward and punishment: The BIS/BAS scales. *Journal of Personality and Social Psychology* 67, 319-333.

Cattell, H.E. and Schuerger, J.M., (2003). Essentials of the 16PF. John Wiley and Sons, Inc., New York,.

Cloninger, C. R. (1987). A systematic method for clinical description and classification of personality variants. *Archives of General Psychiatry*, 44, 573 – 588.

Cloninger, C. R. (1999). A new conceptual paradigm from genetics and psychobiology for the science of mental health. *Australian and New Zealand Journal of Psychiatry*, 33, 174-186

Coccaro, E. (1989). Central serotonin and impulsive aggression. *British Journal of Psychiatry*, 155, 52-62.

Cools, R., Robersts, AC., and Robbins, T. W., (2008). Serotoninergic regulation of emotional and behavioural control processes. *Trends in Cognitive Sciences*, 12, 31-40.

Corruble, E., Benyamina, A., Bayle, F., Falissard, B., and Hardy, P. (2003). Understanding impulsivity in severe depression? A psychometrical contribution. *Progress in Neuro-Psychopharmacology and Biological Psychiatry,* 27, 829-833.

Corbett, D., and Wise, R. A. (1980). Intracranial self-stimulation in relation to the ascending dopaminergic systems of the midbrain: A movable electrode mapping study. *Brain research,* 185, 1-15.

Costa, P. T., and McCrae, R. R. (1985). The NEO personality inventory manual. Odessa, FL: Psychological Assessment Resources.

Daruna, J. H., and Barnes, P. A. (1993). A neurodevelopmental view of impulsivity. In W. G. McCown, J. L. Johnson, and M. G. Shure The impulsive client: theory research and treatement. Washington, DC: The American Psychological Association.

Dawe, S., and Loxton, N. J. (2004). The role of impulsivity in the development of substance use and eating disorders. *Neuroscience and Biobehavioral Reviews*, 28, 343-351.

Deakin, J.F.W., and Graeff, F.G. (1991). 5-HT and mechanisms of defence. *Journal of Psychopharmacology,* 5, 305–315

Depue, R. A. (1995). Neurobiological factors in personality and depression. *European Journal of Personality* 9, 413–39.

Depue, R. A. (1996). Neurobiology and the structure of personality: Implications for the personality disorders. In: Major theories of personality disorders, ed. J. Clarkin and M. Lenzenweger. Guilford Press.

Depue, R. A., and Collins, P. F. (1999). Neurobiology of the structure of personality: Dopamine, facilitation of incentive motivation, and extraversion. *Behavioral and Brain Sciences*, 22, 491–569.

Dickman, S. J. (1990). Functional and dysfunctional impulsivity: Personality and cognitive correlates. *Journal of Personality and Social Psychology*, 58, 95–102.

Ebstein, R. P., Nemanov, L., Klotz, I., Gritsenko, I., and Belmaker, R. H. (1997). Additional evidence for an association between the dopamine D4 receptor (D4DR) exon III repeat polymorphism and the human personality trait of Novelty Seeking. *Molecular Psychiatry*, 2, 472-477.

Elliot, A. J., and Thrash, T. M. (2002). Approach-avoidance motivation in personality: Approach and avoidance temperaments and goals. *Journal of Personality and Social Psychology*, 82, 804-818.

Fisher, S. L., and Ford, J. K. (1998). Differential effects of learning effort and goal orientation on two learning outcomes. *Personnel Psychology*, 51, 392-420.

Fossati, A., Feeney, J., Carretta, I., Grazioli, F., Milesi, R., Leonardi, B., et al. (2005). Modeling the relationships between adult attachment patterns and borderline personality disorder: the role of impulsivity and aggressiveness. *Journal of Social and Clinical Psychology*, 24, 520-537.

Fowles, D. C. (1980). The three arousal model: Implication of Gray's two factor learning theory for heart rate, electrodermal activity and psychopathy. *Psychophysiology*, 17, 87-104.

Gillihan, S., Farah, M., Sankoorikal, G., Breland, J., and Brodkin, E. (2007). Association between serotonin transporter genotype and extraversion. *Psychiatric Genetics*, 17, 351-354.

Goldstein, R. Z., Tomasia, D., Rajaramb, S., Cottonea, L. A., Zhangb, L., Maloneya, T., Telanga, F., Alia-Kleina, N., and Volkow, N. D. (2007). Role of the anterior cingulate and medial orbitofrontal cortex in processing drug cues in cocaine addiction. *Neuroscience,* 144, 1153-1159.

Golimbet, V., Alfimova, M., Gritsenko, I., and Ebstein, R. (2007). Relationship between dopamine system genes and extraversion and novelty seeking. *Neuroscience and Behavioral Physiology*, 37, 601-606.

Gray, J. A. (1982).The neuropsychology of anxiety: an enquiry into the function of the septo-hippocampal system. NY:OUP

Gray, J. A. (1987). The neuropsychology of emotion and personality. In S. M. Stahl, S. D. Iverson, and E. C. Goodman (Eds), Cognitive neurochemistry. Oxford: OUP

Gray, J. A., and McMaughton, N. (2000). The neuropsychology of anxiety. Oxford: OUP.

Gunnar, M. R. (1998). Quality of early care and buffering of neuroendocrine stress reactions: Potential effects on the developing human brain. *Preventative Medecine*, 27, 208-211.

Ham, B., Lee, Y., Kim, M., Lee, J., Ahn, D., and Choi, M. et al. (2006). Personality, dopamine receptor D4 exon III polymorphisms, and academic achievement in medical students. *Neuropsychobiology*, 53, 203-209.

Hogan, R. (1986). Hogan Personality Inventory manual. Minneapolis, MN: National Computer Systems.

Hurtig, T., Ebeling, H., Taanila, A., Miettunen, J., Smalley, S., McGough, J., et al. (2007). ADHD and comorbid disorders in relation to family environment and symptom severity. *European Child and Adolescent Psychiatry*, 16, 362-369.

Hurtz, G., and Donovan, J. (2000). Personality and job performance: The big five revisited. Journal of Applied Psychology, 85, 869-879.

Jackson, D. N. (1967). Personality Research Form Manual. Goshen, NY: Research Psychologists Press.

Jackson, C. J. (2001). Comparison between Eysenck and Gray's models of personality in the prediction of motivational work criteria. *Personality and Individual Differences*, 31, 129–144.

Jackson, C. J. (2005). An applied neuropsychological model of functional and dysfunctional learning: Applications for business, education, training and clinical psychology. Cymeon: Australia.

Jackson, C. J. (2008). Measurement Issues Concerning a Personality Model Spanning Temperament, Character, and Experience. In G. J. Boyle, G. Matthews and D. Saklofske (Eds.) The SAGE Handbook of Personality Theory and Assessment: Personality Measurement and Testing (Vol 2, pp. 73-94). London: Sage Publishers.

Kelley, A., and Stinus, L. (1984). Neuroanatomical and neurochemical substrates of affective behaviour. In N. A. Fox, R. J. Davidson (Eds), Affective development: A psychobiological perspective (pp. 1-75). Hillsdale, NJ, Lawrence Erlbaum.

Keltikangas-Jarvinen, L., Raikkonen, K., Ekelund. J., and Peltonen, L. (2004). Nature and nurture in novelty seeking. *Molecular Psychiatry,* 9, 308-311.

King, I. M., and Chassin, L. (2004). Mediating and moderated effects of adolescent behavioural undercontrol and parenting in the prediction of drug use disorders in emerging adulthood. *Psychology Addictive Behaviors* 18, 239 – 249.

Kozlowski, S. W. J., Gully, S. M., Brown, K. G., Salas. E., Smith, E. A., and Nason, E. R. (2001). Effects of training goals and goal orientation traits on multi-dimensional training outcomes and performance adaptability. *Organizational Behavior and Human Decision Processes*, 85, 1-31.

Lesch, K. P., Bengel, D., Heils, A., Sabol, S. Z., Greenberg, B. D., Petri, S., et al. (1996). Association of anxiety-related traits with a polymorphism in the serotonin transporter gene regulatory region. *Science*, 274, 1527-1531.

Linnoila, V., and Virkkunen, M. (1992). Aggression, suicidality, and serotonin. *Journal of Clinical Psychiatry*, 53, 46-51.

Matthews, G., and Gilliland, K. (1999). The personality theories of H. J. Eysenck and J. A. Gray: A comparative review. *Personality and Individual Differences*, 26, 583-626.

Osher, Y., Hamer, D. and Benjamin, J. (2000). Association and linkage of anxiety-related traits with a functional polymorphism of the serotonin transporter gene regulatory region in Israeli sibling pairs. *Molecular Psychiatry*, 5, 216-219.

Peirson, A. R., Heuchert, J. W., Thomala, L., Berk, M., Plein, H., and Cloninger, C. R. (1999). Relationship between serotonin and the Temperament and Character Inventory. *Psychiatry Research*, 89, 29-37.

Preacher, K. J., Rucker, D. D., and Hayes, A. F. (2007). Assessing moderated mediation hypotheses: Theory, methods, and prescriptions. *Multivariate Behavioral Research*, 42, 185-227

Simpson, J. A., Collins, W. A. ran, S., and Haydon, K. C. (2007). Attachment and the experience and expression of emotions in romantic relationships : A developmental perspective. *Journal of Personality and Social Psychology*, 92, 355 – 367.

Spoont, M. (1992) Modulatory role of serotonin in neural information processing: Implications for human psychopathology. *Psychological Bulletin* 112:330–50.

Stellar, J. R., Kelley, A. E., and Corbett, D. (1983). Effects of peripheral and central dopamine blockade on lateral hypothalamic self-stimulation: Evidence for both reward and motor deficits. *Pharmacology, Biochemistry and Behavior*, 18, 433-442

Strobel, A., Wehr, A., Michael, A., and Brock, B. (1999). Association between the dopamine D4 receptor (DRD4) exon III polymorphism and measures of novelty seeking in a German population. *Molecular Psychiatry*, 4, 378-384.

Svrakic, D., Draganic, S., Hill, K., Bayon, C., Przybeck, T., and Cloninger, C. (2002). Temperament, character, and personality disorders: Etiologic, diagnostic, treatment issues. *Acta Psychiatrica Scandinavica*, 106, 189-195.

Tellegen, A. (1985). Structures of mood and personality and their relevance to assessing anxiety, with an emphasis on self-report. In: A. H. Tuma, and J. D. Maser (Eds) Anxiety and anxiety disorders. (pp. 681 – 706). Hillsdale, NJ: Earlbaum.

Thakore, J., O'Keane, V., and Dinan, T. (1996). d-Fenfluramine-induced prolactin responses in mania: Evidence for serotonergic subsensitivity. *American Journal of Psychiatry*, 153, 1460-1463.

VandeWalle, D., Brown, S. P., Cron, W. L., and Slocum, J. W. (1999). The influence of goal orientation and self-regulation tactics on sales performance: A longitudinal field test. *Journal of Applied Psychology*, 84, 249–259.

VandeWalle, D. M., and Cummings, L. (1997). A test of the influence of goal orientation on the feedback-seeking process. *Journal of Applied Psychology*, 82, 390-400.

Winstanley, C. A., Eagle, D. M., and Robins, T. W. (2006). Behavioral models of impulsivity in relation to ADHD: Translation between clinical and preclinical studies. *Clinical psychology Review*, 26, 379-395.

Zuckerman, M. (1994). Behavioral expressions and biosocial bases of Sensation Seeking. New York: Cambridge University Press.

In: Impulsivity: Causes, Control and Disorders
Editor: George H. Lassiter

ISBN 978-1-60741-951-8
© 2009 Nova Science Publishers, Inc.

Chapter VIII

Mood Disorders of Female Delinquents in a Juvenile Detention Center: Its Relationship with Impulsivity and Depression Assessments

Michio Ariga[1], Toru Uehara[2]*, Kazuo Takeuchi[3], Yoko Ishige[4], Reiko Nakano[5] and Masahiko Mikuni[4]
1. Administrative Institution National Center for Persons with Severe Intellectual Disabilities, Nozominosono, Takasaki, Gunma, Japan
2. General Health Support Center, Gunma University, Maebashi, Gunma, Japan
3. Department of Education, Saitama University, Saitama, Japan
4. Department of Psychiatry and Human Behavior,
Gunma University Graduate School of Medicine, Maebashi, Gunma, Japan
5. Haruna Female Detention Center (Haruna Joshi Gakuen),
Shinto, Gunma, Japan

Abstract

Backgrounds: This study aims to compare depression between female participants of adolescent offenders and students, and to clarify relationships of mood variables with comorbidity and impulsivity in a Japanese delinquent sample. *Methods*: 64 females are randomly interviewed at a detention center, and diagnosis was determined using a structured method. The five self-ratings including depression (the DSD), impulsivity (the BIS11), and eating attitudes (the EAT26), were collected. 167 high school and college female students were recruited to compare the DSD. *Results*: By the DSD, the major depressive episodes (MDE) were higher in the offenders than in the controls. In the offenders using a structured interview, 18 (28.1%) were diagnosed with MDE, 21.9% were having dysthymia, and 6.3% had current manic or hypomanic episode. The

---

* Address correspondence to: Toru Uehara, 4-2 Aramaki, Maebashi, Gunma 371-8510, Japan. Tel/fax: 81-27-2207162, e-mail: toruaki@gunma-u.ac.jp.

offenders with MDE showed higher on the DSD significantly than those without mood disorders. Offenders with mood disorders had higher comorbidity including anxiety disorders. The DSD scores were significantly predicted by the EAT26 and the inappropriate attention scores of the BIS11. *Conclusions*: Depression and mania may be associated with antisocial behaviors in female delinquents. Eating problems and impulsivity were risk factors of depression in female adolescent offenders.

Keywords: depression, hypomania, suicidality, offender, impulsivity

1. Introduction

Mood disorder is one of the important issues related to adolescent health problems, and large-scale representative studies have already reported (e.g., Teplin et al., 2002). A recent review reported that mood disorders are relatively common among adolescents, particularly juvenile offenders (Ryan and Redding, 2004). For instance, in a study of approximately 1,550 youths committed to Virginia's Department of Juvenile Justice, McGarvey and Waite (2000) found that 38 percent of males and 30 percent of females reported a history of medication use for a mood disorder. An epidemiologic study of juvenile detainees in Illinoi, any mood disorders were indicated 42% of prevalence (Abram et al., 2003). Especially among female offenders, more than 20% met criteria for a major depressive episode (Teplin et al., 2002). In depressive adolescents, intensify of symptoms when they are placed in correctional settings might be a stronger trigger to impulsive suicide attempts comparing in community settings (Ryan and Redding, 2004). Thus, the identification of depressive disorders in the incarcerated adolescents is urgent, and a comparison with general population is necessary. Additionally, considering a firm link between high risk of suicide and depression, it is all the more important to investigate major depressive episode in adolescence.

Practically, mood disorders may contribute to exacerbate delinquent and disruptive behaviors in a variety of ways, and particularly mania could lead to risk-taking and sensation-seeking behaviors (Dailey et al., 2005). In an epidemiologic study of a community sample of 1,700 adolescents, Lewinsohn et al. (1995) found high rates of comorbid disruptive behavior in participants with bipolar disorders. At an urban juvenile detention center, adolescents with mania had much higher rates of substances abuse other than alcohol or marijuana (Pliszka et al., 2000). The authors hypothesize that mood liability, particularly hypomania, must play a critical role to induce delinquent in female adolescents. According to this context, it could be reasonable to speculate a substantial relationship between mood disorders (such as depression, hypomanic, or dysphoric mania) and antisocial behaviors such as impulsive acts or substance use disorders (SUD) in young females.

On the other hand, Dixon et al. indicated that female offenders have higher experiences of traumatic events such as sexual abuse or domestic violence (2005), and it is already clear that childhood trauma may be closely associated to depression (Cauffman et al., 1998). Although the evidence was supported by the study about PTSD in a juvenile classification house in Japan (Yoshinaga et al., 2005), we can not find out any systematic studies of mood disorders in detention centers or reform schools. Only a series of studies by Matsumoto et al.

(2005) investigated self-harm or mutilation and a depressive assessment in a Japanese juvenile detention center, and they only suggested a relationship between depressive mood and a type of self harms. Therefore, a psychiatric investigation in female offenders is necessary, and it might contribute an improvement of correctional education to clarify the prevalence and characteristics of the disorders.

The first aim of the present study is to compare prevalence of major depressive episode (MDE) and dimensional scores of depression using a structured self-rating questionnaire between samples of female students and adolescents with delinquency. And we attempt to clarify point prevalence of mood disorders and suicidality in female offenders in Japan using a structured interview. Through the investigations in comparison with background characteristics and comorbidity between participants with and without mood disorders, we examine relationships among mood variables and impulsivity. Additionally, eating attitudes, parenting styles, trauma, and substance use problems were included as confounding factors. Finally, we intend to determine what factors could be associated with depressive symptoms in female adolescent offenders.

2. Methods

2.1. Participants

Sixty four female adolescent offenders were randomly selected from a consecutive sample at a young female detention centre (reformatory) in Japan as follows. During November 2004 to June 2006, 181 delinquent adolescents entered the detention centre. Among those offenders, we excluded candidates who had already been administered neuroleptics (major tranquilizers, antidepressants, lithium, methylphenidate, or anticonvulsants) or who were in a severe physical or psychiatric condition. That design was intended to avoid bias caused by medications, which induce reduction of symptoms, when a structured interview was conducted for quantifying natural prevalence, to receive reliable informed consent, and to consider physical situations under a burden of this investigation. Of the candidates, 17 cases were excluded based on medication; the final candidates for the pool used for random selection were 164. No subjects were excluded because of a severe physical or psychiatric illness, and subjects with only a psychiatric history were included in the study. Finally, 64 participants completed the initial screening interview and the reporting questionnaires. Those participants' ages were 16–19 years (mean = 17.2, S.D. = 1.0). Before incarceration, approximately one-half (55%) of offenders had lived separately from immediate family. Of all offenders, 61% had left school before grade 10; one-third (33%) of offenders had not been admitted to high school. The remaining offenders had been enrolled in high school. This investigation was conducted as a usual medical service to maintain mental health for offenders in the reformatory school. Written informed consent for participation in this study was obtained from all participants, and the institutional head and the Chief Director of Correction (Haruna Joshi Gakuen, administered by the Tokyo Regional Office of the Correction Bureau, the Ministry of Justice, and in Japan) approved the study.

Healthy female control participants were recruited from another epidemiological study sample (Takeuchi, 2003), and it consisted of college and high school students from Gunma prefecture, Japan. Participants were 168; their ages were 15 - 19 (mean = 17.9, S.D. = 0.4). This epidemiological study was conducted to promote mental health in youth in this prefecture.

Characteristics of delinquent participants have already summarized in the other previous reports (Ariga et al., 2008), and they featured family history of psychiatric disease, past history of psychiatric problems, recidivism records, SUD, and trauma exposures of the participants. Briefly, in all, 49 participants reported traumatic exposure, and sexual abuse was the most common in this female sample. Regarding SUD, illegal use of methamphetamine (MAP) and marijuana was the highest, followed by inhalants (excluding alcoholic abuse or dependence). Regarding the offense profile of the sample participants, 41% of the offenders had been detained for drug-related crimes, 30% for violent crime (e.g., assault, robbery), and 22% for pre-delinquent behaviors (e.g., prostitution or "sugar daddy business"). Approximately 10% of the girls were multiple offenders; 60% had been arrested twice or more.

2.2. Procedures

In the control group, the aim and content of the investigation were explained and the two self-rating questionnaires; the DSM-scale for depression (DSD; Roberts et al. 1995), and the Eating Attitudes Test 26 (EAT26; Garner and Garfinkel, 1979) were administered by their teachers. Subsequently, students were asked to complete them simultaneously, and instruments were collected while protecting their privacy. Finally, 168 participants were considered to have answered adequately.

In the delinquent group, the participants of offenders were interviewed within one month from their admission to obtain demographic information including family composition, past and family history of psychiatric illness, history of substance use (dose, frequency, and duration), record of delinquency or recidivism history, and traumatic events. Educational attainment and intelligence quotient (IQ: The Binet test was already measured in a juvenile classification home) was investigated individually. During assessment, the interviewer was blind to the participants' offence and sociodemographic information. Psychiatric interviews were administered by the first, the second, or the fourth author. Finally, each participant was asked to complete four self-report questionnaires within a week.

2.3. Questionnaires and Interviews

The DSD is used to evaluate depressive symptoms dimensionally, and to obtain major MDE diagnose according to the DSM-IV criteria (Chen et al., 1998). The DSD was instructed for participants to choose one of four responses for the latest two weeks. The Japanese version consists of 27 items (the original version consists of 31 items including impairment and bereavement items) assessing categories such as depressive mood

/anhedonia, appetite/weight, sleep, agitation, fatigue, guilt, concentration, and suicide. A 4-item Likert scale (1 for none, 2 for sometimes, 3 for occasionally, and 4 for always according to frequency) was applied from item 1 to 26 except for item 27, which asked how to change body weight during recent 2 week with a response on 1 for increasing very much, 3 for no change, and 5 for decreasing very much. To rate MDE positively, the following algorithm is required simultaneously: 1) a positive item requires 4 points (1 or 5 points on the item 27) for at least a 2-week duration; 2) a positive item should be checked at least as either depressive mood (item1-2) or anhedonia (item 3-4); 3) at least four other positive items should vary over the remaining seven categories. The total DSD scores are also calculated as a simple sum for 26 items, which reflect the depressive severity; the Japanese version was made by Doi et al. (2001). The EAT-26 contains three subscale: dieting, overeating (binge eating), and oral control. The dieting factor relates to avoidance of fattening foods and a preoccupation with being thinner. The bulimia and food preoccupation factors consist of items reflecting thoughts about food as well as those indicating bulimia. The oral control factor represents one's self-control in eating and the pressure perceived from others to gain weight. The Japanese version was already developed and used universally (Ujiie and Kono, 1994). The Barratt impulsiveness scale 11th version (BIS-11; Patton et al., 1995) has three factors: motor impulsivity, no planning, and inappropriate attention. It contains 30 items, each of which is answered on a four-point Likert scale; impulsiveness level is calculated by summing up the scores for each item. The Japanese version had already been developed by Someya et al. (2001). The parental bonding inventory (PBI) has been widely used to evaluate the parental situations of participants all over the world (Parker, 1979ab). It was developed in order to assess paternal and maternal parenting styles recognized respectively by offenders using a two-dimensional subscale: care and control. The Japanese version had already been developed and applied widely (Kitamura and Suzuki, 1993).

Psychiatric diagnosis was determined using the Japanese version of the Mini International Neuropsychiatric Interview for children and adolescents (MINI-kids) consisting of 23 modules (Sheehan et al., 1998), which was translated by Otsubo et al. (2005). The MINI-kid screens 23 axis-I DSM-IV disorders; for most modules, 2-4 screening questions are used to rule out a diagnosis when answered negatively. Positive responses to screening questions are examined through further investigation of other diagnostic criteria. It can provide MDE, manic or hypomanic episode (current and past), and dysthymia diagnosis according to DSM-IV, and also indicate risk of suicide (suicidality). A comorbid diagnoses was allowed among respective mood disorders. Before the investigation, the raters were trained using the standard manual of the MINI-kid.

2.4. Data Analysis

First, the overall prevalence of MDE was measured using the DSD algorithm, and total DSD scores between the sample of delinquency and normal controls were compared applying analysis of variance (ANOVA) and non-paired t-test. Next, the more precise point prevalence with some DSM-IV mood disorders (MDs) was investigated, and the percentages of participants with some MDs were examined including having current and past diagnosis of mania or hypomania. Consecutively, we compared the individual factors including psychiatric comorbidity rated using the MINI-kids, self-ratings, experiences of traumatic event, and history of substance use among participants with and without MDE, current manic or hypomanic episodes, and dysthymia by Fisher's exact probability (chi-square test) or ANOVA (Bonferroni's multiple comparison were conducted as a post hoc test). On the MINI-kids, an absence of hospitalization due to interpersonal problems over at least one week is required when a participant is explored as a hypomanic episode. Therefore, the present study deals hypomania into the same category with manic episode. Finally, linear multiple regression analysis was conducted using the DSD scores as a dependent variable. Independent valuables were selected from the dimensional scores using stepwise method. A probability level of 0.05 or less was chosen to indicate significance (two tailed). A Japanese version of SPSS was used for statistical analyses.

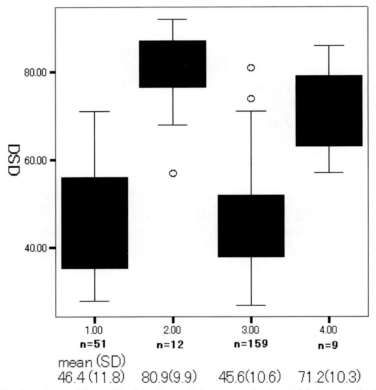

1: negative offenders 2: positive offenders 3: negative controls 4: positive controls (MDE diagnosis using the DSD algorism).

Figure 1. Comparisons of total scores between the participants with positive and negative using the DSD algorithm in the offenders and the normal control students. Significant differences among the positive and negative participants in the delinquent and control group were indicated (F=53.6, P<.001). The offenders with positive (80.9) were higher than the offenders and the controls with negative (46.4 and 45.6, respectively), and the controls with positive (71.2) were higher than the offenders and the controls with negative diagnosis of MDE using the DSD. Between the delinquents and controls, differences were not significant for the corresponding groups.

3. Results

3.1. Comparisons of the DSD with Normal Control

Point prevalence of MDE was 9 (5.4%) in a sample of normal control, and 12 (18.8%) in a sample of delinquency (Fisher's exact probability, $p<0.003$). Figure 1 summarizes comparisons of total scores between the subject with positive and negative by the DSD algorithm in offenders and normal controls. We found significant differences between the positive and negative subjects in the both group ($F=53.6$, $P<0.001$), but differences between the delinquent and control sample were not significant for corresponding groups as regards the positive or negative diagnosis of MDE.

Table 1. Comparisons of dimensional scores among mood disorders

Variables	Subscale scores or subcategory	MDE		Dysthymia		Manic episode#		No MDs		F
		mean	S.D.	mean	S.D.	mean	S.D.	mean	S.D.	
Age		17.2	1.0	16.8	0.5	17.3	1.5	17.3	1.0	0.8
IQ		84.5	14.2	85.9	10.5	84.7	19.2	91.8	13.0	0.8
Number of recidivism history		1.5	0.5	1.8	0.5	1.3	0.6	1.6	0.5	1.4
DSD***		68.2	16.4	55.8	17.2	57.0	25.5	44.0	11.9	10.9 (MDE>no MDs)
EAT-26	Diet	10.8	7.7	12.1	7.2	16.0	20.2	6.9	7.1	2.2
	Binge-eating	3.6	4.3	1.5	1.7	5.3	8.4	1.9	2.8	1.7
	Oral control	2.5	2.5	3.6	2.5	3.7	4.0	1.9	2.6	1.2
	Total	16.8	11.5	17.3	9.7	25.0	32.1	10.8	10.6	2.2
BIS-11	Iat	21.1	5.4	19.3	1.4	24.3	7.0	19.8	4.7	1.6
	Im	29.4	5.7	27.4	3.4	30.0	8.0	27.5	6.4	0.5
	Inp	30.8	5.6	28.4	3.5	28.3	7.6	30.5	5.3	0.6
	Total	81.4	11.4	75.0	4.7	82.7	22.6	77.8	13.7	0.6
PBI	Paternal care	19.6	10.2	15.9	8.0	27.0	5.3	14.9	8.9	2.4
	Paternal op	22.1	8.0	25.6	5.9	21.7	5.5	25.0	7.5	0.9
	Maternal care	13.4	11.5	13.9	9.6	16.3	10.4	10.7	8.1	0.7
	Maternal op	23.8	8.7	22.6	6.8	22.0	5.2	27.3	7.4	1.5
Ages of trauma exposures$ (only significant factors were indicated)	Fire or bombing**	0.1	0.5	0	0	1.7	2.9	0.1	0.6	4.3(manic>oth)
	Childhood abuse*	0.8	1.2	1.1	1.6	0.3	0.6	0.2	0.4	2.8

mean and S.D. (standard deviation), ANOVA and post hoc Bonferroni test, ***: $P<0.001$ **: $P>0.01$, *: $P<0.05$
DSD; DSM scale for depression   Iat ; Inappropriate attention   PBI; parental bonding inventory
EAT-26; eating attitudes test   Im ; Motor impulsivity,   op; overprotection
BIS-11; Barraett impulsiveness scale   Inp ; No planning
MDE; major depressive episode   oth; the other subjects   MDs; mood disorders
$; Ages were separated 5 degrees according to older experience of trauma (gradual from 0 to 4)
Subjects with double depression and mixed state were included in the MDE group.
#; Including hypomanic episode ($n = 1$)

3.2. Point Prevalence of Mood Disorders

Point prevalence of MDE diagnosed by DSM-IV was 28.1% ($N=18$), and 14 (21.9%) were diagnosed as dysthymia. Five participants have concurrent diagnosed with MDE and dysthymia as a double depression. And percentages of currently manic ($N=3$) or hypomanic

(N=1) episode were 6.3%. Regarding mood-related problems, the rate of the offender with suicidality was extremely high (48.4%, N=31), and 46.9% were having a past episode of mania (N=19) or hypomania (N=11). Totally, 38 participants (59.4%) have some kinds of abnormal mood problems. One participant showed mixed state and she had both diagnoses of MDE and mania. Depressive symptoms were dominant for the participant, thus she was included as a MDE in the following analysis. Manic and hypomanic episodes were integrated as 'mania' in the following text and table.

Table 2. Comorbidity with mood disorders

Categorical factors$ and Diagnosis (determined by the MINI-kids)	Sub category	MDE N=18 %		Dysthymia N=8 %		Manic episode# N=3 %		No MDs N=35 %	
Trauma exposure**		18	100.0%	7	87.5%	3	100.0%	21	60.0%
Cocaine use*		0	0.0%	3	37.5%	0	0.0%	0	0.0%
Marijuana use*		12	66.7%	1	12.5%	0	0.0%	16	45.7%
Panic Disorder**	History	9	50.0%	1	12.5%	0	0.0%	2	5.7%
	Current	9	50.0%	1	12.5%	0	0.0%	1	2.9%
Agoraphobia		6	33.3%	1	12.5%	0	0.0%	3	8.6%
SA**		10	55.6%	1	12.5%	1	33.3%	5	14.3%
Social phobia**		9	50.0%	1	12.5%	1	33.3%	3	8.6%
Specific phobia*		3	16.7%	4	50.0%	1	33.3%	3	8.6%
OCD*		7	38.9%	1	12.5%	1	33.3%	3	8.6%
PTSD**		11	61.1%	3	37.5%	2	66.7%	5	14.3%
Alcohol	Abuse	13	72.2%	3	37.5%	1	33.3%	22	62.9%
	Dependence	13	72.2%	2	25.0%	1	33.3%	23	65.7%
Substance	Abuse	10	55.6%	5	62.5%	0	0.0%	23	65.7%
	Dependence	7	38.9%	4	50.0%	0	0.0%	20	57.1%
Tic Disorders	Tourette	0	0.0%	0	0.0%	1	33.3%	0	0.0%
	Motor	0	0.0%	0	0.0%	0	0.0%	1	2.9%
	Vocal	0	0.0%	0	0.0%	0	0.0%	0	0.0%
	Transient	1	5.6%	0	0.0%	0	0.0%	0	0.0%
ADHD*	Combined*	7	38.9%	3	37.5%	1	33.3%	3	8.6%
	Inattentive	0	0.0%	0	0.0%	0	0.0%	6	17.1%
	Hyperactive/impulsive	1	5.6%	0	0.0%	0	0.0%	1	2.9%
Conduct Disorder		14	77.8%	7	87.5%	2	66.7%	23	65.7%
Oppositional Defiant Disorder		1	5.6%	0	0.0%	0	0.0%	2	5.7%
Psychosis*	Current	8	44.4%	2	25.0%	0	0.0%	5	14.3%
	Lifetime	8	44.4%	3	37.5%	0	0.0%	8	22.9%
	Mood disorders with psychotic features*	0	0.0%	2	25.0%	2	66.7%	0	0.0%
AN		2	11.1%	1	12.5%	1	33.3%	4	11.4%
BN		2	11.1%	0	0.0%	1	33.3%	5	14.3%
GAD**		0	0.0%	2	25.0%	0	0.0%	0	0.0%
PDD		1	5.6%	0	0.0%	0	0.0%	1	2.9%

*: P<0.05, **: P<0.01, chi-square test　　　　　$: Only significant factors were indicated.
SA: separation anxiety, OCD: obsessive compulsive disorder, PTSD: posttraumatic stress disorder
ADHD: attention deficit hyperactivity disorder, GAD: generalized anxiety disorder
PDD: pervasive developmental disorder　　　　　MDE: major depressive episode
Subjects with double depression and mixed state were included in the MDE group.
#: Including hypomanic episode (n = 1)　　　　　MDs: mooe disorders

3.3. Factors Associated with Mood Disorders

We compared comorbidity, background features, and self-rating measures according to mood disorders diagnosis using one-way ANOVA (table 1) and chi-square test (table 2) and. Among MDE, dysthymia, and current mania, we did not find significant differences of all mean scores of all the self-report questionnaires except for the DSD and dimensional factors such as IQ, number of arrest, or age. The offenders with MDE showed greater scores on the DSD significantly than those without mood disorders ($F=11.6$, $p<0.0001$). Trauma experiences made two significant differences on age distributions of the first exposure; participants with mania showed older exposure on fire or bombing ($F=4.3$, $P=0.007$). Ages of childhood abuse differed among the groups, whereas an individual significance was not revealed.

When it comes to comorbid diagnosis, participants showed significant differences on comorbidity with current ($p=0.001$) and past history (0.001) of panic disorders (PD), separation anxiety (SA) (0.010), social phobia (0.006), specific phobia (0.038), obsessive compulsive disorder (OCD) (0.050), PTSD (0.003), mixed attention deficit hyperactivity disorder (ADHD) (0.038), psychosis with mood disturbance (.041), and generalized anxiety disorder (GAD) (.002) according to the diagnosis. In comparison of offenders with MDE, dysthymia, and current mania, participants with MDE showed 50.0% ($n=9$) comorbidity of current and past history of PD. 55.5 % ($n=10$) of MDE and 33.3% of mania ($n=1$) were diagnosed as SA, and nine participants with MDE (50.0%) and one mania (33.3%) also had social phobia. Dysthymia participants had higher comorbidity of specific phobia (50.0%). Participants with MDE showed 38.9% ($n=7$), and mania showed 33.3% ($n=1$) of comorbidity with OCD. Percentages of PTSD gradually increased to mania (66.6%), MDE (61.1%), dysthymia (37.5%), and from participants without mood disorders (14.3%). Combined ADHD was detected 38.9% in MDE, 37.5% in dysthymia, and 33.3% in mania participants. Psychosis with mood disturbance was co-existed higher in participants with mania (66.7%, $n=2$), and GAD ($n=2$) was diagnosed only as dysthymia. In addition, one who had a transient tic was included in MDE, and only one participant who had Tourett's syndrome was diagnosed as current mania. In comparisons of trauma experiences, every mood disorders showed higher rates of trauma exposure (87.5 - 100%) than those without the disorders (60.0%). Regarding history of SUDs, participants with dysthymia were more likely to report usage of cocaine ($n=3$ and 37.5% vs. 0%; $P=0.045$) than the others, and marijuana ($n=12$ and 66.7% vs. from 12.5 % to 0%; $P=0.026$) than those with dysthymia and mania. Except these factors, no significant correlation was apparent among the offenders with mood disorders in background characteristics including family history or past history of psychiatric illness, profile of recidivism, and SUDs.

Table 3. Prediction of the depressive symptoms

	Dependent valiable	Variables entered	Standardized coefficients	t	R^2	F
$n = 64$	the DSD				0.47	17.0***
df (1,60)		total of the EAT	0.48	4.8***		
		Ia of the BIS	0.24	2.3*		
		IQ	-0.27	2.8**		

Multiple linear regression, stepwise method, **: $P<0.001$, **: $P<0.01$, *: $P<0.05$
DSD: DSM scale for depsression
EAT-26: Eating attitudes test
BIS-11: Barraett impulsiveness scale
Ia: Inappropriate attention

3.4. Correlation with the DSD

To predict depressive symptoms assessed by the DSD, we conducted multiple regression analysis using stepwise method. First, the total scores were used as a dependent variable, and dimensional scores of the questionnaires, age, and IQ were entered accordingly as independent variables. Significant variables were selected if the p value of each variable was under 0.05, and deleted for $p > 0.10$. Finally, we obtained a significant regression model to predict the DSD scores ($F = 17.0$, $P<0.001$); the total scores of the EAT, the inappropriate attention scale scores of the BIS, and IQ were correlated as significant variables ($t = 4.8$, 2.3, and 2.8; $P<0.001$, 0.05, and 0.01, respectively).

4. Discussion

The present study surveyed a comparison of overall prevalence and severity of depression using a convenient self-rating between the sample with female delinquents and control adolescents in Japan. And percentages of positive subjects with MDE were higher in the offenders than in the control students. Interestingly, between the sample with delinquency and normal control, this study showed no significant differences of the DSD scores in subjects with MDE positive, and also with negative. These results indicated importance to diagnose MDE in adolescence generally, and depressive severity is identical both in delinquents and control students. And this survey led us to emphasize that an adequate investigation to diagnose and treat depression must be contribute subtle improvement on correctional education and mental health in juvenile detention centers.

Surprisingly, participants with any mood disorders or liability were totally recognized 59.4% using a structured interview in the female adolescent offenders, and the precise rate of MDE was remarkably high (28.1%). And as Renaud et al. (2005) reported in a youth centers population that previous suicide attempt was 53.6% and higher rates of indicators of MDE, SUD, and disruptive behaviors were associated with suicide completion, we also reported high risk of suicidality in the sample (48.4%); therefore, it is crucial to prevent suicide based on detection and therapeutic intervention for depression and impulsivity in adolescent delinquents. On the other hand, including participants having current and past history of mania or hypomania, approximately 50% of the offenders have some sort of manic episodes. The results support that mood swing such as manic and hypomanic state could be a trigger to impulsive or simplistic acts in vulnerable adolescents. Consequently, it should be noticed that demand of adequate diagnosis and treatment is urged targeting mood disorders for female adolescents in custody.

Regarding factors associated with MDE, dysthymia, or mania, it is reasonable that comparisons of dimensional scores showed the highest on the DSD in the participants with MDE. However, other instruments did not reach significance among the offenders with or without mood disorders. The results were caused by a ceiling effect; which means that the offenders with delinquency may tend to be naturally high on evaluations of impulsivity, abnormal eating, or adverse parenting. It is curious that statistical significance is revealed on age distributions of the first trauma exposure of 'fire or bombing' and 'childhood abuse'. Older exposure of explosive trauma might affect manic swing in adult, whereas it remains further examinations.

Regarding comorbidity and other categorical factors, striking differences were shown on comorbidity between the offenders with and without mood disorders. Specifically, the participants with MDE were more likely to report several anxiety disorders including current and lifetime panic disorder than those without MDE. Other anxiety disorders tended to be highly diagnosed with both MDE and mania. Interestingly, PTSD comorbidity was demonstrated similar increases in MDE and mania. It has already been reported that anxiety symptom has a close relationship with depression psychopathology (e.g., Devane et al., 2005), and it is also important to consider mood swing (including hypomanic episode) as a part of anxiety-mood spectrum in female delinquents. According to high rates of GAD comorbidity in the participants with dysthymia, chronic mild depression might be associated with persistent generalized anxiety. And in a view of clinical observation, it is natural that ADHD co-exists more in the participants with mania. Additionally, MDE and dysthymia were highly complicated in ADHD. Adolescents with ADHD may be vulnerable to mood reactivity or liability due to their impulsivity or attention disturbance. Based on the analysis about trauma experiences, every mood disorders were closely related to existence of trauma exposures. Regardless of variety of trauma, traumatic events may influence to mood liability. And MDE offenders had more occasional history of usage on marijuana than those with the other mood disorders. On the other hand, dysthymia was related to cocaine use. Speculatively, dysthymic offenders may have burdened prolonged distress mood; dysphoria occasionally could turn into impulsivity, at last it might induce to use illegal drugs such as marijuana or cocaine. It is still unclear to explain why they choose downer drugs and there were many marijuana users in the participants without mood disorders.

Regarding prediction of depressive severity by multiple regression analysis, we found three significant variables correlated with the DSD; IQ, the EAT26 total score, and inappropriate attention of the BIS. Many reports indicated biological and phenomenological associations between depression and eating disorders (e.g., Kaye et al., 2000), and we have already mentioned in the other analysis that abnormal eating problem has a strong relationship with depression (Uehara et al., 2008). Additionally, attention deficit or impulsivity assessed by the BIS showed highly predictive to depression. Actually, inappropriate attention may be a risk to bring about stressful events, and they could cue to be depressive consecutively.

In the present study, we could not support hypothesis that relationship between depression and SUD except for marijuana and cocaine. And despite adverse parental attitudes have been pointed out to be related to depression or several psychopathology (e.g., Parker, 1979ab), the PBI scores did not differ among these offenders. The participants in this study consist of offenders; therefore, we have to consider that they may be with generally experiences of various drug uses, and many of them grew in dysfunctional parenting situations. Further studies should include comparisons with control females. Although mood swing actually interact antisocial attitudes, recidivism history did not differ among participants with or without mania. We have to apply more detailed assessments, and data form more participants should be examined.

In conclusion, the present study indicates high prevalence of MDE in a female sample with delinquency, and they have depression more compared with matched control students. The psychopathology of mood disorders was also common in this sample, and history of mania was extremely high level. The anxiety disorders were frequently diagnosed with MDE simultaneously. Abnormal eating and inappropriate attention may be risks of depression. The need for appropriate intervention should be suggested for adolescent female offenders in custody including the prevention of depression and manic liability.

References

Abram, K.M., Teplin, L.A., McClelland, G.M., Dulcan, M.K. 2003. Comorbid psychiatric disorders in youth in juvenile detention. *Archives of General Psychiatry*, 60, 1097-1108.

American Psychiatric Association, 1994. Diagnostic and Statistical Manual for Mental Disorders Forth Edition (DSM-IV). APA, Washington D.C.

Ariga, M., Uehara, T., Takeuchi, K., Ishige, Y., Nakano, R., Mikuni, M. 2008. Trauma Exposures and Posttraumatic Stress disorder in female adolescents with delinquency. *Journal of Child Psychology and Psychiatry*, 49, 79-87.

Cauffman, E., Feldman, S. S., Waterman, J., and Steiner, H. 1998. Posttraumatic stress disorder among female juvenile offenders. *Journal of the American Academy of Child and Adolescent Psychiatry,* 37, 1209-1216.

Chen, I.G,, Roberts, R.E., Aday, L.A., 1998. Ethnicity and adolescent depression: the case of Chinese Americans. *Journal of Nervus and Mental Diseases,* 186, 623-630.

Dailey, L.F., Townsend, S.W., Dysken, M.W., Kuskowski, M.A. 2005. Recidivism in medication-noncompliant serious juvenile offenders with bipolar disorder. *Journal of Clinical Psychiatry*, 66, 477-84.

Devane, C.L., Chiao, E., Franklin, M., Kruep, E.J. 2005. Anxiety disorders in the 21st century: status, challenges, opportunities, and comorbidity with depression. *American Journal of Management Care* 11(Suppl), S344-53.

Dixon, A., Howie, P., and Starling, J. 2005. Trauma exposure, posttraumatic stress, and psychiatric comorbidity in female juvenile offenders. *Journal of the American Academy of Child and Adolescent Psychiatry,* 44, 798-806

Doi, Y., Roberts, R.E., Takeuchi, K., Suzuki, S. 2001. Multiethnic comparison of adolescent major depression based on the DSM-IV criteria in a U.S.-Japan study. *Journal of the American Academy of Child and Adolescent Psychiatry*, 40, 1308-1315.

Garner, D. M., Olmsted, M. P., Bohr, Y., and Garfinkel, P. E. 1982. The Eating Attitudes Test: psychometric features and clinical correlates. *Psychological Medicine*, 12, 871-878

Kaye, W.H., Gendall, K.A., Fernstrom, M.H., Fernstrom, J.D., McConaha, C.W., Weltzin, T.E., 2000. Effects of acute tryptophan depletion on mood in bulimia nervosa. *Biol. Psychiatry* 47, 151-157

Kitamura, T., and Suzuki, T. 1993. A validation study of the Parental Bonding Instrument in a Japanese population. *Japanese Journal of Psychiatry and Neurology*, 47, 29-36

Lewinsohn, P.M., Klein, D.N., Seeley, J.R. 1995. Bipolar disorders in a community sample of older adolescents: prevalence, phenomonology, comorbidity, and course. *Journal of the American Academy of Child and Adolescent Psychiatry*, 34, 454–463.

Matsumoto, T., Yamaguchi, A., Chiba, Y., Asami, T., Iseki, E., Hirayasu, Y. 2005. Self-burning versus self-cutting: patterns and implications of self-mutilation; a preliminary study of differences between self-cutting and self-burning in a Japanese juvenile detention center. *Psychiatry and Clinical Neurosciences*, 59, 62-69.

McGarvey, E.L., Waite, D. 2000. Mental health needs among juveniles committed to the Virginia Department of Juvenile Justice. Development, *Mental Health and Law* 20, 1–24

Otsubo, T., Tanaka, K., Koda, R., Shinoda, J., Sano, N., Tanaka, S., Aoyama, H., Mimura, M., Kamijima, K. 2005. Reliability and validity of Japanese version of the Mini-International Neuropsychiatric Interview. *Psychiatry and Clinical Neurosciences*, 59, 517-526.

Parker, G., Tupling, H., and Brown, L. B. 1979a. A parental bonding instrument. *British Journal of Medical Psychology*, 52, 1-10.

Parker, G., 1979b. Parental characteristics in relation to depressive disorders. *British Journal of Psychiatry*, 134, 138-147.

Patton, J. H., Stanford M. S., and Barratt, E. S. 1995. Factor structure of the Barratt Impulsiveness Scale. *Journal of Clinical Psychology*, 51, 768-774.

Pliszka, S.R., Sherman, J.O., Barrow, M.V., Irick, S. 2000. Affective disorder in juvenile offenders: A preliminary study. *American Journal of Psychiatry*, 157, 130-132.

Renaud, J., Chagnon, F., Turecki, G., Marquette, C. 2005. Completed suicides in a youth centres population. *Canadian Journal of Psychiatry* 50, 690-4.

Roberts, R. E., Roberts, C. R., and Chen Y. W. 1995. Ethnocultural differences in prevalence of adolescent depression. 123rd Annual Meeting of American Public Health Association, San Diego.

Ryan, E.P., Redding, R.E. 2004. A review of mood disorders among juvenile offenders. *Psychiatry Service* 55, 1397-1407.

Sheehan, D. V., Lecrubier, Y., Sheehan, K. H., Amorim, P., Janavs, J., Weiller, E., Hergueta, T., Baker, R., Dunbar, G.C. 1998. The Mini-International Neuropsychiatric Interview (M.I.N.I.): the development and validation of a structured diagnostic psychiatric interview for DSM-IV and ICD-10. *Journal of Clinical Psychiatry*, 59 Suppl 20: 22-33; Quiz 34-57.

Someya, T., Sakado, K., Seki, T., Kojima, M., Reist, C., Tang, S.W., Takahashi, S. 2001. The Japanese version of the Barratt Impulsiveness Scale, 11th version (BIS-11): its reliability and validity. *Psychiatry and Clinical Neurosciences*, 55, 111-114.

Takeuchi, K., 2003. An epidemiological study of relationships between depression and eating abnormality in adolescence. Research accomplishment report of the Grant-in-Aid for Scientific Research (No. 14570354), Japan.

Teplin, L.A., Abram, K.M., McClelland, G.M., Dulcan, M.K., Mericle, A.A. 2002. Psychiatric disorders in youth in juvenile detention. *Archives of General Psychiatry* 59, 1133-1143.

Uehara, T., Ariga, M. 2008. Eating disorders and female delinquency: a cross sectional study of adolescents at a female detention center. *Japanese Journal of Child Adolescent Psychiatry,* 49(English Supplement), 23-36.

Ujiie, T., and Kono, M. 1994. Eating Attitudes Test in Japan. *Japanese Journal of Psychiatry and Neurology*, 48, 557-565.

Yoshinaga, C., Kadomoto, I., Otani, T., Sasaki, T., Kato, N. 2004. Prevalence of post-traumatic stress disorder in incarcerated juvenile delinquents in Japan. *Psychiatry and Clinical Neurosciences,* 58, 383-388.

In: Impulsivity: Causes, Control and Disorders
Editor: George H. Lassiter

ISBN 978-1-60741-951-8
© 2009 Nova Science Publishers, Inc.

Chapter IX

The Impact of Impulsivity on Adolescent Performance in an Emotional Go/No-Go Task

Miguel Ángel Muñoz[1], Marlen Figueroa[1], Eduardo García[1],
Martina Carmelo[1], Mercedes Martínez[2], Ana M. Rodríguez[3],
Rocío Sanjuan[1] and Sonia Rodríguez-Ruiz[1]*

1. University of Granada, Granada, Spain
2. University of Islas Baleares, Palma de Mallorca, Spain
3. Primary Care Center, Pediatric Service, Barcelona, Spain

Abstract

Background. Impulsivity and emotional drive constitute distinctive markers of adolescence, characterized in many instances by sensation seeking and risk taking behaviors. On the other hand, the Go/No-Go task is possibly the experimental paradigm most often used when studying impulsivity and behavioral inhibition in the laboratory. Thus, the aim of this study is to explore the effect of impulsivity on adolescent performance in an emotional Go/No-Go task. *Method.* We administered a set of questionnaires on trait impulsivity (Plutchik Impulsivity Scale; Plutchik and Van Praag, 1989) to a non-clinical sample of 1190 adolescents (from 14 to 18 years old) and selected 49 participants at the two end of the impulsivity continuum: high (n=21) and low impulsive adolescents (n=28). We further tested these extreme groups on neuropsychological measure of motor impulsivity (emotional Go/No-go task). The emotional Go/No-go task provides a measure of motor impulsivity since the participant has to inhibit a behavioural response (press a key) to specific and emotionally relevant stimuli. *Results.* The Go/No-go task indicates that high impulsive adolescents display

* Correspondence to: Sonia Rodríguez-Ruiz, Departamento de Personalidad, Evaluación y Tratamiento Psicológico, Facultad de Psicología, Universidad de Granada, Campus de la Cartuja s/n, 18071, Granada (Spain), Phone: (+ 34) 958 24 37 53 (Lab), (+ 34) 958 24 62 50 (Office), Fax: (+ 34) 958 24 37 49, E-mail: srruiz@ugr.es.

faster reaction times (both for hits and false alarms) while viewing affective (pleasant and unpleasant) and non-affective pictures, whereas low impulsive participants exhibit faster reaction times only to affective pictures. *Discussion.* High impulsive adolescents revealed impaired emotional responses to the pictures compared to participants with low impulsivity. In sum, the preset study suggests a negative relationship between impulsivity and emotional processing in adolescent population.

Keywords: impulsivity, emotional Go/No-Go task, emotional processing, affective pictures

1. Introduction

In the last few decades, research on impulsivity has advanced considerably, particularly as it pertains to its relationship with psychopathology (e.g., substance abuse, attention deficit/hyperactivity disorder, conduct disorder, eating disorders) (Luengo, Otero, Romero, E., and Gómez-Fraguela, 1996; McCown, Johnson and Shure, 1993; Wood et al., 1995). Despite the lack of universal agreement regarding the concept of "impulsivity", most would concur in defining impulsivity as the inability to think or reflect when confronting a conflictive situation, resulting in failure to anticipate the consequences of one's actions, a rushed style when making decisions, difficulties in planning one's future behavior and/or inability to exert self-control (McCown and DeSimone, 1993).

Impulsivity and emotional drive constitute distinctive markers of adolescence, characterized in many instances by sensation seeking and risk taking behaviors. Impulsive actions have been associated with immaturity of frontal brain mechanisms underlying inhibition of automatic behaviors (Nederkoorn, Van Eijs and Jansen, 2004). From that perspective, impulsivity in adolescence can be seen as the result of a certain stage of brain development. Numerous studies show that maturation of prefrontal cortex begins in adolescence (Sadurni and Rostan, 2004), together with a progressive increase in connectivity between orbito-frontal cortex and various limbic structures, such as the amygdala, the hippocampus, and the caudate nuclei. Ultimately, these connections enable an adult to exert control over emotional responses that can be considered automatic (Weinberger et al., 2005).

The Go/No-Go task is possibly the experimental paradigm most often used when studying impulsivity and behavioral inhibition in the laboratory. The task requires that the subject respond as fast as possible to a frequently presented stimulus (Go), while inhibiting a response when the infrequent, non-target stimulus is presented (No-Go). Developmental studies of children and adolescents (9-17 years of age) demonstrate that age is inversely correlated with the rate of false alarms (i.e., responses to No-Go stimuli), such that the rate of this type of erroneous responses decreases as children grow older (Hooper et al., 2004).

In a variant of the Go/No-Go task designed to study the effect of emotional factors on behavioral inhibition, Go and No-Go stimuli consist of images with distinct emotional valence. Thus, the emotional Go/No-Go task provides not only a measure of behavioral inhibition, but also an evaluation of the emotional effect over such inhibition or impulsivity. For instance, Hare and his colleagues (2005) used faces with different emotional expressions and showed that fearful faces resulted in slower reaction times (RTs), while happy faces evoked faster motor responses, which were more difficult to inhibit. In a more recent study, Schulz et al. (2007) obtained significant differences in subjects' responses when viewing happy, sad, and neutral faces. While responses were comparably fast when happy and neutral faces were presented, sad faces resulted in slower RTs than happy faces.

The objective of the present study was to investigate the effect of impulsivity on adolescent performance in an emotional Go/No-Go task. We anticipated that highly impulsive adolescents would sacrifice accuracy to speed, thus committing more errors (i.e., a higher number of false alarms). Also, since impulsivity has been associated with a number of externalizing psychopathologies characterized by dull emotional responses, we anticipated that emotional valence would affect adolescents with low impulsivity more than highly impulsive adolescents.

2. Method

2.1. Participants

The study included 49 adolescents with an average age of 15.83 years. Participants were selected from a larger sample of adolescents that volunteered their participation in a study of healthy habits and impulsivity. Subject selection was carried out according to scores from the *Impulsivity Scale* [IS] (see Table 1). Two groups of adolescents were chosen: (a) subjects with IS scores that were higher than 26, which constituted the *High Impulsivity* group; and (b) subjects with IS scores that were lower than 10, which constituted the *Low Impulsivity* group.

Subject selection was carried out in participating schools, after obtaining permission to participate from school principals, as well as parent representatives of the schools. All participating subjects were given a numerical code by which they were identified throughout the day. No identifying information was obtained, thus ensuring confidentiality of the data.

Table 1. Number of subjects, average age (standard deviation), and mean impulsivity (IS) scores (standard deviation) of the High Impulsivity and Low Impulsivity groups

	♂ Males (N=17)	♀ Females (N=32)	Total (N=49)
High Impulsivity (N=21; ♂: 8; ♀: 13)	Age: 16.25 (±2.05) IS: 29.25 (±3.49)	Age: 15.38 (±1.04) IS: 29.84 (±2.70)	Age: 15.71 (±1.52) IS: 29.61 (±2.95)
Low Impulsivity (N=28; ♂: 9; ♀: 19)	Age: 15.88 (±1.36) IS: 6.77 (±2.43)	Age: 15.94 (±1.26) IS: 6.89 (±2.30)	Age: 15.92 (±1.27) IS: 6.85 (±2.30)

2.2. Procedure

Emotional Go/No-Go Task (Newman, Widom and Nathan, 1985)

A computerized version of the Go/No-Go task was used. Slides had an affective content from three levels of valence: Pleasant, Unpleasant, and Neutral. The experimental session was divided in three blocks, each containing 100 trials and 2 different images. Participants were asked to hit the space bar as quickly as possible upon seeing the frequent image of the two images included in each block. They were also required to withhold their responses to the infrequent image. Target images were signaled to the subject at the beginning of each block.

Following completion of the first 50 trials of each block, a sound announced that subjects needed to switch responses, as the target image had changed for the remaining 50 trials. Feedback was given on each trial, indicating whether the response was correct, omitted, or was a false alarm.

Images were presented for 400 ms and inter-image intervals varied between 400, 450, 500, 550, and 600 ms. Seventy percent of trials required a response (Go trials) and the remaining 30% were No-Go trials that involved response inhibition. The higher rate of Go trials induced a response set that made inhibition more difficult.

Blocks were always presented in the same order: 1. Neutral block, with 2 images of neutral emotional valence; 2. The second block contained one of the neutral images from the previous block and a second, pleasant image; 3. The last block included the same neutral image from the second block and a second, unpleasant image. All images were taken from the International Affective Picture System (IAPS; Lang et al., 1995; Moltó, et al., 1999; Vila et al., 2001).

Impulsivity Scale [IS] (Plutchik and Van Praag, 1989)

Plutchik's *Impulsivity Scale* is a self-report questionnaire that contains 15 items and evaluates an individual's tendency to behave impulsively. Responses are given in a Likert scale with 4 values, ranging from "Never" to "Almost Always". The scale has good internal validity and reliability ($\alpha = .73$) (De Leo and Heller, 2004; Kingsbury et al., 1999; Plutchik and Van Praag, 1989; Ystgaard et al., 2003). The Spanish version of the scale (Portilla et al., 2005) was used for this study.

High (≥ 26) and low (≤ 10) IS scores were used to select those adolescents that would be administered the Go/No-Go task. Subjects had already finished filling a number of self-report questionnaires on eating habits, substance use, and attentional behavior. The Go/No-Go task was administered after the questionnaires had been completed and lasted a total of 20 minutes.

2.3. Statistical Analyses

All statistical tests were carried out by means of the Statistical Package for the Social Sciences (SPSS 15). Most analyses entailed a mixed ANOVA design with 2 levels of impulsivity (High vs. Low) as a between-subject factor, and all other variables as within-subject repeated measures factors. P-values of within subject tests were corrected using the Greenhouse-Geisser correction. Results are presented with the original degrees of freedom but corrected p-values. Significant interactions were subjected to post-hoc Bonferroni tests with an overall alpha level of 0.05.

Participants that were deemed outliers on the Go/No-Go task, due to very low hit rates or excessive numbers of false alarms (High Impulsivity: N=10; Low Impulsivity: N=11), or extreme RT values (High Impulsivity: N=2; Low Impulsivity: N=3), were not included in the corresponding analyses.

3. Results

3.1. Hits and False Alarms

Hit rates for each subject were analyzed with a mixed model ANOVA design 2(x3x5), where *Group* was the between-subject variable (High vs. Low Impulsivity) and there were 2 within-subject, repeated-measures factors: *Valence* with 3 levels (Pleasant, Neutral, Unpleasant) and *Block* with 5 levels (B1/6, B2/7, B3/8, B4/9, B5/10).

This first analysis revealed significant main effects of *Group* (F[1, 26]=4.361, p<0.05), *Valence* (F[2, 52]=24.062, p<0.0001) and *Block* (F[4, 104]=14.987, p<0.0001), as well as a significant interaction *Valence x Block* (F[8, 208]=2.693, p<.05). The main effect of *Group*, as shown in Figure 1, is due to the higher hit rate obtained by subjects in the High Impulsivity group when compared to those in the Low Impulsivity sample.

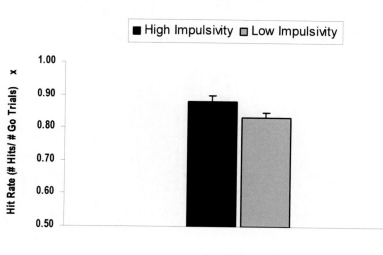

Figure 1. Hit Rates in the Go/No-Go task for each Impulsivity Group.

HIT RATE

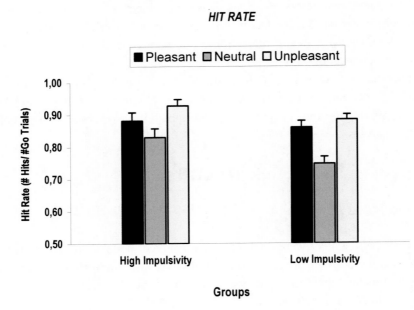

Figure 2. Hit rates in the Go/No-Go task for each level of Valence (Pleasant, Neutral, Unpleasant) for High and Low Impulsivity groups.

FALSE ALARMS

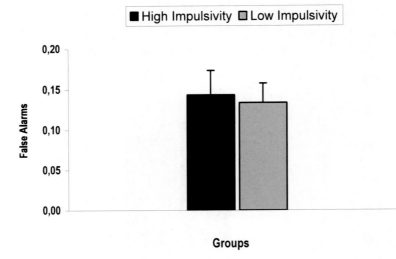

Figure 3. False Alarm rates in the Go/No-Go task for the two Impulsivity groups.

Post-hoc comparisons for the *Valence* factor revealed that hit rates were higher for pleasant than neutral images (*pleasant*=0.87 vs. *neutral*=0.79, p<0.001), as well as for unpleasant than neutral images (*unpleasant*=0.91 vs. *neutral*=0.79, p<0.001), with no significant differences in hit rate between pleasant and unpleasant images (p>0.10) (see Figure 2).

This effect indicates that affective images with a higher level of arousal (i.e., pleasant and unpleasant) potentiate performance and increase the number of hits, when compared with neutral images, which are significantly less activating. This happens for both highly impulsive and much less impulsive adolescents. Thus, it seems that the arousal level of affective images is responsible for the enhanced performance observed in all subjects.

Like in the case of hit rates, analysis of False Alarm (FA) rates was carried out with a mixed model 2(x3x5) ANOVA design, with the same between- and within-subject factors. Results of the ANOVA showed significant effects of *Valence* ($F_{[2, 52]}=3.568$, $p<0.05$) and *Block* ($F_{[4, 104]}=2.902$, $p<0.05$). There were no significant interactions.

Figure 3 shows that the High Impulsivity group made more errors than the Low Impulsivity group, but the difference did not reach statistical significance.

Post-hoc comparisons indicated that both groups issued fewer FAs when presented with pleasant or unpleasant images than when responding to neutral targets (*High Impulsivity*: pleasant=0.10; neutral=0.18; unpleasant=0.15; *Low Impulsivity*: pleasant=0.10; neutral=0.17; unpleasant=0.13). Still, these effects were minor and only approached statistical significance when comparing pleasant and neutral images (p=0.07) (see Figure 4).

Once again, this result shows that affective images that are highly arousing (i.e., pleasant and unpleasant images), compared with neutral images that are less activating, lead to lower rates of FAs in both high and low impulsivity individuals. Moreover, there is a trend towards a valence effect such that only pleasant and neutral images appear to differ somewhat in the way they affect performance. It seems as if a positive valence, paired with a higher level of arousal, facilitates accuracy in detection and responding for all participants in this Go/No-Go task.

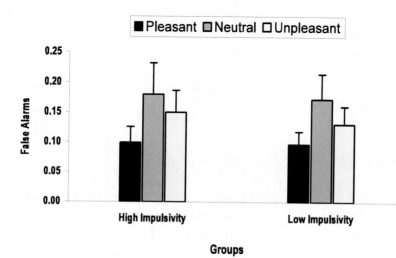

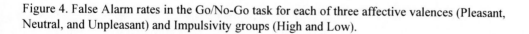

Figure 4. False Alarm rates in the Go/No-Go task for each of three affective valences (Pleasant, Neutral, and Unpleasant) and Impulsivity groups (High and Low).

Table 2. Mean rates of Hits and False Alarms, and Signal Detection Theory measures of sensitivity (d') and criterion (β) in the Go/No-Go task for High and Low Impulsivity groups

	Hits	False Alarms	d' (Sensitivity)	β (Criterion)
High Impulsivity	0.88	0.14	2.26	1.08
Low Impulsivity	0.83	0.13	2.08	1.13

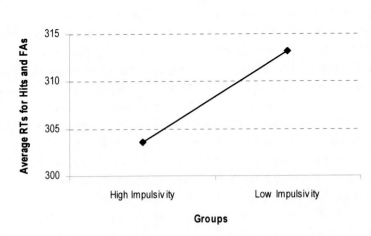

Figure 5. Average Reaction Times (RTs) for Hits and FAs in the Go/No-Go task for the two Impulsivity groups.

Table 2 includes average hit and FA rates for all trials in all blocks and valences of the Go/No-Go task and indicates that, while both High Impulsivity and Low Impulsivity subjects committed approximately the same number of FA errors, highly impulsive adolescents outperformed less impulsive individuals in terms of correct responses or hits. Average d' (i.e., sensitivity) and β (i.e., criterion) values for the two groups tend to suggest that differences may be due to variations in perceptual discriminability, rather than more or less conservative response styles.

3.2. Reaction Times for Hits and False Alarms

Reaction times (RTs) were analyzed by means of a mixed model 2(x3) ANOVA design, with two levels of the between-subjects factor *Group* (High Impulsivity vs. Low Impulsivity) and 3 levels of the within-subject repeated measures factor *Valence* (Pleasant, Neutral, and Unpleasant). The main effect of *Group* approached statistical significance ($F[1, 42]=3.293$, $p=0.07$), while the interaction *Group x Valence* was statistically significant ($F[2, 84]=3.056$, $p<0.05$). Figure 5 illustrates how the High Impulsivity group tends to have faster RTs overall than the Low Impulsivity group (High Impulsivity=304 ms vs. Low Impulsivity=313 ms).

REACTION TIMES

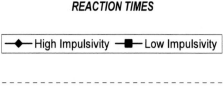

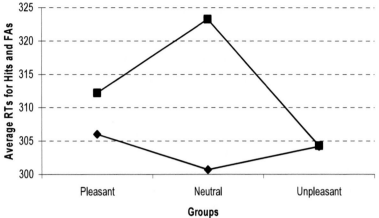

Figure 6. Average Reaction Times (RTs) for each of three affective Valences (Pleasant, Neutral, Unpleasant) and two Groups (High Impulsivity and Low Impulsivity) in the Go/No-Go task.

Separate ANOVAs conducted for each group showed a main effect of *Valence* for the Low Impulsivity group (F[2, 48]=4.017, p<0.05) and no significant differences due to affective valence for the High Impulsivity group (F[2, 36]=0.386, p=0.682) (see Figure 6).

Post-hoc comparisons for the factor *Valence* and the Low Impulsivity group revealed significantly faster RTs for hits and FAs when unpleasant images are presented in comparison with neutral slides (unpleasant = 304 ms vs. neutral = 303 ms; p<0.05). No other difference was significant (pleasant vs. neutral, p=0.289; pleasant vs. unpleasant, p=0.81). Therefore, although the overall trend for the Low Impulsivity group was to respond faster to all affective images, whether pleasant or unpleasant, this difference, possibly due to a greater arousal level, only reaches statistical significance when comparing unpleasant and neutral images and only in the Low Impulsivity group.

4. Discussion

Results obtained in this study demonstrate that the rate of correct responses or hits is higher in adolescents endorsing a higher number of impulsivity items in a self-report questionnaire. Although a trend was observed for High Impulsivity subjects to make more False Alarms in this affective Go/No-Go task, such tendency was not significantly reliable and, thus, should not be discussed. Still, it seems appropriate that highly impulsive adolescents would tend to show less inhibitory control and, consequently, a higher rate of responding, both correct and incorrect (Perales et al., under review).

There were significant differences in the rate of hits and false alarms as a function of the affective valence of the pictures included in the Go/No-Go task used here (i.e., pleasant, neutral, and unpleasant). Both the High Impulsivity and the Low Impulsivity groups emitted higher hit rates when responding to the affective images that were more activating or arousing (i.e., pleasant and unpleasant slides) when compared to neutral images with less activating content. In the case of False Alarm rates, it was just the difference between pleasant and neutral images that reached statistical significance for both groups. These results indicate that higher activation or arousal, paired with a positive emotional valence, may enhance task performance, as hit rate increased with the more activating pleasant and unpleasant slides, while false alarms decreased with pleasant images.

In terms of reaction times in the Go/No-Go task, there was a trend towards faster responses in both hits and false alarms in the High Impulsivity group with respect to the Low Impulsivity group. On the other hand, when reaction times are considered as a function of affective valence, the Low Impulsivity group showed significant differences that were absent in the High Impulsivity group. Highly impulsive adolescents were fast responders, regardless of the affective content of the target images. In contrast, adolescents that endorsed fewer impulsivity items in the IS demonstrated slower hit and false alarm reaction times when the pictures were activating or arousing (i.e., pleasant or unpleasant) than when they were neutral, with significant differences between unpleasant and neutral images. As was the case with accuracy data (i.e., hits and false alarms), arousal level and unpleasant valence of the images speeded up the performance of low impulsivity participants. High impulsivity adolescents were not capable of adjusting their responses to the eliciting stimuli as a function of their affective valence or emotional intensity (i.e., arousal).

These results partly corroborate previous data obtained with distinct versions of the emotional Go/No-Go task (Hare et al., 2005; Schulz et al., 2007). Those studies found higher false alarm rates associated with positive valence (i.e., happy facial expressions), as well as longer reaction times in response to negative valence stimuli (i.e., facial expressions of fear or sadness). It should be noted, however, that the pleasant image used in the present study depicted a fun activity (i.e., skydiving in a group) and was chosen to match the level of arousal of the pleasant and unpleasant (i.e., the face of a sad child) images. Therefore, differences found between the Go/No-Go task used here and those used in previous studies might be due to variations in methodology.

Nevertheless, other investigations that have used various types of tasks (e.g., dot-probe paradigms with affective images or image visualization) have found that processing of emotional stimuli can have either positive or negative effects on performance. For instance, healthy controls show faster reaction times while detecting negative or threatening faces versus neutral faces (Ishai, Pessoa, Bikle and Ungerleider, 2004; Öhman, Lundqvist and Esteves, 2001) or while detecting relevant fearful faces among irrelevant pictures (Öhman, Flykt and Esteves, 2001).

Alternatively, presentation of stimuli with emotional content can at times increase reaction times. For instance, when participants have to determine the orientation of a visual stimulus, their responses are slower if the stimuli are presented right before an affective image (Hartikainen, Ogawa and Knight, 2000). Similarly, the appearance of an unpleasant image in the center of the screen slows down discrimination of peripheral stimuli (Tipples and Sharma, 2000). In conclusion, it could be stated that contrasting effects in terms of task performance when processing emotional stimuli could be related to the methodology employed in that particular study (e.g., the type of stimuli).

Some limitations should be acknowledged in the present study. Firstly, the number of participants in each of the two impulsivity groups was relatively small. Additionally, adolescents are notoriously variable and it would probably be easier to find larger differences in performance with older subjects. In fact, other studies have found out that the range of ages in the sample significantly affects performance in the Go/No-Go task (Crone, Vendel and Van der Molen, 2003; Hooper et al., 2004).

Acknowledgments

The present research was supported by a grant from the Junta de Andalucía (research group HUM-388).

References

Crone, E. A., Vendel, I., and Van der Molen, M. W. (2003). Decision-making in disinhibited adolescents and adults: Insensitivity to future consequences or driven by immediate reward? *Personality and Individual Differences, 34,* 1–17.

De Leo, D. and Heller, T., (2004). *Suicide in Queensland, 1999–2001: Mortality Rates and Related Data.* Australian Institute for Suicide Research, Brisbane.

Hare, T. A., Tottenham, N., Davidson, M. C., Glover, G. H., and Casey, B. J. (2005). Contributions of amygdala and striatal activity in emotion regulation. *Biological Psychiatry, 57,* 624–632.

Hartikainen, K.M., Ogawa, K.H., and Knight, R.T. (2000). Transient interference of right hemispheric function due to automatic emotional processing. *Neuropsychologia, 38,* 1576-1580.

Hooper, C., Luciana, M., Conklin, H., and Yarger, R. (2004). Adolescents' Performance on the Iowa Gambling Task: Implications for the Development of Decision Making and Ventromedial Prefrontal Cortex. *Developmental Psychology, 40 (6),* 1148-1158.

Ishai, A., Pessoa, L., Bikle, P.C., and Ungerleider, L.G. (2004). Repetition suppression of faces is modulated by emotion. *Proceedings of the National Academy of Sciences of the United States of America, 101,* 9827-9832.

Kingsbury, S., Hawton, K., Steinhardt, K., and James, A. (1999). Do adolescents who take overdoses have specific psychological characteristics? A comparative study with psychiatric and community controls. *Journal of the American Academy of Child and Adolescent Psychiatry, 38,* 1125–1131.

Lang P.J. (1995). The emotion probe: Studies of motivation and attention, *American Psychology, 50,* 372-385.

Luengo, M.A., Otero, J.M., Romero, E., and Gómez-Fraguela, J.A. (1996). Efectos de la necesidad de búsqueda de sensaciones sobre la involucración en el consumo de drogas de los adolescentes. *Análisis y Modificación de Conducta, 22 (86),* 683-708.

Nederkoorn C, Jansen E, Mulkens S, and Jansen A (2006) Impulsivity predicts treatment outcome in obese children. *Behaviour Research and Therapy*, 45, 1071–1075.

Newman JP, Widom CS, Nathan S (1985) Passive avoidance in syndromes of disinhibition: psychopathy and extraversion. *J. Person Soc. Psychol.* 48:1316–1327

McCown, W., and DeSimone, P. (1993). Impulsivity: A historic overview. In J. McCown, and M. Shure (Eds.), *The impulsive client: Theory, research, and treatment.* Washington, DC: American Psychological Association.

McCown, W. G., Johnson, J. L., and Shure, M. B. (1993). The impulsive client: theory, research, and treatment. Washington, DC: *American Psychological Association.*

Moltó, J., Montañés, S., Poy, R., Segarra, P., Pastor, M.C., Tormo, M.P., Ramírez, I., Hernández, M.A., Sánchez, M., Fernández, M.C., and Vila, J. (1999). Un nuevo método para el estudio experimental de las emociones: The International Affective Picture System (IAPS). Adaptación española. *Revista de Psicología General y Aplicada, 52,* 55-87.

Öhman, A., Flykt, A., and Esteves, F. (2001). Emotion drives attention: Detecting the snake in the grass. *Journal of Experimental Psychology: General, 130,* 466-478.

Öhman, A., Lundqvist, D., and Esteves, F. (2001). The face in the crowd revisited: A threat advantage with schematic stimuli. *Journal of Personality and Social Psychology, 80,* 381-396.

Perales, J.C., Verdejo-García, A., Moya, M., Pérez-García, M. and Lozano, O. (en revisión). Bright and Dark sides of Impulsivity: Performance of individuals with high and low trait impulsivity on neuropsychological tasks. *Brain and Cognition.*

Plutchik, R., and Van Praag, H., (1989). The measurement of suicidality, aggressivity and impulsivity. *Prog. Neuro-Psychofarmacol. and Biol. Psychiat, 13,* 23-24.

Portilla, M.P.G., Bascarán, M.T., Sáiz, P.A., Bousoño, M., and Bobes, J. (2005). *Evaluación de la Impulsividad.* Ars Medica: Barcelona.

Sadurni, M. and Rostán, C. (2004). La importancia de las emociones en los periodos sensibles del desarrollo. *Infancia y Aprendizaje, 27,* 105-114.

Schulz, K., Fan, J., Magidina, O., Marks, D., Hahn, B., and Halperin, J., (2007). Does the emotional go/no-go task measure behavioral inhibition? Convergence with measures on a non-emotional analog. *Archives of Clinical Neuropsychology, 22,* 151–160.

Tipples, J. and Sharma, D. (2000). Orienting to exogenous cues and attentional bias to affective pictures reflect separate processes. *British Journal of Psychology, 91,* 87-97.

Vila, J., Sánchez, M., Ramírez, I., Fernández, M.C., Cobos, P., Rodríguez, S., Muñoz, M.A. Tormo, M.P., Herrero, M., Segarra, P., Pastor, M.C., Montañés, S., Poy, R., and Moltó, J. (2001). El Sistema Internacional de Imágenes Afectivas (IAPS): Adaptación española. Segunda parte. *Revista de Psicología General y Aplicada, 54* (4), 635-657.

Weinberger, D.R., Elvevag, B. and Giedd, J.N. (2005). *The adolescent brain: A work in progress.* Washington, DC: National Campaign to Prevent Teen Pregnancy.

Wood, P., Cochran, J., Pfefferbaum, B., and Arneklev, B. (1995) Sensation-seeking and delinquent substance use: an extension of learning theory. *The Journal of Drug Issues, 25,* 173-193.

Ystgaard, M., Reinholdt, N., Husby, J., and Mehlum, J., (2003). Deliberate self harm in adolescents. *Tidsskrift for Den Norske Laegeforening (Norwegian Medical Journal) 123*, 2241–2245.

Reviewed by Lourdes Anllo-Vento (University of California, San Diego, USA) and Jaime Vila Castellar (University of Granada, Spain).

In: Impulsivity: Causes, Control and Disorders
Editor: George H. Lassiter

ISBN 978-1-60741-951-8
© 2009 Nova Science Publishers, Inc.

Chapter X

A Comparison of the Eysenck Impulsiveness Questionnaire and the Dickman Impulsivity Inventory in a Flemish Sample

L. Claes, H. Vertommen and N. Braspenning
Department of Psychology, Catholic University Leuven,
Leuven, Belgium

Abstract

Self-report questionnaires are widely used techniques for measuring impulsiveness. Some have developed as a part of more general personality scales, and others specifically for measuring impulsiveness (Luengo et al., 1991). In this paper we investigated the psychometric properties of one of the latter, the Eysenck Impulsiveness Questionnaire (I.7; Eysenck, Pearson, Easting, and Allsopp, 1985) when applied in a Flemish sample. We present the factor structure of the Dutch I.7 and describe the psychometric properties of the instrument. Further, the characteristics of the I.7 subscales were compared with those reported in the original papers. In addition, the items of another impulsivity questionnaire, namely the Dickman Impulsivity Inventory (DII; Dickman, 1990) and the I.7 items were pooled to investigate the extent to which the two scales measure the same variable(s) and to get a better understanding of the impulsiveness construct.

Keywords: Impulsivity, Venturesomeness, Functional Impulsivity, Dysfunctional Impulsivity

Introduction

The personality trait "Impulsiveness" has undergone several changes in the course of the development of Eysenck's Theory (see e.g., Luengo, Carrillo-de-la-Pena, and Otero, 1991). In 1977, Eysenck and Eysenck established that impulsiviness itself is not a unitary trait, but exists of four independent facets: narrow impulsiveness, risk taking, non-planning and liveliness (Eysenck, 1993; Luengo, et al., 1991). In 1978, factor analysis on three of the four facets of impulsiveness (liveliness not included) and four subscales of the Sensation Seeking Scale of Zuckerman (1993), revealed two factors, being Impulsiveness (Do without thinking) and Sensation Seeking or Venturesomeness (Risk Taking). The Eysenck Impulsiveness Questionnaire was developed to measure both aspects, Impulsiveness and Venturesomeness. The current version of this instrument (I.7) exists of 54 items (Eysenck, Pearson, Easting, and Allsopp, 1985) divided over 3 subscales: 19 items for Impulsiveness, 16 items for Venturesomeness, and 19 filler-items for Empathy (selected from the Empathy Scale of Mehrabian and Epstein, 1972). The I.7 has been translated into different languages, such as French (Caci, Nadalet, Bayllé, Robert, and Boyer, 2003), German (Eysenck, Daum, Schugens, and Diehl, 1990), Spanish (Luengo, Carillo-de-la-Pena, and Otero, 1991; Aluja, and Blanch, 2007) and Dutch (The Netherlands) (Lijffijt, Caci, and Kenemans, 2005).

In this study, we investigate the psychometric properties of the Dutch (Flemish) I.7. The means, standard deviations, reliabilities and sex and age differences were calculated and compared with those reported in other papers. Furthermore, the items of the Impulsivity and Venturesomeness scales of the I.7 were pooled with items of the Functional and Dysfunctional Impulsivity Subscales of the Dickman Impulsiveness Inventory (DII, Dickman, 1990). Dysfunctional Impulsivity is the tendency to act with less forethought when this tendency is a source of difficulty. Functional impulsivity, in contrast, is the tendency to act with relatively little forethought when such a style is optimal. Research of Miller, Joseph, and Tudway (2004) found that Eysenck's Impulsiveness and Dickman's Dysfunctional Impulsivity are measuring a similar facet of impulsivity; however, the results suggest a significant, yet weaker correlation between Venturesomeness and Functional Impulsivity. Comparable findings were mentioned by Claes, Vertommen and Braspenning (2000), who found correlations of 0.73 between Impulsiveness and Dysfunctional Impulsivity and 0.44 between Venturesomeness and Functional Impulsivity. Considering these results, we expect that factor analysis on the items of the I.7 and DII will reveal three factors: being impulsiveness, venturesomeness and functional impulsivity.

Method

Subjects

Subjects were 315 adults, representative for the Flemish population, who were recruited by students in psychology. Each student was given a profile of three persons (s)he had to look for, specifying gender, age and educational level in order to guarantee a good cross-section of the population. There were 159 male (50.5%) and 156 female (49.5%) respondents. Five different age ranges were represented: 18-24 years (16.5%), 25-34 years (25.3%), 35-44 years (25.0%), 45-54 years (18.8%) and 55-65% years (14.0%). With respect to the education level, 9.2% only followed elementary school, 52.8% went to high school and 37.3% followed higher education. The majority of respondents (66.1%) were married or living together with a partner, 30.4% were unmarried, 1.3% divorced and 1.9% widowed. The distribution of the subjects over the gender groups, the age groups and the educational levels corresponds to the distribution of the Flemish population (see Claes, Vertommen and Braspenning, 2000).

Instruments

Eysenck Impulsiveness Questionnaire (I.7)

The I.7 is a self-report inventory that consists of 54 items to be answered with a yes/no format. Eysenck and Eysenck (1978) concluded that the I.7 is an adequate measure of three factors, named Impulsiveness (Imp, 19 items), Venturesomeness (Vent, 16 items) and Empathy (Emp, 19 items). In this study we are only interested in the first two subscales. Impulsivity is measured with items such as 'I often buy things on impulse'. Venturesomeness exists of items such as 'I quite enjoy taking risks'.

Dickman Impulsivity Inventory (DII)

The DII-short (Dickman, 1990) is a self-report questionnaire developed to measure two types of impulsivity, namely Functional and Dysfunctional Impulsivity. It consists of 23 items to be answered with a true/false answer format. Eleven items were written to tap functional impulsivity and exist of items such as 'People have admired me because I can think quickly'. Another 12 items were designed to tap dysfunctional impulsivity and exist of items such as 'I often say whatever comes into my head without thinking first'.

The two scales have been translated into Dutch and retranslated into English by a native speaker of English. Differences between the original versions and the retranslations were discussed in order to improve the quality of the Dutch translations (see Claes, Vertommen and Braspenning, 2000).

Results

Factor Structure of the I.7

The correlation matrix of the 19 impulsiveness and the 16 venturesomeness items was factor-analyzed using the Principal Axis Method with Oblique Rotation (oblimin with delta set to 0). The criterion for factor extraction was an eigenvalue equal or greater than 1.

The first two factors explained 31% of the total variance (Table 1) and represented the two expected components 'Venturesomeness' (20% of variance) and 'Impulsivity' (11% of variance). Fifteen of the sixteen items that loaded on Factor 1 had been written by Eysenck et al. (1985) to measure Venturesomeness, whereas 18 of the 19 items that loaded on Factor 2 had been developed to measure Impulsivity. Only two items of Factor 1 had a loading smaller than 0.30, namely item 2 and item 49. This can be explained by the fact that item 49 was designed to tap 'Impulsiveness'. The lower loading of item 2 in this study and in the study of Eysenck et al. (1985) may be due to its content that was not referring to an activity that was full of risks as do the other items.

Table 1. Results of the factor analysis with oblique rotation of the Dutch and English I.7

Items	This study (2008)		Eysenck et al. (1985)	
	Factor 1 Vent	Factor 2 Imp	Factor 1 Vent	Factor 2 Imp
39. Would you like to go scuba diving?	**0.71**	-0.04	**0.63**	-0.11
20. Would you like to learn to fly an aeroplane?	**0.71**	-0.03	**0.61**	-0.06
36. Would you enjoy the sensation of skiing very fast down a high mountain slope?	**0.71**	-0.03	**0.65**	-0.13
06. Would you enjoy parachute jumping?	**0.71**	-0.00	**0.63**	-0.05
30. Do you sometimes like doing things that are a bit frightening?	**0.69**	0.04	**0.66**	-0.02
01. Would you enjoy water skiing?	**0.62**	0.01	**0.57**	-0.12
17. Do you welcome new and exciting experiences and sensations, even if they are a little frightening and unconventional?	**0.61**	0.12	**0.61**	0.01
47. Would you be put off a job involving quite a bit of danger?	**-0.60**	-0.04	**-0.59**	-0.02
04. Do you quite enjoy taking risks?	**0.59**	0.12	**0.60**	0.09
12. Do you think hitch-hiking is too dangerous way to travel?	**-0.57**	-0.05	**-0.39**	-0.03
14. Do you like diving off the high-board?	**0.53**	0.06	**0.37**	-0.02
46. Do you like to go pot-holing?	**0.52**	0.03	**0.50**	-0.02
41. Would you enjoy fast driving?	**0.49**	0.08	**0.50**	0.09
28. Do you find it hard to understand people who risk their necks climbing mountains?	**-0.40**	0.07	**-0.47**	0.25
02. Usually do you prefer to stick to brands you know are reliable, to trying new ones on the change of findings something better?	-0.17	-0.05	-0.24	-0.01
49. When people shout at you, do you shout back?	-0.17	0.13	0.03	0.28
19. Do you usually think before doing anything?	0.08	**-0.74**	0.13	**-0.55**
22. Do you often do things on the spur of the moment?	-0.07	**0.73**	0.19	**0.54**
42. Do you usually work quickly, without bothering to check?	-0.09	**0.69**	0.00	**0.43**
25. Do you mostly speak before thinking things out?	-0.18	**0.68**	-0.18	**0.63**
07. Do you often buy things on impulse?	-0.14	**0.67**	0.17	**0.46**
11. Do you often get into a jam because you do things without thinking?	-0.02	**0.64**	-0.02	**0.64**
16. Are you an impulsive person?	-0.02	**0.60**	0.15	**0.61**
44. Before making up your mind, do you consider all the advantages and disadvantages?	-0.01	**-0.59**	-0.11	**-0.51**
27. Do you often get so 'carried away' by new and exciting ideas that you never think of possible snags?	0.10	**0.57**	0.16	**0.51**

Table 1. (Continued)

Items	This study (2008)		Eysenck et al. (1985)	
	Factor 1 Vent	Factor 2 Imp	Factor 1 Vent	Factor 2 Imp
52. Do you usually make up your mind quickly?	0.15	**0.44**	0.08	**0.28**
31. Do you need to use a lot of self-control to keep out of trouble?	-0.00	**0.41**	0.12	**0.36**
48. Do you prefer to 'sleep on it' before making decisions?	-0.14	**-0.40**	-0.22	**-0.28**
26. Do you often get involved in things you later wish you could get out off?	0.20	**0.38**	-0.04	**0.48**
43. Do you often change your interest?	0.19	**0.34**	0.17	**0.30**
09. Do you generally do and say things without stopping to think?	0.11	**0.31**	-0.12	**0.70**
38. Do you think an evening out is more successful if it is unplanned or arranged at the last moment?	0.04	0.16	0.18	0.20
33. Would you agree that almost everything enjoyable is illegal or immoral?	0.00	0.13	0.07	0.29
35. Are you often surprised at people reactions to what you do or say?	0.04	0.09	0.00	0.39
34. Generally do you prefer to enter cold sea water gradually, to diving or jumping in?	0.07	0.09	-0.31	0.07

Note. Factor loadings above 0.30 are printed in bold.

On Factor 2, there were 4 items with a loading smaller than 0.30. The lower loading of item 34 can be due to the fact that it was designed to measure 'Venturesomeness'. The lower loadings of item 33, 35, and 38 can be explained by their content; they don't refer to an action without thinking before as do the other items.

Taking together we can say that the result of the oblique factor solution yields a similar factor pattern to that found by Eysenck et al. (1985). Further evidence on this topic has been gathered by means of a Procrustes congruence rotation. We found a great concordance between the results in our study and the study of Eysenck et al. (1985). Congruence coefficients are good for both subscales, namely 0.93 for Venturesomeness and 0.92 for Impulsivity.

Scale Characteristics of the I.7

Means and standard deviations of both subscales are presented in Table 2 and can be compared with the means and standard deviations reported by Eysenck et al. (1985). The results show that males and females in this study are on average less impulsive and less venturesome than their counterparts in the study of Eysenck et al. (1985). This can be due to the fact that the subjects in our sample (M_{age} = 38 years) are older than those in Eysenck's sapmle (M_{age} = 26), and as we will show later, impulsivity and venturesomeness scores decrease when age increases.

Table 2. Means and standard deviations of I.7 impulsiveness and venturesomeness scores obtained by Eysenck et al. (1985) and in this study

Scale	This study (2008)						Eysenck et al. (1985)			
	Total sample		Male		Female		Male		Female	
	M	SD	M	SD	M	SD	M	SD	M	SD
Impulsiveness	4.63	3.50	4.33	3.13	4.94	3.85	7.93	4.12	9.02	4.19
Venturesomeness	6.26	4.20	7.62	4.28	4.87	3.66	10.31	3.73	8.69	3.91

Table 3. Internal consistency coefficients and correlations of the I.7 impulsiveness and venturesomeness subscales obtained by Eysenck et al. (1985) and in this study

Scale	This study (2008)						Eysenck et al. (1985)			
	Total sample		Male		Female		Male		Female	
	1	2	1	2	1	2	1	2	1	2
Impulsiveness	*0.79*	0.31	*0.75*	0.29	*0.82*	0.44	*0.84*	0.35	*0.83*	0.38
	(0.83)	(0.33)	*(0.77)*	(0.32)	*(0.87)*	(0.46)				
Venturesomeness		*0.85*		*0.84*		*0.81*		*0.85*		*0.84*
		(0.87)		*(0.87)*		*(0.84)*				

Notes. 1. Italicized values on the diagonal are internal consistency coefficients (Cronbach's alpha's).
2. Values without brackets are calculated on the scales as defined by the original author (N_{imp}=19, N_{vent}=16), values between brackets are based on the results of our own analyses [N_{imp}=15 (elimination of items 33, 34, 35 and 38); N_{vent}=14 (elimination of items 2 and 49)].

Internal consistency coefficients and subscale intercorrelations are presented in Table 3. As revealed by Table 3, the reliability analysis indicates sufficient internal consistency of both subscales and shows that the Cronbach's alpha coefficients of the Dutch study are almost the same as those of Eysenck et al. (1985) study in the female sample, respectively 0.82 versus 0.83 for the impulsiveness subscale and 0.81 versus 0.84 for the venturesomeness scale. Only the alpha coefficient of the impulsiveness subscale calculated in the Flemish male sample is lower (0.75) compared to the alpha coefficient (0.84) in Eysenck et al. (1985). The alpha coefficient of the venturesomeness subscale of the male participants is comparable in both studies (0.84 and 0.85).

Compared with Eysenck et al. (1985) results, the correlation between both subscales is slightly higher in the female Flemish sample (r = 0.44 > $r_{Eysenck}$ = 0.38) and slightly lower in the male Flemish sample (r = 0.29 > $r_{Eysenck}$ = 0.35).

Relationship between I.7 Scales and Demographics

The relationships between the I.7 subscales and the demographic variables, Sex and Age were explored by means of a multivariate analysis of variance (MANOVA) followed by univariate analysis of variance (ANOVAs) and Scheffé's post hoc tests for the significant effects. We found a significant effect of Sex on Venturesomeness, which was a consequence of the fact that men reported significantly more risk-taking and adventure-seeking behaviours [$F(1, 297)$=42.18, p<0.001] than women. The effect of Sex on Impulsiveness was not significant.

We also found a significant effect of Age on Venturesomeness [$F(1, 297)=42.18$, $p<0.001$], the effect of Age on Impulsiveness showed the same tendency but was not statistically significant. The results show that Venturesomeness and Impulsiveness decrease, when age increases.

The Components of Impulsiveness as measured by I.7 and DII

Finally, we performed a joint factor analysis of the I.7-Items (N=35) and the DII-items (N=23). The result of this factor solution can be found in Table 4.

Table 4. Results of the factor analysis with oblique rotation on the I.7 impulsiveness and venturesomeness items and the DII functional and dysfunctional impulsivity items

Item	Scale	Factor 1	Factor 2	Factor 3
9.	Dysf-Imp	**0.71**	0.08	0.11
19.	Imp	**-0.68**	-0.06	0.15
1.	Dysf-Imp	**0.66**	-0.14	-0.07
22.	Dysf-Imp	**-0.66**	-0.20	0.20
7.	Dysf-Imp	**0.65**	-0.03	0.16
25.	Imp	**0.64**	-0.08	-0.16
22.	Imp	**0.63**	0.05	-0.17
11.	Imp	**0.63**	0.18	0.19
42.	Imp	**0.62**	0.05	-0.11
18.	Dysf-Imp	**0.62**	0.14	0.20
7.	Imp	**0.60**	0.00	-0.14
21.	Dysf-Imp	**0.60**	-0.05	-0.06
13.	Dysf-Imp	**0.56**	0.16	0.02
10.	Dysf-Imp	**0.55**	0.26	0.16
16.	Imp	**0.54**	0.06	-0.15
44.	Imp	**-0.53**	-0.12	0.18
27.	Imp	**0.51**	0.25	-0.01
17.	Dysf-Imp	**0.51**	0.05	0.34
14.	Dysf-Imp	**-0.50**	0.05	-0.03
31.	Imp	**0.42**	0.19	0.24
23.	Dysf-Imp	**0.30**	-0.11	0.28
9.	Imp	0.25	0.15	-0.16
49.	Imp	0.16	-0.13	0.12
38.	Imp	0.14	0.08	0.00
36.	Vent	0.00	**0.72**	-0.02
6.	Vent	0.04	**0.71**	-0.05
39.	Vent	-0.00	**0.70**	-0.04
20.	Vent	0.02	**0.70**	-0.07
30.	Vent	0.11	**0.69**	-0.10
1.	Vent	0.03	**0.63**	-0.00
17.	Vent	0.13	**0.60**	-0.16
4.	Vent	0.11	**0.58**	-0.21

Table 4. (Continued)

Item	Scale	Factor 1	Factor 2	Factor 3
14.	Vent	0.11	**0.56**	-0.08
47.	Vent	-0.10	**-0.56**	0.30
12.	Vent	-0.07	**-0.52**	0.29
46.	Vent	0.05	**0.49**	-0.16
41.	Vent	0.07	**0.49**	-0.12
16.	F-Imp	-0.00	**0.45**	-0.23
43.	Imp	0.28	**0.33**	0.06
28.	Vent	0.08	**-0.32**	0.18
26.	Imp	0.31	**0.32**	-0.03
34.	Vent	0.05	0.10	-0.00
11.	F-Imp	-0.02	-0.14	**0.73**
6.	F-Imp	0.21	0.22	**-0.58**
52.	Imp	0.32	0.13	**-0.58**
2.	F-Imp	-0.02	-0.13	**0.55**
19.	F-Imp	-0.11	0.01	**-0.52**
48.	Imp	-0.32	-0.11	**0.51**
8.	F-Imp	0.29	-0.05	**0.49**
12.	F-Imp	0.11	-0.18	**0.47**
15.	F-Imp	0.18	0.38	**-0.46**
4.	Dysf-imp	-0.18	-0.23	**0.45**
20.	F-Imp	0.03	0.07	**-0.45**
5.	F-Imp	0.21	0.16	**-0.41**
3.	F-Imp	0.11	-0.04	**0.31**
2.	Vent	-0.03	-0.11	0.21
35.	Imp	0.10	0.13	0.14
33.	Imp	0.12	0.06	0.14

Notes. 1. Factor loadings above 0.30 are printed in bold.
2. Imp = I.7 Impulsiveness, Vent = I.7 Venturesomeness; F-Imp = Functional Impulsiveness; Dysf-Imp = Dysfunctional Impulsiveness.

The first factor accounts for 17.3% of the total variance. Twenty four of the in total 58 items loaded on Factor 1. Eleven of these items were developed by Dickman to measure Dysfunctional Impulsivity and the other 13 items were written by Eysenck to measure Impulsiveness. All these items refer to human behaviour without adequate thought, and are supposed to be indicators of Dysfunctional Impulsivity, as in literature (dysfunctional) impulsive behaviour is defined as 'behaviour with no thought whatsoever' (English, 1928), 'action of instinct without recourse to ego restraint' (Demont, 1933).

Factor 2 explains 10.4% of the total variance and exists of 18 items. The items that load significantly on this factor are almost all written by Eysenck to measure 'Venturesomeness'. These items refer to thrill and adventure seeking.

The third factor that emerged from the factor analysis, exists of 16 items. Most of these items were written by Dickman to assess Functional Impulsivity and refer to the action of quick decision taking when such a response style is functional. Dickman (1990) called this factor 'Functional Impulsivity'. However, Eysenck (1993) suggested that it might be better to name functional impulsivity 'spontaneity' to indicate its separateness from dysfunctional impulsivity.

Discussion

The current study presents the validation of the Flemish version of the Eysenck Impulsiveness Questionnaire (I.7; filler items excluded). As expected, a two factor solution emerged, each factor representing one of the two types of impulsivity as defined by Eysenck et al. (1985), named Impulsivity and Venturesomeness. Except for two items (items 49 and 34), all items are found to belong to the same subscales in both versions, which again indicates that the internal factor structure of the I.7 is consistent across the Flemish and English samples. This concordance between both versions of the I.7 was also demonstrated after congruence rotation, which yields very high (> 0.90) congruence coefficients for both subscales. The fact that the items 49 and 34 did not fit the original structure could be due to their content which was not in line with the other items. In the original study of Eysenck, these items also had lower factor loadings if compared with the other items of the same factor.

The internal consistency of both I.7 scales proved to be good, respectively 0.93 and 0.92 for Venturesomeness and Impulsivity. As in the original study by Eysenck, the correlation (r=0.30) between the two subscales is moderate so we cannot conclude that impulsiveness and venturesomeness are completely independent personality factors.

We further found significant sex and age differences which are in line with the results of previous research. Eysenck et al. (1985) found a decrease in impulsivity with age and showed that men are even more impulsive/risk taking than women (Eysenk et al., 1985; Leungo et al., 1991). Our data confirmed that venturesomeness (and to some degree impulsiveness) decrease with increasing age; and that males are more risk-taking than females.

Finally, the results of the joined factor analysis of the I.7 and the DII revealed three factors referring to Dysfunctional Impulsivity, Venturesomeness and Functional Impulsivity. The fact that Venturesomeness and Functional Impulsivity form two different factors is not surprisingly, as their content is very different. Miller, Joseph and Tudway (2004) clearly mentioned that Venturesomeness includes items which describe acts of risky behaviour, the consequences of which may be life threatening. On the contrary, Functional Impulsivity focuses on cognitive processes, of which the consequences of being impulsive are less dangerous and can be even positive. Finally, the three factors Dysfunctional Impulsivity, Venturesomeness and Functional Impulsivity are regularly described in literature (e.g., Barratt, 1985; Corulla, 1987; Gerbing, Ahadi, and Patton, 1993; Luengo et al., 1991). For example, Gerbing, Ahadi, and Patton (1987) performed a factor analysis on different self-report and behavioural measures of impulsiveness, and found three factors: being 'Impulsive', 'Thrill Seeking' and 'Quick Decisions'. Also Miller, Joseph, and Tudway (2004) factor-analyzed items of four impulsiveness measures and found three components of impulsiveness: being 'Non-Planning Dysfunctional', 'Functional Venturesomeness' (which in our study was divided into two components), and 'Drive/Reward Responsiveness'.

Given that impulsiveness comprises different facets, it seems important to define which aspect of impulsiveness one wants to measure, before deciding which instrument one wants to use.

References

Aluja, A., and Blanch, A. (2007). Comparison of impulsiveness, venturesomeness and empathy (I7) structure in English and Spanish sampes: Analysis of different structural equation models. *Personality and Individual Differences, 43*, 2294-2305.

Barratt, E.S. (1985). Impulsiveness subtraits, arousal and information processing. In J.T. Spence and C.E. Itard (Eds.), *Motivation, emotion and personality* (pp. 137-146). North Holland: Elsevier Science.

Caci, H., Nadaleet, L., Bayllé, F.J., Robert, F., and Boyer, P. (2003). Cross cultural study of the impulsivenes-venturesomeness-empathy questionnaire. *Comprehensive Psychiatry, 44*, 381-387.

Claes, L., Vertommen, H., and Braspenning, N. (2000). Psychometric properties of the Dickman Impulsivity Inventory. *Personality and Individual Differences, 29*, 27-35.

Corulla, W.J. (1987). A psychometric investigation of the Eysenck Personality Questionnaire (revised) and its relationship to the I.7 Impulsiveness Questionnaire. *Personality and Individual Differences, 8*, 651-658.

Dickman, S. (1990). Functional and dysfunctional impulsivity: Personality and cognitive correlates. *Journal of Personality and Social Psychology, 58*, 95-102.

Demont, L. (1933). *A concise dictionary of psychiatry and medical psychology.* Philadelphia: Lippincott.

English, H. (1928). *A student's dictionary of psychological terms.* Yellow Springs, OH: Antioch Press.

Eysenck, H.J. (1993). The nature of impulsivity. In W.G. McCown, J.L. Johnson, and M.B. Shure (Eds.), The impulsive client: Theory, Research, and Treatment (pp. 57-69). Washington, DC: American Psychological Association.

Eysenck, S.B.G. (1993). The I.7: Development of a measure of impulsivity and its relationship to superfactors of personality. In W.G. McCown, J.L. Johnson, and M.B. Shure (Eds.), The impulsive client: Theory, Research, and Treatment (pp. 141-149). Washington, DC: American Psychological Association.

Eysenck, S.B.G., and Eysenck, H.J. (1978). Impulsiveness and Venturesomeness: Their position in a dimensional system of personality description. *Psychological Reports, 43*, 1247-1253.

Eysenck, S.B.G., Daum, I., Schugens, M.M., and Diehl, J.M. (1990). A cross-cultural study of impulsiveness, venturesomeness and empathy: Germany and England. *Zeitschrift für Differentiell und Diagnostische Psychologie, 11*, 209-213.

Eysenck, S.B.G., Pearson, P.R., Easting, G., and Allsopp, J.F. (1985). Age norms for impulsiveness, venturesomeness and empathy in adults. *Personality and Individual Differences, 6*, 613-619.

Gerbing, D.W., Ahadi, S.A., and Patton, J.H. (1987). Towards a conceptualization of impulsivity: components of the I.7 Impulsiveness Questionnaire and the Barratt Impulsiveness Scale. *Personality and Individual Differences, 12*, 657-667.

Lijffijt, M., Caci, H., and Kenemans, J.L. (2005). Validation of the Dutch translation of the I7 questionnaire. *Personality and Individual Differences, 38*, 1123-1133.

Luengo, M.A., Carrillo-de-la-Pena, M.T., and Otero, J.M. (1991). The components of impulsiveness: A comparison of the I.7 Impulsiveness Questionnaire and the Barratt Impulsiveness Scale. *Personality and Individual Differences, 12*, 657-667.

Mehrabian, A., and Epstein, N. (1972). A measure of emotional empathy. *Journal of Personality, 40*, 525-543.

Miller, E., Joseph, S., and Tudway, J. (2004). Assessing the component structure of four self-report measures of impulsivity. *Personality and individual differences, 37*, 349-358.

Zuckerman, M. (1993). Sensation seeking and impulsivity: A marriage of traits made in biology. In In W.G. McCown, J.L. Johnson, and M.B. Shure (Eds.), The impulsive client: Theory, Research, and Treatment (pp. 71-91). Washington, DC: American Psychological Association.

In: Impulsivity: Causes, Control and Disorders
Editor: George H. Lassiter

ISBN 978-1-60741-951-8
© 2009 Nova Science Publishers, Inc.

Chapter XI

Psychological and Biological Basis of Impulsive Behavior

*Michio Nomura**
Graduate School of Integrated Arts and Sciences,
Hiroshima University, Japan

Abstract

It has been suggested that impulsive behavior is caused by dysfunctional serotonergic 5-HT neurotransmissions in the central nervous system (CNS). A substantial body of evidence has supported this hypothesis by demonstrating that acute tryptophan depletion, a procedure that transiently decreases 5-HT neurotransmission, has been reported to increase impulsive behaviors. Recently, the conclusions of several studies have been in apparent conflict with the function of the 5-HT2A receptor (one of three major types of the 5-HT receptor family) in impulsivity. We examined whether the polymorphism in the 5-HT2A receptor gene promoter is involved in impulsivity using a Go/No-go task in 71 normal volunteers. Impulsivity was defined as the number of commission errors (responding when one should not) recorded during a Go/No-go task; a larger number of commission errors indicate greater difficulty in inhibiting impulsive behavior. The participants of the A-1438A allele group for the 5-HT2A receptor gene made more commission errors under the PR condition (withholding responses to active stimuli were punished and withholding responses to passive stimuli were rewarded) than those in the G-1438G group. From these results, we suggest the possible involvement of the A-1438A polymorphism of the 5-HT2A receptor gene promoter in impulsive behavior.

Keywords: Impulsivity; 5-HT2A receptor; Gene Polymorphism; Neuroimaging; Go/No-go task

---

* Address for correspondence: Michio Nomura, 1-7-1, Kagamiyama, Higashi-Hiroshima, 739-8521, Japan. E-mail: nomura@hiroshima-u.ac.jp.

Introduction

Impulsivity and Serotonin

Impulsive behavior is a multidimensional personality trait that comprises a wide spectrum of human behaviors; it is one of the defining characteristics of a number of psychiatric diagnoses. It may contribute to antisocial personality disorders and poor impulse control in borderline cases (Stein, Hollander, and Liebowit, 1993; Tremblay, et al., 1994). In addition, impulsivity is related to an important aspect of risk assessment in a wide range of clinical situations such as pathological gambling and eating disorders (Barratt, 1994; Hart and Dempster, 1997; Leyton, et al., 2001). Moreover, it has often been implicated as a key aspect in the risk assessment of affective liability, self-injury, and suicidal behavior (Plutchik and Van Praag, 1995).

It has been suggested that impulsive behavior is caused by dysfunctional serotonergic 5-HT neurotransmissions in the central nervous system (CNS). Serotonin (5-HT) has been reported to have a wide range of biological effects on human behavior, and dysfunctional 5-HT neurotransmissions in the CNS may cause behavioral diseases that are characterized by impulsivity. A substantial body of evidence has supported this 5-HT hypothesis by demonstrating that acute tryptophan depletion, which transiently decreases 5-HT neurotransmission, has been reported to increase impulsive and aggressive behaviors (Cleare and Bond, 2000; Walderhaug, et al., 2002). It has also been reported that the administration of the serotonin-releasing drugs d,l-fenfluramine and paroxetine decreases impulsivity in conduct disorder participants (Cherek and Lane, 2000). Furthermore, 5-HT depletions were found to impair impulsive motor action and not delay aversion (Winstanley, et al., 2004). In conclusion, these clinical, behavioral, and pharmacological observations appear to support the hypothesis that functional alteration in 5-HT neurotransmissions is involved in impulsive motor action in humans.

The 5-HT2A Receptor Gene and Impulsive Behavior

The 5-HT family of receptors has three major types: 5-HT2A, 5-HT2B, and 5-HT2C. These receptors are similar in terms of their molecular structure, pharmacology, and signal transduction effects. The 5-HT2A receptors are widely distributed, with high levels in the frontal cortex, where postsynaptic activation may modulate executive functions and impulsive behaviors. For instance, although negative data have been also reported (van Heeringen et al., 2003), greater 5-HT2A binding in the prefrontal cortex has been correlated with suicide (Oquendo et al., 2006). In addition, rat studies showing abnormalities in the 5-HT2A receptor gene may be related to impulse control in continuous performance tasks (Winstanley et al., 2004). The 5-HT2A receptor antagonist ketanserin has been tested in the five-choice serial reaction time task (5-csrtt) and shown to decrease premature responding when administered peripherally or into the medial prefrontal cortex (Passetti, Dalley, and Robbins, 2003). Furthermore, administering the 5-HT2A antagonist DOI [1-(2,5-dimethoxy-

4-iodophenyl)-2-aminopropane] enhanced premature responding in the 5-csrtt (Koskinen and Sirvio, 2001).

Recently, the conclusions of several studies have been in apparent conflict with the function of 5-HT2A receptor gene polymorphism for impulsivity. Several studies have demonstrated associations between the promoter region of the 5-HT2A receptor A-1438G genotypes and psychiatric disorders characterized by impulsive behavior (Nishiguchi, et al., 2001) in alcohol dependents (Preuss, et al., 2001) and in obsessive and compulsive disorder patients. For instance, an association between the A-1438G genotype and crime commission by Swedish males has been reported (Berggard, et al., 2003). Furthermore, elevated A allele frequencies, associated with increased promoter function (Parsons, et al., 2004), were reported to be associated with susceptibility to anorexia nervosa.

On the other hand, the results of several reports that examined the associations between 5-HT2A receptor gene polymorphisms and impulsive behavior remain controversial. This is because no correlations between them have been detected in diseases such as anorexia nervosa (Ziegler, et al., 1999) that are characterized by impulsivity, and healthy participants evaluated by psychometric self-report personality trait measures such as the Temperament and Character Inventory (TCI) (Kusumi, et al., 2002). The inconsistency among these findings may have developed because of inadequate statistical powers and the use of categorical diagnostic criteria alone that does not provide adequate measures for identifying psychiatric phenotypes and subtle individual differences between the mental characteristics of healthy and clinical participants. Thus, the etiology of these complex diseases, including subtle differences, should be considered and elucidated using a direct behavioral study that examines the relationship between genetic factors and susceptibility to impulsive diseases rather than by the psychometric self-report approach to impulsivity.

Methods

This behavioral study revealed two aspects of impulsivity: the reward-delay impulsivity that is defined as the inability to delay reward, leading to an increased tendency to select immediate small rewards over larger delayed ones (Monterosso and Ainslie, 1999); and the rapid-response impulsivity that is the failure to correctly respond to the environment and social context leading to commission errors, e.g., in a test that requires careful examination of the stimuli such as in the Go/No-go tasks. The Go/No-go tasks possess reasonable temporal stability and tend to have high test-retest reliability. Our previous study (Nomura, et al., 2006) revealed an association between 5-HT2A receptor gene polymorphism and rapid-response impulsive behavior by using a Go/No-go task in healthy volunteers.

Seventy-one unrelated Japanese volunteers (39 males: 28.7 ± 9.7 years) with normal visual acuity, either unaided or with correction, participated in this study. All participants were drug-free for at least four weeks before the blood sampling, had no history of physical or psychiatric illness and gave written informed consent after receiving a detailed description of the study. The research protocol was approved by the ethics committee of the Hokkaido University Graduate School of Medicine. The participants filled out a Japanese version of the TCI, a self-report measure for four temperament dimensions (Novelty seeking, Harm avoidance, Reward dependence, and Persistence) and three character dimensions (Self-directedness, Cooperativeness, and Self-transcendence) as defined by Cloninger's psychobiological model of personality (Cloninger, Svrakic and Przybeck,.1993). Next, the participants performed a reward-punishment Go/No-go task. In this behavioral task, participants were instructed in such a way as to learn to respond to "active" stimuli (two numbers paired with a reward) and inhibit their response to "passive" stimuli (two numbers paired with a punishment) by trial and error. Four conditions of the Go/No-go task were performed by each participant. Under the reward-only condition, both responses to active stimuli and withholding responses to passive stimuli were rewarded. Under the punishment-only condition, both withholding responses to active stimuli and responses to passive stimuli were punished. In the reward-punishment condition, responses to active stimuli were rewarded and responses to passive stimuli were punished. In the punishment-reward condition, withholding responses to active stimuli were punished and withholding responses to passive stimuli were rewarded. By using visual feedback after each response, correct responses were rewarded with the word "CORRECT" on a computer screen, implying that according to the condition participants were given 10 yen as monetary feedback, while incorrect responses were punished by the word "WRONG" implying that 10 yen were subtracted from the participants' earnings.

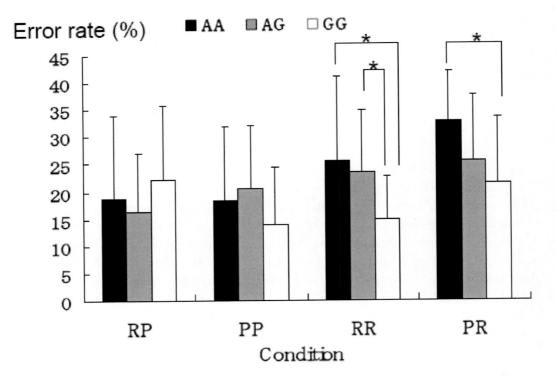

Figure 1. Commission error rates (%) under four conditions in each of the three allele groups (AA: A-1438A, AG: A-1438G, and GG: G-1438G). Bar graphs indicate the results of statistical analysis (asterisk, p <0.05). Mean ± SD. RR: reward-only condition, PP: punishment-only condition, RP: reward-punishment condition, and PR: punishment-reward condition.

Error rate (%)

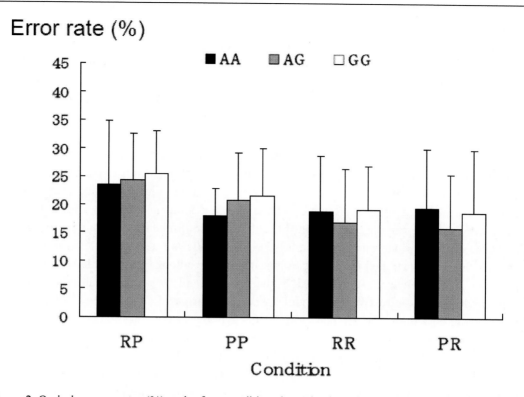

Figure 2. Omission error rates (%) under four conditions in each of the three allele groups (AA: A-1438A, AG: A-1438G, and GG: G-1438G). Mean ± SD. RR: reward-only condition, PP: punishment-only condition, RP: reward-punishment condition, and PR: punishment-reward condition.

To test the hypothesis that the 5-HT2A receptor gene is involved in impulsive behavior, DNA was extracted from lymphocytes isolated from whole blood samples (20 ml) of the participants by standard methods. Briefly, 3.8 % Na-citrated whole blood samples were centrifuged at 1,000 × g for 20 minutes and the middle layer was separated for lymphocyte preparation by further centrifugation. Briefly, we analyzed this polymorphism (1438G/A) in the promoter region of the 5-HT2A receptor gene using the following two kinds of primer: 5'-AAGCTGCAAGGTAGCAACAGC-3' and 5'-AACCAACTTATTTCCTACCAC-3'. The 468 base pair (bp) products obtained were digested with MspI, which cuts the 1438 allele into two fragments of 244 and 224 bp. The fragments were separated on a 3 % agarose gel plate.

Results and Discussion

The present study demonstrated that the observed genotype distributions were consistent with the Hardy-Weinberg equilibrium, and that no significant differences existed with regard to age, education, and gender ratio across genotypes. A two-way analysis of variance (ANOVA) of the commission errors revealed that the A-1438A group made significantly more commission errors than the G-1438G group, which collapsed under all four conditions (see Figure 1). The analysis also showed that the A-1438A group made significantly more PR commission errors than the G-1438G group (Tukey HSD post hoc test, $p < 0.05$), and that the

A-1438A and G-1438A groups appeared to make relatively more RR commission errors than the G-1438G group (Tukey HSD post hoc test, $p < 0.05$).

On the other hand, a two-way ANOVA of the omission errors revealed no significant main effects or interactions, indicating that this 5-HT2A receptor gene polymorphism had no effect on omission errors (see Figure 2). The TCI scores showed no significant relationship between the 5-HT receptor A-1438G genotypes and the seven personality dimension scores, except self-directedness.

The increased number of commission errors indicates the possible role of G-1438A polymorphism of the 5-HT2A receptor gene in susceptibility to impulsive behaviors in an aspect that incorporates the failure of response inhibition. This is in accordance with a previously proposed hypothesis which stated that a dominant response set for reward is formed by making response inhibition difficult when confronted by stimuli associated with response cost (Newman and Wallace, 1993). The results are also consistent with previous studies that demonstrate increased commission errors among psychopaths (Newman and Kosson, 1986; Newman, Widom and Nathan, 1985) and aggressive male adolescents as compared to non-aggressive male adolescents (LeMarquand, et al., 1998). Further, our findings support these reports and lead to the hypothesis that the 5-HT2A receptor gene polymorphism is also involved in the impulsive behavior of healthy participants.

In addition, the present results showed no significant group differences during either RP or PP conditions. One possible assumption is that this result indicates punishment for errors during Go/No-go trials in A-1438A group reduced commission errors. This interpretation is in line with the demonstration that acute depletion of the 5-HT precursor tryptophan in healthy participants enhanced the ability to predict punishment and improved behavioral performance as shown by Cools, Robinson, and Sahakian (2008). In their study, participants were presented with two visual patterns, one of which was associated with reward, the other with punishment. The outcome was presented after the participants made their predictions and they made significantly fewer punishment prediction errors after the acute depletion of tryptophan than the controls did. On the basis of these findings our findings lead to the hypothesis that the reduced 5-HT functions in the A-1438A group and, in sum, provide a link between the 5-HT2A receptor gene polymorphism and the impulsive behavior of healthy participants.

Genetics and Functional Brain Neuroimaging

Brain neuroimaging studies have shown that behavioral (motor response) inhibition is linked to the activation of cortex sites such as the right ventral frontal cortex (Rubia, et al., 2005) and the dorsolateral frontal cortex, whose activation negatively correlates with impulsivity (Asahi, et al., 2004). Several reports also show that impulsivity is characteristic of damage to the ventral frontal lobe in monkeys (Iversen and Mishikin, 1970) and humans (Godefroy and Rousseaux, 1996), and that lesions in the ventral frontal lobe have been known to cause sociopathic syndromes (Damasio, Tranel and Damasio, 1990; Grafman, et al., 1996). This observation has led to suggestions that controlling 5-HT function may contribute to ventral frontal lobe function, lesions in which lead to impulsive behavior. In fact, by using positron emission tomography (PET) with selective neurotransmitter radiotracers, Leyton et al. (2001) reported that a male with borderline personality disorder showed significant negative correlations between [11C]MTrp trapping (a measure of serotonergic responsiveness) and the number of commission errors in the ventral frontal lobe during the Go/No-go task. By using PET imaging with [18F]altanserin to characterize 5-HT2A receptor binding, Kaye et al. (2001) revealed a reduction in ventral frontal cortex 5-HT2A binding in women who had recovered from bulimia nervosa, which is characterized by impulsive behavior. Together with our findings, these observations indicate the possible involvement of the 5-HT2A receptor gene polymorphisms in 5-HT2A receptor expression in the ventral and medial frontal cortex.

Conclusion

The results of the present study suggest the possible involvement of A-1438A polymorphism of the 5-HT2A receptor gene in impulsive behavior. Psychological studies with concurrent biochemical and pharmacological measurements of both 5-HT2A receptor functions in humans—in particular those investigating the effect of gene polymorphisms—appear to be useful in clarifying the relationships between personality traits and vulnerability to impulsive behaviors. However, further studies will have to be performed to clarify the pathophysiological mechanism of impulsive behavior. Neural circuits (including the 5-HT system) in the regional brain, which are the underlying cause of impulsive behavior, remain to be elucidated.

References

Asahi, S., Okamoto, Y., Okada, G., Yamawaki, S., Yokota, N. (2004). Negative correlation between right prefrontal activity during response inhibition and impulsiveness: A fMRI study. *Eur. Arch. Pschiatry Clin. Neurosci*, 254, 245–251.

Berggard, C., Damberg, M., Longato–Stadler, E., Hallman, J., Oreland, L., kan Garpenstrand, H. (2003). The serotonin 2A -1438 G/A receptor polymorphism in a group of Swedish male criminals. *Neurosci Lett.*, 347, 196–198.

Bjork, J. M., Moeller, F. G., Dougherty, D. M., Swann, A. C.,. Machado, M. A. and Hanis, C. L. (2002). Serotonin 2a receptor T102C polymorphism and impaired impulse control. *Am. J. Med. Genet.*, 114, 336–339.

Cherek, D. R., and Lane, S. D. (2000). Fenfluramine effects impulsivity in a sample of adults with and without a history of conduct disorder. *Psychopharmacology*, 152, 149–156.

Cleare, A. J., and Bond, A. J. (2000). Experimental evidence that the aggressive effect of tryptophan depletion is mediated via the 5-HT1A receptor. *Psychopharmacology*, 147, 439–441.

Cloninger, C. R., Svrakic, D. M., and Przybeck, T. R. (1993). A psycho–biological model of temperament and character. Arch. *Gen. Psychiatry.*, 50, 975–590.

Cools, R., Robinson, O. J., and Sahakian, B. (2008). Acute tryptophan depletion in healthy volunteers enhances punishment prediction but does not affect reward prediction. *Neuropsychopharmacology*, 33, 2291–2299.

Damasio, A. R., Tranel, D and Damasio, H. (1990). Individuals with psychopathic behaviour caused by frontal damage fail to respond autonomically to social stimuli. *Brain Behav. Res.*, 41, 81–94.

Godefroy, O., and Rousseaux, M. (1996). Divided focus attention in patients with lesion of the prefrontal cortex. *Brain Cogn.*, 30, 155–174.

Grafman, J., Schwab, K., Warden, D., Pridgen, A., Brown, H. R., and Salazar, A. M. (1996). Frontal lobe injuries, violence, and aggression: A report of the Vietnam Head Injury Study. *Neurology*, 46, 1231–1238.

Hart, S. D. and Dempster, R. J. (1997). Impulsivity and Psychopathy. In: Webster, C. D., Jackson, M. A., editors. Impulsivity; theory, assesment and treatment. 212–232. Guilford Press, New York.

Iversen, S. D., and Mishikin, M. (1970). Perseverative interference in monkeys following selective loss of the inferior prefrontal convexity. *Exp. Brain Res*, 11, 376–386.

Kaye, W. H., Frank, G. K., Meltzer, C. C., Price, J. C., McConaha, C. W., Crossan, P. J., Klump, K. L., and Rhodes, L. (2001). Altered serotonin 2A receptor activity in women who have recovered from bulimia nervosa. *Am. J. Psychiatry*, 158, 1152–1155.

Koskinen, T., Sirvio, J. (2001). Studies on the involvement of the dopaminergic system in the 5-HT2 agonist (DOI)-induced premature responding in a five-choice serial reaction time task. *Brain Research Bulletin.*, 54, 65–75.

Kusumi, I., Suzuki, K., Sasaki, Y., Kameda, K., Sasaki, T., and Koyama, T. (2002). Serotonin 5–HT receptor gene polymorphism, 5–HT receptor 2A function and personality traits in healthy participants: a negative study. *J. Affect. Disorder.*, 68, 235–241.

Leyton, M., Okazawa, H., Diksic, M., Paris, J., Rosa, P., Mzengeza, S., Young, S. N., Blier, P., and Benkelfat, C. (2001). Brain regional α–[^{11}C]methyl–L–tryptophan trapping in impulsive participants with borderline personality disorder. *Am. J. Psychiatry*, 158, 775–782.

McMurran, M., Blair, M., and Egan, V. (2002). An investigation of the correlations between aggression, impulsiveness, social problem–solving, and alcohol use. *Aggressive Behav..* 28, 439–445.

Monterosso, J., and Ainslie, G. (1999). Beyond discounting: possible experimental models of impulse control. *Psychopharmachology*, 146, 339–347.

Oquendo, M. A., Russo, S. A., Underwood, M. D., Kassir, S. A., Ellis, S. P., Mann, J. J., and Arango, V. (2006). Higher postmortem prefrontal 5-HT2A receptor binding correlates with lifetime aggression in suicide. *Biol. Psychiatry*, 59, 235-243.

Parsons, M. J., D'Souza, U, M., Arranz, M. J., Kerwin, R. W., and Makoff, A. J. (2004). The -1438A/G polymorphism in the 5-hydroxytryptamine type 2A receptor gene affects promoter activity. *Biol. Psychiatry*, 56, 406-410.

Passetti, F., Dalley, J. W., and Robbins, T. W. (2003). Double dissociation of serotonergic and dopaminergic mechanisms on attentional performance using a rodent five-choice reaction time task. *Psychopharmacology*, 165, 136–145.

Newman, J. P., and Kosson, D. S. (1986). Passive avoidance learning in psychopathic and non psychopathic offenders. *J. Abnorm. Psychol.*, 95, 252–256.

Newman, J. P., and Wallace, J. F. (1993). Diverse pathways to deficient self–regulation: Implications for disinhibitory psychopathology in children. *Clin. Psychol. Rev.*, 13, 699–720.

Newman, J. P., Widom, C. S., and Nathan, S. (1985). Passive avoidance in syndromes of disinhibition: Psychopathy and extraversion. *J. Pers. Soc. Psychol.*, 48, 1316–1327.

Nishiguchi, N., Matsushita, S., Suzuki, K., Murayama, M., Shirakawa, O., and Higuchi, S. (2001). Association between $5HT_{2A}$ receptor gene promoter region polymorphism and eating disorders in Japanese patients. *Biol. Psychiatry*, 50, 123–128.

Nomura, M., Kusumi, I., Kaneko, M., Masui, T., Daiguji, M ., Ueno, T.,. Koyama, T., and Nomura Y. (2006). Involvement of a polymorphism in the 5-HT2A receptor gene in impulsive behavior. *Psychopharmacology* (Berl), 187, 30–35.

Plutchik, R., and Van Praag, H. M. (1995). The nature of impulsivity: Definitions, ontology, genetics, and relations to aggression. In Hollander, E., Stein, D., editors. Impulsivity and Aggression. 7–24. Wiley, New York.

Preuss, U. W., Koller, G., Bondy, B., Bahlmann, M., and Soyka, M. (2001). Impulsive traits and $5–HT_{2A}$ receptor promoter polymorphism in alcohol dependents: possible association but no influence of personality disorders. *Neuropsychobiology*, 43, 186–191.

Rubia, K., Lee, F., Cleare, A. J., Tunstall N., Fu, C. H., Brammer, M., and McGuire, P. (2005). Tryptophan depletion reduces right inferior prefrontal activation during response inhibition in fast, event-related fMRI. *Psychopharmacology*, 179, 791–803.

Stein, D. J., Hollander, E., and Liebowit, M. R. (1993). Neurobiology of impulsivity and the impulse control disorders. *J. Neuropsychiatry*, 5, 9–17.

Tremblay, R. E., Pihl, R. O., Vitaro, F., and Dobkin, P. L. (1994). Predicting early onset of male antisocial behavior from preschool behavior. *Arch. Gen. Psychiatry*, 51, 732–739.

Van Heeringen, C., Audenaert, K., Van Laere, K., Dumont, F., Slegers, G., Mertens, J., and Dierckx, R. A.. (2003). Prefrontal 5-HT2a receptor binding index, hopelessness and personality characteristics in attempted suicide. *J Affect Disord.*, 74, 149-158.

Walderhaug, E., Lunde, H., Nordvik, J. E, Landro, N. I., Refsum, H., and Magnusson, A. (2002). Lowering of serotonin by rapid tryptophan depletion increases impulsiveness in normal individuals. *Psychopharmacology*, 164, 385−391.

Winstanley, C. A., Dalley, J. W., Theobald, D. E. and Robbins, T. W. (2004 a). Fractionating impulsivity: contrasting effects of central 5-HT depletion on different measures of impulsive behavior. *Neuropsychopharmacology*, 29, 1331–1343.

Winstanley, C. A., Theobald, D. E., Dalley, J. W., Glennon, J. C., and Robbins, T. W. (2004 b). 5-HT2A and 5-HT2C receptor antagonists have opposing effects on a measure of impulsivity: interactions with global 5-HT depletion. *Psychopharmacology* (Berl), 176, 376-385.

Ziegler, A., Hebebrand, J., Gorg, T., Rosenkranz, K., Fichter, M., Herpertz-Dahlmann, B., Remschmidt, H., and Hinney, A. (1999). Further lack of association between the 5-HT2A gene promoter polymorphism and susceptibility to eating disorders and a meta-analysis pertaining to anorexia nervosa. *Mol. Psychiatry*, 4, 410–412.

In: Impulsivity: Causes, Control and Disorders
Editor: George H. Lassiter

ISBN 978-1-60741-951-8
© 2009 Nova Science Publishers, Inc.

Chapter XII

The Relationship between Impulsiveness and Rejection Behavior in the Ultimatum Game

Haruto Takagishi, Taiki Takahashi and *Toshio Yamagishi*
Department of Behavioral Science, Faculty of Letters,
Hokkaido University, Japan

Abstract

The purpose of this study is to examine the relationship between impulsiveness and behavioral responses in an economic game known as the ultimatum game. Thirty-one participants played the role of the responder in repeated one-shot ultimatum game. Following the ultimatum game, participants filled out the Barratt Impulsive Scale (BIS-11; Patton et al., 1995). Results showed that the higher the participant scored on impulsiveness, the more likely they were to accept highly unfair offers. This result implied that rejection behavior in the ultimatum game is less impulsive than accepting behavior.

Introduction

Recent studies in neuroeconomics have employed economic game experiments in order to elucidate neural correlates of social decision-making. Impulse control in social interactions has been studied with the ultimatum game, in which one player (the proposer) proposes a way to split a sum of money with another person (the responder). If the responder accepts the offer, both players are paid accordingly. If the responder rejects the offer, neither player is

* Corresponding author: Taiki Takahashi, 1Department of Behavioral Science, Faculty of Letters, Hokkaido University. N.10, W.7, Kita-ku, Sapporo, 060-0810, Japan. TEL +81-11-706-3057, FAX +81-11-706-3066. e-mail: taikitakahashi@gmail.com.

paid. Responders tend to reject offers less than 20% of the total stake, despite the fact that such retaliation is costly, and rejection decisions are predicted by the intensity of the aversive response to the unfair offer (Sanfey et al., 2003). Neuroeconomic studies have implied that several types of impulses are associated with the responses in the ultimatum game. For instance, Sanfey et al. (2003) conducted a neuroimaging study in the ultimatum game. They observed the anterior insula activation in the responders who faced unfair offers in the ultimatum game. The authors stated that unfair offer-induced negative emotional impulses (e.g., anger and disgust), which are represented in the anterior insula activities, made the participants reject the unfair offers. Furthermore, it has been interpreted that the dorsolateral prefrontal cortex (DLPFC) activity represents the cognitive control of the impulse to reject. The interpretation implies that interfering or disrupting DLPFC activity reduces the control of the impulse and should, thus, increase the rejection rate. Knoch et al. (2006) examined this hypothesis by reducing the activation in right and left DLPFC with low-frequency repetitive TMS. Surprisingly, the study found that rTMS of right DLPFC increases the acceptance rate of unfair offers relative to a placebo stimulation, whereas rTMS of left DLPFC did not affect behavior significantly. This finding suggests that right DLPFC is not involved in controlling the impulse to reject unfair offers but in controlling the impulse that pushes subjects towards accepting unfair offers, that is, with controlling economic self-interest. Interestingly, the disruption of right DLPFC only affects subjects' fairness-related behaviors but not their fairness judgments, that is, they still judge low offers as unfair, but they nevertheless accept them more frequently and more quickly. These findings suggest the importance of the examination of what types of impulsive tendencies are associated with the responses in the ultimatum game.

If people have social preferences the brain must compare social motives and economic self-interest and resolve conflict between them. Several studies indicate that the prefrontal cortex plays a decisive role in such conflict resolution. For example, in the contrast between costly punishment condition and costless punishment of players who behaved unfairly, the ventromedial prefrontal cortex (VMPFC) has been implicated (de Quervain et al 2004), consistent with the hypothesis that this area is involved in the integration of separate benefits and costs in the pursuit of behavioral goals (Ramnani and Owen, 2004). The crucial role of VMPFC in decisions involving social preferences is also supported by evidence that subjects with brain lesions in VMPFC reject ultimatum game offers more frequently (Koenings and Tranel, 2007), suggesting that the cost of rejecting positive offers has less weight in the decision process if VMPFC is impaired.

A recent neuroimaging study suggests that the ventrolateral prefrontal cortex (VLPFC) also play an important role in the processing of decisions involving social preferences (Tabibnia et al., 2008). The study examined the neural circuitry involved in the recipient's behavior in an ultimatum game where the rejection of low positive offers involves a motivational conflict between fairness and economic self-interest. The study finds that anterior insula is more active during rejected trials. In addition, the right VLPFC is more activated (relative to a resting baseline) when unfair offers are accepted, which might indicate that this region downregulates the resentment associated with unfair offers.

A neuropsychopharmacological study (Crockett et al., 2008) examined the role of serotonin in the ultimatum game rejection. Serotonin has long been implicated in social behavior, including impulsive aggression, but its precise involvement in impulse control is controversial. Because social interactions in game-theoretic experiments can evoke strong emotions, it is plausible that serotonin modulates impulsivity via emotion regulation mechanisms. Emotion regulation during social interactions has been studied with the ultimatum game experiment. The effect of manipulating serotonergic functioning on rejection behavior in the ultimatum game was examined with an acute tryptophan depletion (ATD) method. ATD significantly increased rejection rates, and this effect was restricted to unfair offers. However, it is still controversial whether lowered serotonin levels are actually associated with impulsivity or not (Evers et al., 2006). Taken together, it is important to examine how a rejection rate in the ultimatum game is associated with self-report impulsivity scales, for a better understanding of neuropsychological processing underlying rejection of unfair offer in the ultimatum game. Therefore, we have examined the relationship between The Barratt impulsiveness scale (BIS) scores and rejection rates in the ultimatum game. If the rejection in the ultimatum game is (less deliberative) impulsive behavior, BIS scores should positively be correlated with the rejection rate in the ultimatum game. On the contrary, if the acceptance in the ultimatum game is impulsive behavior, BIS scores should negatively be correlated with the rejection rate in the ultimatum game.

Methods

Participants

Thirty-one participants (Male=21, Female=10) at Hokkaido University participated in the study. Participants completed the experiment individually in small experimental booths equipped with individual computers.

The Ultimatum Game

Participants played the role of the responder in a repeated one-shot ultimatum game. At the beginning of the game, the proposer received 1,000 yen (= \$10) from the experimenter, and made an offer regarding how to divide money between him/herself and the responder. After the proposer had made her allocation decision, the responder decided whether to accept or reject the proposer's offer. If the responder accepted the proposer's offer, then each player could receive money according to the proposer's offer. However, if the responder rejected the offer, then both players received nothing. In this experiment, the proposer was absent: all proposer's decisions were programmed by the experimenter in advance. Participants played the ultimatum game a total of ten times as the responder, each time with a new proposer. Participants faced five 500/500 offers, two 700/300 offers, two 800/200 offers and one 900/100 offer in randomized order. The earnings of each participant were determined by the outcomes from two of the ten games which were determined by the computer.

The Barratt Impulsiveness Scale

Following the ultimatum game, participants filled out The Barratt Impulsiveness Scale (BIS-11; Patton et al., 1995; The Japanese version of the Barratt Impulsiveness Scale 11th version; Someya et al., 2001). The BIS-11 is a self-reported questionnaire which measures the tendency toward impulsiveness as a personal trait. It contains a 30 items and is composed of three subscales (Attentional Impulsiveness, Motor Impulsiveness and Non-planning Impulsiveness). The experiment took about one hour to complete.

Results

Rejection by the Responder

Figure 1 shows the mean rejection rates for each proposal. Results clearly show that fair offers were accepted and unfair offers were rejected with high probability (Figure 1). The mean rejection rate in the unfair offers (300, 200, and 100 yen) were higher than those fair offers (fisher's exact test; $p<.01$).

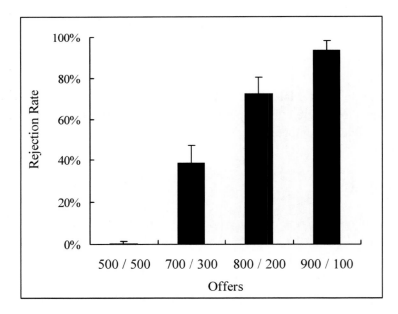

Figure 1. Rejection rate for each offer. Horizontal axis indicates the offer by the proposer. Vertical axis indicates the rate of rejection by the responder. Error bars indicate standerd error.

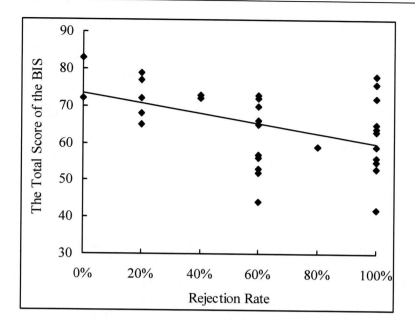

Figure 2. Scatter plot of the BIS and rejection rate. Horizontal axis indicates the rejection rate of the responder. Vertical axis indicates the Barratt Impulsiveness Scale score.

Table 1. Internal consistency of the BIS-11

	Cronbach's alpha
Total BIS	0.81
Attentional Impulsiveness	0.58
Moror Impulsiveness	0.63
Non-planning Impulsiveness	0.68

Table 2. The mean level of the BIS-11 and the subscales

	Male		Female	
	M	SD	M	SD
Total BIS	64.48	9.76	65.70	11.92
Attentional Impulsiveness	17.76	3.49	16.10	3.54
Moror Impulsiveness	22.19	3.91	24.10	4.86
Non-planning Impulsiveness	24.52	4.79	25.50	5.28

Table 3. Correlations among the BIS-11 and rejection rate

	Rejection rate	
Total BIS	-.446	*
Attentional Impulsiveness	-.198	
Moror Impulsiveness	-.351	†
Non-planning Impulsiveness	-.494	**

** $p<.01$, * $p<.05$, † $p<.10$.

Relationship between the Rejection of Unfair Offers and BIS-11

The mean level of the BIS-11 score is 64.9 (SD=10.31), and Cronbach's alpha coefficients were .81 for the combined BIS-11 measure, and .58, .63, and .68 for the Attentional Impulsiveness, Motor Impulsiveness, and Non-planning Impulsiveness subscales, respectively (Table 1). These results were very similar to the precious studies in Japan (Someya et al., 2001). There were no sex differences in the mean level of the BIS-11 or its subscales (Table 2).

Next, we conducted a correlation analysis to examine the relationship between the rejection of unfair offers and impulsiveness as a personal trait. A significant negative correlation between the BIS-11 score and the mean rejection rates of unfair offers was observed (r=-.45, $p<.05$; Figure 2). When correlations were examined in subscales, significant correlations were observed between the means rejection rates of unfair offers and Non-planning impulsiveness (r=-.49, $p<.01$; Table 3). These results showed that the higher the participant scored on impulsiveness, especially non-planning impulsiveness, the more likely they were to accept highly unfair offers.

Discussion

This study is the first to demonstrate the negative relationships between self-reported impulsiveness scores (Barratt impulsiveness scale scores) and the rejection in the ultimatum game. Our results indicate that acceptance, rather than rejection, in the ultimatum game is associated with impulsiveness. Impulsiveness is a dimensional personality trait that is important for a wide range of different human behaviors.

Although a strict definition of impulsiveness is difficult to establish, biological, psychological and social studies have regarded impulsiveness as 'a predisposition toward rapid, unplanned reactions to internal or external stimuli without regard to the negative consequences of these reactions to the impulsive individual or to others' (Moeller et al., 2001). Recent laboratory investigations of impulsiveness showed two dominant models: (1) Reward-delay impulsivity, which is the inability to delay reward and leads to an increased tendency to choose immediate small rewards over larger delayed ones (Monterosso and

Ainslie, 1999); and (2) Rapid-response impulsivity, which is the inability to conform responses to environmental context and leads to errors of commission on tests that require careful checking of stimuli (Evenden, 1998). The latter model appeared to be more closely related to trait impulsiveness, which was measured by the Barratt Impulsiveness Scale (BIS), a popular self-reporting impulsiveness scale (Patton et al., 1995).

Asahi et al. (2004) examined the relationship between the Barratt Impulsiveness Scale (BIS-11) and prefrontal activity during response inhibition. The aim of the study (Asahi et al., 2004) was to investigate the association between regional cerebral activation in Go/No–Go task and impulsiveness. Activated regions included the right middle frontal gyrus and the inferior parietal lobe, which is consistent with previous neuroimaging studies. A negative correlation was observed between the motor impulsiveness of BIS-11 and No-Go-related activation in the right dorsolateral prefrontal cortex (RDLPFC). Their results suggest that the RDLPFC is the area most sensitive to differences in individual motor impulsiveness and its activity may be an indicator of the individual capacity for response inhibition. In our present study, there was a tendency that motor impulsiveness was negatively correlated with the rejection rate in the ultimatum game, indicating that subjects with small capacity for response inhibition accepted the unfair offer in the ultimatum game. This interpretation is consistent with Knoch et al's study (2006) that disrupting DLPFC decreased the rejection rate in the ultimatum game. Taken together, it is supposable that during the responder's decision in the ultimatum game, an impulse to accept unfair offer may conflict with negative emotions (e.g., anger and disgust) induced by the unfair offer. Therefore, more impulsive subjects may tend to accept unfair offers more frequently.

Lee et al (2008) conducted an event-related fMRI study on risk taking by individuals of high or low impulsiveness. The impulsiveness was also assessed with the Barratt Impulsiveness Scale. The study reported that a stronger activation in the insula-orbitofrontal-parietal regions was found in the high impulsiveness group compared to the low impulsiveness group. The levels of activation in the lateral prefrontal and anterior cingulated regions did not differ between the two groups. Furthermore, Huettel et al (2006) demonstrate by fMRI that individuals' preferences for risk (uncertainty with known probabilities) and ambiguity (uncertainty with unknown probabilities) predict brain activation associated with decision making. Activation within the lateral prefrontal cortex was predicted by ambiguity preference and was also negatively correlated with an independent clinical measure of behavioral impulsiveness (Barratt Impulsiveness Scale), suggesting that this region implements contextual analysis and inhibits impulsive responses. Therefore, the relationship between Barratt Impulsiveness Scale scores, decision under uncertainty, and rejection in the ultimatum game should be examined in future studies, in order to elucidate the role of impulsiveness in decision-making in economic games.

Regarding the relationships between behavioral inhibition and decision-making the economic games, Scheres and Sanfey (2006) studied a personality dimension that may influence economic decision-making, the Behavioral Activation System, (BAS) which is composed of three components: Reward Responsiveness, Drive, and Fun Seeking. In order to assess economic decision making, they utilized two commonly-used tasks, the ultimatum game and dictator game. Individual differences in BAS were measured by completion of the Behavioral Inhibition/Activation System Scales (BIS/BAS), and correlations between the

BAS scales and monetary offers made in the two tasks were computed. They observed that higher scores on BAS Drive and on BAS Reward Responsiveness were associated with a pattern of higher offers on the ultimatum game, lower offers on the dictator game, and a correspondingly larger discrepancy between ultimatum game and dictator game offers. These findings are consistent with an interpretation that high scores on Drive and Reward Responsiveness are associated with a strategy that first seeks to maximize the likelihood of reward, and then to maximize the amount of reward.. Therefore, future study should examine the relationship between Barratt Impulsiveness Scale scores and the discrepancy between the ultimatum game and dictator game offers, for a better understanding of the role of response inhibition in decision-making in the economic games.

References

Asahi S, Okamoto Y, Okada G, Yamawaki S, Yokota N. (2004) Negative correlation between right prefrontal activity during response inhibition and impulsiveness: A fMRI study. E*ur. Arch Psychiatry Clin. Neurosci*, 254, 245-251.

Crockett MJ, Clark L, Tabibnia G, Lieberman MD, Robbins TW. (2008) Serotonin modulates behavioral reactions to unfairness. *Science* 320, 1739.

de Quervain DJ, Fischbacher U, Treyer V, Schellhammer M, Schnyder U, Buck A, Fehr E. (2004) The neural basis of altruistic punishment. *Science*, 305, 1254-1258.

Evenden JL (1998) The pharmacology of impulsive behaviour in rats IV: the effects of selective serotonergic agents on a paced fixed consecutive number schedule. *Psychopharmacology*, 140, 319–330.

Evers EA, van der Veen FM, van Deursen JA, Schmitt JA, Deutz NE, Jolles J. (2006) The effect of acute tryptophan depletion on the BOLD response during performance monitoring and response inhibition in healthy male volunteers. *Psychopharmacology*, 187, 200-208.

Huettel SA, Stowe CJ, Gordon EM, Warner BT, Platt ML. (2006) Neural signatures of economic preferences for risk and ambiguity. *Neuron*, 49, 765-775.

Knoch D, Pascual-Leone A, Meyer K, Treyer V, Fehr E. (2006) Diminishing reciprocal fairness by disrupting the right prefrontal cortex. *Science*, 314, 829-832.

Koenigs M, Tranel D.(2007) Irrational economic decision-making after ventromedial prefrontal damage: evidence from the Ultimatum Game. *Journal of Neuroscience,* 27, 951-956.

Lee TM, Chan CC, Han SH, Leung AW, Fox PT, Gao JH. (2008) An event-related fMRI study on risk taking by healthy individuals of high or low impulsiveness. *Neurosci Lett,* 438, 138-141.

Moeller FG, Barratt ES, Dougherty DM, Schmitz JM, Swann AC (2001) Psychiatric aspects of impulsivity. *Am. J. Psychiatry*, 158, 1783–1793.

Monterosso J,Ainslie G (1999) Beyond discounting: possible experimental models of impulse control. *Psychopharmacology*, 146, 339–347.

Patton JH, Stanford MS, Barratt ES. (1995) Factor structure of the Barratt impulsiveness scale.*J. Clin. Psychol*, 51, 768-774.

Ramnani N. and Owen A.M. (2004) Anterior prefrontal cortex: insights into function from anatomy and neuroimaging. *Nat. Rev. Neurosci*, 5, 184-194.

Sanfey AG, Rilling JK, Aronson JA, Nystrom LE, Cohen JD.(2003) The neural basis of economic decision-making in the Ultimatum Game. *Science*, 300, 1755-1758.

Scheres A, Sanfey AG. (2006) Individual differences in decision making: Drive and Reward Responsiveness affect strategic bargaining in economic games. *Behav. Brain Funct*, 2:35.

Someya T, Sakado K, Seki T, Kojima M, Reist C, Tanf SW, Takahashi S. (2001) The Japanese version of the Barratt Impulsiveness Scale, 11th version (BIS-11): its reliability and validity. *Psychiatry and Clinical Neurosciences*, 55, 111-114.

Tabibnia G, Satpute AB, Lieberman MD. (2008) The sunny side of fairness: preference for fairness activates reward circuitry (and disregarding unfairness activates self-control circuitry). *Psychol. Sci*, 19, 339-347.

In: Impulsivity: Causes, Control and Disorders
Editor: George H. Lassiter

ISBN 978-1-60741-951-8
© 2009 Nova Science Publishers, Inc.

Chapter XIII

The Construct of Impulsivity within the Context of Gender-Specific Adversity and Resilience during Adolescence: Guidelines for Future Work

Roberto Mejia[1], Christian Heidbreder[2],
Yolanda Torres de Galvis[1] and Lenn Murrelle[3]

1. School of Medicine, Universidad CES,
Medellin, Colombia
2. Global Research & Development, Reckitt Benckiser Pharmaceuticals,
Richmond, Virginia
3. ELM International Research Consultants, LLC,
Richmond, Virginia

This commentary proposes areas for future development of impulsivity, a construct denoting the inability to inhibit impulsive responses to achieve a goal or to wait for a desired goal. Impulsivity is a multifactorial construct encompassing several processes that include an inability to delay gratification, an inability to withhold a response, acting before all of the relevant information is provided, and decision making that is risky and inappropriate. Delay of gratification and inability to withhold a response are also often referred to as cognitive and motor impulsivity, respectively. Cognitive impulsivity may result from deficits in attention, an inability to discriminate reward magnitude, disruptions in time perception, a misunderstanding of response contingencies, an inability to consider future events, or a distortion in the value of long-term consequences. Similarly, apparent deficits in motor impulsivity may result from disruptions in sensory, motor, or timing abilities, even if the ability to withhold an automatic (pre-potent) response is intact.

There are typically three broad classes of tests to measure impulsivity: (1) measures of response inhibition based on the suppression of a pre-potent response (Logan et al., 1997);

(2) measures of delay discounting, which define impulsivity in terms of choice preference for a small reward available immediately (or after a short delay) over a larger reward available in the future (Bickel and Marsch, 2001; Reynolds, 2006); and (3) measures of cognitive impulsivity that refers to decision-making processes. One component of cognitive impulsivity is referred to as "reflection impulsivity" or the tendency to collect and assess information before making complex decisions (Kagan, 1966). Reflection impulsivity may be related to what other authors have referred to as "non-planning impulsivity" (Patton et al., 1995) or "lack of premeditation" (Whiteside and Lynam, 2001). Additional measures to assess cognitive impulsivity also include tasks during which the subject has to select between a conservative option and a more risky option that offers a "superficially seductive" gain (Bechara, 2003; Knoch and Fehr, 2008).

Though research on impulsivity has expanded in recent years, it is our belief that investigators should increase the study of impulsivity as a theoretical construct in the context of gender-specific experiences of significant adversity during adolescence. First, we address the need to understand gender differences in impulsivity associated with cognitive and behavioral variables outside traditional constructs reflecting impulse control problems (i.e., ADHD, substance use disorders, frontal lobe dementia, borderline personality disorder, eating disorders, obsessive-compulsive disorders, pathological gambling, and disruptive behavior disorders) and briefly describe the importance of studying gender differences in measures of impulsivity and their relation to behavioral risk and adverse contextual circumstances. Second, we examine the role of impulsivity in adaptive functioning. Specifically, we suggest the use of a resilience framework to examine impulsivity as either a moderator or mediator process and to study the relevance of this framework for prevention research.

Gender, Adolescent Adversity, and Impulsivity

Research to date has shown gender differences in cognitive and behavioral variables associated with impulsivity such as inhibitory control and representations of aggression among adolescents and young adults (Driscoll, Zinkivskay, Evans, and Campbell, 2006), as well as information processing, adolescent aggression, and social cognition in the context of personality (Calvete and Cardeñoso, 2004; Fite, Goodnight, Bates, Dodge, and Pettit, 2008). However, even fewer studies have focused on gender differences in impulsivity when adolescents are exposed to a variety of adverse life circumstances such as interparental conflict, single parenthood, maltreatment, neighborhood violence and poverty (Hayaki, Stein, Lassor, Herman, and Anderson, 2005; Waldeck and Miller, 1997). Expanded research effort is needed to understand the interactions between gender and impulsivity when at-risk youths in the community (i.e., non-clinical populations) are exposed to adverse life events. Research conducted in the field of resilience (Luthar, 1999; Spencer, 1999) has shown that male adolescents have greater vulnerability to the negative effects of community influences than girls. Therefore, identification of protective mechanisms or processes that "buffer" these adverse effects among at-risk adolescents (i.e., youths who display lower impulsive responses despite being exposed to accumulating life stressors) is warranted. Improved understanding of impulsivity as an "underlying process" (Luthar and Cicchetti, 2000; Masten, 2001; Rutter,

2000) that either increases vulnerability to adjustment problems or plays, in some, a protective role in everyday life and adaptive functioning is long overdue in the field. Studies which explore gender differences in the natural changes in impulsivity across adolescence will provide valuable information to prevention programs among disadvantaged or at-risk youths. Similarly, future research should examine gender differences in impulsive responses among youths exposed to adverse events using appropriate indices and scores (e.g., aggregate competence/vulnerability scores) coupled with impulsivity scores from laboratory-based tasks (Olson, Schilling, and Bates, 1999).

Impulsivity can serve both as a mediator of risk (i.e., a process underlying vulnerability) or as a protective mediating factor. While there is clinical evidence of the detrimental effects of impulsivity on decision-making, other studies have yielded results showing an association with enhanced decision-making (Franken and Muris, 2005). This apparent inconsistency may well have to do with the nature of the study populations or the fact that most of these studies have only employed one specific test to measure impulsivity and/or decision-making. In the next section, we discuss specific contributions of resiliency models using impulsivity as a mediating factor and briefly discuss implications for developing prevention programs targeting at-risk youths.

Exploration of Impulsivity as a Process Underlying Protective/Vulnerability Factors

Research on impulsivity would benefit from increased focus on elucidating developmental processes to understand protective or vulnerability mechanisms and co-morbidities. In order to frame the construct of impulsivity within a resilience model, investigators should delineate its contribution in multiple dimensions of competence/adaptation that are intertwined with traditional psychological problems. For example, Luthar, Doernberger, and Zigler (1993) showed that among adolescents who experienced significant adversity, some youths displayed successful academic adaptation, but struggled in other domains such as presenting increased symptoms of depression and posttraumatic stress disorder.

The adolescent period is accompanied by relative deficiencies in inhibitory capacity. Several models have emphasized how the major neurodevelopmental trajectories during the adolescent period may convey vulnerability to high-risk behaviors via the relative immaturity of frontal cortical control systems coupled with the relative maturity of striatal systems responsible for reward processing and motivation (see e.g. Chambers et al., 2003). This imbalance makes adolescence a period during which the activity of the reward system prevails over that of the systems governing avoidance or self-control (see e.g. Ernst et al., 2006). Hence, impulsivity can be reliably linked with behavioral problems and positive outcomes when adolescents are exposed to adverse circumstances (Mejia, Kliewer, and Williams, 2006). In this study, Mejia and colleagues used structural equation modeling (SEM) to examine mediating pathways of impulsivity and substance use problems between family violence/maltreatment and violent and prosocial behavior in a Colombian sample of 1,152 school youths and a convenience group of 148 juvenile offenders aged 11-19 years.

Impulsivity was measured using a 9-item scale assessing whether youths were angry and slammed doors, could not sit still long, had difficulty following directions, or engaged in risky behaviors in their lifetime. Substance use problems encompassed eleven indicators assessing whether youths disregarded social rules while under the influence of drugs, fought because of their drug use, hurt someone while under the influence of drugs, or had an accident while using drugs in the past year. The presence of mediation was determined by testing indirect and direct effects using chi-square fit indexes. Although substance use problems and impulsivity mediated the relation between maltreatment and violent behavior, the direct effect was greater than were the indirect effects. Conversely, the effects of family violence and maltreatment were directly and inversely associated with prosocial behavior (i.e., a measure of adaptive functioning) rather than mediated by impulsivity (see Figure 1).

It is possible that links between impulsivity and aggressive responses (White et al., 1994) or its relation to affiliation with deviant peers (Goodnight et al, 2006) can be attributed to a cognitive deficit in the response evaluation step, which considers both immediate and long-term consequences of an action or response (Dodge et al., 2002); this step is crucial in processing information that leads to optimal or suboptimal decisions (i.e., aggressive responses among impulsive youths) as a result of exposure to multiple stressors. Recently, Fite et al., (2008) examined how individual differences in social cognition and personality interact in predicting later aggressive behavior among 585 adolescents. Using longitudinal data and multiple reporters, their study tested the interaction of impulsivity between Social Information Processing (SIP) and aggressive behavior. Findings indicated that response evaluation at age 13 was positively predictive of adolescents' later aggressive behavior for high-impulsive and medium-impulsive adolescents, but failed to significantly predict aggression among low-impulsive adolescents. Authors concluded that high-impulsive adolescents may be less likely to use specific details unique to each social situation they encounter and rather rely upon their default cognitive-processing patterns than low-impulsive teens.

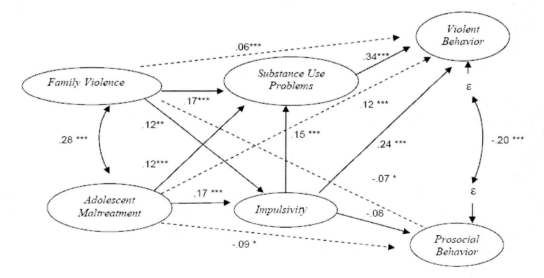

Figure 1. Impulsivity and substance use problems as mediators of the association between family violence/maltreatment and violent and prosocial behavior.

Conclusions

A central task for future studies in this field is to understand gender differences in impulsive responses when adolescents are exposed to multiple contextual stressors as well as identifying risk and protective processes that interact with impulsivity during adolescence. Conducting research to identify gender-specific factors that contribute to high impulsive responses seems warranted among adolescents exposed to high-risk circumstances. Similarly, another important area for future research relates to the relationships between operational models of impulsivity (e.g., response inhibition, delay-discounting, and cognitive impulsivity including reflection impulsivity and tests of risky decision-making).

Future work should also consider modeling meditational processes (e.g., impulsivity, substance use problems) between a variety of contextual stressors and multiple outcomes such as violent and prosocial behaviors. Studying associations of adversity, impulsive responses, and adaptive and maladaptive functioning can inform prevention and intervention research (Cowen and Durlak, 2000; Weissberg and Greenberg, 1998). We are optimistic that research on impulsivity can move forward when additional protective mechanisms (i.e., mediators) are identified and incorporated into prevention programs that simultaneously promote positive adaptation and minimize the negative effects of highly impulsive behaviors

References

Bechara, A. (2003) Risky business: emotion, decision-making, and addiction. *Journal of Gambling Studies* 19, 23–51.

Bickel, W.K., Marsch, L.A. (2001). Toward a behavioral economic understanding of drug dependence: delay discounting processes. *Addiction,* 96, 73–86.

Calvete, E., and Cardeñoso, O. (2004). Gender Differences in Cognitive Vulnerability to Depression and Behavior Problems in Adolescents. *Journal of Abnormal Child Psychology,* 33(2), 179-192.

Chambers, R.A., Taylor, J.R., Potenza, M.N., (2003). Developmental neurocircuitry of motivation in adolescence: a critical period of addiction vulnerability. *American Journal of Psychiatry,* 160, 1041–1052.

Cowen, L.C., and Durlak, J.A. (2000). *Social policy and prevention in mental health. Development and Psychopathology, 12*: 815-834

Dodge. K.A., Laird, R., Lochman, J.E., Zelli, A., and Conduct Problems Prevention Research Group. (2002). Multidimesional latent construct analysis of children's social information-processing patterns: correlations with aggressive behavior problems, *Psychological Assessment, 14*: 60-73.

Driscoll, H., Zinkivskay, A., Evans, K., and Campbell, A. (2006). Gender differences in social representations of aggression: The phenomenological experience of differences in inhibitory control? *British Journal of Psychology, 97(2),* 139-153.

Ernst, M., Luckenbaugh, D.A., Moolchan, E.T., Leff, M.K., Allen, R., Eshel, N., London, E.D., Kimes, A., (2006). Behavioral predictors of substance-use initiation in adolescents with and without attentiondeficit/ hyperactivity disorder. *Pediatrics,* 117, 2030–2039.

Fite, J.E., Goodnight, J.A., Bates, J.E., Dodge, K.A., and Pettit, G.S. (2008). Adolescent aggression and social cognition in the context of personality: impulsivity as a moderator of predictions from social information processing. *Aggressive Behavior, 34(5),* 511-520.

Goodnight, J.A, Bates, J.E, Newman, J.P., Dodge, K.A., and Pettit, G.S. (2006). The interactive influences of friend deviance and reward dominance on the development of externalizing behavior during middle adolescence. *Journal of Abnormal Child Psychology, 34(5),* 573-583.

Franken, I.H.A., Muris, P. (2005). Individual differences in decision making. *Personality and Individual Differences,* 39: 991–998.

Hayaki, J., Stein, M.D., Lassor, J.A., Herman, D.S., and Anderson, B.J. (2005). Adversity among drug users: relationship to impulsivity. *Drug and Alcohol Dependence, 78,* 65-71.

Kagan, J. (1966) Reflection-impulsivity: the generality and dynamics of conceptual tempo. *Journal of Abnormal Psychology,* 71, 17–24.

Knoch, D., Fehr, E. (2008) Resisting the power of temptations: the right prefrontal cortex and self-control. *Annals of the New York Academy of Sciences,* 1104, 123–134.

Logan, G., Schachar, R., Tannock, R. (1997) Impulsivity and inhibitory control. *Psychological Science,* 8, 60–64.

Luthar, S. S. and Cicchetti, D. (2000). The construct of resilience: Implications for interventions and social policies. *Development and Psychopathology, 12,* 857-885.

Luthar, S. S. (1999). *Poverty and children's adjustment.* Thousand Oaks, CA: Sage.

Luthar, S.S., Doernberger, C.H., Zigler, E. (1993). Resilience is not a unidimensional construct: Insights from a prospective study on inner-city adolescents. *Development and Psychopathology, 5,* 703-717.

Masten, A. (2001). Ordinary magic: Resilience processes in development. *American Psychologist, 56,* 227-238.

Olson, S.L., Schilling, E.M., and Bates, J.E. (1999). Measurement of impulsivity: Construct coherence, longitudinal stability, and relationship with externalizing problems in middle childhood and adolescence. *Journal of Abnormal Child Psychology, 27,* 151-165.

Patton, J.H., Stanford, M.S., Barratt, E.S. (1995) Factor structure of the Barratt impulsiveness scale. *Journal of Clinical Psychology,* 51, 768–774.

Reynolds, B. (2006) A review of delay-discounting research with humans: relations to drug use and gambling. *Behavioral Pharmacology,* 17, 651–667.

Rutter, M. (2000). Resilience reconsidered: Conceptual considerations, empirical findings, and policy implications. In J. P. Shonkoff and S. J. Meisels (Eds.), *Handbook of early childhood intervention (2nd ed).,* pp. 651-682. New York: Cambridge.

Spencer, M. B. (1999). Social and cultural influences on school adjustment: The application of an identity-focused cultural ecological perspective. *Educational Psychologist, 34,* 43-57.

Waldeck, T., and Miller, L.S. (1997). Gender and impulsivity differences in licit substance use. *Journal of Substance Abuse, 9,* 269-275.

Weissberg, R.P., and Greenberg, M.T. (1997). School and community competence-enhancement and prevention programs. In *Handbook of child psychology,* edited by William Damon., pp. 651-682. New York: John Wiley.

White, J. L., Moffitt, T. E., Caspi, A., Bartusch, D. J., Needles, D. J., and Stouthamer-Loeber, M. (1994). Measuring impulsivity and examining its relationship to delinquency, *Journal of Abnormal Child Psychology, 103(2),* 192-205.

Whiteside, S.P., Lynam, D.R. (2001) The five factor model and impulsivity: using a structural model of personality to understand impulsivity. *Personality and Individual Differences,* 30, 669–689.

Index

A

abnormalities, 35, 37, 45, 208

absorption, 5

abstinence, ix, 6, 83, 94, 96, 115

abusive, 53

accidents, vii, 1, 4, 5, 19

accuracy, 151, 183, 187, 190

acetate, 48

acetic acid, 128

achievement, 163

acid, 21, 69, 77, 128, 132, 140

activation, 9, 10, 11, 18, 22, 23, 25, 48, 66, 91, 108, 112, 113, 114, 128, 136, 143, 152, 153, 154, 161, 162, 190, 208, 212, 215, 218, 223

activity level, 112

acute, xi, 12, 13, 14, 20, 26, 60, 67, 68, 74, 78, 98, 100, 179, 207, 208, 212, 219, 224

acute stress, 100

adaptability, 164

adaptation, 229, 231

adaptive functioning, 228, 229, 230

addiction, 12, 15, 17, 18, 19, 22, 23, 25, 55, 71, 72, 88, 94, 99, 154, 163, 231

ADHD, 7, 28, 43, 57, 125, 128, 129, 132, 133, 134, 135, 136, 138, 139, 141, 142, 143, 144, 145, 146, 147, 150, 159, 163, 165, 175, 177, 228

adjustment, 66, 69, 88, 100, 123, 229, 232

administration, 12, 13, 15, 27, 28, 94, 96, 103, 128, 208

adolescence, xi, 5, 64, 65, 124, 168, 176, 180, 181, 182, 228, 229, 231, 232

adolescent female, 178

adolescents, vii, xi, 7, 23, 24, 28, 29, 50, 55, 57, 64, 74, 79, 84, 103, 109, 120, 123, 128, 132, 134, 135, 136, 142, 144, 145, 159, 168, 169, 171, 176, 177, 178, 179, 180, 181, 182, 183, 184, 187, 188, 189, 190, 191, 193, 212, 228, 229, 230, 231, 232

ADS, 66

ADT, 68

adult, 53, 57, 118, 130, 137, 158, 163, 177, 182

adulthood, 5, 7, 9, 65, 164

adults, 4, 23, 25, 28, 47, 50, 55, 57, 62, 75, 80, 102, 103, 109, 132, 145, 191, 196, 204, 213, 228

adverse event, 229

advertisements, 11

affective disorder, 56, 65, 66, 67, 68, 74, 79, 80

affective intensity, 115

African-American, 138

age, 4, 7, 8, 12, 13, 63, 64, 65, 66, 67, 72, 74, 164, 175, 176, 177, 182, 183, 196, 199, 201, 203, 211, 230

agents, 224

aggregation, 48

aggression, viii, 6, 9, 19, 23, 35, 53, 59, 60, 61, 62, 64, 65, 66, 68, 69, 71, 72, 73, 74, 75, 76, 78, 79, 133, 135, 137, 138, 139, 141, 142, 146, 153, 162, 214, 215, 219, 228, 230, 231, 232

aggressive behavior, 40, 62, 64, 65, 67, 68, 70, 72, 75, 139, 142, 208, 230, 231

aggressiveness, 73, 78, 130, 134, 137, 163

agonist, 214

alcohol, vii, viii, ix, 1, 2, 3, 4, 5, 6, 7, 8, 10, 11, 12, 13, 14, 15, 16, 17, 18, 19, 20, 21, 23, 24, 25, 26, 27, 28, 29, 50, 53, 59, 64, 66, 71, 72, 76, 81, 94, 98, 101, 105, 110, 111, 112, 115, 116, 117, 120, 121, 122, 124, 131, 132, 133, 135, 138, 140, 141, 142, 145, 146, 147, 168, 209, 214, 215

alcohol abuse, 9, 17, 20, 21, 23, 24, 64, 66, 124

alcohol consumption, vii, 1, 3, 4, 5, 6, 10, 11, 13, 14, 16, 20, 24, 25, 111, 120 alcohol dependence, vii, 1, 5, 27, 28, 29, 50, 53, 71, 72, 81, 132, 135, 142, 145, 146, 147

alcohol problems, 7, 9, 20

alcohol use, vii, ix, 1, 2, 3, 4, 5, 7, 8, 17, 18, 20, 21, 28, 29, 72, 105, 110, 111, 115, 116, 120, 121, 122, 214

alcohol withdrawal, 72, 138

alcoholics, 6, 8, 13, 18, 20, 23, 25, 26, 27, 72, 76, 100, 102, 111, 119, 132, 134, 143, 146

alcoholism, 7, 8, 20, 25, 26, 27, 69, 72, 79, 132, 135, 138, 143, 144, 145, 146

algorithm, 90, 91, 171, 172, 173

allele, xii, 138, 144, 146, 207, 209, 210, 211

alleles, 68, 144

alpha, 185, 200, 221, 222

alternative, 88, 90, 91, 92, 95, 97, 98, 107, 117, 125, 130, 158

alternative behaviors, 117

alternatives, 106

alters, 23, 26

ambiguity, 223, 224

American Psychiatric Association, 32, 35, 37, 41, 43, 47, 178

American Psychological Association, 118, 120, 161, 162, 192, 204, 205

amino, 21

amino acid, 21

amphetamine, 10, 23, 137

AMS, 27

amygdala, 18, 22, 25, 35, 47, 112, 113, 119, 182, 191

analog, 192

analysis of variance, 171, 200, 211

analytical framework, 121

anatomy, 225

anger, 112, 116, 117, 133, 218, 223

anger management, 116, 117

animals, 130, 153

anorexia, 209, 215

anorexia nervosa, 209, 215

ANOVA, 171, 175, 184, 185, 187, 188, 211, 212

antagonist, 15, 208

antagonistic, 26

antagonists, 15, 16, 28, 35, 39, 41, 42, 44, 125, 128, 134, 215

antecedents, 22, 37, 38, 40

anterior cingulate cortex, 120

anticonvulsants, 35, 169

antidepressant, 65, 75

antidepressants, viii, 46, 59, 67, 169

antipsychotics, 34, 35, 39

antisocial alcoholism, 133, 142

antisocial behavior, xi, 146, 168, 215

antisocial behaviour, 135, 145

antisocial personality, 70, 78, 208

antisocial personality disorder, 70, 78, 208

anxiety, viii, x, 25, 31, 32, 33, 34, 35, 36, 37, 38, 39, 40, 41, 42, 43, 44, 46, 47, 51, 54, 59, 68, 76, 107, 122, 124, 152, 154, 163, 164, 165, 168, 175, 177, 178

Anxiety, 52, 54, 56, 57, 67, 124, 152, 165, 178

anxiety disorder, viii, x, 32, 35, 39, 42, 47, 59, 124, 165, 168, 177, 178

anxiolytic, 15

APA, 150, 178

appetite, 171

application, 27, 115, 117, 122, 232

applied psychology, 161

applied research, ix, 84, 149, 161

appraisals, 102

argument, 11, 150, 156

Aristotle, 60, 73

arousal, 9, 36, 41, 43, 44, 48, 61, 112, 113, 163, 187, 189, 190, 204

arrest, 175

Asian, 132

assault, 72, 170

assertiveness, 116

assessment, 13, 48, 49, 55, 60, 62, 65, 71, 73, 74, 76, 77, 79, 102, 108, 109, 114, 117, 125, 140, 169, 170, 208

ataxia, 5

athletes, 29

Atlas, 122

atrophy, 69, 76, 79

attachment, 159, 162, 163

Attention Deficit Disorder, 130

Attention Deficit Hyperactivity Disorder, 7

attention problems, 55

attentional bias, 12, 20, 24, 57, 192

attitudes, x, 50, 114, 167, 169, 178

AUDs, vii, 1, 3

Australia, 3, 63, 149, 164

Austria, 5

autism, 32, 33, 34, 35, 45, 47, 49, 51, 52, 53, 54, 56

automaticity, 13

autopsy, 64

autosomal recessive, 69

availability, 16

averaging, 107

aversion, 42, 52, 208
avoidance, 8, 9, 20, 64, 123, 130, 152, 153, 154, 163, 171, 192, 210, 214, 215, 229
avoidant, 36
awareness, 22, 60, 61
axon, 132, 135

B

babies, 159
back, 2, 22, 198
bargaining, 225
BAS, 22, 124, 152, 153, 154, 158, 161, 162, 223
basal ganglia, 34, 54
base pair, 211
base rate, 94, 95, 96
base rates, 94
BD, viii, 59, 60
beating, 9
beer, 2, 14
behavior rehearsal, 58
behavior therapy, 47, 49, 50, 54, 123
behavioral assessment, 103
behavioral change, 116
behavioral dimension, 78, 84
behavioral disorders, ix, 83
behavioral problems, 54, 229
Behavioural Inhibition System (BIS), 152
behaviours, ix, 6, 7, 8, 9, 10, 11, 14, 17, 20, 80, 127, 130, 131, 132, 133, 135, 150, 154, 155, 159, 160, 161, 200
Belgium, 195
beliefs, 7
belongingness, 73
benchmarks, 3
benefits, 103, 120, 218
benzodiazepines, 154
bereavement, 170
beta-blockers, 55
beverages, 2, 4
bias, 29, 88, 89, 129, 169
binding, 21, 23, 77, 138, 139, 208, 213, 214, 215
binge drinking, vii, 1, 4, 5, 6, 8, 13, 16, 19, 22, 27, 28
binge eating disorder, 116
bingeing, 8, 13
biological processes, 44, 130
biological systems, 151
biosynthesis, 132

bipolar, viii, 54, 59, 61, 66, 67, 76, 78, 79, 80, 81, 131, 168, 178
bipolar disorder, viii, 54, 59, 61, 66, 67, 78, 80, 131, 168, 178
BIS, xii, 22, 64, 65, 66, 67, 68, 70, 71, 72, 140, 152, 153, 154, 162, 171, 176, 177, 180, 217, 219, 220, 221, 222, 223, 225
blocks, 11, 29, 92, 184, 188
blood, 3, 12, 24, 209, 211
blood pressure, 3
blood sampling, 209
body image, viii, 32, 33, 38, 40, 44, 46
body weight, 32, 171
Bohr, 179
BOLD, 224
bonding, 171, 179
borderline, 61, 70, 71, 72, 74, 77, 79, 122, 132, 133, 135, 138, 139, 140, 141, 143, 146, 163, 208, 213, 214, 228
borderline personality disorder, 61, 70, 71, 72, 74, 77, 79, 122, 132, 133, 135, 138, 139, 141, 143, 146, 163, 213, 214, 228
Borderline Personality Disorder, 114
boredom, 106, 107
Boston, 25
bottom-up, 113
boys, 138
brain, vii, viii, 5, 6, 18, 26, 31, 32, 35, 37, 42, 44, 47, 55, 56, 68, 69, 74, 77, 84, 86, 88, 97, 98, 100, 103, 112, 113, 114, 118, 120, 122, 128, 132, 136, 141, 182, 192, 213, 218, 223
brain abnormalities, 35
brain damage, 88, 97, 128
brain development, 182
brain injury, 100, 102, 103
brainstem, 35
Brazilian, 142
breakdown, 69
buffer, 228
bulimia, 116, 118, 121, 124, 133, 139, 141, 171, 179, 213, 214
bulimia nervosa, 116, 118, 121, 124, 133, 139, 141, 179, 213, 214
burdensomeness, 73
burning, 179

C

caffeine, 26
Canada, 118

candidates, 169

cannabis, 13

caregivers, 159

Caribbean, 147

case study, 43

catechol, 145, 146

catecholamines, 135

Catholic, 2, 195

causal interpretation, 96

causal relationship, 68, 95

ceiling effect, 177

central executive, 99

central nervous system, xi, 14, 146, 207, 208

cerebellum, 38, 46

cerebral cortex, 35, 68

cerebrospinal fluid, 69, 73, 77, 79, 128, 132, 137

CES, 227

child molesters, 51

childhood, 9, 62, 64, 65, 70, 71, 103, 138, 145, 146, 168, 175, 177, 232

children, 7, 12, 21, 22, 34, 35, 36, 49, 50, 51, 52, 53, 54, 55, 57, 64, 74, 102, 109, 110, 114, 125, 129, 133, 135, 137, 139, 143, 144, 145, 150, 171, 182, 192, 215

chocolate, 7

cholinergic, 129

chorea, 32

chromosome, 68, 134

cigarette smoke, 23, 78, 100, 102, 103

cigarettes, 13

cingulated, 112, 223

cirrhosis, vii, 1, 4, 5

citalopram, 56

classes, 227

classical, 60, 133

classification, 100, 162, 168, 170

clients, 115, 117

clinical assessment, viii, 59, 124

clinical presentation, 33, 45

clinical psychology, 164

clinical trial, 80

clinically significant, 43

clinician, 77, 114, 115, 117

close relationships, 162

clusters, 8, 21, 32, 37, 80, 118, 150, 154

CNS, xi, 14, 27, 47, 55, 135, 207, 208

Co, 122, 229

cocaine, 23, 25, 26, 94, 102, 119, 135, 138, 147, 163, 175, 177, 178

cocaine abuse, 26, 102

cocaine use, 177

Cochrane, 28

coding, 79, 132, 133, 134, 135, 136

cognitive behavioral therapy, 33, 54, 116

cognitive deficit, 230

cognitive effort, 6

cognitive function, 5, 17, 22

cognitive impairment, 24, 25, 101

cognitive level, 40

cognitive load, 88, 89, 90, 91, 92, 99

cognitive models, 13

cognitive process, 16, 17, 154, 203

cognitive psychology, 115

cognitive research, 154

cognitive style, 140

cognitive therapy, 40, 57

coherence, 232

cohort, 20, 21

college students, 26, 27, 28, 63, 108, 109, 110, 111, 120

Colombia, 227

commodity, 87

communication, 35, 116

communication skills, 116

community, 39, 81, 114, 133, 134, 135, 168, 179, 191, 228, 232

co-morbidities, 229

comorbidity, viii, x, 31, 32, 33, 34, 37, 39, 40, 43, 45, 46, 47, 48, 51, 52, 55, 57, 58, 62, 67, 70, 167, 169, 172, 175, 177, 178, 179

competence, 17, 159, 229, 232

competition, 101

complexity, 14, 18, 22, 123

complications, 61

components, 116, 120, 152, 154, 157, 197, 203, 205, 223

composition, 170

compulsion, 7, 15

compulsive behavior, 33, 34, 35, 36, 39, 41, 43, 44, 45, 48, 51

computation, 91

computed tomography, 56, 69

concentrates, 20

concentration, 16, 24, 69, 74, 77, 79, 132, 140, 171

conceptualization, 107, 116, 149, 205

conceptualizations, x, 49, 106, 149

concordance, 129, 199, 203

conditioning, 41, 42, 53, 122

condom, 26, 111, 117, 119

conduct disorder, 21, 22, 24, 28, 43, 75, 131, 132, 138, 182, 208, 213
confabulation, 5
confidentiality, 183
conflict, xi, 11, 19, 64, 93, 115, 207, 209, 218, 223
conflict resolution, 19, 218
confrontation, 60
confusion, 5
congruence, 199, 203
connectivity, 182
conscientiousness, ix, 105, 109, 110
consciousness, viii, 59
consensus, 132
consent, 169, 209
constraints, ix, 83, 84, 86, 87, 88, 89, 90, 92, 94, 95, 97, 99
construct validity, 110, 123
construction, 124
consumption, vii, 1, 2, 3, 4, 5, 6, 10, 11, 13, 14, 16, 20, 24, 25, 28, 111, 120
contaminants, 39
contamination, 39, 45
contiguity, 97
contingency, 13
control condition, 88, 89, 92, 96
control group, 170, 172
controlled studies, 39, 70
conversion, 5
Coping, 121
correlation, 63, 89, 95, 98, 107, 129, 130, 175, 196, 197, 200, 203, 213, 222, 223, 224
correlation analysis, 222
correlation coefficient, 63
correlations, 44, 99, 107, 130, 196, 200, 209, 213, 214, 222, 223, 231
cortex, 17, 22, 34, 39, 40, 42, 44, 99, 112, 113, 118, 122, 128, 136, 163, 208, 212, 218
cost-effective, 53
costs, 86, 97, 103, 120, 218
Council of Europe, 25
counseling, 123
counseling psychology, 123
covering, 136
craving, 16, 23, 25, 27, 53, 119
CRC, 29
creative process, 102
crime, 209
crimes, 170
criminal activity, 5
criminality, vii, x, 131, 149

criminals, 141, 213
critical period, 231
cross-cultural, 204
cross-sectional, 94, 111
CSF, 74, 75, 146
CT, 25
cues, 9, 10, 11, 14, 15, 17, 26, 27, 48, 50, 117, 163, 192
cultural influence, 129, 232
culture, 4, 125
cycling, ix, 60
cyproterone acetate, 48
Czech Republic, 5

D

dances, 6
danger, 198
dating, 2
deafness, 69, 79
death, 63, 72, 73
deaths, vii, 1, 3
decision making, ix, xii, 22, 23, 83, 84, 88, 92, 94, 98, 100, 101, 102, 106, 112, 113, 131, 159, 223, 225, 227, 232
decision-making process, 17, 97, 228
decisions, 12, 22, 60, 87, 88, 89, 92, 95, 96, 102, 121, 123, 125, 151, 152, 159, 182, 199, 218, 219, 228, 230
declarative knowledge, 97
deficiency, 5, 48
deficit, ix, 22, 23, 28, 51, 61, 75, 98, 127, 128, 131, 132, 135, 138, 139, 141, 142, 143, 144, 145, 146, 175, 177, 182
deficits, ix, xii, 23, 41, 42, 83, 94, 95, 96, 97, 98, 100, 105, 109, 110, 128, 165, 227
definition, x, 4, 84, 106, 107, 114, 127, 136, 155, 158, 222
degradation, 133, 135
degrees of freedom, 185
delinquency, vii, x, 149, 150, 169, 170, 171, 173, 176, 177, 178, 180, 233
delinquent adolescents, 169
delinquent behavior, 170
delinquent group, 170
delinquents, xi, 168, 172, 176, 177, 180
delivery, 13, 17
dementia, 4, 5, 228
demographics, 72
Denmark, 5

Department of Health and Human Services, 26, 167

dependent populations, 13, 20

dependent variable, 172, 176

deposits, 4

depressants, viii, 59

depressed, 62, 65, 68, 69, 71, 74, 138

depression, x, 9, 43, 63, 64, 65, 66, 68, 69, 72, 75, 76, 77, 78, 80, 116, 117, 120, 122, 162, 167, 168, 169, 170, 173, 176, 177, 178, 179, 180, 229

depressive disorder, 35, 64, 66, 67, 69, 76, 81, 168, 179

depressive symptoms, 169, 170, 176

desensitization, 53

detainees, 168

detection, 136, 176, 187

detention, x, 167, 168, 169, 176, 178, 179, 180

developing countries, vii, 1, 3

developmental disorder, 39, 47, 54

developmental process, 229

deviation, 96, 183

diabetes, 69, 76, 79

diabetes insipidus, 69

diabetes mellitus, 69, 76, 79

diagnostic criteria, 34, 39, 47, 61, 65, 171, 209

Diamond, 100

diet, 5

dieting, 116, 117, 122, 171

diets, 5

difficult goals, 155

discipline, 108

discomfort, 37, 115

discount rate, 26, 76, 102

discounting, ix, 13, 14, 23, 24, 26, 27, 80, 83, 84, 85, 86, 87, 88, 89, 90, 91, 92, 93, 94, 95, 97, 99, 100, 101, 102, 103, 119, 214, 224, 228, 231, 232

discounts, 86

discriminant analysis, 103

discrimination, 16, 137, 190

diseases, 208, 209

disequilibrium, 27, 144

disinhibition, 5, 6, 7, 8, 9, 10, 11, 12, 13, 14, 17, 18, 19, 20, 21, 22, 27, 28, 36, 84, 94, 123, 131, 143, 192, 215

disorder, vii, viii, ix, 1, 5, 7, 9, 18, 20, 21, 28, 31, 32, 34, 35, 36, 38, 39, 40, 42, 44, 45, 46, 48, 49, 50, 51, 52, 53, 54, 55, 57, 58, 59, 61, 62, 66, 67, 69, 70, 71, 75, 76, 77, 78, 94, 96, 98, 100, 116, 119, 122, 123, 127, 128, 130, 131, 135, 138, 139, 141, 142, 143, 144, 145, 146, 168, 175, 178, 179, 182, 209, 229, 231

disposition, 94, 108, 109, 120, 121

dissatisfaction, 37

dissociation, viii, 59, 214

distraction, 112

distress, 35, 40, 43, 115, 116, 117, 118, 121, 124, 177

distribution, 69, 85, 87, 95, 121, 130, 197

diuretics, 116

diving, 198, 199

dizygotic, 129, 130

dizygotic twins, 130

DNA, 144, 211

domestic violence, 168

dominance, 89, 232

doors, 230

dopamine, x, 15, 17, 24, 25, 34, 41, 47, 69, 113, 127, 128, 133, 134, 135, 136, 137, 138, 140, 143, 144, 145, 146, 147, 153, 154, 155, 161, 163, 165

dopamine agonist, 34

dopamine antagonists, 15

dopaminergic, x, 15, 113, 127, 128, 129, 132, 134, 135, 136, 145, 151, 153, 162, 214

dopaminergic neurons, 153

dorsolateral prefrontal cortex, 218, 223

Down syndrome, 35

DRD4 gene, 144

drinking, vii, 1, 2, 3, 4, 5, 6, 7, 8, 10, 11, 13, 14, 15, 16, 17, 18, 19, 20, 21, 22, 23, 24, 26, 27, 28, 29, 53, 108, 111, 116, 120, 121

drug abuse, 7, 8, 24, 25, 121, 132, 133, 135

drug abusers, 132

drug addict, 8, 119

drug addiction, 8, 119

drug dealing, 155

drug dependence, 24, 73, 119, 231

drug use, ix, 5, 6, 12, 13, 28, 94, 105, 111, 164, 178, 230, 232

drug-related, 170

drugs, 13, 15, 99, 112, 119, 134, 137, 150, 177, 208, 230

DSM, 32, 46, 47, 52, 55, 56, 61, 65, 66, 67, 69, 72, 75, 79, 118, 150, 170, 171, 173, 178, 179

DSM-II, 47, 55, 79, 118

DSM-III, 47, 55, 79, 118

DSM-IV, 52, 61, 65, 66, 67, 69, 72, 75, 79, 170, 171, 173, 178, 179

duration, 70, 170, 171

dysphoria, 177

dysregulation, 116, 118, 141

dysthymia, x, 43, 167, 171, 172, 173, 175, 177

dysthymic disorder, 43

E

earnings, 210, 219
eating, vii, ix, x, 7, 48, 105, 110, 111, 116, 118, 119, 121, 122, 123, 124, 127, 141, 162, 167, 169, 171, 177, 178, 180, 182, 184, 208, 215, 228
eating behavior, 111, 118
eating disorders, vii, ix, 48, 105, 117, 122, 123, 141, 162, 177, 180 182, 208, 215, 228
ecological, 232
economic resources, 36
economic status, 4, 132, 135
economics, 103
ecstasy, 123
Education, 27, 167
EEG, 21, 27
ego, 38, 41, 43, 202
electrophysiology, 26
elementary school, 197
e-mail, 31, 167, 217
emission, 56, 69, 119, 122, 123, 213
emotion, ix, 41, 102, 105, 108, 109, 111, 112, 113, 114, 115, 116, 118, 119, 120, 123, 124, 163, 191, 204, 219, 231
emotion regulation, 41, 115, 119, 124, 191, 219
emotional, xi, 36, 37, 61, 93, 95, 98, 107, 112, 113, 114, 115, 123, 141, 162, 181, 182, 183, 184, 190, 191, 192, 205, 218
emotional experience, 112, 113, 114
emotional reactions, 36, 123
emotional responses, xi, 182, 183
emotional state, 61, 115
emotional stimuli, 107, 190, 191
emotional valence, 182, 183, 184, 190
emotional well-being, 114
emotionality, 106
emotions, 61, 112, 113, 114, 115, 118, 128, 164, 219
empathy, 204, 205
employment, 98
encephalopathy, 5
encoding, 76, 133
encouragement, 2
endocrine, 44
endocrine system, 44
endophenotypes, 27
engagement, 63, 96, 110, 114, 116
England, 28, 76, 102, 204
entorhinal cortex, 35

environment, 9, 11, 14, 21, 86, 115, 116, 124, 129, 130, 145, 155, 156, 158, 159, 160, 209
environmental conditions, 98
environmental context, 223
environmental factors, 5, 129, 159
environmental influences, 21
environmental issues, 129
environmental stimuli, 153
enzymes, 136
epidemiology, 47
epigenetic, 129
epinephrine, 135
equilibrium, 211
error detection, 136
ethanol, 10, 23, 25, 26
ethics, 73, 209
etiology, ix, 40, 45, 53, 84, 98, 209
Europe, 28
evening, 199
examinations, 177
excitability, 60, 122, 134
excitation, 44
excitotoxic, 24
execution, 10, 13, 16, 24, 26
executive function, 13, 41, 42, 57, 208
executive functioning, 41, 42
executive functions, 13, 208
executive processes, 89, 101, 103
exercise, 116
exposure, 33, 41, 42, 53, 57, 64, 115, 119, 158, 159, 161, 170, 175, 177, 178, 230
Exposure, 45, 53, 57
externalization, 140
externalizing, 114, 124, 145, 183, 232
externalizing behavior, 114, 145, 232
externalizing problems, 232
extraction, 197
extraversion, 8, 106, 120, 130, 134, 137, 143, 162, 163, 192, 215
extroversion, 122
eyes, 5

F

facial expression, 190
factor analysis, 49, 109, 196, 198, 201, 202, 203
failure, vii, viii, 35, 40, 41, 59, 84, 152, 156, 160, 182, 209, 212
fairness, 218, 224, 225
fairness judgments, 218

faith, 2

false alarms, xi, 182, 183, 185, 189, 190

familial, viii, 31, 32, 37, 40, 42, 44, 45, 46, 48, 50, 129, 130

familial aggregation, 48

family, xi, 7, 8, 11, 14, 20, 22, 25, 33, 34, 37, 40, 43, 45, 48, 50, 52, 54, 55, 71, 116, 129, 137, 138, 139, 144, 163, 169, 170, 175, 207, 208, 229, 230

family environment, 163

family history, 20, 55, 71, 170, 175

family members, 11, 33, 129

family studies, 34, 37, 40, 43, 45

family violence, 229, 230

fasting, 116

fatigue, 171

fax, 167

fear, 33, 34, 40, 41, 60, 112, 152, 190

feedback, 18, 97, 122, 165, 210

feelings, 9, 16, 37, 38, 40, 41, 73, 93, 115, 124

females, x, 64, 139, 167, 168, 178, 199, 203

fire, 175, 177

first degree relative, 20, 35, 53

fluid, 69, 73, 74, 75, 77, 79, 80, 128, 132, 137

fluoxetine, 49, 56, 57

fluvoxamine, 51, 54

fMRI, 213, 215, 223, 224

FMRI, 55

focusing, 15, 21, 34, 107, 115, 129, 136

food, 18, 87, 150, 155, 171

Ford, 159, 163

forebrain, 153

forensic, 132

formal education, 159

Fox, 18, 24, 25, 65, 80, 164, 224

framing, 101

fraternal twins, 129

freedom, 185

Freud, 60, 75

Friday, 4

frontal cortex, 17, 18, 34, 89, 128, 182, 208, 212

frontal lobe, 12, 15, 16, 17, 86, 89, 94, 101, 103, 128, 212, 228

frontal lobes, 15, 16, 17, 103

frustration, 37, 93

functional analysis, 38

functional aspects, 38

GABRA2, 21, 24

gambling, vii, x, 12, 17, 32, 35, 36, 37, 39, 40, 41, 42, 46, 47, 48, 50, 51, 52, 53, 54, 57, 76, 94, 108, 110, 111, 112, 120, 121, 122, 123, 134, 135, 144, 146, 149, 208, 228, 232

games, 219, 223, 225

ganglia, 34, 54

ganglion, 33

gauge, 13

gel, 211

gender, 4, 8, 21, 63, 196, 211, 228, 231

gene, xi, 21, 23, 27, 29, 68, 76, 79, 132, 133, 134, 135, 136, 138, 139, 140, 141, 142, 143, 144, 145, 146, 147, 164, 207, 208, 209, 211, 212, 213, 214, 215

gene promoter, xi, 140, 141, 143, 207, 215

generalization, 131

generalized anxiety disorder, 43, 175

generation, 34, 77

genes, x, 68, 69, 127, 128, 129, 130, 131, 132, 133, 135, 136, 138, 139, 140, 141, 142, 143, 145, 147, 163

genetic factors, 129, 130, 136, 209

genetic linkage, 74

genetics, 22, 52, 76, 162, 215

Geneva, 28, 29

genome, 129

genotype, 68, 76, 132, 133, 134, 135, 138, 140, 142, 143, 145, 163, 209, 211

genotypes, 209, 211, 212

Germany, 204

girls, 76, 170, 228

glucose metabolism, 57

goal-directed, 9, 10, 15, 128, 137

goal-directed behavior, 137

goals, 112, 113, 115, 117, 119, 155, 163, 164, 218

government, vii, 1, 2, 3, 114

grass, 192

Greenhouse, 185

group therapy, 58

groups, xi, 4, 8, 15, 39, 44, 45, 62, 64, 66, 71, 72, 73, 172, 173, 175, 181, 183, 186, 187, 188, 190, 191, 197, 210, 211, 212, 223

guidance, 119, 137

guidelines, 3

guilt, 9, 40, 171

gyrus, 35, 128, 223

G

GABAergic, 129

H

haplotype, 29, 68, 141
haplotypes, 146
harm, 8, 9, 20, 36, 40, 44, 64, 73, 112, 117, 132, 133, 134, 140, 141, 169, 193
Harm Avoidance, 150, 152, 153
Harvard, 76
hazards, 11
head injury, 66
health, 4, 5, 20, 25, 26, 33, 45, 168, 179
Health and Human Services, 26
health problems, 4, 168
health services, 5
heart, 73, 163
heart rate, 73, 163
heavy drinkers, 16
heavy drinking, 4, 7, 24, 26
hedonic, 15
height, 146
hepatitis, 4
heritability, 21, 129, 130, 145
heroin, 94, 145
Heroin, 26, 76, 102
heterogeneity, 35, 43, 53, 145
heterogeneous, 131
high risk, 25, 67, 73, 115, 168, 176
high school, x, 167, 169, 170, 197
high scores, 224
higher education, 197
high-risk, 73, 78, 94, 95, 96, 97, 115, 117, 229, 231
hip, xi, 182
hippocampal, 163
hippocampus, 35, 68, 182
hips, 159
Hiroshima, 207
Holland, 204
homogenous, x, 149, 151
hopelessness, 62, 66, 67, 71, 72, 73, 215
hospitalization, 98, 172
hospitals, 61
host, 3, 4, 11, 21
hostility, 66, 67, 74, 107, 135
House, 25
human, 16, 22, 23, 27, 28, 47, 74, 94, 100, 101, 102, 103, 119, 120, 124, 128, 132, 137, 142, 143, 150, 151, 152, 154, 156, 163, 165, 202, 208, 222
human behavior, 208, 222
human brain, 28, 74, 163
human cognition, 100

human subjects, 74, 95, 102
humans, 23, 25, 27, 56, 74, 95, 112, 153, 208, 212, 213, 232
hyperactivity, ix, 6, 22, 28, 51, 66, 75, 127, 128, 130, 131, 135, 138, 139, 141, 142, 143, 144, 145, 146, 175, 182, 231
hyperbolic, 85, 102
hypersensitivity, 17, 23
hypnotic, 49
hypochondriasis, viii, 32, 33, 44, 47, 49, 57
hypothalamic, 165
hypothalamus, 5, 44
hypothesis, xi, 23, 66, 70, 77, 88, 89, 90, 94, 95, 96, 97, 98, 99, 108, 128, 130, 160, 178, 207, 208, 211, 212, 218
hysteria, 6

I

ICD, 36, 72, 79, 179
id, 40, 63, 66, 72, 177, 178
identical twins, 129, 130
identification, 21, 109, 117, 136, 168, 228
identity, 115, 232
IDS, 118
IGT, 97
illegal drug use, 111, 125
illegal drugs, 177
imagery, 123
images, 4, 182, 184, 186, 187, 189, 190
imaging, 22, 28, 33, 37, 42, 44, 48, 51, 54, 56, 57, 100, 213
imitation, 21
immediate gratification, ix, 83
impairments, 5, 94, 95, 96, 97, 98
impulsiveness, xi, xii, 60, 61, 62, 63, 64, 65, 68, 71, 78, 79, 88, 106, 108, 121, 123, 129, 130, 131, 132, 133, 134, 135, 136, 137, 140, 141, 147, 171, 195, 196, 197, 200, 201, 203, 204, 205, 213, 214, 215, 217, 219, 220, 222, 223, 224, 232
in situ, 86, 87, 151
in vivo, 76
inattention, 84
incarceration, 169
incentive, 15, 17, 120, 162
incidence, 95
inclusion, 106, 115
income, 66
independence, 123
independent variable, 176

Indian, 51
Indiana, 105
indication, 129
indicators, 69, 87, 176, 202, 230
indices, 5, 156, 229
indirect effect, 97, 156, 157, 159, 230
individual differences, 25, 100, 102, 103, 113, 121, 150, 151, 152, 205, 209, 230
inert, 15
infancy, 99, 158
infections, 6
inferences, 122
inferior frontal gyrus, 128
information processing, 11, 12, 13, 24, 113, 124, 140, 151, 165, 204, 228
informed consent, 169, 209
inheritance, x, 5, 127, 145
inhibition, x, xi, 6, 9, 10, 11, 13, 17, 23, 25, 36, 41, 42, 44, 48, 54, 61, 71, 100, 127, 128, 130, 136, 139, 141, 145, 154, 158, 162, 181, 182, 184, 192, 212, 213, 215, 223, 224, 227, 231
inhibitors, 33, 52, 53, 55, 56
inhibitory, 6, 7, 9, 11, 17, 24, 25, 71, 103, 106, 123, 152, 153, 154, 158, 189, 228, 229, 231, 232
inhibitory effect, 153
inhuman, 79
initiation, 231
injuries, 28, 98, 214
injury, 5, 19, 27, 66, 100, 102, 103, 208
insight, 5, 6, 117
instability, 76, 114
instinct, 202
instruction, 41
instruments, 73, 124, 131, 170, 177
insulin, 69
integration, 6, 49, 218
integrity, 50
intellectual functioning, 53
intelligence, viii, 59, 170
interaction, 35, 92, 112, 116, 129, 153, 156, 159, 185, 188, 230
interaction effect, 92
interactions, 114, 185, 187, 212, 215, 217, 219, 228
interference, 12, 92, 101, 191, 214
internal consistency, 200, 203
internal validity, 184
internal working models, 159
internet, 37
interparental conflict, 228
interpersonal conflict, 115

interpersonal relationships, 5, 114
interval, 91
intervention, 53, 115, 116, 118, 119, 176, 178, 231, 232
interview, x, 49, 52, 64, 65, 70, 74, 75, 79, 108, 109, 167, 169, 176, 179
interviews, 170
intoxication, vii, 1, 26, 94, 110
intron, 140
introversion, 122
intrusions, 92
inventories, 73
iodine, 69
Iowa Gambling Task, 97, 191
IQ, 170, 175, 176, 177
Ireland, 5
irritability, 37, 72, 130
isoforms, 74
isolation, 11, 131
Israel, 139, 141, 144
Italy, 59, 127
item parameters, 92

J

Japan, 167, 168, 169, 170, 176, 179, 180, 207, 217, 222
Japanese, x, 53, 140, 141, 167, 169, 170, 171, 172, 179, 180, 209, 215, 220, 225
Jefferson, 141
job performance, 150, 159, 161, 163
judge, 218
judgment, 98, 102
jumping, 110, 198, 199
juvenile delinquents, 180
juveniles, 179

K

Kant, 60, 76
Kentucky, 105
King, 37, 46, 51, 52, 142, 144, 149, 164
kleptomania, 35, 37, 39, 41, 42, 46, 47, 50, 51, 52, 53
Korean, 139, 144, 145

L

laboratory studies, 95

large-scale, 168
latency, 10, 12, 129
late-onset, 100
laws, 155
laxatives, 116
learning, 5, 9, 13, 15, 18, 22, 97, 99, 101, 116, 117, 119, 123, 155, 158, 159, 160, 161, 163, 164, 192, 214
learning environment, 159, 160, 161
learning outcomes, 163
learning styles, 155
lending, 115
lesions, 15, 17, 23, 24, 38, 128, 153, 212, 218
life stressors, 62, 98, 228
lifestyle, 115
lifetime, 37, 64, 65, 66, 67, 70, 71, 135, 177, 214, 230
ligand, 69
likelihood, 44, 72, 95, 98, 113, 114, 157, 158, 224
Likert scale, 171, 184
limbic system, 15, 35, 39
limitation, 150, 154, 156
limitations, 136, 154, 156, 157, 161, 191
linear, 10, 16, 156, 157, 160, 172
linkage, 145, 146, 164
links, vii, 1, 8, 14, 15, 45, 46, 159, 230
lithium, 70, 73, 75, 76, 77, 78, 80, 169
Lithium, 54, 76
liver, vii, 1, 4, 28
liver cirrhosis, 4, 28
loading, 197, 199
localization, 143
locomotor activity, 23, 130
locus, 27, 68, 134, 141, 144
locus coeruleus, 68
London, 1, 25, 29, 164, 231
long period, 7
longitudinal study, 34, 145
long-term memory, 101
losses, viii, 59
lover, 42
low risk, 67
lymphocyte, 211

M

M.I.N.I, 79, 179
magnetic, 51, 54, 100, 122
magnetic resonance imaging, 51, 54, 100
maintenance, ix, 5, 53, 54, 80, 83, 96, 120
Maintenance, 122
major depression, 43, 61, 66, 70, 71, 72, 75, 77, 78, 142, 179
major depressive disorder, 35, 66, 67, 69, 76, 81
maladaptive, ix, 54, 87, 105, 106, 110, 112, 114, 115, 118, 231
males, 52, 64, 81, 125, 134, 168, 199, 203, 209
Malta, 48, 50
maltreatment, 228, 229, 230
management, 114, 115, 116, 117, 122
mania, xi, 52, 65, 66, 67, 80, 153, 165, 168, 172, 174, 175, 177, 178
manic, x, 65, 67, 167, 171, 172, 173, 177, 178
manic episode, 172, 177
manic symptoms, 65
MANOVA, 200
MAO, 140
mapping, 162
marijuana, 168, 170, 175, 177, 178
marriage, 205
Maryland, 102
mastery, 155
maternal, 130, 135, 171
matrix, 108, 119, 197
maturation, 182
meanings, 12
measurement, 36, 50, 73, 102, 124, 136, 152, 158, 192
measures, vii, 7, 12, 19, 24, 63, 64, 65, 66, 70, 71, 72, 73, 84, 100, 103, 108, 118, 122, 125, 129, 130, 132, 133, 134, 135, 136, 138, 151, 165, 175, 185, 188, 192, 203, 205, 209, 215, 220, 227, 228
media, 4
medial prefrontal cortex, 208
mediation, 46, 97, 156, 164, 230
mediators, 230, 231
medical student, 163
medication, 24, 42, 45, 78, 128, 136, 168, 169, 178
medications, 34, 35, 38, 41, 44, 53, 56, 169
memory, ix, 5, 13, 17, 18, 19, 22, 23, 25, 83, 84, 86, 87, 88, 89, 90, 91, 92, 94, 95, 96, 97, 98, 99, 100, 101, 102, 103, 117
memory capacity, 13, 92, 94, 96, 100, 101
memory deficits, ix, 23, 83, 94, 95, 96, 97, 98, 100
memory processes, 88
men, 4, 7, 10, 16, 21, 26, 52, 65, 66, 67, 69, 75, 135, 147, 200, 203
mental disorder, 47, 161
mental health, 73, 162, 169, 170, 176, 231
mental retardation, 134, 143

mesocorticolimbic, 15
meta-analysis, 47, 134, 135, 144, 161, 215
metabolism, 57, 143
metabolite, 80, 128, 132
metabolites, 146
methamphetamine, 137, 170
methodological implications, ix, 84
methylphenidate, 51, 75, 169
mice, 130, 134, 137, 143
Michigan Alcoholism Screening Test, 71
midbrain, 15, 162
minerals, 5
Mini International Neuropsychiatric Interview, 67, 171
Minnesota, 124
minority, 10
misconception, 3
misunderstanding, xii, 227
modeling, 96, 102, 229, 231
models, 13, 15, 18, 19, 22, 84, 90, 95, 97, 99, 108, 109, 116, 125, 150, 151, 153, 154, 157, 161, 162, 164, 165, 204, 214, 222, 224, 229, 231
moderates, 86
modulation, viii, 13, 59, 68, 112, 113, 114, 128
modules, 115, 171
molecular structure, 208
money, 6, 14, 27, 40, 96, 155, 217, 219
monkeys, 17, 130, 137, 212, 214
monoamine, 80, 134, 136, 142, 143, 146
monoamine oxidase, 134, 142, 143, 146
monoaminergic, 145
mood, viii, ix, x, 35, 39, 41, 42, 59, 60, 64, 66, 68, 69, 71, 73, 74, 78, 80, 81, 108, 111, 114, 115, 117, 120, 124, 125, 140, 146, 165, 167, 168, 169, 170, 171, 173, 174, 175, 176, 177, 178, 179
mood disorder, ix, x, 39, 60, 64, 69, 78, 80, 140, 146, 168, 169, 171, 173, 174, 175, 176, 177, 178, 179
mood states, 108, 117
morbidity, 79, 122
morning, 14
morphometric, 54
mortality, 4
mortality rate, 4
mothers, 129
motivation, x, 9, 10, 15, 18, 19, 22, 24, 25, 37, 50, 93, 99, 103, 119, 120, 149, 152, 153, 154, 155, 156, 159, 160, 161, 162, 163, 191, 229, 231
motives, 15, 111, 218
motor behavior, 38

motor task, 48
mountains, 198
movement, 5
mPFC, 113
MTMM, 108, 110
multidimensional, 84, 95, 106, 107, 128, 131, 208
multiple regression, 67, 172, 176, 177
multiple regression analysis, 172, 176, 177
multivariate, 64, 200
muscle, 123
mutations, 69, 70, 79
myopia, 11, 23, 26, 28
myopic, 102

N

National Academy of Sciences, 25, 27, 191
National Institutes of Health, 26
natural, 13, 18, 62, 121, 124, 169, 177, 229
natural environment, 124
natural science, 121
nausea, 42
negative attitudes, 72
negative consequences, 6, 8, 9, 12, 19, 20, 40, 61, 94, 121, 222
negative emotions, ix, 40, 105, 223
negative life events, 114
negative mood, 111, 115, 117
negative outcomes, vii, x, 110, 111, 149
negative reinforcement, 15, 18, 96
negative relation, xi, 159, 182, 222
negative valence, 190
neglect, 70, 101, 106, 153
negligence, 62
Netherlands, 5, 196
network, 44
neural mechanisms, 44
neuroanatomy, 56
neurobehavioral, 152
neurobiological, 136, 153, 158
neurobiology, 77
neurochemistry, 49, 163
neurodegeneration, 5
neurodegenerative, 69
neuroeconomics, 217
neuroendocrine, 163
neuroimaging, 136, 147, 212, 218, 223, 225
neuroimaging techniques, 136
neuroleptics, 34, 169
neuronal degeneration, 5

neurons, 15, 21, 79, 103, 128, 153

neuropsychiatric disorders, ix, 127

neuropsychology, 163

neuroticism, 106, 121, 130, 150

neurotoxicity, 76

neurotransmission, xi, 69, 134, 207, 208

neurotransmitter, 68, 112, 113, 114, 118, 124, 213

New England, 54

New York, 27, 47, 52, 53, 56, 73, 74, 75, 77, 79, 80, 99, 100, 101, 102, 103, 119, 120, 121, 122, 123, 161, 162, 165, 214, 215, 232

New Zealand, 53, 162

Ni, 100, 138, 141, 143

nicotine, 6, 13

Nielsen, 140

non-clinical, xi, 33, 40, 125, 181, 228

non-human, 94

nonsmokers, 78, 102

non-violent, 69, 143

nonwhite, 66

norepinephrine, 41, 133, 135

normal, xi, 4, 6, 7, 35, 50, 53, 54, 70, 75, 81, 88, 96, 99, 103, 128, 138, 150, 156, 171, 172, 173, 176, 207, 209, 215

normal children, 54

normal development, 103

norms, 155, 204

Notre Dame, 149

novel stimuli, 107

novelty, 6, 8, 9, 20, 64, 106, 107, 134, 143, 144, 163, 164, 165

novelty seeking, 6, 9, 20, 64, 106, 107, 134, 143, 144, 163, 164, 165

Novelty Seeking, 143, 150, 152, 153, 163

nuclear, 141

nuclei, 68, 182

nucleus, 15, 25, 35, 41, 46

nucleus accumbens, 15, 25

O

obese, 132, 139, 192

obesity, 135, 146

observations, 47, 208, 213

observed behavior, 86, 99

obsessive-compulsive, viii, 31, 32, 35, 37, 41, 45, 46, 47, 48, 49, 50, 51, 52, 53, 54, 55, 56, 57, 125, 228

Obsessive-compulsive, 36, 39, 45, 49, 50, 51, 53

obsessive-compulsive disorder, viii, 31, 32, 37, 47, 48, 49, 50, 51, 52, 53, 54, 55, 56, 57, 228

occupational, 43

OCD, viii, 31, 32, 33, 34, 35, 36, 37, 38, 39, 40, 41, 42, 43, 44, 45, 46, 47, 48, 50, 175

offenders, x, 69, 132, 167, 168, 169, 170, 171, 172, 173, 175, 176, 177, 178, 179, 229

Oklahoma, 25

olanzapine, 50

older adults, 62

omission, 212

opiates, 13, 28

opioid, 15, 16, 21, 23, 27, 29, 35, 39, 41, 42, 44, 77, 144

Opioid, 28

Oppositional Defiant Disorder, 145

optimization, 90, 91, 92, 99

oral, 171

orbitofrontal cortex, 17, 22, 39, 42, 44, 113, 118, 136, 163

organ, 4

organism, 15, 87

organizational behavior, 121

orientation, 112, 113, 163, 164, 165, 190

outliers, 185

outpatient, 65

outpatients, 33, 58

overeating, 150, 171

P

pain, 103

pairing, 91

panic disorder, 43, 57, 175, 177

paradoxical, 73

paralysis, 5

parameter, 85, 87, 91, 93

paraphilia, 37, 43, 44, 46, 49, 52

parental attitudes, 178

Parental Bonding Instrument, 179

parenthood, 228

parenting, 164, 169, 171, 177, 178

parenting styles, 169, 171

parents, 12, 29, 35, 51

parietal lobe, 223

Paris, 214

Parkinson, 113, 119

paroxetine, 52, 138, 139, 208

passive, xii, 207, 210

paternal, 171

pathogenesis, 33, 41, 77

pathological gambling, 32, 35, 36, 37, 39, 40, 41, 42, 46, 47, 48, 50, 51, 52, 54, 57, 121, 123, 134, 135, 144, 146, 208, 228

pathology, 25

pathophysiological, 213

pathophysiology, 61, 129, 130

pathways, x, 15, 33, 113, 127, 151, 153, 157, 160, 215, 229

patients, vii, viii, x, 8, 12, 23, 24, 27, 33, 34, 35, 36, 37, 38, 39, 40, 41, 43, 44, 45, 47, 48, 49, 50, 51, 53, 57, 59, 60, 61, 62, 65, 66, 67, 68, 69, 70, 71, 72, 73, 74, 76, 77, 78, 79, 80, 81, 84, 89, 94, 98, 99, 100, 115, 118, 124, 127, 128, 131, 132, 133, 134, 135, 137, 138, 139, 140, 141, 145, 209, 214, 215

PBI, 171, 178

pediatric, 45, 47

peer, 62, 116, 230

per capita, 3

perception, xii, 4, 100, 121, 159, 227

perseverance, 108, 109, 110, 111, 118, 131

personal control, 115

personal problems, 4

personal relations, 5

personal relationship, 5

personality, ix, x, xi, 6, 7, 8, 9, 13, 18, 19, 20, 22, 23, 24, 25, 43, 60, 61, 64, 65, 66, 67, 69, 70, 71, 75, 79, 100, 105, 106, 107, 108, 114, 115, 116, 117, 118, 119, 120, 121, 124, 125, 127, 128, 130, 131, 133, 134, 137, 138, 139, 141, 143, 144, 150, 151, 152, 154, 155, 158, 161, 162, 163, 164, 165, 195, 196, 203, 204, 208, 209, 210, 212, 213, 214, 215, 222, 223, 228, 230, 232, 233

personality characteristics, 107, 115, 215

personality dimensions, 79, 150, 151, 161

personality disorder, x, 9, 24, 43, 61, 65, 66, 69, 70, 71, 75, 114, 118, 127, 128, 131, 133, 134, 138, 141, 143, 150, 162, 165, 215

personality factors, 62, 203

personality research, 152, 161

personality scales, xi, 195

personality traits, ix, 7, 8, 9, 20, 22, 61, 64, 105, 114, 130, 139, 141, 144, 150, 213, 214

personality type, 20

pessimism, 73

PET, 213

PFC, 113

pharmacological, 6, 18, 32, 33, 34, 35, 38, 39, 42, 44, 45, 55, 56, 67, 123, 208, 213

pharmacological treatment, 32, 34, 35, 38, 39, 42, 45, 55, 56, 123

pharmacology, 77, 137, 208, 224

pharmacotherapy, 49, 56, 78

phenomenology, 48, 52, 57

phenotype, 6, 50, 80, 141, 143, 144, 145, 146

phenotypes, 6, 11, 13, 18, 20, 21, 22, 49, 209

phenotypic, viii, 31, 32, 33

Philadelphia, 204

phobia, 175

photon, 56, 69

physical well-being, 114

physics, 101

physiological, 50, 107

physiological arousal, 50

pilot study, 48, 50, 51, 55, 56, 141

pituitary, 27, 44

placebo, 10, 16, 19, 25, 38, 39, 48, 49, 50, 51, 52, 55, 56, 70, 76, 80, 218

planning, viii, 6, 22, 59, 64, 66, 73, 106, 107, 108, 109, 113, 131, 171, 182, 196, 220, 221, 222, 228

plasma, 75

platelet, 134, 139

Platelet, 140

Plato, 60, 78

play, 20, 21, 33, 41, 68, 94, 110, 112, 113, 118, 150, 151, 153, 158, 168, 218

pleasure, 36, 41, 43, 57, 103

poisoning, 128

Poland, 71

polymorphism, xi, 21, 23, 27, 138, 139, 140, 141, 142, 143, 144, 145, 146, 147, 163, 164, 165, 207, 209, 211, 212, 213, 214, 215

polymorphisms, 69, 70, 138, 139, 140, 141, 143, 145, 163, 209, 213

poor, 5, 35, 60, 94, 110, 112, 117, 150, 151, 154, 155, 208

poor performance, 110

population, xi, 40, 42, 63, 71, 75, 77, 78, 96, 115, 129, 140, 145, 165, 168, 176, 179, 182, 196

positive correlation, 63, 69

positive emotions, 112, 117

positive feedback, 18

positive mood, 108, 111, 117, 120

positive relationship, 16, 156, 159

positron, 119, 122, 123, 213

positron emission tomography, 119, 123, 213

postmortem, 214

postsynaptic, 208

posttraumatic stress, 98, 100, 119, 123, 178, 229

posttraumatic stress disorder, 98, 100, 119, 123, 229
post-traumatic stress disorder, 180
poverty, 228
power, 21, 99, 154, 232
powers, 209
pragmatic, 102
preclinical, 125, 165
prediction, 73, 155, 164, 177, 212, 213
predictive validity, 110
predictors, 8, 49, 64, 67, 76, 231
pre-existing, vii, 1, 160
preference, ix, 53, 83, 85, 96, 97, 223, 225, 228
prefrontal cortex, viii, 17, 22, 23, 24, 40, 46, 47, 59, 100, 113, 119, 120, 128, 182, 208, 214, 218, 223, 224, 225, 232
premack principle, 122
preschool, 215
presentation order, 89
press, xi, 89, 90, 91, 92, 94, 101, 181
pressure, 3, 115, 116, 171
prevention, x, 33, 41, 43, 45, 53, 57, 114, 115, 122, 149, 160, 178, 228, 229, 231, 232
preventive, 117
primary care, 159
primary caregivers, 159
primate, 17
primates, 118
priming, 6, 10, 11, 13, 16, 19, 24, 51
priming paradigm, 19
prisoners, 63, 73
privacy, 170
proactive, 90, 92, 99, 101
proactive interference, 90, 92, 99, 101
probability, 85, 87, 90, 93, 94, 96, 103, 123, 125, 172, 173, 220
probands, 33, 35, 37, 39, 42, 43, 61, 130
probe, 190, 191
problem behaviors, 110, 111, 114
problem drinking, 26, 80, 121
problem solving, 43, 112, 116
production, 2
productivity, 5
program, 7, 73, 121
prolactin, 74, 165
promoter, xii, 68, 138, 139, 140, 141, 143, 146, 207, 209, 211, 214, 215
promoter region, 139, 140, 141, 146, 209, 211, 215
property, 103
prophylactic, 80
prophylaxis, 73

prosocial behavior, 229, 230, 231
prostitution, 170
protective factors, 62
protective mechanisms, 228, 231
protective role, 229
protein, 76, 79, 132
proteins, 5
protocol, 209
provocation, 123
proxy, 64, 65
psychiatric diagnosis, 49
psychiatric disorder, viii, 39, 40, 43, 45, 47, 48, 53, 60, 61, 62, 69, 102, 136, 178, 209
psychiatric disorders, viii, 39, 40, 43, 45, 47, 48, 53, 60, 61, 69, 102, 136, 178, 209
psychiatric illness, 169, 170, 175, 209
psychiatric morbidity, 79
psychiatric patients, 134
psychobiology, 55, 162
psychological problems, 229
psychology, 102, 151, 161, 165, 196, 204, 232
psychometric properties, xi, 195, 196
psychopathic, 214
psychopathic offenders, 214
psychopathology, 42, 50, 54, 60, 61, 62, 65, 72, 103, 124, 128, 138, 139, 140, 147, 150, 165, 177, 178, 182, 215
psychopaths, 102, 212
psychopathy, 163, 192
psychopharmacological, 14, 33, 72
psychopharmacology, 55
psychosis, 175
psychostimulants, 128
psychotherapeutic, 67
psychotherapy, 38, 49, 58
psychotic, 67, 80
psychoticism, 8, 106
PsycInfo, 62
PTSD, 66, 168, 175, 177
puberty, 56
Public Health Service, 68, 80
punishment, 9, 102, 128, 152, 162, 210, 211, 212, 213, 218, 224
P-value, 185
pyromania, 35

Q

quality of life, x, 22, 51, 127
query, 101

questionnaire, xi, 11, 63, 65, 74, 109, 122, 125, 169, 184, 189, 195, 197, 204, 205, 220

questionnaires, xi, 8, 169, 170, 175, 176, 181, 184, 195

R

radiopharmaceutical, 69
random, 88, 89, 90, 91, 92, 93, 96, 99, 169
randomness, 93
range, x, 6, 21, 85, 115, 127, 191, 208, 222
raphe, 128
rash, ix, 105, 108, 109, 111, 112, 113, 114, 116, 117, 118, 120
rat, 23, 208
rating scale, 76, 132
ratings, x, 138, 167, 172
rationality, 124
rats, 15, 103, 137, 224
reaction time, xi, 71, 133, 182, 190, 208, 214
reactivity, viii, 59, 177
reading, 11
reality, 108, 151
reasoning, 17, 97, 101, 102, 158
receptor agonist, 134
receptors, 17, 21, 133, 135, 208
recidivism, 170, 175, 178
recognition, 15, 108, 114, 116, 128
reconditioning, 51
recovery, 5
recurrence, ix, 60
reflection, viii, 59, 60, 128, 129, 137, 228, 231
reflexive responses, 16
regional, 69, 213, 214, 223
regression, 72, 158, 176
regression analysis, 72
regulation, 36, 41, 61, 101, 115, 119, 120, 122, 123, 124, 162, 165, 191, 215, 219
reinforcement, 14, 17, 18, 19, 23, 38, 96, 137, 159
reinforcers, 18, 24
rejection, xii, 62, 70, 217, 218, 220, 221, 222, 223
relapse, 6, 16, 28, 71, 81, 96, 102, 115
relapses, 115
relatives, 33, 34, 35, 37, 39, 44, 79, 130
relaxation, 38, 116, 117
relevance, 124, 151, 155, 165, 228
reliability, 74, 180, 184, 200, 209, 225
Reliability, 179
remission, 75
repetitive behavior, 32, 34, 35, 45, 46, 51, 54

replication, 144
reporters, 230
resentment, 218
resilience, 228, 229, 232
resolution, 19, 218
resources, 36, 88, 123
response time, 129
responsiveness, 113, 213
restructuring, 38, 40, 41, 43, 116
retaliation, 218
retrograde amnesia, 5
reversal training, 34, 39, 45
rewards, ix, 10, 12, 13, 16, 18, 20, 26, 76, 77, 83, 84, 85, 86, 87, 88, 89, 90, 92, 93, 94, 95, 96, 97, 99, 101, 102, 103, 209, 222
Reynolds, 13, 27, 84, 94, 103, 111, 125, 228, 232
RFLP, 146
risk assessment, 62, 208
risk behaviors, 94, 95, 96, 97, 98, 229
risk factors, viii, xi, 8, 9, 20, 59, 64, 68, 78, 112, 115, 117, 168
risks, 18, 21, 107, 178, 198
risk-taking, 17, 41, 106, 107, 110, 112, 118, 125, 168, 200, 203
risperidone, 55
robbery, 155, 170
rodent, 151, 214
romantic relationship, 159, 164
Rome, 59, 67
Rouleau, 75, 142
Royal Society, 120

S

sadness, 190
safety, 52, 112
sales, 165
sample, x, xi, 25, 33, 34, 35, 36, 37, 39, 40, 42, 43, 55, 57, 63, 65, 66, 67, 70, 109, 129, 130, 133, 134, 135, 141, 142, 145, 160, 167, 168, 169, 170, 171, 173, 176, 178, 179, 181, 183, 185, 191, 195, 199, 200, 213, 229
sampling, 209
Sarin, 27
Saturday, 4
scarcity, 87
Schizophrenia, 60, 65, 66, 74, 79, 146
schizophrenic patients, 132, 135, 139
school, x, 7, 8, 49, 74, 110, 138, 167, 168, 169, 170, 183, 197, 229, 232

school adjustment, 232
school performance, 110
scores, x, 13, 64, 65, 66, 67, 70, 71, 72, 140, 168, 169, 171, 172, 173, 175, 176, 177, 178, 183, 184, 199, 200, 212, 219, 222, 223, 224, 229
search terms, 62
searches, 62
searching, 63
sedation, 24
sedative, 16, 19
selecting, 85, 90, 93, 96, 97
selective attention, 17, 41
selective serotonin reuptake inhibitor, 33, 52, 56
Self, x, xi, 16, 57, 75, 123, 142, 149, 158, 159, 161, 179, 195, 210
self-control, 61, 62, 77, 112, 123, 124, 128, 171, 182, 199, 225, 229, 232
self-destructive behavior, 63
self-discipline, 108
self-efficacy, 27, 53
self-esteem, 116
self-image, 114
self-interest, 218
self-management, 122
self-mutilation, 50, 179
self-regulation, 165
self-report, 8, 16, 26, 54, 77, 100, 119, 124, 130, 133, 150, 165, 170, 175, 184, 189, 197, 203, 205, 209, 219, 220, 222, 223
SEM, 229
semantic, 12
semantic content, 12
sensation, ix, xi, 6, 8, 20, 29, 36, 39, 40, 41, 105, 106, 107, 108, 109, 110, 111, 117, 118, 119, 121, 131, 138, 156, 168, 181, 182, 198
sensation seeking, ix, xi, 6, 8, 20, 105, 106, 107, 108, 109, 110, 111, 117, 118, 119, 121, 131, 138, 157, 181, 182
sensations, 8, 34, 36, 38, 198
sensitivity, 9, 23, 27, 188
sensitization, viii, 32, 33, 42, 44, 46, 50, 73
separateness, 203
separation, 175
series, 12, 17, 49, 52, 54, 58, 85, 108, 168
serotonergic, xi, 68, 69, 72, 74, 77, 113, 132, 135, 140, 146, 151, 165, 207, 208, 213, 214, 219, 224
serotonin, x, 33, 41, 52, 53, 55, 56, 68, 69, 74, 75, 76, 77, 79, 103, 113, 127, 128, 132, 133, 136, 137, 138, 139, 140, 141, 142, 143, 146, 153, 158, 162, 163, 164, 165, 208, 213, 214, 215, 218

Serotonin, 28, 68, 75, 128, 132, 133, 138, 139, 141, 208, 213, 214, 218, 224
SERT, 131, 132, 136
services, 5, 121
SES, 159
severity, viii, 37, 59, 65, 66, 67, 68, 71, 72, 97, 114, 135, 145, 146, 163, 171, 176, 177
sex, 11, 18, 28, 64, 67, 111, 119, 140, 155, 196, 203, 222
sex differences, 222
sexual abuse, 71, 168, 170
sexual activities, 6, 43
sexual behavior,11, 43, 44, 48, 55, 111, 124, 125
sexual intercourse, 96
sexually transmitted infections, 6
shape, 11, 116
shaping, 11
shares, 42
short-term, 12, 100, 139
short-term memory, 100
siblings, 21, 57, 164
signal transduction, 208
signalling, 15
signals, 113
signs, 94, 116, 117
similarity, 93, 137
simulation, 89
single nucleotide polymorphism, 21
singular, 92
sites, 69, 212
skills, 35, 112, 114, 115, 116, 117
skills training, 116
skin, 37, 38, 39, 46, 48, 49, 54, 57
skin picking, 37, 38, 39, 46, 49, 54, 57
sleep, 171, 199
smokers, 23, 78, 100, 102
smoking, 6, 23, 26, 102, 103, 125, 132, 135, 140
SNP, 21
sociability, 106, 130
social anxiety, 36, 50
social behavior, 1, 55, 219
social cognition, 228, 230, 232
social consequences, 36
social context, 209
social deviance, 8
social impairment, 37
social information processing, 232
social learning, 121
social phobia, 35, 43, 56, 69, 175
social psychology, 121

social rules, 230

social skills, 35

social status, 155

social support, 41

somatic marker, 23

somatization, 68

Spain, 181, 193

specificity, 78

SPECT, 48

spectrum, viii, 21, 31, 32, 37, 44, 46, 47, 48, 49, 50, 51, 53, 54, 76, 177, 208

speech, 55

speed, 183

spheres, 7

spiritual, 2

sports, 20

SPSS, 172, 184

SRIs, 33

stability, 100, 129, 209, 232

stabilizers, 41, 42, 68

stages, 24, 61, 65

standard deviation, 183, 196, 199, 200

statistical analysis, 62, 210

Statistical Package for the Social Sciences, 184

stimulant, 14, 23

stimulus, 10, 14, 16, 115, 182, 190

storage, 100

strains, 130, 137

strategies, 10, 24, 38, 42, 49, 52, 90, 91, 92, 99, 115, 122, 155, 157, 158, 160

strength, 4, 32, 132

stress, viii, 59, 63, 78, 98, 100, 116, 119, 123, 124, 163, 178, 180, 229

stress reactions, 163

stressful events, 178

stressors, viii, 59, 61, 62, 68, 98, 228, 230, 231

striatum, 15, 37, 46, 68, 119, 128

structural equation model, 158, 204, 229

structural equation modeling, 229

students, x, 26, 27, 28, 48, 63, 108, 109, 110, 111, 120, 163, 167, 169, 170, 172, 176, 178, 196

subgroups, 65

subjective, 12, 16, 19, 26, 28, 63, 87, 90, 96, 125

substance abuse, vii, x, 28, 41, 43, 61, 66, 67, 70, 78, 80, 84, 94, 98, 103, 116, 127, 128, 129, 131, 133, 134, 135, 136, 145, 150, 182

substance addiction, 23, 100

Substance P, 68

substance use, ix, 8, 22, 26, 28, 83, 84, 94, 95, 96, 98, 100, 115, 162, 168, 169, 170, 172, 184, 192, 228, 229, 230, 231, 232

substances, 94, 95, 96, 97, 99, 122, 168

substitution, 21

substrates, 45, 73, 164

suffering, 12, 14, 17

sugar, 2, 170

suicidal, viii, x, 6, 59, 60, 61, 62, 63, 64, 65, 66, 67, 68, 69, 70, 71, 72, 73, 74, 75, 76, 77, 78, 79, 80, 117, 127, 132, 133, 135, 138, 140, 142, 144, 146, 208

suicidal behavior, viii, x, 59, 60, 61, 62, 63, 64, 65, 67, 68, 69, 70, 71, 72, 73, 74, 75, 77, 78, 80, 127, 138, 142, 146, 208

suicidal ideation, viii, 60, 63, 66, 68, 74, 75, 76, 77, 117

suicide, viii, 59, 60, 61, 62, 63, 64, 65, 66, 67, 68, 69, 70, 71, 72, 73, 74, 75, 76, 77, 78, 79, 80, 81, 128, 131, 132, 133, 134, 137, 138, 139, 140, 141, 142, 168, 171, 176, 208, 214, 215

suicide attempters, 63, 66, 69, 71, 75, 77, 80, 132, 133, 134, 139, 142

suicide attempts, viii, ix, 59, 60, 61, 63, 65, 67, 69, 70, 71, 72, 73, 74, 75, 76, 78, 79, 80, 81, 139, 142, 168

suicide completers, 81

suppression, 9, 24, 26, 191, 227

Surgeon General, 68, 80

Surgery, 50

susceptibility, 61, 107, 141, 209, 212, 215

Sweden, 25

symbolic, 40, 61

symptom, 44, 55, 68, 123, 135, 163, 177

symptomology, viii, 31, 32

symptoms, 7, 28, 35, 39, 41, 42, 43, 46, 51, 54, 65, 66, 67, 68, 110, 116, 118, 121, 125, 131, 135, 136, 139, 145, 146, 168, 169, 170, 174, 176, 229

syndrome, 5, 15, 32, 33, 34, 45, 48, 49, 50, 54, 55, 56, 57, 69, 76, 79, 134, 135, 144, 145, 175

synthesis, 152

T

tactics, 165

targets, 10, 187

task difficulty, 92

task performance, 10, 99, 190, 191

taxonomic, 150, 151, 152

taxonomy, 150

TBI, 98
teachers, 170
teaching, 38, 40, 102, 114, 115, 159
teens, 230
telephone, 63
temperament, 64, 65, 78, 106, 119, 145, 152, 162, 209, 213
temporal, 80, 84, 86, 87, 88, 90, 91, 92, 93, 97, 209
tension, 40, 41
test-retest reliability, 209
Texas, 24
thalamus, 5
theft, 41, 155
therapy, 33, 34, 38, 53, 57, 58, 116, 117, 118
Thiamine, 5
thinking, 60, 62, 73, 102, 106, 107, 108, 196, 197, 198, 199
threat, 192
threatened, 77
threatening, 63, 190, 203
three-dimensional, 69
threshold, viii, 18, 59
tic disorder, 34, 45, 50
tics, 34, 47, 56
time consuming, 88
time frame, 89, 106
time periods, 85
timing, xii, 227
tobacco, 3, 94
Tokyo, 169
tolerance, 8, 19, 115, 116, 117, 118
top-down, 113
TPH, 131, 132, 133, 136, 140
training, 15, 34, 40, 45, 102, 115, 116, 129, 164
traits, ix, 25, 34, 60, 62, 64, 70, 73, 105, 106, 108, 109, 110, 111, 112, 113, 114, 117, 118, 121, 122, 123, 124, 125, 129, 130, 131, 133, 134, 135, 136, 137, 141, 143, 150, 151, 153, 158, 159, 160, 161, 164, 205, 215
trajectory, 62
tranquilizers, 169
transcendence, 210
transcranial magnetic stimulation, 122
transformations, 102
transgenic, 134
transgenic mice, 134
translation, 205
transmembrane, 76, 79
transmission, 68, 130, 143, 144
trauma, 70, 168, 169, 170, 175, 177
traumatic brain injury, 98, 100, 102, 103
traumatic events, 168, 170, 177
travel, 198
treatment programs, 115, 116, 117
trial, 10, 47, 49, 50, 51, 55, 56, 58, 80, 89, 92, 93, 184, 210
trial and error, 210
trichotillomania, 32, 35, 36, 37, 38, 39, 46, 48, 49, 52, 53, 54, 56, 57, 58
tricyclic antidepressant, 38, 46
tricyclic antidepressants, 46
Trp, 68
true/false, 197
tryptophan, xi, 68, 74, 75, 78, 133, 139, 140, 141, 179, 207, 208, 212, 213, 214, 215, 219, 224
Tryptophan, 68, 73, 81, 119, 132, 136, 137, 140, 141, 215
Tryptophan (Trp), 68
Tukey HSD, 211
Tukey HSD post hoc, 211
twin studies, 22, 129
Twin studies, 129
twins, x, 127, 129, 130, 136, 137
two-dimensional, 171
two-way, 211, 212
typology, 24, 115

U

uncertainty, 223
unconditioned, 28
undergraduate, 102
underlying mechanisms, 99
United Kingdom, 3
United States, 3, 191
univariate, 64, 200
unpredictability, viii, 59
US Department of Health and Human Services, 26

V

valence, 184, 187, 189, 190
validation, 77, 79, 107, 119, 120, 122, 179, 203
validity, 9, 32, 76, 107, 108, 110, 123, 124, 179, 180, 184, 225
values, 72, 85, 86, 87, 88, 89, 90, 91, 93, 94, 95, 96, 184, 185, 188, 200
variability, 37, 67, 73, 87, 95, 96, 97, 99, 136, 146

variables, x, 8, 13, 24, 37, 62, 65, 67, 72, 86, 95, 98, 99, 117, 136, 156, 167, 169, 176, 177, 184, 200, 228

variance, ix, 68, 83, 90, 107, 108, 111, 130, 136, 150, 157, 158, 171, 197, 200, 202, 211

variation, 113, 130, 133, 136, 137, 140, 141, 142, 143, 145, 151, 152

vasopressin, 75

vasopressin level, 75

vein, 4

ventrolateral prefrontal cortex, 218

veterans, 119

victims, 64, 65, 138, 141

Vietnam, 119, 214

violence, 138, 214, 228, 230

violent, 6, 41, 69, 72, 75, 77, 128, 131, 132, 133, 135, 138, 139, 143, 147, 170, 229, 230, 231

violent behavior, 77, 132, 138, 147, 230

violent crime, 170

violent offenders, 69, 77, 132, 135

visible, 38, 158

visual acuity, 209

visual stimulus, 137, 190

visualization, 190

vitamin B1, 5

vitamins, 5

vomiting, 42, 116, 124

vulnerability, 34, 69, 94, 116, 138, 145, 162, 213, 228, 229, 231

W

war, 67

warrants, 151

Warsaw, 71

water, 155, 198, 199

wealth, 155

weight reduction, 122

Weinberg, 211

well-being, 114

Wernicke's encephalopathy, 5

white matter, 42

wine, 2

Wisconsin, 17, 24

withdrawal, 15, 96

women, 4, 7, 8, 10, 16, 20, 25, 26, 56, 57, 67, 111, 116, 121, 132, 133, 134, 140, 141, 200, 203, 213, 214

working memory, ix, 13, 17, 22, 23, 83, 84, 86, 87, 88, 89, 90, 91, 92, 94, 95, 96, 97, 98, 99, 100, 101, 102, 103

workplace, 159

World Health Organisation, 3, 28, 29, 142

X

X-linked, 143

Y

yeast, 2

yes/no, 197

yield, 89

young adults, 4, 23, 25, 28, 132, 228

Z

ziprasidone, 54